Settling in a Changing World

Amsterdam Archaeological Studies 19

Other titles in the AAS series:

1. N. Roymans (ed.): *From the Sword to the Plough. Three Studies on the Earliest Romanisation of Northern Gaul*
    Open Access edition: http://dare.uva.nl/record/19675

2. T. Derks: *Gods, Temples and Ritual Practices. The Transformation of Religious Ideas and Values in Roman Gaul*
    Open Access edition: http://dare.uva.nl/aup/en/record/172370

3. A. Verhoeven: *Middeleeuws gebruiksaardewerk in Nederland (8e – 13e eeuw)*
    Open Access edition: http://dare.uva.nl/aup/en/record/172373

4. F. Theuws / N. Roymans (eds): *Land and Ancestors. Cultural Dynamics in the Urnfield Period and the Middle Ages in the Southern Netherlands*
    Open Access edition: http://dare.uva.nl/aup/en/record/172372

5. J. Bazelmans: *By Weapons made Worthy. Lords, Retainers and Their Relationship in* Beowulf
    Open Access edition: http://dare.uva.nl/aup/en/record/172337

6. R. Corbey / W. Roebroeks (eds): *Studying Human Origins. Disciplinary History and Epistemology*
    Open Access edition: http://dare.uva.nl/aup/en/record/172272

7. M. Diepeveen-Jansen: *People, Ideas and Goods. New Perspectives on 'Celtic barbarians' in Western and Central Europe (500-250 BC)*
    Open Access edition: http://dare.uva.nl/aup/en/record/172273

8. G.J. van Wijngaarden: *Use and Appreciation of Mycenean Pottery in the Levant, Cyprus and Italy (ca. 1600-1200 BC). The Significance of Context*
    Open Access edition: http://dare.uva.nl/aup/en/record/172274

9. F.A. Gerritsen: *Local Identities. Landscape and community in the late prehistoric Meuse-Demer-Scheldt region*
    Open Access edition: http://dare.uva.nl/aup/en/record/172320

10. N. Roymans: *Ethnic Identity and Imperial Power. The Batavians in the Early Roman Empire*
    Open Access edition: http://dare.uva.nl/aup/en/record/172930

11. J.A.W. Nicolay: *Armed Batavians. Use and significance of weaponry and horse gear from non-military contexts in the Rhine delta (50 bc to ad 450)*
    Open Access edition: http://dare.uva.nl/aup/nl/record/397232

12. M. Groot: *Animals in ritual and economy in a Roman frontier community. Excavations in Tiel-Passewaaij*
    Open Access edition: http://dare.uva.nl/aup/en/record/301388

13. T. Derks & N. Roymans: *Ethnic Constructs in Antiquity. The role of power and tradition*
    Open Access edition: http://dare.uva.nl/aup/en/record/301890

14. T. D. Stek: *Cult places and cultural change in Republican Italy. A contextual approach to religious aspects of rural society after the Roman conquest*
    ISBN 978 90 8964 177 9

15. P. A.J. Attema, G.-J. L.M. Burgers & P. M. van Leusen: *Regional Pathways to Complexity. Settlement and land-use dynamics in early italy from the bronze age to the republican period*
    ISBN 978 90 8964 276 9

16. E.M. Moormann: *Divine Interiors. Mural paintings in Greek and Roman sanctuaries*
    ISBN 978 90 8964 261 5

17. N. Roymans / T. Derks (eds): *Villa Landscapes in the Roman North. Economy, Culture and Lifestyles*
    ISBN 978 90 8964 348 3

18. N. Roymans / G. Creemers / S. Scheers (eds): *Late Iron Age Gold Hoards from the Low Countries and the Caesarian Conquest of Northern Gaul*
    ISBN 978 90 8964 349 0

Settling in a Changing World

VILLA DEVELOPMENT IN THE NORTHERN PROVINCES OF THE ROMAN EMPIRE

DIEDERICK HABERMEHL

AMSTERDAM UNIVERSITY PRESS

This book meets the requirements of ISO 9706: 1994, Information and documentation – Paper for documents – Requirements for permanence.

Cover illustration: A sculptural model of a villa from Fontoy (France). After Gebus/Klag 1990, 88.
Cover design: Kok Korpershoek, Amsterdam
Lay-out: Bert Brouwenstijn, ACASA Amsterdam

ISBN: 978 90 8964 506 7
e-ISBN: 978 90 4851 822 7
NUR: 682
© Diederick Habermehl, Amsterdam University Press, Amsterdam, 2013

TO MY FATHER

CONTENTS

PREFACE

This study is the result of my research, carried out as a PhD-researcher at the Archaeological Centre of the VU University and the research institute CLUE between 2006 and 2010. I successfully defended the original thesis in September 2011. My research forms part of a broader research programme titled 'Roman villa landscapes in the North: Economy, Culture and Lifestyles'. This programme was financed by the Netherlands Organisation for Scientific Research (NWO), for which my gratitude. Furthermore, without the support of a considerable number of people, this study would not have been written. First and foremost I would like to express great gratitude to my *promotor* Prof. Nico Roymans for his support, trust and the good atmosphere of both academic and personal interaction. Special thanks also to Ton Derks, my *co-promotor*, for always being there for advice and a critical view. Both were part of the villa research group also including myself and my two direct PhD-colleagues: Karen Jeneson and Laura Crowley. Without these latter two the four years of research would not have been so inspiring, fun and unforgettable. One of the things I will always remember is our tour on foot through the 'villa landscape' from Tongres to Cologne. I would like to thank my other 'roommates' Stijn Heeren and Philip Verhagen and my colleagues at the archaeological centre and VUhbs: Henk Hiddink, Joris Aarts, Jean-Paul Crielaard, Mieke Prent, Antoine Mientjes, Mikko Kriek, Fokke Gerritsen, Ingmar Elstrodt, Julie Van Kerckhove, Cees Koot, Elbrich de Boer, Mara Wesdorp, Maaike Groot and Wouter Vos for their support and their contribution to a marvellous working atmosphere. Thanks also to Jan Slofstra, Fokke Gerritsen, Laura Kooistra, Gerard Tichelman, Anouk Veldman, Lourens van der Feijst and Jeremy Taylor for their contribution in the form of discussion, data or figures. I am grateful to Prof. Greg Woolf, for his stimulating role as advisor of the research programme, and to Prof. Wim De Clercq, Prof. Tom Bloemers, Prof. Jürgen Kunow, Henk Hiddink as well as some anonymous reviewers for their valuable comments on an earlier version of the manuscript. Thanks to Bert Brouwenstijn for his work on the layout of this book; to Jaap Fokkema for his work on the distribution maps and to Leonie Abels and Annette Visser (Wellington, NZ) for correcting the English. Outside the professional context I would like to thank my parents, Nico Habermehl and Jeannette Habermehl-Van 't Land, for their great support, interest and love. Last but certainly not least I would like to thank Koen van Leeuwen for his love and support.

Diederick Habermehl

1 Introduction

Settling in a changing world, local inhabitants forging a new place for themselves in the rapidly evolving environment of the Roman provinces that affected each and every dimension of their lives – this is the core theme of the study before you. Generally speaking, the development of the northernmost provinces of the Roman empire involved creating a new administrative structure that included *civitates* and their capitals, the development of many other urban and rural centres connected by a network of well-constructed roads and a series of military camps, concentrated mainly along the Rhine. This can be linked to significant changes in the economic, social, cultural, demographic and political spheres. New markets opened up, new institutions of power were created, new lifestyles were introduced and people's mobility increased significantly. Particularly within the context of their local settlements, the rural population dealt with this changing world and created a new place within it by changing both the ways in which they inhabited and worked the landscape and how they related to each other. These processes can be studied by exploring the development trajectories of rural settlements. After all, the adoption of new materials, forms, objects and spatial concepts can be regarded as a way of redefining relationships within local communities as well as between communities and the outside world. This study is about individual people, families and communities actively creating a new place for themselves within the changing world of the Roman provinces and empire.

Where then do villas fit in? The fact that I have not yet mentioned the word 'villa' may already reveal my reservations about the term. These reservations stem from the difficulties surrounding the definition and use of the term, its limitations and its complex background. Although this theme will be discussed in more detail below, I would like to begin by saying that the phenomenon generally referred to as 'villa' is only part of a broader and more complex rural development. In my view, the strict and essentialistic use of a villa definition for both data selection and analysis could limit the scope of research and the understanding of the true complexity of the processes at hand. This is not to say that we should, or even could, ignore the term altogether. The study of monumental villas has been and will continue to be an undeniable and vital part of provincial Roman archaeology. However, we must always be aware of the problematic nature of the term and the more complex realities concealed beneath the surface.

1.1 GENERAL

1.1.1 KEY OBJECTIVES AND BASIC CHARACTERISTICS

The general objective of this study is to analyse developments and processes of change within rural settlements in the northern provinces of the Roman empire. Two main parts can be identified. The first relates to the detailed reconstruction, visualisation and analysis of development trajectories in internal settlement organisation and house building. The second concerns the interpretation of these processes from a multi-dimensional approach, which is introduced at greater length below. A detailed and well-structured analysis of the wealth of settlement data, inventoried in Appendix 1 and further discussed in chapter 2, has the potential to improve our understanding of the complex and various ways in which people dealt with and were affected by the changing world of the developing Roman provinces.

It would be true to say that the vast dataset produced by existing research on villas and rural settlements has by no means been used to its full potential. For the European continent in particular, there is a lack of broader synthesising studies, while existing studies are generally poorly informed on a theoretical level and are strongly empirical and descriptive in character. With this in mind, my study was designed to include the following basic characteristics:

- a development perspective
- a broad empirical approach
- a long-term approach
- a large research region covering four modern-day countries
- a theoretically informed and interpretative study with a social focus

Firstly, development – a diachronic approach – is central to this study. The key aim is to understand change and development in its physical as well as its socio-cultural and economic dimensions. Compared to synchronic studies, such an approach could yield a better understanding of complex phenomena by exploring backgrounds and implications in more detail, rather than confining itself to structural features.

Secondly, the empirical approach goes beyond the scope of most traditional villa studies. As previously mentioned, data selection is not based on an *a priori* villa definition. As a result, all types of rural settlements are included, both synchronically and diachronically. This broad approach enables us to shed more light on the regional variety in processes of change, without being limited to the well-known typical monumental villa settlements.

Thirdly, this study takes a longer-term approach, including not only the period when monumental villa settlements were at their peak, but also the Late Iron Age and Early Roman period. By exploring longer lines of development, we can gain a greater understanding of the complexity of developments in rural settlements. It enables us to explore both continuity and rapid transformation.

Fourthly, the area defined as the research region is a fairly extensive one, covering parts of no less than four modern-day nations (the Netherlands, Germany, Belgium and France). The result is a large dataset containing a vast quantity of high-quality research that may be consulted for detailed analysis. The defined region covers not only the loess region traditionally regarded as the 'villa landscape', but also the more northerly sand and clay areas.

Lastly, it is important to emphasise the interpretative character of this study and its explicit use of theoretical insights from both archaeology and social studies. The general focus of this study is a social one. This is because processes of change cannot be understood unless we specifically involve people as active and creative agents in our analysis.

Viewed as part of the broader field of academic research, this archaeological study can contribute to the debate in its own way, significantly complementing other kinds of research on the Roman past. The study of developments in spatial organisation and architecture can shed light on the dynamics and character of social and economic relationships in a way that other fields of research, such as iconography, epigraphy and ancient history, cannot.

I.I.2 RESEARCH PROGRAMME

The present study is part of a broader research programme entitled 'Villa landscapes in the Roman North: Economy, Culture and Lifestyles'. This programme entails four parts – three thematic studies and a synthesising study.[1] The general objective is to present a picture of the origins, development and social interpretation of Roman villa landscapes in the region between Cologne and Bavay at the northern frontier of the Roman empire, as well as to develop a new interpretive model of villa landscapes that does justice to both the socio-economic and cultural dimensions.[2]

The thematic studies differ in terms of their perspective, their methodology, their selection and use of sources. The first study aims to reconstruct and analyse the entire settlement landscape, including burial and infrastructural evidence. Using the results of all types of archaeological research plus other types of research, it seeks to generate a model of settlement specific to the loess regions in the north. It uses GIS technology to store, analyse and visualise the archaeological and environmental data. The third thematic study focuses on the privileged burials associated with villa settlements. Striking because of their monumental markers, associated grave gifts and/or iconography, these elements provide considerable insight into various aspects of the lifestyles and identities constructed by the deceased and their survivors.

The present study could in some respects be seen as occupying an intermediate position between the other two thematic studies and it overlaps with both. As each settlement is embedded in a settlement landscape, knowledge acquired about the position of settlements within this landscape could provide additional insight into the significance of settlements and their development. Soil type, geographical position, the spatial relationship to towns and military camps, and the nature of the broader settlement system could all be important aspects. Graves are intimately connected with the communities inhabiting rural settlements and can tell us more about social differentiation and the active way in which people constructed new social identities and new lifestyles – a topic also discussed in this study. The integration of this study into the broader research programme widens the analytical horizon, something that I will attempt to do throughout the study.

The fourth part of the programme presents an overarching perspective, integrating the themes discussed in the above studies and also raising a number of new topics. The approach taken combines several dimensions (economic, social, institutional, individual, long-term and short-term) and covers several disciplines (archaeology, classical studies and social studies). The programme as a whole is able to offer a uniquely wide, synthesising and multi-dimensional view on significant developments in the provincial countryside during the first centuries AD.

1.1.3 FRAMEWORKS

This initial chapter introduces the frameworks for the study. The first section specifies the geographical and chronological frameworks and broadly outlines both the research region and research period. Next, the theoretical and conceptual foundations critical to the analyses carried out in this study are explored. The dataset and methodology are then examined, while the last section explains the structure of the study.

---

[1] The other two thematic studies within the research programme are being conducted by Karen Jeneson (in prep.; for an overview of the preliminary results, see Jeneson 2011) and Laura Crowley (in prep.; for an overview of the preliminary results, see Crowley 2011). The synthe-

sising volume contains synthesising papers as well as case studies by several authors (Roymans/Derks 2011).

[2] NWO (Netherlands Organisation for Scientific Research) research proposal 'Roman Villa Landscapes in the North: Economy, Culture and Lifestyles' (nr. 360-60-060).

Geographically, this study covers the northwestern, continental part of the empire, broadly extending between the Rhine *limes* in the east and Channel coast of northern France in the west.[3] This extensive region encompasses parts of four modern-day countries and a multitude of regions (see fig. 1.1). The first broad division that can be made is between the sand and clay areas in the north (covering large parts of the Netherlands and Germany just south and west of the Lower Rhine and Flanders) and the loess belt running from the Cologne region through the southernmost part of the Netherlands and Belgium towards the French Picardy region. In Germany and Belgium this loess belt is bordered to the south by the mountainous region of the Eifel-Ardennes. It is in this rather narrow loess belt that the main route runs between Cologne and Bavay and all the way to Boulogne-sur-Mer and Amiens. This loess zone is also generally regarded as the 'villa landscape', where intensive wheat production took place and monumental villas dominated the landscape. As mentioned previously, this study explicitly chooses to look beyond these supposed 'villa landscapes' and to include the northern sand and clay areas, as well as parts of the Eifel-Ardennes. This allows us to better understand the differentiation in rural settlement development and to place these developments in context.

The total research region thus covers an area of around 350 by 200 km. It is a region of considerable geographical diversity. By understanding this diversity, we can also understand the background to the developments reconstructed in the following chapters. The research region will therefore now be explored from a geographical perspective.

I . 2 . I   A   D I V E R S I T Y   O F   L A N D S C A P E S

Geographical regions can be defined on the basis of a number of factors, including soil type, relief, altitude, geological structure, hydrology, climate and vegetation. To a degree closely related, these factors vary considerably between regions, defining the physical characteristics and potential of the different landscapes. The research region can be divided into a number of landscapes from north to south: a mainly flat sandy region of Pleistocene origin and clay and peat regions of Holocene origin, a hilly to flat Pleistocene loess region and a mountainous region of pre-Quatenary origin (the Eifel-Ardennes massif).[4] The northernmost region is dominated by sand, clay and peat soils. During the Roman period, extensive, largely uninhabitable peat bogs could be found in the western parts of the Netherlands, behind the coastal strip in particular. The central and eastern river area, dominated by river sediments, was generally more suitable for habitation. This is a relatively fragmented landscape consisting of old river arms, levees, backlands and peaty areas. South of the river area is what is referred to as the Meuse-Demer-Scheldt (MDS) region, covering both Dutch and Belgian Brabant and Limburg. This region is dominated by sandy soils that also extend into adjacent Germany. The sandy soils are mineralogically poor, limiting their natural fertility. The landscape is generally flat. Towards the south, these sandy landscapes are bordered by the loess-dominated landscapes.[5] In Belgium, the transi-

---

[3]   The research region covers the modern provinces and departments of Nordrhein-Westfalen, Rheinland-Pfalz (Germany), Zuid-Limburg (the Netherlands), Vlaams Limburg, Luik, Vlaams Brabant, Waals Brabant, Henegouwen/Hainaut, Namen/Namur (Belgium) and Nord-Pas-de-Calais, Somme, Aisne and Oise (France).

[4]   Denis 1992; Derks 1998, 55.

[5]   Loess itself is a very fine-grained homogenous aeolian

sediment from the Ice Age, providing a fertile basis for agriculture, especially the predominantly calcium-rich loess soils (Mücher 1973; Denis 1992, 252). One of the definitions for loess soils, based on particle size, is that 80% should be of a fraction between 0.002-0.05 mm and the proportion of $CaCO_3$ should be around 10% (Denis 1992, 252). The big disadvantage of this soil type, however, is its strong sensitivity to erosion. Because of

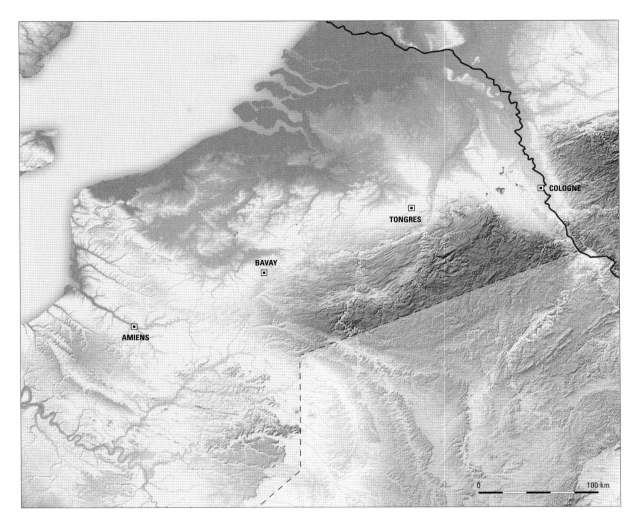

Fig. 1.1. The modern geography of the research region with four main Roman-period centres and the *limes* along the Rhine. The general division into landscapes is shown by different shades of grey.

tion between sand and loess soils follows the line from Ghent and Mechelen towards Hasselt. In Dutch Limburg, the loess extends up to around Sittard. In Germany, it extends sharply northward up to about Duisburg. The core of the loess region is a flat or hilly landscape intersected by river and brook valleys. In the German region, the loess landscape consists of a number of generally flat plains. Known as *Rheinische Lössbörden*, they are intersected by the rivers Rur and Erft, running through broad, slightly hilly and reasonably inhabitable valleys.[6] The Erft valley at least was inhabited intensively, as detailed

its highly uniform particle size and the lack of elements such as clay minerals and humus, loess erodes at a slope of only 3%. The entire topsoil will erode at a slope of at least 8% (Berendsen 1997, 21; Kooistra 1996, 91. These figures apply to bare soils, as is the case for much of the arable land).

[6] East of and parallel to the Erft is the small Ville mountain chain. Between the Ville and the Rhine we find river terraces. Cologne is situated here, directly alongside the river. Further to the west, between the Erft and Rur,

the Titzer Platte stretches out and, directly west of the Rur, the Aldenhovener Platte. An important geographical feature with a prominent position in this study is the Hambacher Forst, officially named Bürgewald. This was a vast forest area during the Middle Ages but was inhabited during the Roman period. Today it is characterised by large-scale opencast mining activities for lignite extraction, presenting both a great threat to and a unique opportunity for archaeology.

archaeological surveys have demonstrated.[7] Towards the west, the Dutch loess region or *Limburger Börde*[8] consists of a number of plateaus,[9] separated by brook and river valleys, of which Geul, Wurm and Meuse are the most important. The Limburg area is more articulated and fragmented than the German loess plains. The plateaus are between 120 and 200 m above sea level, while the valleys are up to 80-150 m lower in some cases. The highest parts of the plateaus have little or no loess cover, limiting their agricultural potential.[10] In the Belgian loess region, it is also possible to define a number of plateaus, particularly the Haspengouw, Henegouwen and Brabant plateaus. The Haspengouw stretches out west of the Meuse and is bordered by the Gete river to the east. These Belgian plateaus are situated at an altitude of between 100 and 200 m above sea level. The river valleys cutting through the plains are relatively shallow and poorly articulated. The southernmost part of the research area is formed by the French Picardy region, consisting of three departments – Somme, Aisne and Oise. This region is characterised by highly fertile loess plains stretching over a large area. To this day, the region is vital for the large-scale production of wheat.

Towards the south, the loess landscapes are bordered by the higher and mountainous regions of the Eifel-Ardennes. In the Belgian region, the wide Meuse-Samber valley forms the dividing line between the loess region and the Condroz, Herve and Fagne-Famenne plateaus.[11] These plateaus, which mark the transition between the loess region and the mountainous regions, are situated at altitudes between 200 and 300 m above sea level and are more articulated.[12] In the German region, the North Eifel forms such a transition zone, quite similar to the Condroz region.

Apart from soil type, altitude and relief, climatological conditions are yet another key factor. The climate in the relatively low loess landscapes is fairly mild and moist with early springs and many sunny days, making it very suitable for agriculture. In the region near Cologne, the average annual temperature is above 10 degrees Celsius.[13] Conditions in the more southerly mountainous regions are different, however. With its longer and harsher winters, this region is much less suitable for arable farming. Less climate-dependent activities such as livestock farming and pottery, glass and chalk production are consequently of greater importance here.[14]

1.2.2 A CULTURAL LANDSCAPE

A prominent feature of the research region is the road that runs east-west from Cologne to Boulogne-sur-Mer and Amiens. This road was the essential link between urban centres and smaller rural centres or *vici*. After a phase of mainly military use, from the 1st century AD onwards, the road became a mainly economic artery, connecting the fertile agricultural areas with urban centres and military troops along the Rhine. Secondary roads leading to this main artery linked rural settlements in the hinterland to the wider and rapidly changing outside world. The road network was thus an essential element in the development of the provincial countryside.

Several towns and many roadside settlements, or rural centres, were situated along the main road, including Bavay, Liberchies, Tongres, Maastricht, Jülich and Cologne.[15] Such settlements generally

[7] See Jeneson in prep.; Hinz 1969b.

[8] Tietze *et al.* 1990, 117.

[9] A number of plateaus are defined in Renes 1988.

[10] Examples are the Brunsummerheide and Vrouweheide areas; see Renes 1988, 19.

[11] Directly south of Dutch Limburg is the Herve plateau, characterised by a subsoil of horizontal chalk layers. To the west are the Fagne-Famenne and Condroz regions.

The latter is characterised by a series of long ridges with depressions in between. The former region is situated at a lower elevation, generally around 150 m below the highest parts of the Condroz (Denis 1992, 133-134).

[12] Denis 1992, 131.

[13] Tietze *et al.* 1990, 247.

[14] Eck 2004, 26.

[15] Stuart/De Grooth 1987, 17.

served as economic, religious and administrative centres. Although quite a few places along the road are known from the *Itinerarium Antonini Augusti*,[16] archaeological research has demonstrated that more places were in fact located there. It seems highly likely that they were of lesser importance as they are not mentioned in the *Itinerarium*. We should also bear in mind that not all centres were located along the main road. Aquae Granni (Aachen), for example, was situated 16 km south of the route between Cologne and Bavay.

Another important road ran along the northern border of both the research region and the Roman empire. This *limes* road linked the many auxiliary and legionary camps as well as civilian centres such as Xanten. In the northern regions, the military presence unquestionably exerted a major influence over the hinterland directly south of the Rhine.[17]

With regard to the pre-Roman background, it should be mentioned that much of the research region is situated north of the *oppida* zone, which featured major fortified settlements with centre functions of various kinds, controlled by elites. This has led many to assume that societies in the northern region were more egalitarian and less complex. However, recent research has demonstrated that for this region too, we should consider the possibility of places with a supra-local importance, controlled by elite figures.[18]

1.2.3 CHRONOLOGICAL FRAMEWORK

To understand the complex changes in rural settlements, it is essential to focus on both short-term transformations and longer lines of development. Confining ourselves to the High Empire, the period when monumental villa settlements were at their peak, would be unhelpful. Instead, the chronological scope should be broadened to include the later Iron Age (see fig. 1.2 for a chronological table). The structure and development of rural settlements in the last centuries BC and the transition period between the Iron Age and the Roman period can provide useful insights into the longer lines of settlement development and into continuities and discontinuities. The Late Empire, at the other end of the timeline, is not a period of focus in this study. A large number of villa settlements no longer survived as agricultural settlements after the 3rd century AD. The re-use of abandoned buildings for artisan production has been documented in many cases. These later phases will largely be left unconsidered.

1.3 VIEW ON VILLA AND SETTLEMENT

This study has so far been critical of the villa concept commonly used in archaeological studies. This section will explore in more detail existing research on villas and the general category of rural settlements. It will also explain the approach adopted by that research. Most importantly, it will discuss how the present study relates to existing lines of research.

---

[16] Bagacum (Bavay), Vodgoriacum (Waudrez), Germiniacum (Liberchies), Atuatuca Tungrorum (Tongres), Coriovallum (Heerlen), Iuliacum (Jülich), Tiberiacum (Thorr?) and Colonia (Cologne) are mentioned.

[17] Heeren 2009; Vos 2009; Roymans 2010.

[18] Roymans 2005. For the Dutch region, a location of supra-local importance can perhaps be identified at Kessel. In the German and Belgian plains, fairly large enclosed sites could possibly be regarded as a kind of lowland fortification with certain centre functions.

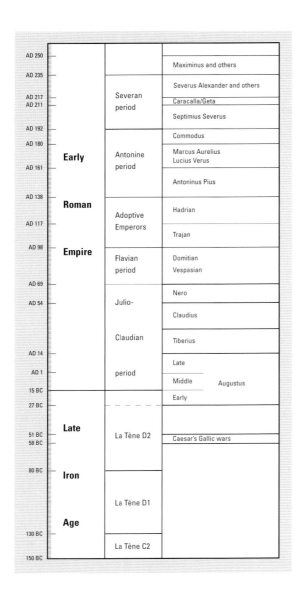

Fig. 1.2. Chronological table outlining the chronological framework of this study and the chronological terminology used.

1.3.1 VILLA RESEARCH: A RICH TRADITION

Traces of monumental villa houses have been a central feature of studies of the Roman period for centuries. Over time, however, academic objectives, views and interpretations have been subject to considerable change.

The earliest interest in villas as traces of a past culture had a personal, mainly socio-political background. From the 16th century onwards, the Renaissance triggered an immense interest in the classical past. As a result, contemporaneous aristocrats sought to appropriate the Roman past by associating themselves with Roman elites in order to legitimise and strengthen their social dominance. Classical texts were associated with physical traces of villas found in the landscape. Consequently, the ideal of an Arcadian rural life, as opposed to the hectic urban life, was revived. This development began in 16th-century Italy, but can be identified in for example 17th- and 18th-century Holland and England as well.[19]

Up to the 20th century, Roman provincial villas were considered the luxurious residences of a Roman elite. Students of these monumental remains had a profoundly Romano-centric and elite-oriented perspective. In the early years of the 20th century, the work of Mommsen and Haverfield pleaded for a more complex perspective, elucidating the interaction between the Roman occupiers and local populations.[20] The central concept here was 'romanisation', then regarded as the process whereby local indigenous cultures were influenced by Roman culture to such an extent that the Roman element eventually took over the culture in question. This view also influenced villa archaeology, as illustrated by the important excavations at Mayen. In that research, conducted in the 1920s, Franz Oelmann identified a post-built structure under the monumental 'Roman' villa. Oelmann concluded that the villa had evolved from the indigenous post-built house that had preceded it.[21] A few years later, such a post-built predecessor of a monumental house was also identified by Fremersdorf at Cologne-Müngersdorf. He specifically refers to the indigenous background of the inhabitants of the villa: 'Obwohl die beschriebenen Bauten nach ihren Abmessungen, nach Art und Technik einen rein römischen Eindruck machen, glaube ich, das der Besitzer des Kölner Gutshofes kein Römer, sondern ein Mann aus der einheimischen Bevölkerung

---

[19] See Dyson 2003; Bentmann/Müller 1990; Glaudemans 2000; Hingley 2000.

[20] Mommsen 1886; Haverfield 1905/1906.

[21] Oelmann 1928.

gewesen ist…'.[22] However, there was still little nuance in the attention to the indigenous people. The use of this absolute and uniform concept of culture meant that 'Roman' and 'native' were dichotomised. Furthermore, the archaeological focus was generally still confined to the most monumental parts of the settlements, the main house, and thus to the upper circles of society.

It was also Oelmann and Fremersdorf who first introduced socio-economic research themes for villa settlements. However, it was not until the 1960s and 1970s that this approach was developed further. British authors Rivet and Percival attempted to reconstruct the villa's social and economic structure and function, mainly on the basis of classical-Roman texts by Columella, Cato and Varro.[23] Later authors refer to this historical orientation as the 'Italic' or 'historical' model.[24]

To go beyond this Italic model, Slofstra and Wightman examined other, and in their opinion more reliable, sources. Slofstra has employed anthropological modelling, while Wightman relied on parallels from the earlier medieval period.[25] Villas in this period were regarded as elements within a broader socio-economic system, which Slofstra even labelled a 'villa system'. The social characteristics of the villa main house were also studied from another perspective. Smith interpreted spatial structure in quite direct social terms, concluding that a social continuity existed between pre-Roman and Roman times.[26] This direction was continued by a number of authors, including Hingley, Clarke, Scott and Samson, all of them British.[27]

Since the 1990s, the academic focus has shifted from broader, longer-term processes and structures to micro-processes, diversity and individuality.[28] New perspectives on the house and household have emerged as a result of this focus on the processes of everyday life.[29] The house is regarded as a locus for day-to-day social and economic interaction, production and reproduction of social identities. Social perspectives on material culture also placed additional emphasis on consumption and its social significance.[30]

Following this broad sketch, it is important to highlight some of the shortcomings of existing studies. First of all, there is a general lack of synthesising studies on rural settlement within the research region. Apart from some regional overviews, true syntheses that systematically analyse the wealth of available settlement data are simply not available.[31] Secondly, there is a general focus on the most monumental buildings or development phases. As a result, non-monumental settlements or settlement phases tend to be excavated less frequently and to feature less in villa studies. Secondary houses and economic buildings that are an integral part of settlements are often given insufficient attention. As a final point, it is important to mention the generally limited theoretical and interpretative quality

[22] Fremersdorf 1933, 47-48.

[23] Rivet 1969; Percival 1976.

[24] Slofstra (1983, 87) speaks of the Italic model, involving the interpretation of provincial phenomena on the basis of sources from the Italic region. Both Rivet (1969, 179-182) and Percival (1976, 119-144) use classical sources and could thus be said to be employing an Italic model. Slofstra and Wightman (1978) harbour strong doubts about the value of such a model for the reconstruction of the situation in the northern provinces of the Roman empire. Hingley (1989, 3) has also stressed the strongly historical interpretative frameworks within which archaeological finds and phenomena are being interpreted.

[25] Slofstra 1983; Wightman 1978.

[26] Smith 1978, 1997. For a critical discussion of Smith's approach, see Scott 1990 and Samson 1990.

[27] Hingley 1989; Clarke 1999; Samson 1990; Scott 1990.

[28] Taylor 2001, 48; Hodder 2004, 36.

[29] Hodder 2004, 26.

[30] The consumption perspective occupies an important position in the studies by Millet (1990), Woolf (1998), Hingley (2005) and Martins (2005).

[31] In this respect, the northern sand and clay area is a well-researched region, as settlement data have been used for a number of synthesising studies (Gerritsen 2001; Roymans 1996; Verwers 1998; Theuws/Roymans 1998). For northern France, some regional overviews are available as well (Bayard/Collart 1996; en Redjeb/Duvette/Quérel 2005). Many of the excavations, however, have not been well-published.

of the continental studies. All too often, excavated settlements are not analysed beyond the empirical level. The lack of synthesising studies is matched by an absence of interpretations on a social, economic or cultural level. Theoretical concepts developed in British archaeological studies are only rarely employed within the scope of continental villa studies.

This study seeks to remedy these shortcomings by choosing a broad, synthesising approach that incorporates a wealth of settlement data from four countries. As already mentioned, the full range of rural settlements and buildings can be included in the analysis because no *a priori* villa definition is used. A further explicit objective is to shed light on the non-elite rural population. This study also has a significantly interpretative character. It uses theoretical insights developed in among others British archaeology, together with models and insights from social studies, to create a new understanding of the complex processes of change in the countryside in the northern Roman provinces. The next section will introduce the central theoretical concepts and themes.

1.3.2 VILLA, 'VILLA' OR...? A PROBLEMATIC DEFINITION

Defining the term 'villa' has been somewhat problematic throughout villa studies. Although seemingly self-evident, it is difficult to define and demarcate the villa phenomenon, and this is complicated further by the multitude of perspectives from which it has been studied.

The Latin word *villa* was originally employed by classical authors to refer to a particular settlement or house form. In antiquity, however, the use of this term had already become rather vague and inconsistent.[32] This study will use the word 'villa' solely as a modern archaeological term and not in its historical Latin sense.

In archaeological studies, the villa as a house has been associated with a high degree of 'Roman-ness', an investment of wealth and display of status in architectural form.[33] Over time, alongside morphology, social or economic characteristics have also been taken as the primary basis for defining a villa. In archaeological practice, the term 'villa' has been applied to a broad array of structures. In general, a distinction may be made between morphological and relational definitions.[34] A relational definition is highly interpretative in character and focuses on the functional purpose of villa settlements within economic and social structures. Such definitions are often shaped within strongly historical interpretative frameworks, constructed on the basis of a limited and biased collection of historical sources.[35] A morphological definition focuses mainly on building material and architectual form. Generally, houses with stone foundations and elements of Mediterranean architecture are regarded as villas.

The archaeological substance of these definitions has often faded, however. As Hingley argues, 'If the term 'villa' is to be more useful than merely a description of building form, a great deal more must be discovered concerning the origin and nature of the settlements on which these buildings are found. The alternative – forcing inadequate evidence into a predetermined and over-simplistic historical framework – will not create a true picture of the economic and social background and lifestyle of the rural elite of Roman Britain'.[36] An alternative definition is an archaeological one. This is the approach adopted by Woolf, who has defined the villa mainly as a 'style of consumption', by which new archi-

[32] Classical authors on the villa include Columella (4-70 AD): De re rustica (I.6.1-3); Cato (234-149 BC): De agricultura (I.4.1); Horatius (65-8 BC): Odes (I.17), Epistularum (I.7 and 10); Plinius minor (ca. 61–112): Epistulae (II.17, V.6).

[33] See Hingley 1989, 45-46.

[34] Hingley (1989) distinguishes a historical and an archaeo-logical definition.

[35] See Hingley (1989, 3) for a critical view on such historical interpretative frameworks. Other frameworks are based on anthropological or ethnological parallels (Slofstra 1983; Wightman 1978).

[36] Hingley 1989, 22-23.

tectural forms, materials and objects are being consumed, in relation to social and economic strategies.[37] But even then, both developments and their outcomes may vary considerably across the broad research region. In many cases, this has led to a discussion on whether or not to call a settlement or house a villa.[38] In my opinion, such arguments are essentially useless, as it is much more important to reconstruct and understand developments rather than their outcomes and their place in a classification system. Similarly, it has been suggested that we abandon the term villa altogether. We would then no longer speak of villas but only of farms, which differ in various ways.[39] Although this is theoretically interesting, it seems neither possible nor desirable to attempt to ignore the word villa, mainly because of its strong roots in archaeology. The point remains, however, that 'villa' should not be used in an essentialist way and that we should always take into account the broad and complex developments in the countryside. We should also be aware of the potentially misleading and simplistic associations of the term: its Roman-ness, its interpretation as the residence of an elite and its function as a rationally operating enterprise. As we will see, the actual differentiation of rural settlements is so pronounced that such simplifications would undermine our understanding of complex historical realities.

1.4 AN INTERPRETATIVE FRAMEWORK

This being an interpretative study, I need to establish an interpretative course before analysing the data in the following chapters. I will introduce a number of general approaches and assumptions, and then explore several themes in somewhat more detail.

First of all, it should be emphasised that my approach is essentially a social one, as archaeology ultimately concerns people. Apparently neutral concepts such as space, technology and objects are all embedded in the 'social' and should therefore be studied as such.[40] As Hodder states, 'everything is social'; all aspects of daily life can be seen as part of the continuous active negotiation of social roles.[41]

Understanding more of the true complexity of the developments explored in this study also requires a complex approach. In recent decades, quite a number of archaeologists have called for integrated perspectives that combine the strengths of processual and post-processual archaeological approaches.[42] Webster speaks in this context of an eclectic approach.[43] Jan Slofstra developed a suitable model combining several dimensions for the integrated analysis of romanisation processes (fig. 1.3). His model brought together time-space dimensions, micro and macroscale, and the short and long-term. Slofstra also distinguishes between institutional and cultural dimensions. The former relates to political and economic institutions and structure, the latter to more informal social interaction, culture, identity and agency.[44] It is the complex, dialectical interaction between the different dimensions, spheres and scales that lies at the heart of Slofstra's model and that can provide a better understanding of structures, processes and their dynamics.

---

[37] Woolf 1998, chapter 7.

[38] Illustrative in this context is Slofstra's (1991) introduction of the term 'proto-villa'. This underlines the absolute typology applied to rural settlement, in which settlements are either 'native', 'proto-villas' or 'real villas'. Such an abstract model, into which these terms are fitted, does not account for the complex heterogeneity and differentiated processes of change with which the villa phenomenon can be related.

[39] Pers. comm. Greg Woolf, Vaals symposium, 2008.

[40] As Taylor (2001, 49) points out, there is a real danger of confusion between subject and object in archaeological studies: archaeological phenomena, such as house plans, tend to overshadow the societies that created them and in which they played an active role.

[41] Hodder 2004, 26, 36.

[42] Pope 2003; Webster 1996; Slofstra 2002.

[43] Webster 1996.

[44] The commonly used concepts of 'structure' and 'agency' were originally introduced by Giddens (1984).

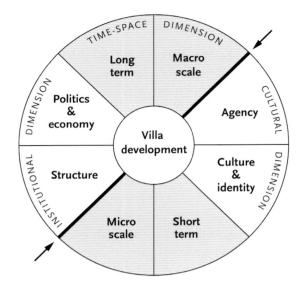

Fig. 1.3. The dimensional model as developed by Slofstra with 'villa development' replacing 'romanisation' as the central theme. After Slofstra 2002, 20 (with modifications).

A dimensional approach, as outlined above, can be applied to this study. To better understand the processes of change within rural settlements, we also need to consider Slofstra's dimensions and their interaction. It is in settlements that the institutional and cultural dimensions interacted, and approaching settlement development from both short and long-term and micro and macroscale could improve our understanding of the backgrounds to and implications of the processes of change.[45] Having explored this general framework, I will now define and explore some more specific themes central to this study's interpretative course.

I.4.I ROME AND THE OTHERS

A key traditional theme in the archaeology of the Roman provinces is the process generally referred to as 'romanisation'. Originally, romanisation was regarded as a unidirectional process in which native people became 'romanised'. More modern approaches to romanisation, however, view it as a complex and multi-vocal, socio-cultural interaction between the Roman occupier and local groups and individuals, shedding light on both Romans and the native population as active and creative agents.[46] This study will link up with these more complex perspectives on romanisation. Studying villa development is particularly suitable for elucidating the processes of change in all their facets and complexity. Following the dimensional model introduced above, we will shed light on the various dimensions of these processes.[47] One important factor is institutional power (both political and military).[48] But we must not overlook more informal and personal change processes and individual creativity. Romanisation was a social process by nature. As Hingley states, "'Roman' culture was brought into being through the creation of relations between peoples within the expanding empire as part of a developing discourse of imperialism."[49] The local settlement was one of the important loci in which these relationships were created, shaped and reproduced, aimed both inwardly and outwardly.

[45] Hendon (2004, 272) argues for a vision of households based on the interaction between 'structure' and 'agency'.

[46] For an extensive discussion of perspectives on romanisation, see Derks 1998; Woolf 1992, 1997, 1998; Slofstra 2004; Hingley 2000, 2005 and Heeren 2009. Especially in British archaeology, a hostile attitude towards the concept of romanisation has developed in recent decades. Several authors have rejected the concept for its colonial background. Although the post-colonial critique has been useful for the development of new ideas and insights, it is in our opinion neither necessary nor preferable to reject the concept of romanisation completely.

[47] See Slofstra 2002.

[48] Slofstra 2004, 52.

[49] Hingley 2005, 51.

From the 1970s and 1980s onwards, more attention was paid to the concept of the house.[50] No longer examined as simply a physical structure, the house was now regarded as the residence of a social group, and consequently as the location for production, consumption and the social practices of everyday life. These day-to-day practices in and around the house were an important social arena for the production and reproduction of social identities and relationships of power. The house and its inhabitants lived in a mutually constituting relationship.[51]

The research theme of house and settlement offers good opportunities for the integral social study of architecture, space and mobile material culture. How were these elements used to produce and reproduce social relationships and identities within the house, as well as between the inhabitants of the house and the outside world?[52] As they are embedded in social practice, architecture and space are regarded as socially significant.[53] In this study, space will be examined on the level of both the individual house and the settlement. How did new types of architecture and new ways of ordering space develop in the countryside and how can this be linked to changing social relationships, identities and production strategies?

Three concepts – 'family',[54] the 'household' and 'community'[55] – are especially important in the social approach to house and settlement. Family is a specific social unit, mostly – although not exclusively – based on biological kinship. A distinction is generally made between nuclear and extended families.[56] Households are the smallest social systems where intensive and important social interaction takes place; they usually consist of people who are relatives and who also live under one roof.[57] 'Community' can be regarded as a more general concept that is manifested on various levels.[58] It is a social network in which social interaction takes place. Communities have an ideological dimension as well; they are constructed in symbolic ways.[59]

I.4.3 MATERIAL CULTURE AND CONSUMPTION

The concept of material culture – the complete material environment created by humans, including non-fixed (mobilia), semi-fixed (for example furniture) and fixed (buildings) elements – has gained traction within archaeology over the last few decades.[60] The complex relationship between people and material culture has been a point of particular interest. 'Material culture is a medium through which people create and negotiate social roles; culture operates through material dimensions'.[61] As such, material culture is not a passive reflection of human behaviour, but an integral and active part of social

[50] The primary studies on this theme came from the ethnological and anthropological disciplines. An important early archaeological study is that of Wilk/Rathje 1982.

[51] See Hendon 2004, 272.

[52] See Allison 1999, 8. Some studies, such as at North Warnborough, attempted to reconstruct domestic social structure on the basis of the distribution of mobile material culture within the house (Hingley 1989, 43-45).

[53] The term 'social space' is used in the literature: Hodder 2004, 272; Hillier/Hanson 1984; Clarke 1999.

[54] Hingley (1989, 6 ff.) uses both family and community as central themes in his study of rural settlements.

[55] A good study with regard to 'community' is that of Cohen (1985).

[56] Hingley 1989, 5-10.

[57] Eriksen 1995.

[58] Sometimes, however, 'community' is related to a particular social level. Hingley (1989, 8-9), for example, regards community as a social level above that of the family. In this view, a community can consist of a group of families, for example.

[59] Eriksen 1995; Cohen 1985.

[60] See Tilley et al. 2006 for a good overview.

[61] Hingley 2005, 73.

processes, playing a key role in the production and reproduction of identities.[62] By viewing settlement and house as material culture, we can shed more light on the complex relationship between people and their settlement environment, as well as on the significant processes of change.

Critically, this increasing attention to material culture is closely linked to emerging views on consumption.[63] Consumption should not be seen as a purely economic phenomenon but also as a socially significant act, or even a strategy. The study of changing consumption patterns can increase our understanding of important social transformations within the studied communities. From this perspective, Woolf in fact regards 'Romanization as a change in patterns of consumption'.[64]

I.4.4 TEMPORALITY

The past is not static but dynamic. While this may appear rather self-evident, temporality has more than once been marginalised in the study of the past. Bearing in mind the research themes defined in this study, I will briefly outline this concept. First of all, it is important to be aware of the time depth and dynamic that is concealed beneath what archaeologists find below the surface. The archaeological record is by definition a palimpsest. In most cases, plans of monumental houses are the result of various phases of construction and reconstruction. What is more, settlement plans cannot be read without considering chronological factors. The explicit aim of this study is to reconstruct and analyse such development trajectories. Another approach goes beyond time as an absolute and measurable entity. What role did time and the past play in the past communities under study, and how did attitudes towards the past change over time?[65]

I.4.5 ELITE AND NON-ELITE

As stated, research has traditionally focused on the most monumental buildings in rural settlements and thus on the higher social echelons with the most conspicuous lifestyles.[66] Only in recent years have we seen the excavation of less monumental settlement complexes within the traditional villa landscapes. In the northernmost regions, the tradition of excavating post-built 'native' settlements has nevertheless been around for much longer. To increase our understanding of changes in rural habitation and the phenomenon of villa development, I consider it essential to know more about the lower echelons of society, the less visible, the non-elite. How did these people live and how did they create a new place for themselves in the changing world? What were their relationships to the elites and how were these created and maintained? With such a broad perspective, it is important to include in the dataset non-monumental houses within monumentalised settlements and simple non-monumental settlements. The simple graves found in or near many settlements could be a further interesting category for the study of non-elite people.

[62] Hodder 2004, 29.

[63] Woolf 1998; Allison 1999; Martins 2005.

[64] Martins 2005, 10; Woolf 1998.

[65] See Hingley 2005 for a short discussion on the historical dimension of material culture.

[66] For a critique on elite-focused research, see Hingley 1989 and Hingley 2000.

For a fuller understanding of developments within rural settlements, their broader context needs to be elucidated as well. The relationships between the rising urban centres and rural settlements are particularly interesting in this respect. Town and country were mutually dependent and were linked to one another in a multitude of ways. First of all, rural settlements were the loci of agricultural production, essential for urban markets. Furthermore, the elite families who held key positions in the *civitas* or provincial administration had close ties to the countryside and probably lived there too, at least for part of the time. They probably owned rural estates. Other countryside inhabitants may have had ties with (fully or partially) town-based landowners through patronage or tenancy relationships. An archaeologically visible phenomenon is the relationship between urban lifestyles and the emerging villa lifestyle. Houses were built, walls were decorated and bathing areas were constructed in an urban fashion. How did this link between town and country evolve over time? And can we actually view villa settlements as links between town and country?

1.5 STRUCTURE OF THIS STUDY

The objectives set out above are developed in the following chapters. Firstly, the next chapter will explore the dataset. Following a discussion of the inventory at the heart of this study, I will explore the basic characteristics and biases of the dataset. The inventory itself is presented in the site catalogue (Appendix 1). The third chapter constitutes the core analysis of this study. It explores developments in rural habitation by reconstructing and analysing a range of development trajectories for both the organisation of settlement space and house building. These analyses are almost purely spatio-morphological in character and pay little attention to social and economic interpretations of the developments reconstructed here. However, the fourth and fifth chapters are completely dedicated to these latter themes. Chapter four approaches matters from a social perspective, exploring developments and transformations as they relate to active and creative human agents operating in the social arenas of their families, settlement communities and broader societies. The chapter tackles a wide range of themes, including the reorganisation of social space, the break with existing building traditions, monumentalisation and the creation of new symbols and lifestyles. To this end, it employs concepts, insights and models from both archaeology and social studies. Chapter five will focus on production and the organisation of production. Again, developments and transformations constitute the central element of the study. Archaeobotanical and archaeozoological data provide information on changing production strategies and internal settlement organisation, while specific economic buildings within these settlements can shed light on changes in the organisation of production. This latter theme is also linked to topics discussed in chapter four. In the final chapter, the synthesis, the insights gained in the preceding chapters are brought together in an attempt to create a high-resolution image of the complex developments in the provincial countryside between the 1st century BC and 3rd century AD. I then make some recommendations for future research on villas and rural settlements in general.

2   Data and research

This chapter will introduce and explore the very essence of this study – the dataset. There are two key themes. Firstly, the choices about the composition of the dataset are made explicit. What sites and data are included in the inventory and what is the rationale behind this? Secondly, the characteristics and biases of the dataset are explored to assess how they influence the results of the analyses.

Unlike most studies, which focus on individual sites or specific regions, this dataset includes settlement data from a variety of regions, covering no less than four modern-day countries and a variety of research traditions, spread across both space and time. This has generated a highly heterogeneous dataset whose backgrounds, characteristics and biases need to be explored before a start can be made on analysing the data.

Firstly, I will discuss the conceptual basis on which the dataset is built – in other words, the choices that are made. I will then explore the differentiated research background of the dataset by looking at the different research volumes through time, the scale of research and also discuss a number of important research traditions. Next, I will define and briefly discuss five subregions, bringing some structure to the dataset. Lastly, I will set the dataset against the main objectives of this study – exploring developments in settlement organisation, house building and their regional differentiation.

2.1   CONSTRUCTING A DATASET

Constructing a dataset is always subject to choices relating to the objectives of the study in question. Before working with the dataset, I therefore need to make these choices explicit. As outlined in the previous chapter, the main objective of the present study is to reconstruct and analyse villa development. This requires the availability of quality archaeological data, including detailed information on morphology (structure, form and material of the built environment) and chronology (a fairly detailed phasing of the development of houses and settlements; absolute and relative dating). In other words, only well-excavated and well-published sites can satisfy this study's objectives. Overall, I could say that the availability of a well-documented house plan, preferably well-dated and adequately phased, is the minimum requirement. Ideally, data on the broader settlement context and longer-term developments should also be available. Survey data is therefore not included in the dataset. Publication is a related requirement, which generally means that only published sites have been included.[1]

Apart from data quality, another objective has profoundly influenced the composition of the dataset. In chapter 1 I argued that an essentialist villa definition has to be avoided for a better understanding of villa development. Parallel to this proposition, no such definition was used for the inventory of rural settlements. This means that rural settlements in general were inventoried without selecting data

---

[1] In general, there was no opportunity to return to primary data. In some cases, 'grey' literature was used (unpublished reports, etc.). For the German region, many sites have only been published in preliminary publications. Detailed phasing and description are lacking here. The same applies to the French region, as many sites have been preliminarily published in the 'Carte archéologique de la Gaule' (CAG) or the 'Bilan scientifique de la région Picardie' (BSR).

on the basis of monumentality or Roman-style architectural elements, for example. As a result, the dataset contains sites that archaeologists will generally regard as 'villas', as well as sites that are referred to as 'native', traditional settlements. In general terms, rural settlement refers to those loci that are the homes of local communities living off and working on the land they inhabit. Defensive sites (*oppida* or similar sites), sites with a clear ritual function and sites with a village-like character and centre functions (traditionally termed *vici*) are not included in the dataset.

2.2 BASIC CHARACTERISTICS: SIZE AND DISTRIBUTION

The result of the inventory, the dataset, is presented in the site catalogue of Appendix 1. Some basic characteristics and a basic description are presented for all sites. The complete dataset consists of 270 sites. To make the extensive dataset more comprehensible and to enhance the picture of regionality, the research area has been divided into the following five subregions.

The northern sand and clay areas: this region comprises the area immediately south of the Roman *limes* (situated along the Rhine), and is dominated by sand and clay soils. It covers the Dutch coastal area, the Dutch and German river area and the sandy plains south of this river area, covering large parts of Dutch Brabant and northern Limburg as well as the northern part of the Rhineland west of the Rhine.

Flanders: this region predominantly covers the sand and clay soils of the northernmost parts of Belgium, extending over large parts of the Flemish provinces of East and West Flanders, Antwerp, Brabant and Limburg, around and west of the cities of Bruges, Ghent and Antwerp.

The Dutch and German loess region: this region comprises the fairly narrow loess belt between the northern sand and clay areas and the mountainous Eifel region in the south. The Dutch loess region covers the southernmost part of the province of Limburg alone.

The Belgian loess region: this region encompasses the loess belt between the northern Dutch and Flemish sand and clay areas and the southern mountainous Ardennes region.

Northwestern France: this region covers the French departments of Nord, Pas-de-Calais, Somme, Oise and Aisne (the latter three together forming the Picardy region).

Table 2.1 presents the number of inventoried sites per subregion. Forty-five sites were included for the northern sand and clay areas, 84 for the Dutch and German loess region, 19 for Flanders, 74 for the Belgian loess region, and 48 for northwestern France. Fig. 2.1 visualises the distribution of these sites within the landscape of the research region. A number of general patterns can be identified. An especially tight cluster of sites can be distinguished in the Dutch and German loess region. For the Dutch region, most of the sites were excavated before 1950, the heyday of villa archaeology in this region. The many sites in the German region can be associated with the research taking place in the mining areas there. In addition, a cluster of sites in the Dutch river area can be linked to the well-developed settlement archaeology of this region.

Region	Number of sites	Percentage of total
Northern sand and clay areas	45	17 %
Flanders	19	7 %
Dutch and German loess region	84	31 %
Belgian loess region	74	27 %
Northwestern France	48	18 %

Table 2.1. Number of sites per subregion.

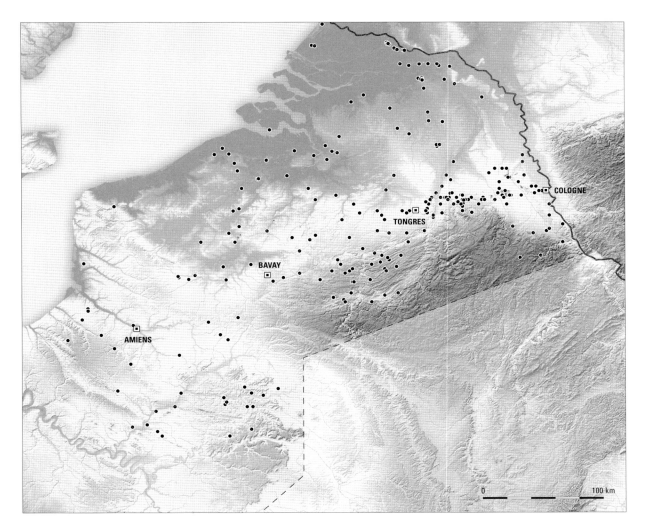

Fig 2.1. General distribution of the inventoried sites.

2.3 THE RESEARCH BACKGROUND

Below I explore the research background of the dataset by looking at some important research traditions throughout the research region, the variability in the volume of research through time and the scale and quality of research.

Within the extensive research region and throughout the 19th and 20th centuries, we can distinguish a number of research traditions that will be discussed below. In general we can say that there has been an significant increase in archaeological research from about the 1960s, linked to significant economic growth and related developments in the landscape. From that time on, much of the research has involved rescue archaeology or development-led archaeology.

The oldest villa research was of a different kind, however. During the 19th and earlier 20th century, a rich archaeological research tradition existed in the Dutch and Belgian loess region.[2] Excavations were commonly led by individuals interested in ancient history (often priests) or by antiquarian societies. The National Museum of Antiquities (Rijksmuseum van Oudheden, Leiden) also took part in these initiatives in Dutch Limburg, especially during the first half of the 20th century.[3] Excavations generally focused on the most monumental parts of rural settlements, usually main houses with stone foundations and bath buildings. Unfortunately, the lack of detailed phasing and lack of attention to less monumental settlement phases and the broader settlement context have rendered this kind of research less useful for the objectives of this study.

From about the 1970s onwards, a tradition of settlement research arose in the Dutch sand and clay areas. This research consisted of large-scale excavations embedded in long-term research projects, initiated and led by the State Archaeological Service (ROB)[4] and several universities. From the late 1970s and 1980s, ROB launched research projects that highlighted the Dutch Kromme Rijn and eastern river areas.[5] The various universities had their own core research regions. Leiden University focused on the region surrounding the town of Oss, while the University of Amsterdam (UvA) and the VU University Amsterdam (VU) concentrated on the Meuse-Demer-Scheldt (MDS) and Kempen regions, particularly the surroundings of Weert and Someren. The VU University Amsterdam has also directed its focus on the Dutch river area (e.g. excavations at Tiel-Passewaaij and Geldermalsen-Hondsgemet). In recent years, the existing tradition of settlement archaeology has continued within commercial archaeology, predominantly in relation to the large-scale expansion of cities (many of them 'Vinex' neighbourhoods) and infrastructural developments.

Intensive development-led archaeology also emerged in northern France, especially from the 1990s.[6] With the creation of the INRAP institute, many excavations have been carried out in regions that saw the large-scale development of roads, railroads and commercial areas (labelled Zone d'Activité Commerciale (ZAC) in French), providing opportunities for archaeology to significantly expand the knowledge about rural settlement in these regions. In northern France in particular, large areas have been surveyed and excavated, generating unique new insights into the structure and development of the rural landscape and settlement, without an *a priori* focus on the most monumental and visible settlement traces. Pre-monumental and non-monumental settlement traces, the broader settlement context and the relationship between pre-Roman and Roman-period rural settlement are potential themes that can be studied using the results of this research.

Rescue archaeology in the German part of the research region, west of Cologne, is associated with developments that are still more far-reaching and destructive. From the 1970s in particular, large-scale opencast mining has destroyed large tracts of land, offering unique opportunities for archaeological research. In the three main mining areas of Inden, Garzweiler and Hambach, an extraordinarily

[2] See De Maeyer 1937, 1940; Braat 1934, 1941.

[3] Well-known archaeologists associated with this museum are Braat, Remouchamps and Holwerda.

[4] The Rijksdienst voor het Oudheidkunding Bodemonderzoek (ROB) is now known as the Cultural Heritage Agency/Rijksdienst voor het Cultureel Erfgoed (RCE).

[5] Vos 2009, 6-9.

[6] See Haselgrove 2007.

large number of settlements were completely excavated, and entire stretches of land were thoroughly examined.

2.3.2 VARIABILITY IN THE VOLUME OF RESEARCH

Because the quality of documentation is a key factor, it is generally the more recent data – mainly excavations carried out from the 1970s-1980s onwards – that is best suited to meeting the objectives of this study. Although much older research presents us with some fairly useful plans, it generally lacks detailed information on the chronology, development and broader settlement context. With this in mind, it would be interesting to gain a picture of the temporal pattern of research. A research period has therefore been determined for each site, divided into three chronological groups: before 1950, 1950 to 1979, and after 1980. For the region as a whole, it appears that of the sites included in the dataset, 48 were excavated before 1950, 51 between 1950 and 1979 and no fewer than 171 after 1980 (see table 2.2).

Period	Northern sand and clay areas	Dutch and German loess region	Flanders	Belgian loess region	Northwestern France
Before 1950	2	23	0	23	0
1950s-1970s	7	19	3	19	3
1980s-2000s	36	42	16	32	45

Table 2.2. Overview of the sites used in this study per period of research per modern-day country.

Fig. 2.2 visualises the distribution of sites in relation to the period in which the excavation was carried out (see also table 2.2). Interestingly, relatively much recent research has been conducted in northern France and Flanders, while in the Dutch and Belgian loess region there was a rich research tradition before 1950.

2.3.3 SCALE AND QUALITY OF RESEARCH

Another important variable is the scale of research, which varies from almost completely excavated landscapes to fragmentarily documented traces of individual buildings. This variable is generally related to the data's value to this study. Table 2.3 presents an overview of the scale of research, divided into four classes. The category of A-sites comprises large-scale excavations whereby complete settlements were excavated. Overall, good-quality chronological data on developments in settlement organisation and house building is available for these sites. The B-category contains partially excavated settlements. Here, excavation reaches beyond the level of the individual building, but the entire settlement complex is not documented. Sites classified in category C include settlements where only the main house was excavated. In many cases, the development trajectory of house building could be reconstructed. Lastly, category-D sites are fragmentarily excavated sites that nonetheless provide useful data on settlement morphology, chronology or development. Of course, many more category-D sites can be found within the research region, but these were not classified as useful for the present study and were therefore not included in the inventory.

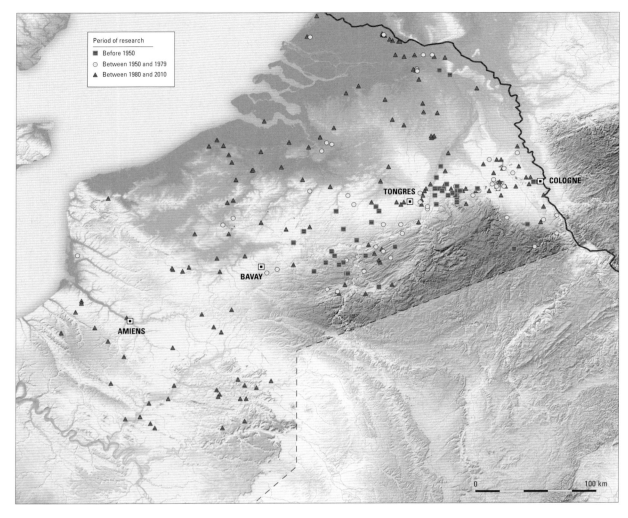

Fig. 2.2. Distribution of sites, related to the period of research: before 1950, 1950 to 1979, and 1980 to 2010. Also see table 2.2.

It should be emphasised that the scale of excavation and publication are not necessarily related. A fuller publication of quite some important large-scale excavations in France and Germany is eagerly awaited. This means that some large-scale research can at this time be used only to a limited extent for the research questions in this study.

Data class	Number of sites	Percentage of total
A-sites	60	22%
B-sites	92	34%
C-sites	94	35%
D-sites	24	9%

Table 2.3. Overview of the variety of scale of research within the dataset. Four classes of data quality have been defined.

Fig. 2.3 visualises the distribution of sites in relation to the scale of research. Much large-scale research (A-category) has been done in the German loess region, the northern sand and clay areas and north-

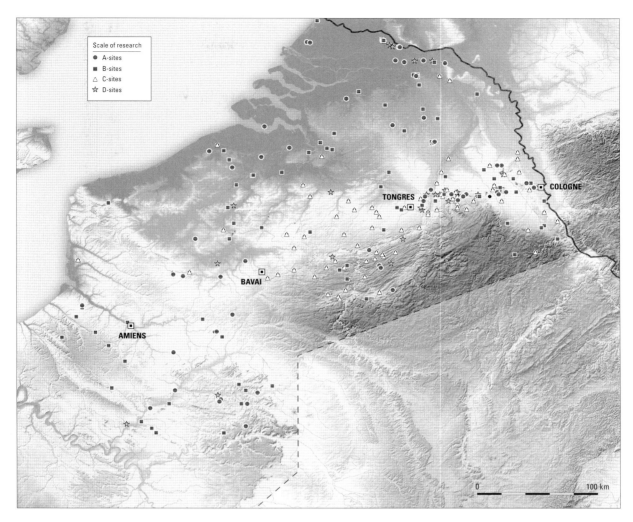

Fig. 2.3. Distribution of sites, related to the scale of research: A-, B-, C- or D-sites. Also see table 2.3.

western France. C-category sites are concentrated in the Belgian, Dutch and German loess belt. We see that sites in category A and B are in fact predominant in the regions that saw a substantial amount of recent research.

2.4 REPRESENTATIVITY AND BIASES

For a proper assessment of the analysis results, it is essential to be aware of potential biases in the data-set. Of course, the picture presented here does not necessarily reflect historical reality. All kinds of factors may potentially affect – and have affected – the way in which we reconstruct rural settlement in the Roman period.

The first important bias concerns the nature of the research. Key factors include the research focus, the choices that are made, the available documentation techniques, and the leading motivations for research. As previously discussed, the general tendency to excavate the most monumental traces of rural settlement is one key issue. This has created a bias whereby non-monumental settlement traces have been neglected. A reduction in this bias has only begun in recent decades, with the excavation of non- monumental or barely monumentalised settlements such as Heerlen-Trilandis, Veldwezelt,

Kesselt, Onnaing, Arras and Bohain-Vermandois. In addition, pre-monumental settlement phases are being documented in increasing detail. At many older excavations, these pre-monumental phases were not recognised, which means that only part of the settlement's development can be studied. The advantage of development-led archaeology is that no *a priori* choice is made with regard to excavation; modern developments rather than academic choices determine what is excavated. [7] This reduces the bias towards larger, monumental complexes and allows us to learn more about the variety and complexity of rural settlements.

A second bias is created by the sometimes severe erosion affecting archaeological records, destroying traces of posts, beams and even stone foundations left in the soil. As stated in chapter 1, loess soil is particularly sensitive to erosion. Sites where only the cellars or hypocausts, the parts of a house with the sturdiest and deepest foundations, are preserved illustrate this type of severe erosion particularly well. [8]

A further bias concerns the access, or lack of access, to research published as 'grey literature'. Compared to my home country, the Netherlands, it was more difficult to gain access to these publications from the other countries in the research area.

2.5 QUESTIONING THE DATASET: HOUSE ARCHITECTURE, SETTLEMENT LAYOUT AND REGIONAL DIFFERENTIATION

The dataset explored in this chapter offers many possibilities for studying interesting themes as well as new entry points for reconstructing broader processes within settlement development in the research region and the longer time period from the Late Iron Age to the Late Roman empire. The dataset is used as the basis for these analyses in the following chapters.

As previously stated, the main subject of this study is the reconstruction of both long-term and short-term development trajectories in rural settlements. Three main categories can be defined: the reconstruction of developments in settlement organisation, developments in house building, and regional and local differentiation with regard to these developments. In the next chapter, I will first explore the spatial, morphological and architectural dimensions of developments in settlement organisation and house building. In chapters 4 and 5 I will move on to explore the social and economic dimensions of these developments.

[7] Although it should also be reminded that this type of archaeology produces new biases given that development seeks out certain landscape types.

[8] Examples can be found at Veldwezelt, Riemst-Lafelt, Lanaken-Smeermaas, Venette-Bois de Plaisance zones 1 and 4, Amiens-Le Champ Pillard, Beauvais-Rue de Witten-'Les Champs Dolents', Gouvieux-La Flâche, Neuville-Saint-Amand-La Vallée de Neuville and Verneuil-en-Halatte.

3 Exploring villa development

Having explored the frameworks and datasets in previous chapters, I will now focus on the main theme of this study – villa development. Using a great deal of the high-resolution data on rural settlement available, I will attempt to reconstruct long-term development trends as well as short-term transformations on the level of the settlement and associated community. This chapter approaches developments solely from a spatial architectural perspective, focusing on both the organisation of settlement space and house building. The social and economic dimensions of the reconstructed developments will be given little attention here as they are the central themes of chapters 4 and 5 respectively.

As discussed in detail in previous chapters, the approach adopted in this study is a broad, diachronic one, focusing on both long-term and short-term developments. For rural settlements, longer-term developments include trends towards durability, stability, nucleation and structuration. Short-term transformations include the adoption of new materials, building techniques, forms and concepts. In this study I am seeking to explore villa development within the forcefield between continuity and change and therefore between these long-term trends and more rapid transformations of settlement and house construction. The main aim of this chapter is to reconstruct, visualise and analyse settlement and house development trajectories, with the intention of providing additional insight into the complexity of processes of change within the research region.

From an architectural perspective, a 'villa' is traditionally viewed as a monumental, Roman-style house, typically characterised by white plastered walls, red tiled roofs and porticoed façades, or, as a settlement with such a monumental house as the main residence. However, a broader approach as outlined in the introduction is needed in order to understand the complex processes involved in villa development. One basic point involves the non-essentialistic approach to the villa concept. I will purposely avoid discussions about detailed definitions of settlements and villas or about the point at which the concept of a 'true villa' came into being. Much more importantly, I will focus on significant development trajectories in rural settlements, of which the development of stone-built houses, traditionally referred to as villas, is only a part. Nevertheless, it is neither possible nor desirable to avoid the term villa altogether. In general, I will use the term 'villa house' for monumental, multi-roomed houses and 'villa settlement' for well-organised and monumentalised settlement compounds.

In this chapter I will first of all briefly explore how views on villa development have evolved from the early days of Roman archaeology up until the professional discipline of the 21st century. Using the best quality settlement data, I will then reconstruct settlement development trajectories per subregion and attempt to classify settlement types and settlement development trajectories in particular. I will also analyse the general, long lines of settlement development between the Late Iron Age and the Roman period. Next, I will construct a more detailed picture of houses, again reconstructing their development trajectories per subregion, once more followed by an attempt to classify these trajectories. Several specific elements of change will then be studied in greater detail. For the sake of context, I will also explore urban house development. In the concluding section I will assess how these analyses have improved our understanding of villa development as a phenomenon within the forcefield between continuity and change.

Views on the development of villas are intimately connected with ways in which villas are interpreted and defined. It is therefore important to understand how villa development has been studied and understood through the ages.

In the early days of Roman archaeology, a Romanist perspective prevailed, in which the villa was regarded as a phenomenon imported from the Roman world and inhabited by Roman officials, officers and wealthy tradesmen.[1] Excavations were confined to the most monumental parts of the villa, disregarding the broader settlement context and less monumental building phases. As a result, this research supported a colonist view. Indicative here is the interpretation of the large central halls in many provincial villas as open courts, similar to the Mediterranean *atrium*.[2] With regard to the villa, Swoboda thus suggests that '…dieser Typus sich in Italien gebildet und von hier aus seine Verbreitung in die Provinzen gefunden habe'.[3]

From the early 20th century onwards, such Romanist views were challenged by emerging theories of romanisation, identifying processes of social, economic and cultural change in the meeting between the Roman conqueror and native subject peoples.[4] The German scholar Franz Oelmann was a protagonist within the field of villa development. His famous excavation at Mayen-Im Brazil, carried out in the 1920s, demonstrated a traditional wood-built architecture being succeeded by a stone-built villa of the portico-risalith type.[5] For the first time, it became evident that the villa was not simply an exponent of colonisation, but could be linked to a gradual evolution involving native people who had '…früher oder später die überlegene Zivilisation übernommen…'.[6] In the slipstream of this new understanding, Fremersdorf identified early building phases at Köln-Müngersdorf[7] (late 1920s). In addition, in Britain and the Netherlands, wood-built predecessors were documented at Park Street (1943-1945), Ditchley (1935) and Kerkrade-Spekholzerheide (1950). The discrepancy with Italic house building was also recognised for the first time, creating a link to traditional local house building.[8]

These few examples of villa development trajectories, linked to the concept of romanisation, long remained prominent within the study of villas. Two important syntheses on villas, Rivet's[9] and Percival's, are based on the assumption that villa owners and builders were in the majority of cases natives.[10] Both authors principally regard the appearance and significance of the villa in socio-economic terms, in relation to the radically altered economic circumstances of the Roman province.[11] Official tax demands, increased town populations and military consumption, the emergence of new markets and the availability of new material culture stimulated the production of a surplus, creating wealth for investment in house building. Wightman distinguishes between villas that accumulated luxury in stages and those that were luxurious from the start.[12] She argues that radical changes, such as the rebuilding and considerable enlargement of houses, cannot be explained by wealth acquired from the exploitation of nearby farmland alone.[13] Consequently, villa studies started to set its sights on explaining the appearance of the villa in broader socio-economic terms, instead of exploring develop-

[1]   Derks 1998.
[2]   Oelmann 1921, 64-73, 1928, 117 ff. Oelmann argued that this space should be interpreted as a roofed hall. In many cases hearths were situated centrally within this hall, rendering an open-court interpretation improbable.
[3]   Swoboda 1919, 78.
[4]   Haverfield 1905/1906; Mommsen 1886.
[5]   Oelmann 1928.
[6]   Oelmann 1928, 137.
[7]   Fremersdorf 1933.

[8]   De Maeyer 1937, 128-131.
[9]   Rivet 1969.
[10] Percival 1976, 38; Bowen 1969, 1: 'The native Celts supplied more than the background to Roman villas in Britain. It seems likely that they actually owned most of them.'
[11] Rivet 1969, 215.
[12] Wightman 1985, 113.
[13] Wightman 1985, 111.

ments in rural settlements in greater detail. The main focus was still the monumental house, neglecting developments in the organisation of the broader settlement.

In more recent decades, both the quality and extent of rural archaeological excavations have improved dramatically. As a result, much more high-resolution spatial and chronological data on rural settlement has become available to those seeking to answer more complex research questions on settlement and house development. In the German loess region and in northern France in particular, a surge of archaeological activity resulted in much more detailed knowledge of rural settlement and the Roman-period countryside. In northwestern France, rural archaeology concentrated on the evolution from *fermes indigènes*, enclosed indigenous settlements, to villa settlements. This research topic was first touched upon by Roger Agache[14] in his seminal study of the Picardy region. As rural archaeology developed further, this theme was explored in more detail at a conference held in France in 1994, resulting in the publication '*De la ferme indigène à la villa Romaine. La Romanisation des campagnes de la Gaule*'.[15] This study casts light on the development of settlements and houses, including their non-monumental phases and the non-Roman elements of villa development. As a result the Roman part of villa development tended to be downplayed, particularly in comparison to earlier views on villas. For example, comparing provincial and Italic villa houses, Lenz argued that it was unlikely that Italic villas were the inspiration for provincial villa building.[16] In this context, Jan Slofstra's introduction of the concept of 'proto-villa' in 1991 is also of considerable interest.[17] Slofstra defined proto-villas as 'the architectural expression of the status of second-rate native chiefs who were not wealthy enough to build a Roman-style villa.'[18] Although frequently criticised, the term has caught on in archaeological literature to describe houses that displayed certain Mediterranean architectural influences, but failed to live up to what a 'real villa' should look like.[19] While this concept implies an essentialistic view of the villa and neglects the development context, it nevertheless directs attention to the variety and complexity of processes of change and the active role native people played in this. One of the few scholars who challenged this native model of continuous villa development is Gaitzsch, who has argued that the Hambach area was a colonised landscape linked to the foundation of Roman Cologne as a Colonia.[20] According to Gaitzsch, the settlement compounds excavated in the hinterland of Cologne were colonist foundations *ex nihilo*, founded within a more or less regularly organised landscape.[21]

The emergence of a more complex understanding of processes of change within the developing Roman provinces was also reflected in the more theoretical debate within British archaeology. The romanisation concept as an explanatory model for change has come in for much criticism in recent decades. The main objections were its inherent Romano-centrism, the Roman-native dichotomy and the modern-colonial background. The critics argued that the development of new models and concepts is pivotal for post-colonial times. In the meantime, a number of new concepts and models have been introduced, including globalisation, creolisation, network theory and consumption theories.

The present study can be placed within the tradition of settlement archaeology, most strongly developed in the sand and clay landscapes of the Netherlands and the loess landscape of French Picardy. It is this archaeological tradition that provides us with a broader perspective on the villa as part of settlement development, rather than viewing the villa as an isolated object of study. The ever-growing

[14] Agache 1978.

[15] Bayard/Collart 1996.

[16] Lenz 1998.

[17] Slofstra 1991.

[18] Slofstra 1991, 163.

[19] Heimberg 2002/2003; Vos 2003; Köhler 2005; Schuler 2000. Heimberg interprets the simple enclosed settlements of Pulheim-Brauweiler, Frimmersdorf 129, Bedburg-Garsdorf and the 1st-century settlement at Jüchen-Neuholz as proto-villas (Heimberg 2002/2003, 64-67).

[20] Gaitzsch 1986.

[21] Whereas Gaitzsch thought of these colonists as military veterans, other scholars have suggested that these settlers had civil Gallic backgrounds (Lenz 1998; Heimberg 2002/2003).

settlement dataset now allows us to reconstruct development trajectories in more detail, creating a clearer and more nuanced picture of the heterogeneous and complex processes of villa development.

3.2 EXPLORING SETTLEMENT DEVELOPMENT TRAJECTORIES

Having explored some backgrounds and defined some directions, I present in this section a description, visualisation and analysis of development trajectories in settlement organisation. First, as defined in the previous chapter, the available data on settlement development will be explored per subregion. Secondly, all data will be brought together to create a useful classification of settlements and settlement development trajectories in particular. Thirdly, settlement development will be viewed from a long-term perspective, covering both the Late Iron Age and Roman period.

3.2.1 DEVELOPMENTS IN SETTLEMENT ORGANISATION PER SUBREGION

The northern sand and clay areas

In recent decades, the northern sand and clay areas, directly south of the Roman *limes* and covering the Dutch river and coastal area as well as the sandy plains of Dutch Brabant and Limburg, have seen a considerable amount of good-quality, large-scale settlement research.[22] I will now explore this data with a view to reconstructing rural settlement development trajectories in this region.

One of the best-researched micro regions of the Brabant sandy plains is that surrounding the city of Oss.[23] For this region, we can track developments in settlement organisation from the Middle Iron Age right into the Roman period. During the earliest periods, small numbers of farmsteads shifted through seemingly stable settlement territories. Each generation saw farmsteads being rebuilt at a new location. During the later Iron Age, the number of contemporary farmsteads rose to a maximum of four within a single settlement territory, whereas farmsteads were increasingly being rebuilt at the same location.[24] Settlement thus became progressively more stable during this period. At two sites, Oss-Schalkskamp and Almstein, settlement space was even enclosed by ditches, which was unusual for Late Iron Age settlements in this region.[25] After 50 BC, in the transition period between the Late Iron Age and the Roman period, two settlements in the Oss region seem to have remained occupied, although habitation is difficult to trace archaeologically for this phase. In the earlier 1st century AD, the relatively dispersed and unstructured habitation at Oss-Westerveld was reorganised by the creation of a rectangular enclosed settlement compound containing three or four contemporary farmsteads. During the Flavian period, the number of farmsteads increased conciderably to a maximum of possibly ten contemporary farmsteads. Then, around 100 AD, a remarkable change took place. One farmstead was separated from the rest by a rectangular ditch system. Apart from this separation, the architectural character of both the house (a portico-house) and the material culture indicate the special status of its inhabitants.[26] A number of other settlements founded in the Oss region during the 1st century AD – IJsselstraat, Horzak, Mettegeupel and Zomerhof – were also enclosed by ditches. However, none featured special-status farmsteads similar to that in Westerveld. Only the Zomerhof settlement included one particularly large house, prominently positioned on the edge of an open area, potentially indicating a special status.[27]

[22] Several syntheses on this settlement research have been published: Slofstra 1991; Roymans 1996; Roymans/ Theuws 1999; Verwers 1998; Gerritsen 2003; Vos 2009; Heeren 2009.

[23] Wesselingh 2000; Schinkel 1994, 2005; Gerritsen 2003;

Van der Sanden 1990; Jansen/Fokkens 1999.

[24] For an overview, see Gerritsen 2003, 181-189, 194-198.

[25] Wesselingh 2000, 197.

[26] Wesselingh 2000; Gerritsen 2003, 181.

[27] Wesselingh 2000, 198.

A development trajectory quite similar to Oss-Westerveld is documented at Hoogeloon-Kerkak-kers.[28] This settlement was founded in the early 1st century AD as an enclosed compound, probably containing four farmsteads arranged more or less around an open space.[29] Generally, houses seem to have been rebuilt at the same location or nearby. The maximum number of contemporaneously inhabited farmhouses at Hoogeloon was probably four. In the period between around 120 and 150 AD, a significant reorganisation of settlement space took place. A separate compound, possibly measuring about 150 by 150 m, was created by means of a ditch.[30] A multi-roomed house on stone foundations, a drinking hole and a hypothetical corral were found on this compound. The house itself was closely surrounded by a rectangular palisade. The other, traditional houses in the settlement were situated directly outside the separately created compound. Parallel to Westerveld, at Hoogeloon, we come across a combination of spatial segregation within the settlement and architectural developments in house building. What is particularly interesting is that the monumental house stood on a prominent, slightly elevated location within the settlement, the same spot where two consecutive Alphen-Ekeren-type houses were also built in the preceding period. Slofstra suggested that the prominent location, combined with the special character of the material culture associated with these traditional houses, points to the prominent social position of their inhabitants within the local community.[31]

Riethoven-Heesmortel,[32] Nistelrode-Zwarte Molen[33] and Nistelrode-Loo[34] are among other enclosed settlements within the sand region of the Netherlands. The Riethoven settlement was enclosed in the 1st century AD, although the enclosure ditch was backfilled in later phases. Nistelrode-Loo has a development trajectory starting in the Late Iron Age and running into the Roman period. Over time, houses were becoming sturdier and the settlement became increasingly spatially stable. Settlement space was enclosed and internal space organised.[35] The Zwarte Molen settlement started as a single farmstead with a portico-house during the Flavian period. It was not until the 2nd century AD that the settlement was enclosed and evolved into a well-structured entity. A possible clue for the earlier systematic reorganisation of settlement space is the construction of four wells, forming a perfect square with sides measuring exactly 180 Roman feet. The excavators suggest that this phenomenon, dating back to the late 1st century AD, is an indication of the systemic layout of settlement space created by Roman geometricians.[36]

Aside from these enclosed and spatially well-organised settlements, another category of unenclosed and quite spatially dynamic sites demonstrates instead a continuation of the structure of Iron Age settlements. These Roman-period settlements, such as Moergestel[37] and Lieshout-Beekseweg,[38] consisted of loosely structured clusters of two to five farmsteads, situated fairly close together and shifting over short distances, comparable to Late Iron Age settlements like Haps, Someren and Beegden. A loosely structured settlement of this kind also existed at Nederweert-Rosveld, although for a short period of time, probably between 150 and 180 AD, settlement space was reorganised by the construction of a common ditch system.[39]

To the north of this sandy region, in the Dutch river area, several well-documented sites reveal more about settlement development trajectories. One of the older excavations is Wijk bij Duurstede-De Horden (see fig. 3.1 for the development trajectory).[40] Its trajectory may be considered typical for this

[28] Slofstra 1985, 1991; Jeneson 2004.

[29] Awaiting the final publication, Jeneson's (2004) revised phasing is used here.

[30] This reconstruction is suggested by Jeneson (2004).

[31] Slofstra 1985, 1991.

[32] Verwers 1998, 66 ff.; Vossen 1997.

[33] Jansen 2008.

[34] Jansen 2008.

[35] Jansen 2008, 551.

[36] Jansen 2008, 134-136, 551.

[37] Verwers 1998, 66-67.

[38] Hiddink 2005a, 133-136.

[39] See fig. 6.10 in Hiddink 2005b, 96.

[40] This settlement was excavated between 1977 and 1987, and was extensively analysed and published by Wouter Vos (Vos 2002, 2009).

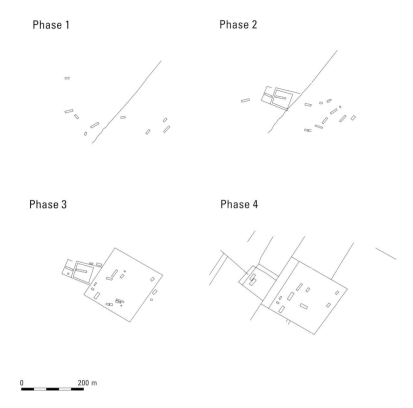

Phase 1   Phase 2

Phase 3   Phase 4

0   200 m

Fig. 3.1. Development trajectory of the Wijk bij Duurstede-De Horden settlement.

northern region, as other excavated sites demonstrate.[41] During the earliest settlement phase, dated to the first half of the 1st century AD, a number of farmsteads clustered within the settlement territory – or, alternatively, as the existence of a dividing ditch suggests, two territories – without being enclosed or organised by a common ditch system. Settlement was organised on the level of the individual farmstead. In a second phase, around the middle of the 1st century AD, one of the farmsteads was enclosed by a ditch, while the others were still quite loosely clustered. Subsequently, in the period 70 to 100 AD, the rest of the settlement was enclosed by a common ditch, forming a squarish settlement compound connected to the earlier enclosure. This organisational structure survived during the 2nd century, although it became integrated into a larger system of ditches organising the surrounding landscape.

As mentioned above, the same development could be identified at several other sites in the region, such as Druten-Klepperheide[42] and Rijswijk-De Bult,[43] as well as the more recently excavated sites of Tiel-Passewaaij[44] and Geldermalsen-Hondsgemet.[45] The settlements of Tiel, Druten and Rijswijk were founded around the beginning of the Common Era, while, at Geldermalsen, habitation went back to the 2nd century BC. During their earliest phases, these settlements consisted of loose clusters of one to four farmsteads without a common ditched enclosure. As at De Horden, space was significantly reorganised during subsequent phases. At Geldermalsen, Druten and Tiel, a settlement was first partly organised by ditches, enclosing single farmsteads. It was not until much later that all farmsteads were integrated into a common ditch system. At Geldermalsen, this development took place around 70 AD, and at Druten somewhere between 80 and 150 AD. The Tiel and Rijswijk settlements were enclosed during the first half of the 2nd century AD. The integration of the enclosed settlement within a wider ditch system, organising the surrounding landscape, as documented at De Horden, was also documented at Tiel-Passewaaij and Rijswijk-De Bult. Off-site excavations near Rijswijk have shown that the landscape was indeed organised by ditches in a systematic manner.

Aside from the sites described above, several settlements within the well-researched microregion of Houten – Houten-Overdam, Houten-Doornkade and Houten-Wulven – also followed patterns of development similar to De Horden.[46] At Houten-Doornkade, a large geometrical ditch system was

[41]   For the reconstructed settlement development trajectory of Wijk bij Duurstede-De Horden, see Vos 2009, 89-99, 104-108.

[42]   Hulst 1978; Maas 2007.

[43]   Bloemers 1978, 1980.

[44]   Heeren 2006, 2009.

[45]   Van Renswoude/Van Kerckhove 2009.

[46]   For an overview, see Vos 2009.

created in the Flavian period at the earliest.[47] Moreover, at Houten-Overdam,[48] a loosely structured cluster of farmsteads was reorganised with the creation of a settlement enclosure, probably during the second half of the 1st century AD. Once more, this enclosure was connected with a larger ditch system, organising the surrounding landscape.

In some of the settlements in the clay region, moves towards spatial segregation, as we established at Oss-Westerveld and Hoogeloon, could also be documented. At Geldermalsen-Hondsgemet and Wijk bij Duurstede-De Horden, separate compounds were defined within the settlement. In the case of Geldermalsen, both the marked entrance to the compound and the recovered material culture indicate the special status of its inhabitants.[49] At Wijk bij Duurstede, the presence of a portico-house probably suggests a similar conclusion. The farmstead first enclosed within the settlement of Druten, dating back to the late 1st century AD, also contained a portico-house, including a stone-lined cellar and walls decorated with painted wall plaster.

Reviewing the settlement data for this northern region, we can make some general observations. During the Late Iron Age and earliest Roman period, settlements consisted of small clusters of farmsteads, in many cases shifting over short distances within a settlement territory. Over time, farmsteads became increasingly stable and settlements increased in size to around five contemporary farmsteads, perhaps a few more. Houses were rebuilt more often in the same location. Continuity between the Late Iron Age and Roman period can be documented with regard to a substantial number of settlements. However, many other settlements were not founded until the early 1st century AD, which appears to have been a period of significant rural population growth. In addition, we observe a significant reorganisation of rural settlements. Some fairly large settlements, like Hoogeloon, Oss-Westerveld and probably Riethoven-Heesmortel, seem to have been enclosed by a common ditch as early as the first half of the 1st century AD. Most settlements, however, were still loosely structured in this period and were reorganised around the middle or the second half of the 1st century AD.[50] In this period, many stable and well-organised settlement compounds developed. Other settlements, such as Tiel-Passewaaij, Rijswijk-De Bult and Nederweert-Rosveld, were not reorganised until later, during the 2nd century AD. In addition to the appearance of settlement enclosures, internal settlement space was reorganised by locating new buildings parallel to the enclosure ditches and surrounding a central open space. For some settlements, internal spatial differentiation and segmentation can be documented as well. In several cases this development is related to shifting patterns of consumption, reflected in the mobile material culture and architectural changes, like the portico-houses that we will discuss in more detail below. This process can be dated to around the late 1st and early 2nd century AD.[51] Aside from these changes, settlements that remained open and only loosely structured also survived. These can be found in the sandy region of Brabant and Limburg, but also in the clay region, such as at Houten-Tiellandt.[52]

---

[47] Vos 2009, 118-126.

[48] Vos 2009, 148 ff.

[49] Van Renswoude/Van Kerckhove 2009, 467.

[50] According to Vos (2009, 133 ff.) almost all settlements in the Kromme Rijn area were being enclosed during the Flavian period.

[51] Apart from spatial segregation and architecture, material culture is another indication for the special position of some farmsteads. Slofstra identified a number of traditional houses within rural settlements that were associated with early imports, probably indicating the special status of its inhabitants; these were Hoogeloon, Riethoven and possibly Donk. Special finds were also associated with the separate compound at Oss-Westerveld. New research

can add to that. At the settlement of Aalter, which was enclosed at an early date, Augustan-Tiberian imports were documented, the earliest in the region. And at both Geldermalsen-Hondsgemet and Den Haag-Wateringse Veld, fragments of military equipment indicate the special position of the inhabitants. The finds show the involvement of the inhabitants in wider networks of exchange or their connection with the Roman military. It is remarkable that these were the settlements with a higher degree of organisation and where changes in house building can sometimes be documented in later phases.

[52] Vos 2009, 133 ff.

Overall, a more differentiated settlement landscape arose, with some settlements developing into large, enclosed and structured entities, while others retained the character of small, open and loosely structured clusters of farmsteads.

Flanders

The subregion of Flanders comprises the Belgian provinces of East and West Flanders, around the Belgian cities of Ghent and Bruges. This region has been subject to an extensive academic synthesis by Wim De Clercq, who used the significant jump in settlement research from the 1990s onwards to shed new light on Roman-period rural settlement.[53]

As for other regions, the transition from the Late Iron Age to the Early Roman period is difficult to grasp, at least archaeologically. There is little data available on settlement activity for this period. According to De Clercq, this is not so much a matter of poor archaeological visibility or a lack of recognisability. Instead, he argues, it could indeed reflect a historical reality. Settlement density was low in this period, as the landscape was largely covered with woods and habitation was concentrated in certain suitable areas. From the Flavian period onwards, however, there was a significant increase in habitation activity and density. Aalter-Langevoorde is one of the few settlements for which actual continuity between the Late Iron Age and the Roman period could be documented.[54] In the 2nd century BC, the first enclosure, possibly with ritual significance, was dug at this site. Probably around the middle of the 1st century BC, a new enclosure was created, covering an area of 150 by 150 m. A traditional Alphen-Ekeren-type house and a number of secondary buildings (including a large nine- and later twelve-post granary) were situated against the northern enclosure ditch. Remarkably early imports found in the enclosure ditches date back to the Augustan period. Along with painted plaster and slate, the latter potentially used for roof covering, these could indicate the special status of the compound's inhabitants. The house was rebuilt in the Flavian period and habitation continued into the 2nd century AD.

Another well-excavated settlement, Bruges-Refuge, consisted of a cluster of two traditional farm-houses during the Early Roman period.[55] In the Flavian period the settlement was reorganised to include four farmsteads, enclosed by a common ditch (fig. 3.2). The houses were situated against the ditches surrounding a central open space. Each house had its own secondary building and well, and in some cases a ditch separated neighbouring farmsteads from each other. Around the middle of the 2nd century, a new house occupied a prominent position on the northern short side of the compound. A remarkable cluster of granaries was situated around this house. Seemingly, the inhabitants of this house occupied a special position within the settlement community and expressed this by constructing the house at this prominent place, while at the same time demonstrating their control over production by means of the granaries. As we will see later, a similar situation was documented at Neerharen-Rekem.

Evergem-Kluizendok is a location with a special character. Three areas – Zandeken (4 ha), Hultjen (12 ha) and Puymeersen (1 ha) – have been excavated at this large site measuring a total of 170 hectares.[56] The sites comprised groups of more or less connected enclosed farmsteads, situated on the slightly higher parts of the fairly low sandy area. Both the excavations and paleo-ecological analysis indicate that the area was not inhabited before the 2nd century AD, when woodland would have dominated the area. A total of 15 farmsteads were documented in the three areas. Although no strictly planned layout seems to have been present, the farmsteads appear to have formed a coherent complex, respecting each other's boundaries. A road seems to have functioned as a structuring element in the area. This layout, combined with the limited time depth of the complex, suggests that the area

53   De Clercq 2009. An English trade edition is in preparation.

54   De Clercq 2009, 220 ff.

55   De Clercq 2009, 225-228.

56   Laloo *et al.* 2008; De Clercq 2009, 229 ff.

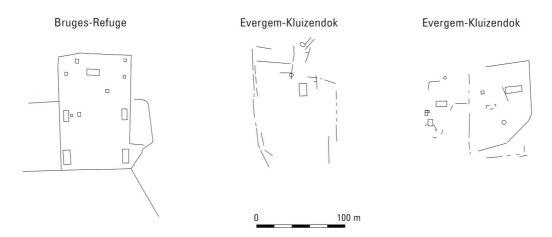

Fig. 3.2. The Bruges-Refuge settlement and two of the enclosed farmsteads of Evergem-Kluizendok.

was colonised in the 2nd century AD. The colonisation of this marginal area was probably linked to increasing pressure on land in this particular period.

For this region, only few indicators exist for the presence of Roman-period open settlements. Only at Wijnegem[57] and Oelegem[58] does this settlement organisation seem plausible.

The Dutch and German loess region

This subregion covers the loess belt between Meuse and Rhine, located between the sandy regions to the north and the mountainous regions of the Eifel-Ardennes massif to the south. The main Roman road from Cologne to Boulogne constituted a central element within this loess region, running almost precisely along the centre line of the loess belt. In the Dutch loess region, settlement archaeology is poorly developed, especially when compared to the more northerly sand and clay areas. A considerable amount of research, especially in the later 19th and earlier 20th century, has focused on the monumental phases of villa settlements, disregarding non-monumental traces and the broader settlement context. Furthermore, techniques for reconstructing settlement development were not yet developed in this period. As a result, there is limited usable data for this region. The situation is completely different, however, in the German part of the loess region. An enormous amount of data on rural settlements has been collected from the 1970s onwards, the indirect result of the large-scale opencast lignite mining carried out in this area. The complete destruction of the landscape has created unique opportunities to excavate entire settlements, even entire landscapes, within the three main extraction areas of Frimmersdorf, Weisweiler and Hambach, as well as the areas that were used for resettling the modern population. Unfortunately, this wealth of data and its inherent academic potential cannot be fully exploited as publication has not kept up with the excavation activities. Only a few sites have been published in detail (Hambach 59, 132, 512, 516 and Frimmersdorf 49 and 131). The majority, however, are published as short notifications in year books like the 'Bonner Jahrbücher' or 'Archäologie im Rheinland'.

As stated, only a small portion of the research carried out in the Dutch loess region meets modern standards and the objectives of this study. Furthermore, two of the better excavations, Maasbracht and Voerendaal-Ten Hove,[59] have only been preliminarily published, limiting their use. In addition, little is known about the Late Iron Age. Fragmentary traces have been documented, but it remains impossible to create a clear picture of Late Iron Age settlement for this region.

[57]   Cuyt 1991.

[58]   De Boe/Lauwers 1979, 1980.

[59]   Willems/Kooistra 1986, 1987, 1988; Willems 1995.

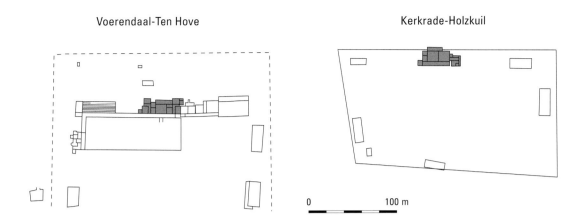

Voerendaal-Ten Hove   Kerkrade-Holzkuil

0   100 m

Fig. 3.3. The settlements of Voerendaal-Ten Hove (left) and Kerkrade-Holzkuil (right).

An interesting exception is the recently excavated settlement of Kerkrade-Holzkuil,[60] especially in terms of the quality of excavation and publication (see fig. 3.14a). It was founded at the end of the 1st century AD as a well-structured, although probably not yet enclosed, settlement. The buildings were basically ordered along two opposing axes, including an open space in between. A pond was created within this central open space. The general layout was maintained during the settlement's occupation. The settlement's main house was positioned centrally on the northwestern building axis and it only gradually evolved into a stone-built house with a monumental façade and bath section (see fig. 3.28a).

The other site that was almost completely excavated is Voerendaal-Ten Hove.[61] This settlement has a longer occupation history than Kerkrade-Holzkuil. The earliest activity on the site probably dates back to the later Iron Age and consists of a seemingly defensive ditched enclosure, comparable to enclosures at Niederzier and Jülich-Bourheim. The first enclosed rural settlement was created somewhere between 50 BC and 50 AD. Small wooden buildings were situated on the enclosed compound. However, the precise organisation of the settlement remains unclear.[62] Around the middle of the 1st century AD, a house on stone foundations was built, occupying a central position on the settlement compound. The secondary buildings were nevertheless still post-built during this phase. Subsequently, around 100 AD, the complex was completely reorganised as the existing house was torn down and a new complex of buildings, including a main residence, granary and bathhouse, was constructed (see fig. 3.3). These buildings were connected by means of a long front portico, creating a remarkably broad and impressive façade.

A much larger amount of settlement data is available for the German loess region.[63] Here, we can also shed some light on what pre-Roman or the earliest Roman-period rural settlement looked like. This habitation consisted of loosely ordered clusters of small, post-built buildings that can be identified as houses, byres and granaries. Together, they formed farmsteads.[64] Unfortunately, it is difficult to establish how many of these farmsteads were in fact contemporary. The well-known Roman-period

[60] Tichelman 2005.

[61] Willems 1986; Willems/Kooistra 1987, 1988; Kooistra 1996.

[62] New, unpublished analyses of the non-monumental phases of the settlement of Voerendaal-Ten Hove have shed somewhat more light on these early settlement phases (these analyses were carried out by students of the VU University in Amsterdam).

[63] For overviews, see Gechter/Kunow 1986; Kunow 1994; Gaitzsch 1986, 2010; Heimberg 2002/2003.

[64] Settlement traces dated to this period were documented at Garzweiler-Köhmbachtal, Eschweiler-Laurenzberg, Weeze-Baal, Jüchen-Neuholz and possibly Pulheim-Brauweiler. Other sites include Lahnstein-Oberlahnstein, Keulen-Porz, Westhoven (Hegewisch 2007, 48) and Eschweiler-Lohn.

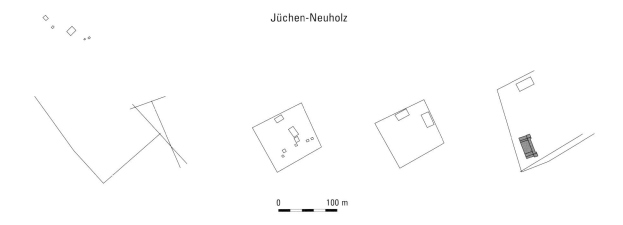

Jüchen-Neuholz

0   100 m

Fig. 3.4. The development trajectory of the settlement of Jüchen-Neuholz.

settlements, however, were all enclosed and well-structured compounds. How, then, did these evolve and are there any indications for continuity of development between the Late Iron Age and the Roman period? Recent excavations could shed some interesting light on this topic. At Jüchen-Neuholz,[65] settlement space seems to have been reorganised from the Augustan period onwards (see fig. 3.4). First, an only fragmentarily known ditch system was created. A wood-built house, larger than its Iron Age predecessors and possibly built on horizontal foundation beams, was situated near these ditches. The first enclosed settlement compound, measuring 80 by 80 m, was created in the first half of the 1st century AD. Eight post-built constructions were situated on the compound in a loosely ordered manner. During the later 1st century, two larger rectangular buildings were constructed directly along the existing enclosure ditches, now creating a more strictly ordered compound. Then, in the 2nd century, a new, larger compound was created, containing a number of new buildings positioned along the enclosure ditches. The main building was a monumental, multi-roomed house on stone foundations. The settlement was destroyed by fire before the end of the 2nd century.

A similar development trajectory could be documented at Pulheim-Brauweiler (see fig. 3.14a).[66] Here, the first settlement phase dates to the latest phase of the Iron Age or earliest Roman period[67] and comprises a loosely ordered cluster of small buildings. Around the middle of the 1st century AD, an enclosed compound was created, containing small buildings oriented to the enclosure ditch. This compound was inhabited until the end of the 1st century AD. Around the same time, a new compound was created just west of the previous one. Three large post-built structures, one building on horizontal foundation beams and four sunken-floor huts were situated parallel to the enclosure ditches and around a central open space. The settlement was inhabited until the middle or the second half of the 3rd century AD.

Aside from these well-documented examples, Late Iron Age or Early Roman settlement activity was also observed at a number of other Roman-period enclosed settlements. Late Iron Age settlement activity was documented at Bedburg-Garsdorf,[68] a mere hundred metres northwest of the Roman-

[65] Andrikopoulou-Strack *et al.* 1999; Frank/Keller 2007.

[66] Andrikopoulou-Strack *et al.* 2000.

[67] In an earlier publication (Archäologie im Rheinland 1999, 82-84) a pre-Roman settlement phase was suggested, but later (Andrikopoulou-Strack *et al.* 2000) this

first phase was redated to the earliest Roman period. However, find material and house building were still heavily rooted in Late Iron Age traditions in this period.

[68] Piepers 1959, 382-384.

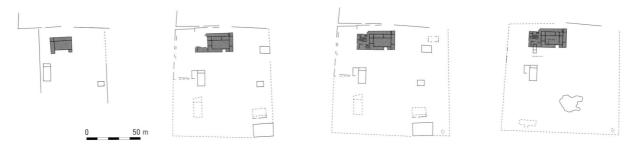

Fig. 3.5. Development of the settlement of Hambach 59 between the middle of the 1st and the 3rd centuries AD.

period settlement. Late Iron Age settlement traces were also documented near the settlement of Frimmersdorf 131.[69] Should we assume continuity here between Late Iron Age and Roman-period habitation? Slight shifts in the location of habitation appear to be a common phenomenon and a possibility that should not be ignored when reconstructing settlement development trajectories.

Some other settlements started as unenclosed farmsteads in the earlier Roman period. Settlements at Niederzier-Steinstrass (Hambach 412)[70] and Jüchen-Auf dem Fuchsberg (Frimmersdorf 129),[71] for example, consisted of a loosely structured cluster of post-built structures in the first half of the 1st century AD. Subsequently, during the second half of the 1st century AD, settlement space was subject to significant reorganisation: a rectangular enclosed compound was created and internal settlement space was structured, while the buildings were ordered along the settlement ditches and around a central open space. Settlements Hambach 512, 516 and probably Rheinbach-Baumarkt also remained unenclosed during their earliest phases, dating back to the middle of the 1st century AD.

Generally, however, the majority of the settlements are assumed to have been founded as well-structured compounds. Settlements such as Frimmersdorf 49,[72] Frimmersdorf 131,[73] Kerpen-Sindorf[74] (dating back to the second half of the 1st century AD), Hambach 403,[75] Bedburg-Garsdorf[76] (middle of the 1st century AD), Hambach 69,[77] Hambach 127[78] (1st century AD) and Jüchen-Neuotzenrath[79] (2nd century) are all classified as the typical compound settlement type (designated as 'Streuhofanlagen' in German literature). One of the most well-studied and published sites is Hambach 59.[80] In the first phase, dated to the 1st century AD, a fairly small, enclosed compound (at least 0.76 ha) contained a simple stone house and two secondary buildings, arranged along the sides (see fig. 3.5). During the second phase, dating back to the 2nd century AD, the compound was considerably extended, covering a surface of 1.5 hectares. The main house was now positioned centrally on the northern enclosure ditch and six secondary buildings were arranged on the compound south of the main house, in an almost axial layout (also see fig. 4.2). Later on, the compound was slightly extended once more, after which the ditches appear to have been backfilled. Apart from the main house, only two or three secondary buildings were in use in this late phase, during the 3rd century.

[69] According to Heimberg (2002/2003, 72-73) pre-Roman traces were also documented at Hambach 403, 512 and 516 and early Roman traces at Sinnersdorf and Rheinbach-Flerzheim.

[70] Archäologie im Rheinland 2007, 69-71.

[71] Archäologie im Rheinland 1997, 53-55.

[72] Köhler 2005.

[73] Köhler 2005.

[74] Archäologie im Rheinland 2002, 87-89.

[75] Bonner Jahrbücher 185, 574-576; Bonner Jahrbücher 186, 617-627.

[76] Piepers 1959, 382-384.

[77] Gaitzsch 1986; Bonner Jahrbücher 183, 652-654.

[78] Archäologie im Rheinland 2000, 73-76.

[79] Archäologie im Rheinland 1999, 82-84. Andrikopoulou-Strack et al. 2000.

[80] Hallmann-Preuss 2002/2003.

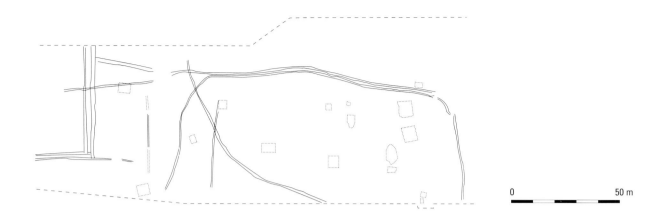

Fig. 3.6. The Late Iron Age enclosed settlement of Brugelette.

This latter settlement thus doubled in compound surface area during its second development phase. A number of other sites were also much enlarged as they evolved. In the second half of the 1st century AD, Hambach 512 grew from a small open farmstead to a 2.5 hectare enclosed compound settlement, after which its area was once more reduced to a single hectare. Such a drop in settlement size was also documented with regard to Hambach 516.[81] In contrast, at Jüchen-Neuholz, the 2nd century compound was considerably larger than that of the 1st century AD.

Another interesting phenomenon is the backfilling of settlement enclosure ditches in the 2nd century AD. From then on, settlement boundaries were marked by palisades or fences, as documented at Hambach 512, 516, 403, 224 and Cologne-Widdersdorf. However, it remains unclear exactly how we should interpret this.

The seemingly large-scale foundation of new settlements in the second half of the 1st century, combined with the reconstructed regular settlement pattern, has led scholars to believe that we are dealing with a colonised landscape in this region.[82] Or could it be that, like Jüchen and Pulheim, more settlements than anticipated had longer development trajectories? Might we have missed earlier, less structured and less monumental settlement phases, predating the development of the well-structured enclosed compound settlements?

Quite unlike the compound settlements described above is the axial complex of Blankenheim-Hülchrath.[83] This highly monumental complex had a strict axial layout with a large main house fronted by two rows of rather large secondary buildings. Unfortunately, it is not possible to establish whether the earliest settlement, dating back to the 1st century AD, was already organised according to the axial layout, such as is the case at Champion-Le Emptinne.[84] The settlement complex eventually comprised six secondary stone-built constructions and a large main house.

The Belgian loess region
The research background for the Belgian loess region is differentiated. Similar to the Dutch loess zone, a strong tradition of monumental villa research existed during the late 19th and early 20th century.[85] Unlike the Dutch region, however, a significant amount of settlement research has been conducted from the 1970s onwards, providing us with a useful set of data for reconstructing settlement development.

[81] Kaszab-Olschewski 2006, 146-147.

[82] Gaitzsch 1986.

[83] Oelmann 1916; Horn 1987, 360-361; Smith 1997, 264 ff.

[84] Horn 1987, 360-361.

[85] For an overview see De Maeyer 1937, 1940.

Other than in the above-mentioned region, where open settlements dominated, Late Iron Age settlements in the Belgian loess zone seem to have been enclosed by ditches.[86] In the better-documented settlements of Chievres-Ladeuze and Brugelette-Mévergnies (fig. 3.6), buildings were arranged loosely on an enclosed compound, still lacking a more strictly ordered layout. Unfortunately, it is not clear whether these enclosed settlements can be identified as single farmsteads that were repeatedly rebuilt at the same location, or that two or more contemporary farmsteads were in fact occupied on the compound.

Late Iron Age habitation activity was documented for quite a number of Roman period settlements.[87] Only for a few sites, however, could real continuity be demonstrated with any degree of certainty. For many other sites, chronological resolution was simply too low to establish the precise relationship between Late Iron Age and Roman-period habitation.[88]

Again, the transition and the earlier Roman period are difficult to grasp archaeologically. At Meslin-l'Évêque,[89] an enclosed settlement with small post-built structures could be dendrochronologically dated to between 40 and 10 BC. At a nearby location, an enclosed farmstead with a fairly large wooden house (20 by 30 m) and a number of smaller secondary buildings survived into the 1st century AD.[90] A monumental villa complex was created at that same location, probably around the third quarter of the 1st century AD. This complex followed the orientation of the pre-Roman settlement, possibly suggesting a degree of continuity in development (see fig. 3.7). For Gesves-Sur le Corria, several earlier, possibly even Late Iron Age, buildings were also documented, with a different orientation from the later monumental house. And at Bruyelle-Haute Éloge, a comparable situation was documented, suggesting continuity between the Iron Age and Roman period.[91] At this site, the later monumental villa complex followed the orientation of earlier settlement ditches. Yet another enclosed settlement, dating back to the end of the pre-Roman Iron Age or the earliest Roman period, was documented at Haccourt.[92] From around the middle of the 1st century AD, this settlement gradually developed into an extensive and highly monumental complex, probably with an axial layout.[93] Unfortunately, however, since the working compound has not been excavated, the exact period in which this axial complex was laid out remains unclear. It may have had a development trajectory similar to that of Meslin-L'Évêque. At Neerharen-Rekem[94] an enclosed settlement existed during the Late Iron Age or Early Roman period.[95] In the Flavian period, a stone house was erected on the location of one of the farmhouses. In addition, several secondary buildings on stone foundations were constructed in front of the main residence, forming a fairly well-structured settlement complex. A similar enclosed settlement with traditional Alphen-Ekeren houses, probably dating back to the 1st century AD, was documented at Lanaken-Smeermaas-Kerkveld.[96] Later again, a house on stone foundations, of which only a cellar and hypocaust have been preserved, was constructed within the settlement. And yet another

[86]   Settlements like Neerharen-Rekem, Engis/Hermal-le-sous-Huy, Leuze-en-Hainaut-Tourpes, Brugelette-Mévergnies, Haccourt, Chievres-Ladeuze, Vechmaal-Middelpadveld, Heers-Vechmaal, Veldwezelt and Ath-Ghislengien all seem to have been enclosed during the Late Iron Age.

[87]   Meslin-l'Évêque, Haccourt, Gesves-Coria, Neerharen-Rekem, Veldwezelt, Bruyelle-Haute Éloge, Vechmaal-Middelpadveld, Broekom, Wange-Damekort and Erps-Kwerps.

[88]   This is the case for settlements at Meslin-l'Évêque, Gesves-Sur le Corria, Neerharen-Rekem, Haccourt, Veldwezelt, and Bruyelle-Haute Éloge.

[89]   Deramaix/Sartieaux 1994; Houbrachts/Zambon 1994;

Braekeleer 1994; Deramaix 2006; Brulet 2009, 309-310.

[90]   Deramaix 2006, 67.

[91]   Corbiau 1997, 319-322; Brulet 2009, 305-309. Only fragmentary traces of Late Iron Age habitation activity have been documented. The layout and character of this settlement phase thus remain relatively unclear.

[92]   De Boe 1973, 1975, 1976, 40.

[93]   De Boe 1973, 112.

[94]   De Boe 1985a.

[95]   The large house (building B in figure 8 in De Boe 1985a) was of a different house type and possibly predated the two-aisled houses that also had a different orientation.

[96]   Pauwels/Creemers 2006, 49-118.

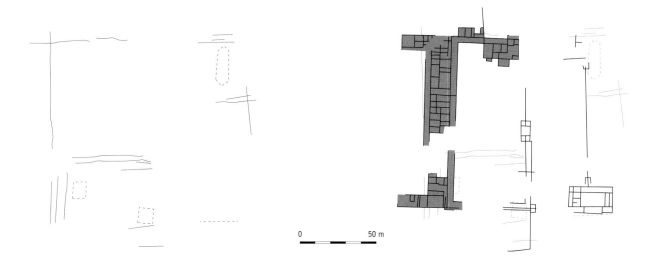

0   50 m

Fig. 3.7. Meslin-L'Evêque. The development of an enclosed settlement with post-built houses into a monumental axially-organised settlement complex.

potentially pre-Roman enclosed settlement was found at Veldwezelt.[97] The discovery of an isolated cellar could suggest that, again, a monumental house was constructed during a later phase. The rest of the settlement was dominated by traditional houses, comparable to the above-mentioned settlement of Hoogeloon.

A number of well-structured sites seem to have been founded *ex nihilo* around the middle or in the second half of the 1st century AD. The complex of Champion-Le Emptinne,[98] for example, was founded with a strict axial layout shortly after the middle of the 1st century AD. The same applies to the settlement of Rochefort-Jemelle,[99] which seems to have been founded as a well-structured complex with a monumental main house around the middle of the 1st century AD. A third example is the settlement of Hamois-Le Hody,[100] founded around the middle of the 1st century AD as a fairly structured compound settlement, comparable to Kerkrade-Holzkuil. The Vezin-Namêche settlement suggests similar features.[101]

Northwestern France

The region of northwestern France, covering the departments of Nord, Pas-de-Calais and the three departments of the Picardy (Somme, Oise and Aisne), has been the subject of well-developed settlement archaeology. This can be linked to various modern developments, including the large-scale extraction of gravel, the development of commercial areas and the construction of roads and railways.[102] This wealth of data provides us with excellent opportunities for reconstructing settlement development. One particular and well-known dataset will not be used in this study, however. The extensive aerial surveys carried out by Roger Agache[103] have provided a large number of villa plans, but the lack of data on chronology and development limits the usefulness of Agache's work for our research. Furthermore, parallel to the German dataset, a great deal of research has only been pre-published in year books or in booklets aimed at a

[97] Pauwels 2007; Vanderhoeven *et al.* 2006.

[98] Van Ossel/Defgnee 2001.

[99] Mignot 2006, 72-75.

[100] Lefert/Bausier/Nachtergael 2000, 2001, 2002.

[101] Robinet 2004.

[102] See Haselgrove 2007 for a more extensive description of the backgrounds of archaeological research in northern France.

[103] Agache 1978.

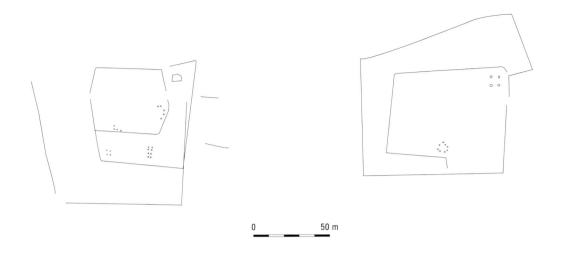

0   50 m

Fig. 3.8. Two examples of 'double compound settlements'. Left: Venette-Bois de Plaisance-Zone 1. Right: Beauvais-Le Brin de Glaine-ZAC du Haut Villé. The inner compound had residential functions, while the outer compound seems to have had different, probably agropastoral functions.

wide audience. Full reports are unavailable or remain as 'grey' literature, making them difficult to access.

In this region, the later Iron Age period and the transition to the earliest Roman period are relatively well known, especially when compared to the subregions discussed above.[104] Pre-Roman settlement activity, dated to the late La Tène D1 and D2 period, was documented for a significant number of settlements.[105] In most cases, these settlement phases consisted of curvilinear or more or less rectangular enclosed compounds. In some cases, settlements with an inner and an outer compound could be identified (see fig 3.8). While the inner compound was residential, the outer probably had agropastoral functions. Examples of this type of settlement include the sites Beauvais-Le Brin de Glaine,[106] Venette-Bois de Plaisance-zone 1,[107] Hordain-La Fosse à Loups,[108] Ploisy-Zone 1[109] and Monchy-le-Preux.[110]

For the Late Iron Age, a clearer picture of the settlement situation within the landscape could be obtained for a number of large-scale excavations. At Arras-Delta 3,[111] in the period between the 2nd century BC and the first centuries AD, several rectangular and trapezoidal enclosures existed, situated only a short distance apart (fig. 3.9). The surface area of these enclosed compounds ranged from 1300 to 6000 m². Similarly, at Onnaing-Toyota,[112] three or four contemporary settlements existed within

[104] Haselgrove 1990, 1995, 1996, 2007; Bayard/Collart 1996. This region is especially well researched as a result of large-scale archaeological aerial research and the archaeological research opportunities created by large-scale gravel extraction, road and rail construction and the development of ZACs, industrial or commercial complexes (Haselgrove 2007, 494-495). In this region, the number of excavated sites grew from 51 to 130 in the ten years up to 1991 (Haselgrove 2007, 494). Another 263 sites from the Late Iron Age were excavated from 1992 onwards. Seventy percent of these sites can be defined as settlements. For a recent overview of settlement research in Picardy, see Ben-Redjeb/Duvette/Quérel 2005.

[105] Roye-Le Puits à Marne I, Gouvieux-La Flâche, Beau-

vais-Le Brin de Glaine, Hordain-La Fosse à Loups, Epaux-Bézu-ZID de l'Omois, Venette-Bois de Plaisance-zone 1, Arras-Delta 3 and Actiparc, Saint Quentin-ZAC du Parcs des autoroutes-A26-A29, Beauvais-ZAC du Haut Villé, Beauvais-'Les champs Dolents, Beaurieux-Les Greves, Monchy-le-Preux

[106] Bilan scientifique de la région Picardie 2004, 60-61.

[107] Bilan scientifique de la région Picardie 2004, 83-85.

[108] Archéologie en Nord-Pas-de-Calais 2007.

[109] Bilan scientifique de la région Picardie 2003, 40-44.

[110] Gricourt/Jacques 2007.

[111] Blancquaert/Prilaux 2003, 17 ff.

[112] Roger/Catteddu 2002.

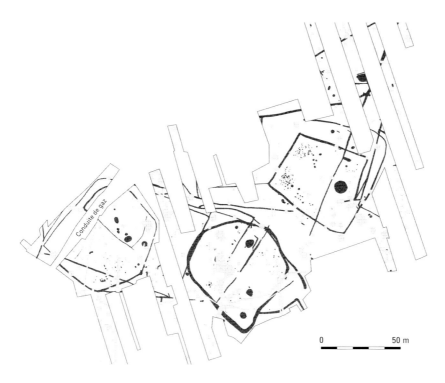

Fig. 3.9. Enclosed farmsteads at Arras-Actiparc-Le Buisson, dated between the Late Iron Age and the High Empire. After Jacques/ Prilaux 2005, 70.

the excavated area, each covering 60 to 80 hectares and situated 800 to 1500 m apart. Some settlements existed without change for one or two generations (sites 4, 6, 17, 19 and 21), while others seem to have shifted over short distances (sites 8/9). However, others again had a longer life span, changing gradually over time (sites 14 and 16). Although it remains difficult to reconstruct internal habitation, the settlement compounds on these sites appear to represent single enclosed farmsteads.

Subsequently, as early as the earliest Roman period, some significant changes in settlement structure occurred, which can be documented at a number of sites. The well-excavated settlements Juvincourt-et-Damary,[113] Monchy-le-Preux,[114] Beaurieux-Les Grèves,[115] Verneuil-en-Halatte,[116] Limé-Les Terres Noires[117] and Famechon-Le Marais[118] saw significant development during this 'période Gallo-Romaine précoce'. Late Iron Age settlement activity has been documented for the latter three sites. Moreover a long-rectangular, axially structured settlement compound was created at all of these sites during the Augustan or Tiberian period, with a main house on one of the short ends, overlooking rows of secondary buildings along one or both of the long sides. At both Famechon and Limé, this new long-rectangular complex was orientated parallel to the Late Iron Age settlement traces.

At Verneuil, settlement space became increasingly organised and segmented over time by means of ditches and palisades (see fig. 3.14b for the development trajectory of this settlement). In the Claudian period, the western U-shaped compound was enclosed by a stone wall, measuring 63 by 71 m. From this phase onwards, the residential compound was thus monumentally separated from the working

[113] Carte archéologique de la Gaule 02, 265-267; Collart 1996, 144-146.

[114] Gricourt/Jacques 2007.

[115] Haselgrove 1996, 155-161; Carte archéologique de la Gaule 02, 118.

[116] Collart 1996, 124 ff.

[117] Bilan scientifique de la région Picardie 1998, 32-34; Carte archéologique de la Gaule 02, 285-291.

[118] Collart 1996, 146-149.

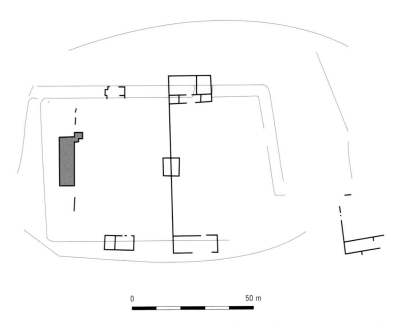

Fig. 3.10. Development of the Roye-Le Puits à Marne I settlement. The grey lines represent the early phases (late 1st century BC-1st century AD); the black lines represent the phases from the 2nd century onwards.

compound. In the course of the 2nd century, several buildings on the working compound were built or rebuilt in stone. However, the main axial structure of the complex was maintained through time. The same applies to Famechon, where the main structure remained the same while the buildings underwent considerable change. In contrast, the Juvincourt and Limé complexes failed to develop into monumental complexes.

At Monchy-le-Preux[119] a La Tène D2 'double compound' settlement was reorganised, probably already during the last decades BC (fig. 3.11). In this period, a new, more or less rectangular enclosure that maintained the existing orientation replaced the La Tène one. This new enclosure covered an area of 5607 m² and contained two new buildings. During the second half of the 1st century, the first changes in house building became apparent with the construction of a multi-roomed house on stone foundations. Although this settlement was not a typical axial complex like the ones described above, it displayed an unmistakable axial layout with a fixed spatial structure.

At Beaurieux-Les Grèves[120] a rectilinear enclosure with several buildings arranged around an open court can be dated to the earliest Roman period. The three larger buildings seem to have been houses, whereas two other buildings were probably barns or byres. At this stage, the settlement displayed an almost axial layout, with a house situated at one of the short ends, overlooking rows of buildings on either side of an imaginary axis. Unlike some other complexes, however, the axial organisation of the settlement did not develop further. During the earlier 1st century AD, the compound was reduced in size and the ditch was finally backfilled in the middle or later 1st century. Around this period or somewhat later, a number of stone buildings were constructed. The main house occupied a central position, flanked by two rows of buildings arranged east-west along the line of the backfilled enclosure ditches.[121]

Another settlement that developed into an axial complex, probably as early as the Augustan period, is Roye-Le Puits à Marne I.[122] Unfortunately, internal habitation is only very fragmentarily known for the periods preceding the 2nd century AD. What is clear, however, is that a rectangular compound

[119] Gricourt/Jacques 2007.

[120] Haselgrove 1996, 155-161; Carte archéologique de la Gaule 02, 118.

[121] Haselgrove 1996, 161.

[122] Collart 1996, Collart pers. comm. 2008.

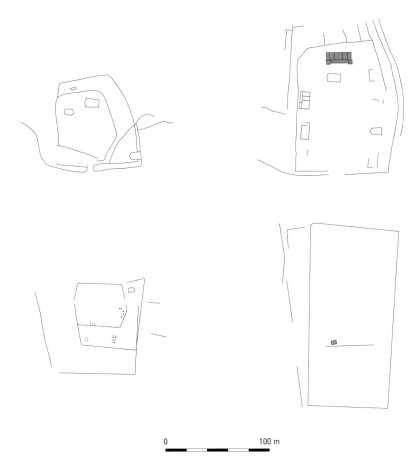

0   100 m

Fig. 3.11. Two axially organised settlement complexes constructed around the middle of the 1st century AD: Venette-Le Bois-de-Plaisance-Zone 1(bottom) and Monchy-le-Preux (top).

was created in the La Tène D2 or Augustan period. Its general form and orientation were continued in the following centuries. It was not until the 3rd century AD that the residential compound at this complex became monumentally separated from the working compound (see fig. 3.10).

Another category of sites seems to have developed into highly structured axial complexes at a later date than the ones described above, not until about the second half of the 1st century AD. They include the following: Saint-Quentin, Venette-Le Bois-de-Plaisance-Zone 1,[123] Epaux-Bézu-ZID de l'Omois,[124] Neuville-St. Amand,[125] Plailly-La Butte Grise,[126] Beauvais-Les Champs Dolents,[127] Roisel-Rue du Nouveau Monde,[128] Monchy-le-Preux,[129] Plailly[130] and Beauvais-ZAC du Haut Villé (see fig. 3.11).[131] Once again it is evident that enclosed and traditionally structured settlements existed prior to the reorganisation of settlement space at most sites. Understanding the relationship between these settlement phases can at times be difficult, however. Indeed, in some cases, such as at Venette-Le Bois-de-Plaisance-Zone 1, the excavators have suggested discontinuity.

[123] Bilan scientifique de la région Picardie 2004, 83-85.

[124] Bilan scientifique de la région Picardie 2004, 28-30.

[125] Bilan scientifique de la région Picardie 2005, 31 ff.

[125] Carte archéologique de la Gaule 60, 375; Gallia Informations 1989, 233-235.

[127] Bilan scientifique de la région Picardie 1996, 50-52; Bilan scientifique de la région Picardie 1999, 46; Bilan

scientifique de la région Picardie 2002, 64-65.

[128] Bilan scientifique de la région Picardie 2004, 119-120.

[129] Gricourt/Jacques 2007.

[130] Carte archéologique de la Gaule 60, 375; Gallia Informations 1989, 233-235.

[131] Bilan scientifique de la région Picardie 2000, 56-57.

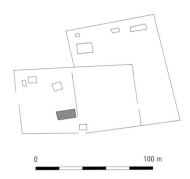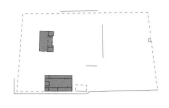

0   100 m

Fig. 3.12. Three settlement phases at Hordain-La Fosse à Loups. From left to right: a Late Iron Age settlement, a 1st-century AD settlement and its 3rd-century successor.

Not all settlements evolved to become highly structured axial complexes. At Onnaing-Toyota,[132] the Roman-period compounds clearly had a larger surface area (up to one hectare), although they essentially appear to have remained single enclosed farmsteads. One of the compounds, number 5, contained a simple house on stone foundations, as well as a granary and a pond. During the first half of the 1st century AD, four relatively dispersed settlements existed. Three of these were already inhabited from the La Tène period onwards. Then, during the second half of the 1st century AD, four new settlements were created, situated within the landscape in an ordered manner and separated by a mere few hundred metres. In the course of the 1st century AD, habitation within the landscape seems to have become increasingly clustered and organised. At Hordain,[133] two Late Iron Age settlements developed into rectangular enclosed compound settlements in the Roman period (see fig. 3.12). In sector 6, a rectangular enclosed compound, measuring 100 by 60 m, was created in the early 1st century AD. Habitation, consisting of one traditional wooden house and a number of secondary buildings, was concentrated on one half of the compound. The other half was clear of built structures and might have been used for agropastoral activities. In the second phase, this divide was marked by a ditch. Then, around the middle of the 1st century AD, the compound was extended to the north and east, doubling its surface area. In this period, the main house was rebuilt as a simple rectangular house on stone foundations. A road was constructed directly to the north of the settlement. Remarkably, after the abandonment of the settlement in the early 2nd century AD, it was re-established in the 3rd century, following the main layout of the 1st-century compound. Three stone buildings were constructed on the residential part of the compound.

The situation at Arras-Delta 3 and Actiparc[134] appears to be comparable to that at Onnaing. Similarly, small compound settlements existed between the Late Iron Age and the middle of the 2nd century AD. These small compounds seem to represent single farmsteads. One of them, measuring 110 by 65 m, was labelled a 'villa' by the authors.[135] This compound contained several buildings, at least one of which was built on stone foundations. Settlement compounds were situated close together, sometimes less than 50 m apart. The construction of a small Roman military fort and a road during the Early Roman period marked the reorganisation of the area.[136]

Continuity between the Late Iron Age and the Roman period could be documented at Gouvieux-La Flâche.[137] Although a Late Iron Age settlement enclosure was documented, probably as a result of severe erosion, internal structures could not be documented. A reorganisation in the 1st century AD

[132] Roger/Catteddu 2002.

[133] Archéologie en Nord-Pas-de-Calais 2007.

[134] Jacques/Prilaux 2005; Blancquaert/Prilaux 2003.

[135] See top left on the map in Blancquaert/Prilaux 2003, 16.

[136] This army camp was only occupied for a short period of

time, probably 64/40-30 BC until the first half of the 1st century AD.

[137] Bilan scientifique de la région Picardie 1997, 57-58; Archéologie en Picardie 1998, nr. 2.

resulted in a more orthogonal layout of the settlement enclosure, now measuring approximately 80 by 80 m. The earliest use of stone, dating back to the 1st or 2nd century AD, is documented with regard to a cellar. The superseding construction, possibly a framework house, was no longer traceable. The general layout of the later settlement consisted of a main house and two rows of secondary buildings, arranged around an open court.

The development of Late Iron Age enclosed settlements into Roman-period structured compound settlements could also be documented at several other sites. Traditional Late Iron Age 'double-compound' settlements existed at Beauvais-Le Brin de Glaine[138] and Ploisy-Le Bras de Fer-zone 1.[139] We see that small rectangular enclosed settlements were constructed in the Roman period (for Ploisy, these small rectangular, organised settlement compounds were created in the 1st century AD at zones 3 and 5). These settlements seem to have been monumentalised only to a limited degree. At Ploisy, during the 2nd century, a stone-lined cellar was constructed.

At Seclin-Hauts Clauwiers[140] there was an only fragmentarily documented Late Iron Age enclosed settlement, which was superseded by an enclosed compound measuring 137 by 144 m in the period between the 1st century BC and AD. This compound had the same orientation as the pre-Roman settlement. In this early phase, buildings were already situated along the enclosure ditches, surrounding a central open space. During the 1st and 2nd centuries AD, the enclosure was extended to 149 by 163 m.

The rather small compound settlement of Bohain-en-Vermandois[141] was founded around the middle of the 1st century AD. The compound was organised by means of internal ditches and most buildings were situated on the central part of the compound. During the second half of the 1st century AD, a traditional house was built in the northeast corner of the compound. In the first half of the 2nd century, a semi-monumental single-aisled house was built against the western enclosure ditch.

In conclusion, for the region of northwestern France, the first element of significance is the high frequency of settlement continuity or semi-continuity. As opposed to the other regions, it is possible to sketch a relatively clear picture of rural habitation during the Late Iron Age and Early Roman period. From the earliest Roman period onwards, quite radical reorganisations of settlement space can be documented for the majority of settlements. The creation of well-structured, long-rectangular axial complexes is particularly significant. This kind of reorganisation may also have involved spatial relocation, as has been suggested at the Saint-Quentin and Venette-Zone 1 sites.[142] Aside from the many axial complexes, we also encounter non-axial compound settlements comparable to those in other regions, with buildings parallel to the enclosure ditches. Many of these compounds are of limited size, possibly even single farmstead settlements. Spatial segregation could be documented for quite a number of settlements. This is particularly evident for the axial complexes, where the main house occupied a prominent position and was in many cases physically separated from the rest of the complex. At some other sites, such as Hordain, a residential area was separated from a part of the compound that seemed to have been used for agropastoral activities. Such divisions are also known from Late Iron Age settlements and the phenomenon might be a continuation of existing patterns. During the Roman period, settlement areas increased significantly. In the La Tène period, a settlement area of 1500 to 6000 m², up to a maximum of 1 hectare, was regarded as normal. In the Roman period, however, a medium-sized settlement measured around 1.5-2 hectares, while axial complexes could measure around 4 to 6 hectares, with the largest of these complexes being much larger (Anthée was around 13 ha and the complex of Limé-Pont d'Ancy-Les Terres Noires exceeded 20 ha). Reviewing the current dataset, we see that small settlements seem to be a minority. We could say, however, that this is a research bias, as these smaller settlements have become an object of study only in recent years.

[138] Bilan scientifique de la région Picardie 2004, 60-61.

[139] Bilan scientifique de la région Picardie 2003, 40-44.

[140] Révillion/Bouche/Wozny 1994.

[141] Archéologie en Picardie 2004, nr. 28.

[142] Ben Redjeb/Duvette/Quérel 2005, 192.

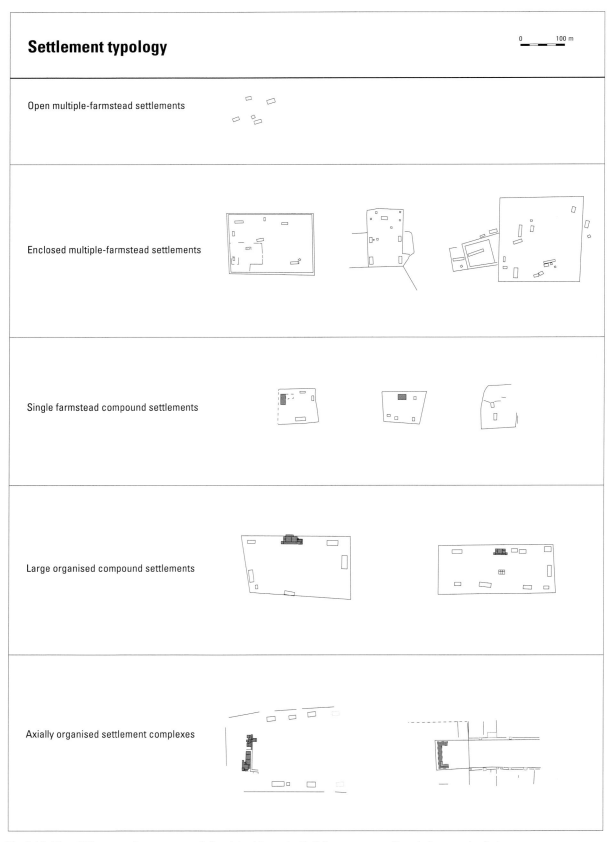

Settlement typology

0 ——— 100 m

Open multiple-farmstead settlements

Enclosed multiple-farmstead settlements

Single farmstead compound settlements

Large organised compound settlements

Axially organised settlement complexes

Fig 3.13. Five different settlement types defined in this study. Buildings on stone foundations are in dark grey.

Having explored the multitude of data on rural settlement development within the various parts of the research region, we will now take a more analytical approach and define a number of general settlement development trajectories. We will in fact create a classification of settlement development and present the development trajectories in diagram form. Needless to say, this is an abstraction of reality; significant variation continues to exist within the categories defined.

Before examining the development trajectories, I will firstly define a number of rural settlement types, ignoring the diachronic dimension for the time being (see fig. 3.13). Five different types have been distinguished:

- Open multiple-farmstead settlement: a loosely ordered cluster of several farmsteads without a common enclosure. Each farmstead consists of a main house and secondary buildings. The farmsteads can shift over short distances within the settlement territory.

- Enclosed multiple-farmstead settlement: several farmsteads organised within a common enclosure. Each farmstead consists of a main house and secondary buildings.

- Enclosed single-farmstead settlement: a single farmstead organised on an enclosed compound, containing a main house and several secondary buildings, organised along the enclosure ditches.

- Large structured compound settlement: enclosed and organised compound with more than one house and several, often fairly large, secondary buildings. Generally, one of the houses had a dominant position within the settlement and was monumentalised. These settlements were organised as coherent compounds, not as a collection of farmsteads.

- Axially organised settlement: long-rectangular settlement complexes strictly organised along a central axis. The main house, situated at one end of and perpendicular to the axis, overlooked two rows of secondary buildings on both sides of and parallel to this axis. In many cases, axial complexes consisted of two separate compounds (residential and working) separated by means of a ditch or even a wall and gate. It could be established for several of these settlements that at least some buildings on the working compound had residential functions.

I will now focus on settlement development trajectories (see figs 3.14a and b). We have already touched upon some of the problems arising with regard to settlement development. One of the main issues is the scale of the research involved, as the reconstruction of development trajectories is dependent on detailed phasing. If non-monumental phases have not been documented, does this reflect historical reality or are they simply not identified because of limited excavation or erosion due to modern ploughing? Furthermore, settlement development can involve locational shifts in habitation, as documented for Jüchen-Neuholz and Pulheim-Brauweiler among others and as suggested for Saint-Quentin. This makes reconstructing settlement development on the basis of limited excavations even more problematic.

Taking this into account, we can attempt to define a number of settlement development trajectories:

- Open farmstead settlements that maintained the same organisation through time. The settlements were not reorganised and virtually maintained a settlement organisation characteristic of the Late Iron Age. These settlements can be found in the northernmost region of the Dutch sand and clay area, for example at Lieshout and Moergestel.

- Open farmstead settlements developing into enclosed multiple farmstead settlements. In some cases, individual farmsteads were enclosed in an intermediate phase. Examples are Wijk bij Duurstede-De Horden, Druten, Tiel-Passewaaij and Geldermalsen-Hondsgemet, all situated within the northern sand and clay area.

- Open farmstead settlements developing into an enclosed compound settlement. The early phases of these settlements date back to the first half of the 1st century AD or earlier. Around the middle of the 1st century AD, the settlements were reorganised on well-structured compounds. Examples include Pulheim-Brauweiler, Frimmersdorf 129, Hambach 512 and 516.

- Settlements founded as a well-structured compound settlement. These settlements were founded in the second half of the 1st or earlier 2nd century AD. Examples are Kerkrade-Holzkuil, Hamois-Le Hody, Jüchen-Neuotzenrath and Hambach 127. The settlement of Champion-Le Emptinne is an example of an axially organised complex that was founded *ex nihilo*.[143] The difficulty with this category is that preceding settlement phases may have been missed, as these were generally less visible archaeologically and habitation might have shifted over short distances.

- Settlements developing from a compound settlement into an axially organised settlement complex. This significant reorganisation of settlement space can sometimes be dated as early as the Augustan period. In other cases, axial complexes seem to develop from around the middle of the 1st century AD. Well-documented examples include Meslin-L'Évêque, Haccourt, Roye, Monchy-le-Preux and Venette-Zone 1.

3.2.3 A LONG DEVELOPMENT LINE

As already argued, a better understanding of villa development also requires the analysis of longer and broader lines of settlement development. In this section we will opt for this broader perspective and look at villa development within the forcefield between continuity and change, spanning the time period between the later Iron Age and the Late Empire. Reviewing the data presented in the preceding sections, we are able to reconstruct some general long-term trends:[144]

- a trend towards nucleation of farmsteads
- a trend towards an increasing spatial stability of settlement
- a trend towards the increasing definition and organisation of settlement space.

The first trend is especially well documented with regard to the northern regions. In the earlier phases of the Iron Age, a dispersed and dynamic settlement system existed, relating to an agricultural system referred to as 'celtic fields'.[145] Farmsteads shifted through the landscape and settlement was not organised beyond the level of the individual farmstead.[146] Unfortunately, the picture is less clear for the more southerly regions. Nevertheless, it has been established that open settlements dominated this region before the 3rd century BC and, in the majority of cases, farmsteads did not seem to have been rebuilt at the same location.[147] From the La Tène C period onwards, some significant changes became

---

[143] Van Ossel/Defgnee 2001.

[144] Roymans/Theuws 1991; Roymans 1996; Haselgrove 1995, 1996, 2007; Bayard/Collart 1996; Gerritsen 2003; Ben Redjeb/Duvette/Quérel 2005.

[145] Gerritsen 2003, 242.

[146] For an analysis of the system of shifting farmsteads in this period, see Gerritsen 2003.

[147] Haselgrove 2007, 504; Séverin *et al.* 2007.

Settlement development trajectories

0 ⊟⊟⊟⊟ 100 m

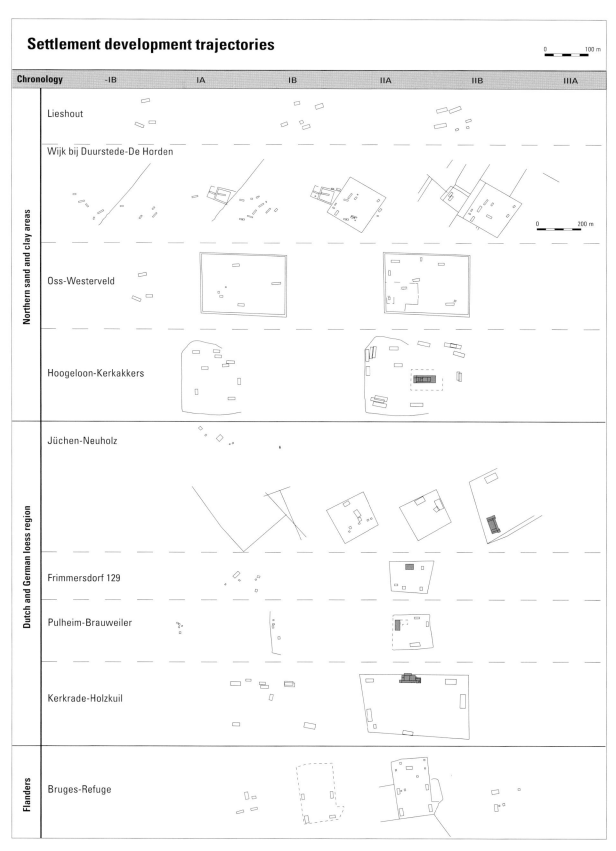

| Chronology | -IB | IA | IB | IIA | IIB | IIIA |

Northern sand and clay areas

Lieshout

Wijk bij Duurstede-De Horden

0 ⊟⊟⊟⊟ 200 m

Oss-Westerveld

Hoogeloon-Kerkakkers

Dutch and German loess region

Jüchen-Neuholz

Frimmersdorf 129

Pulheim-Brauweiler

Kerkrade-Holzkuil

Flanders

Bruges-Refuge

Fig 3.14a. Examples of settlement development trajectories in the northern sand and clay areas, the Dutch and German loess region and Flanders. Buildings on stone foundations are in dark grey.

49

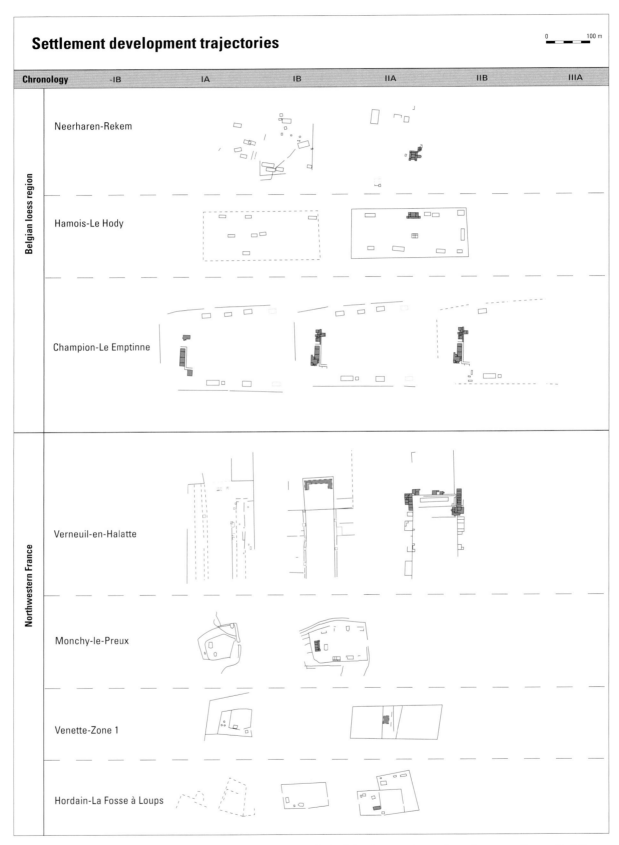

Fig 3.14b. Examples of settlement development trajectories in the Belgian loess region and northwestern France. Buildings on stone foundations are in dark grey.

apparent.[148] In northern France, new ground was colonised for intensive cultivation, and demographic expansion and intensified cultivation is also documented in the Dutch region for the Late Iron Age.[149] Paleo-botanical and paleo-environmental studies have suggested that the later Iron Age was a period of significant agricultural expansion, which was in all probability connected with demographic expansion. In northern France, the growing number of settlements reached its peak in La Tène D1, after which a phase of significant settlement decline set in during the La Tène D2 period, possibly caused by increasing instability and the associated occupation of *oppida*.[150] In the northern regions during the later Iron Age, an increasing number of farmsteads started clustering together, uniting up to five contemporary farmsteads in one cluster. This nucleation trend increased with time during this period and into the Roman period.[151] The picture seems different in the southern region, although it is clear at Arras-Actiparc/Delta 3, Hordain-La Fosse à Loups and Onnaing-Toyota that by the 2nd century BC enclosed farmsteads were being founded at short distances from each other, creating a densely inhabited settlement landscape. For this latter region, however, the data does not permit a reconstruction similar to the one for the northern sand region. The trend towards nucleation was linked to a trend towards increasing stability of habitation within the landscape.[152] Farmsteads went from dynamic units in the earlier Iron Age, shifting through the landscape from generation to generation, to ones that tended to be rebuilt at the same locations in the later Iron Age. This trend continued and intensified into the Roman period, when stable settlement compounds were often inhabited for several centuries.

Over time, settlements thus became stable elements within the landscape that were eventually enclosed by ditches. However, the evolution towards enclosed compounds was not uniform throughout the research region. In northern France, it set in during the La Tène C1 period.[153] From this period onwards, settlements became enclosed, developing into what is generally referred to in the French literature as *fermes indigènes*; or indigenous farms.[154] In the early stage of this development, curvilinear enclosures predominated. From La Tène D onwards, however, an increasing number of enclosures featured a rectangular ground plan. At the same time, the internal settlement became organised in increasingly rigid ways, with buildings arranged along the enclosure ditches, surrounding an open court.[155] The beginnings of this trend can be placed in the earlier Roman period, however, when settlement space was reorganised on a large scale. From this period onwards, larger, rectangular and well-structured settlement compounds were created. Contrary to this continuous trend, habitation hiatuses of one or two generations can sometimes be documented during the latest La Tène period in this region.[156] Nevertheless, this does not seem to imply an actual break in settlement development for the longer term.

In the Belgian loess region, it seems that the trend towards the enclosure of rural settlements can also be dated back to the pre-Roman period.[157] Further north, however, this picture changes. Fig. 3.15 visualises the distribution of open and enclosed sites. Settlements that were already enclosed during the pre-Roman period were clearly concentrated in the southern half of the research region. As described above, various settlements in the northern sand and clay areas started off as loosely structured and

[148] Haselgrove 1996, 2007; Roymans 1996, 49.

[149] In northern France, the slopes of the plateaus were colonised during La Tène C1-2, followed by the plateaus themselves in La Tène D. Haselgrove 2007, 503; Gerritsen 2003, 251.

[150] The appearance of *oppida* seems to relate to the increased instability of rural sites (Haselgrove 2007, 508).

[151] Gerritsen 2003, 182-185, 195.

[152] Schinkel 2005, 538-539; Severin *et al.* 2007; Roger/Catteddu 2002; Gerritsen 2003; Haselgrove 1996, 2007; Blancquaert/Prilaux 2003.

[153] Haselgrove 2007, 513.

[154] Agache (1978) introduced this term for the enclosures he discovered in rural areas of Picardy through his extensive aerial research.

[155] Haselgrove 2007, 506.

[156] Haselgrove 2007, 508.

[157] Leuze-en-Hainaut-Tourpes, Engis/Hermalle-sous-Huy, Brugelette-Mévergnies, Ath-Ghislengien, Chievres-Ladeuze and probably also Neerharen-Rekem, Haccourt, Vechmaal-Middelpadveld and Veldwezelt were already enclosed by ditches in the pre-Roman period.

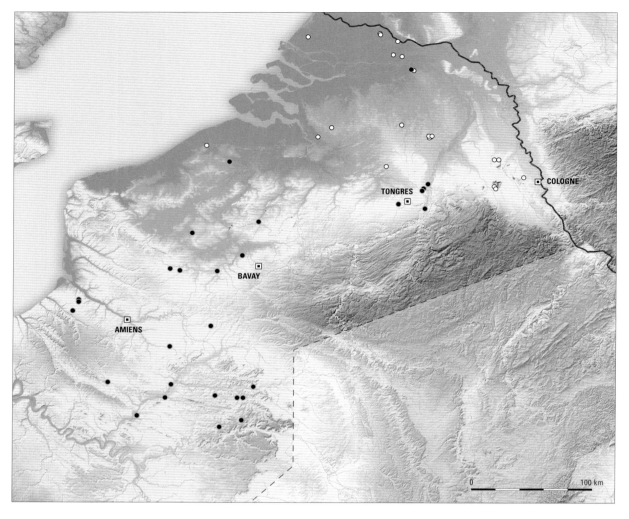

Fig. 3.15. Distribution of open and enclosed sites. The open dots represent open Late Iron Age settlements and settlements founded as open settlements during the first half of the 1st century AD. The closed dots show settlements that were already enclosed during the later pre-Roman period.

unenclosed settlements during the Late Iron Age or Early Roman period and did not become enclosed until around the middle of the 1st century. A similar picture emerges in the German loess region, where settlements like Pulheim-Brauweiler, Hambach 412 and Frimmersdorf 129 were also initially built as open settlements, before being enclosed and spatially organised during the earlier or middle 1st century AD. Viewed from a long-term perspective, however, these enclosures should also be regarded as part of a trend towards stable settlement units within the landscape.

The above discussion of the rise of enclosures has demonstrated the differentiation in settlement development within the research region. These differences went beyond the mere presence or absence of enclosures. A relatively complex and hierarchical settlement system seems to have existed as early as the later Iron Age. Malrain, Matterne and Méniel have created a model of this hierarchy by defining a number of settlement types (see fig. 3.16).[158] The most straightforward category (level 4) entailed small, often single, farmstead settlements, that were not enclosed or organised. The material culture associated with these settlements should be labelled as poor. The two middle categories (levels 3 and 2) were enclosed

[158] Malrain/Matterne/Méniel 2002, 137-145.

52

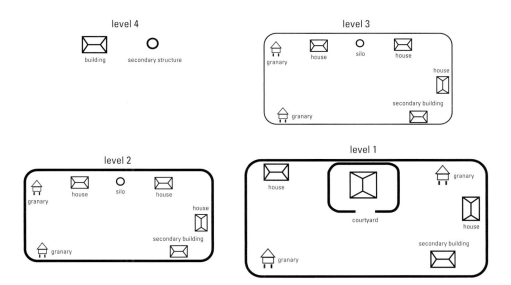

Fig. 3.16. Classification of Iron Age settlements in France according to spatial structure and relating to consumption of mobile material culture and food. After Malrain/Matterne/Méniel 2002, 143.

settlements with more than one house. Space was fairly well organised, although internal divisions were lacking. Certain houses could be built at privileged positions within the settlement, enabling the control and supervision of movement. The level-2 settlements had sturdier settlement enclosures and richer material culture. For the most complex type (level 1), the settlement was enclosed as well as internally organised and subdivided. According to the authors, a separate enclosed compound within the settlement was created for a 'habitation aristocrate'. Such compounds were frequently equipped with monumental entrances. The authors also address the architecture of the house, as well as mobile material culture, as indicators of the higher social standing of the inhabitants. Other houses, granaries and secondary buildings were situated outside the separate compound. Here, it is evident that not only were settlements in the more southerly regions enclosed as early as the later Iron Age, but internal space was also already reorganised in some cases. This reorganisation involved internal subdivision, the creation of spatial hierarchies and, to some degree, monumentalisation. In addition, there were clear differences in the material culture between houses within these settlements. Looking at the development of Roman-period axial complexes then – the category with the most differentiated and structured settlement complexes – we see that this is a phenomenon characteristic of the southern regions, quite parallel to the above-described distribution of settlements that were already enclosed during the Iron Age (see figs 3.15 and 3.17).[159]

The trends outlined here are long, broad and continuous lines of settlement development between the later Iron Age and the Roman period. The processes of nucleation, stabilisation and reorganisation were rooted in the Iron Age and observably continued into the Roman period. Their broad radius is also illustrated by the fact that the same trends can even be observed in settlements north of the research region, such as in Danish Jutland.[160] In that region, we can also identify a trend towards the nucleation of farmsteads, particularly during the last three centuries BC. In this phase, an increasing number of settlements were enclosed by ditches, while settlement stability increased.[161] Furthermore,

[159] Axially organised complexes can be quite clearly separated from settlements that were organised in different ways. Within our dataset, thirty sites (11%) could be identified as axial complexes. At 117 sites (42%), a different type of settlement organisation was documented (in most cases enclosed compound settlements ('Streuhof-Anlagen')) and for the remaining sites (47%), settlement layout could not be reconstructed.

[160] Webley 2007, 457–459; Rindel 1999.

[161] Webley 2007, 455–456.

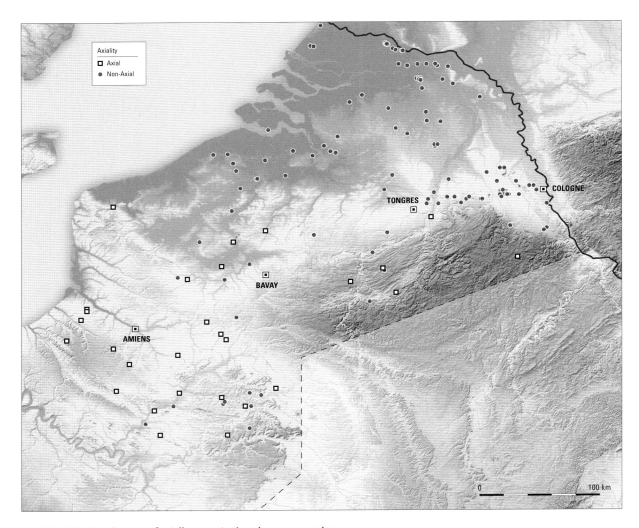

Fig. 3.17. The distribution of axially organised settlement complexes.

during the Roman period, domestic space became increasingly structured and complex, involving the division of space by means of internal fences and the development of units consisting of multiple buildings. According to Webley, both these fences and the appearance of paved paths suggest a heightened concern with guiding and controlling movement within the domestic sphere.[162] During the same period, the size of houses increased and outbuildings became both more common and much larger. Although we must be cautious about making simplistic comparisons, the general trends reconstructed for settlements in Jutland show a striking similarity to those found in our research region.

How then should we understand villa development within these longer-term trends in the organisation of settlement space? As we have established, settlements referred to as villas are stable, enclosed and well-organised compounds. In fact, the development of these compounds fits in with the broader trend of settlements becoming increasingly stable and enclosed. At Hordain, a direct line can be drawn between the rise of the villa settlement and settlement developments from the 2nd century BC onwards, regardless of any direct continuity. Examining broader settlement development, we can clearly distinguish some general trends. The same applies to many other sites, including Onnaing, Arras, Oss-Westerveld and Saint-Quentin-Parc des Autoroutes, to name just a few. In the southern

---

[162] Webley 2007, 458–459.

regions, settlements were already enclosed during the later Iron Age. In the northern regions, settlement became increasingly stable and defined, but they were generally not yet enclosed. In the Roman period, however, these settlements were being enclosed and settlement space was more or less structured. In the southern regions, this structuration of space, initiated in the earliest Roman period, was much more profound, as reflected in the emerging axial complexes. However, the trend towards the structuration of space seems to have set in already during the late pre-Roman period. The monumentalisation of houses (and thus the creation of highly durable structures) was a later development, starting only after settlement space had been reorganised. However, there are indications that already during the later Iron Age and earlier Roman period, houses were being built more sturdily, linked to the increasing spatial stability of settlement. Could the choice of new foundation techniques that increased the house's durability in fact be connected with the rising stability of settlements? Traditionally, scholars have tended to place more focus on the adoption of new architectural forms, communicating Roman-ness. If we view villa development in the forcefield between continuity and change, however, we may discern different patterns that can at least help our understanding of changes in rural settlements. We are not just dealing with specific Roman-period developments; on the contrary, these developments are part of broader, longer-term developments that cover both the later Iron Age and Roman period.

Taking such a long-term approach also offers some clues to understanding regional differentiation in settlement development. As described earlier, it appears that settlements and settlement patterns in the southern parts of the research region were already more complex and differentiated during the later Iron Age, a period in which the northern regions were still characterised by dispersed and dynamic rural habitation, mainly organised on the level of individual farmsteads. This can be related to social and economic realities, the southern regions seemingly being more socio-politically complex. The proximity of the Mediterranean world is probably an important factor here. In the following chapter, we will return to this topic when discussing regional differentiation from a social perspective.

3.3   DEVELOPMENTS IN HOUSE BUILDING: EXPLORING ARCHITECTURAL CHANGE

Having explored development trajectories in settlement organisation, I will now focus on individual houses. Traditionally, it is house building that is most explicitly associated with the 'villa' concept. From the 1st century AD onwards, new techniques, materials, architectural forms and concepts were introduced. In many cases, this resulted in the emergence of characteristic multi-roomed houses on stone foundations with whitewashed walls, red-tiled roofs and a porticoed façade. However, there was considerable variety in house development trajectories that needs to be explored. We will attempt to go beyond the commonly-held view of the simplistic and unproblematic replacement of wooden houses by stone houses.

Parallel to section 3.2.1, house-building developments will first be described in relation to some of the most well-researched sites in each subregion of the research area (3.3.1), while some of their shared characteristics will also be highlighted. In section 3.3.2, we will create a typology for rural houses and their development trajectories on the basis of the evidence presented in this section. Thirdly, specific elements of changes in house building will be discussed in greater detail.

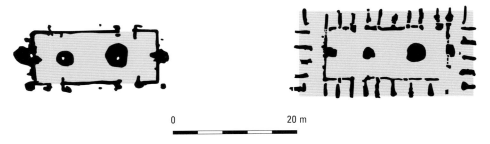

0   20 m

Fig. 3.18. Left: a traditional Alphen-Ekeren-type byre house. Right: the portico-house of Oss-Westerveld. The core of the portico-house is identical to that of the traditional house. The added feature is a wooden portico around the house.

3.3.1 DEVELOPMENTS IN HOUSE BUILDING PER SUBREGION

The northern sand and clay areas

The archaeological study of houses is particularly well developed in this northern region. The general picture is one of continuity of building traditions; the post-built 'Alphen-Ekeren-type' house was built without much change throughout the Roman period. Looking closer, however, we can discern changes in house building in quite a number of cases.

Architectural changes have already been mentioned in relation to Oss-Westerveld and Hoogeloon in the Dutch sand region. At Oss-Westerveld, two-aisled traditional houses dominated the settlement, from at least the early 1st century AD onwards. Around 100 AD, when a separate compound was created within the settlement, a special house was built there.[163] The core of this house was in fact a typical two-aisled Alphen-Ekeren-type house. However, it included a structure around the traditional core that has been interpreted as a wooden portico (see fig. 3.18). The deep foundation of its posts suggests that it had a supporting function, possibly relating to a partly tiled roof for which indications were found. Furthermore, one of the central roof-supporting posts of the house was set on a plank, in fact representing a new foundation technique.

The portico-house is a known phenomenon in the archaeology of these northern regions. Other portico-houses, interpreted as 'certain portico-houses' by Vos, include Tiel-Passewaaij (House 14[164] (1d-2A), portico on all sides), Oosterhout (house 1 (2B), portico on all sides), Breda (House 52 (2nd century), portico on all sides), Harnaschpolder (house 1 (2B/3a), portico on all sides) and Wijk bij Duurstede-De Horden (houses 9 and 25 (2B-3a)).[165] Examining such portico-houses and comparing them to 'traditional' houses nevertheless presents us with a problem of interpretation. In many cases, it is difficult to decide whether the outposts actually represented an element adopted from the Mediterranean architectural lexicon or whether it was an internal development, much more rooted in tradition. With regard to the two houses at Wijk bij Duurstede-De Horden,[166] the fairly large distance between wall and outposts was taken as indicative of a portico structure. Furthermore, it appears that these houses lacked an internal byre, potentially indicating changes in economic practice.[167] Another portico-house from Houten-Wulven[168] was somewhat older, dating back to the Flavian period at the earliest. This particularly long house featured surrounding outposts, positioned 2.5 m from the wall. Although no features of further developments in house building were documented, large quantities of building material and a robber trench could indicate the presence of a house on stone foundations, superseding the portico-house at this site.

[163] For a description of this house (house 78), see Wesselingh 2000, 78-83.

[164] Heeren 2006, 234-236.

[165] For an overview of houses with outposts/portico-houses,

see Vos 2009, 238-239.

[166] Vos 2002, 2009.

[167] Vos 2009, 70.

[168] Vos 2009, 129-130.

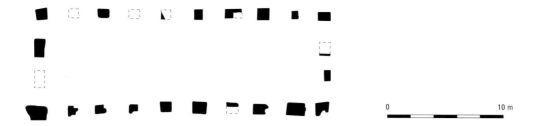

Fig. 3.19. The house on greywacke footings from Lent.

At other settlements, the developments in house building went further than the addition of wooden porticoes. At Houten-Molenzoom,[169] for example, the first habitation phase, dated between about 50 BC to 50 AD, comprised a simple two-aisled house. During later phases, however, new types of single-aisled constructions with supporting posts set in the long walls were constructed. In the first two phases, posts were still set into postholes. Later, however, posts were set on packings of building material and natural stone. The youngest house can be dated to the second half of the 2nd century AD, but its predecessors could potentially be dated back to the 1st century AD.

The settlement of Hoogeloon was also dominated by traditional houses during the 1st century AD. Then, in the first half of the 2nd century, a multi-roomed house on stone foundations (51.5 by 19 m) was built within the settlement, on the exact location of two preceding traditional houses. During a second phase, a bath section and a hypocaust room were constructed within the existing house.

A fairly similar development was documented at Houten-Burgemeester Wallerweg.[170] Two consecutive traditional houses can be dated between 50/75 AD and 150/175 AD. The second house was associated with Roman-style imported objects. Then, in a subsequent phase, after 175 AD, a house on stone foundations, measuring 28 by 11.5 m, was constructed at the same location. The fragmentarily known house seems to consist of a number of rooms fronted by a portico.

Traditional houses also dominated the early phases of the settlement at Druten.[171] It is from the second half of the 1st century AD onwards that significant changes in house building became apparent (for the development trajectory of houses at Druten see fig. 3.28a). House 1 can be measured as 15.5 by 36 m, consisting of a two-aisled house with a surrounding portico. The northern section of the house can possibly be interpreted as a byre. A stone-lined cellar or room on stone foundations, measuring 2 by 2.5 m, was situated in the assumed residential area. As fragments of painted wall plaster indicate, some walls may already have been decorated during this phase. Next, in the period between 80 and 150 AD, three single-aisled houses were constructed, all of them surrounded by outposts that could perhaps be interpreted as porticoes. These single-aisled houses featured heavy wall posts, set in opposite pairs and connected by cross beams. House 12 was particularly remarkable. Here, a long 'gallery' was built at the front of the house, exceeding the width of the house's core.[172] Furthermore, fragments of painted wall plaster, traces of a gutter and the lack of an internal byre all indicate the house's extraordinary character. A multi-roomed house on stone foundations was probably constructed in the second half of the 2nd century. This residence, measuring 32 by 17 m, had a typical plan, consisting of a number of rooms, fronted by a portico-risalith façade.

One house quite similar to the above-mentioned single-aisled houses with heavy wall constructions (those at Houten-Molenzoom and Druten) was documented at Lent (fig. 3.19).[173] This rectangular

[169] Vos 2009, 174-182.

[170] Van Dockum 1990; Vos 2009, 164-174.

[171] Hulst 1978; Maas 2007; Heeren 2009.

[172] Similar houses were found at Hoogeloon and Den Haag-Wateringse Veld.

[173] Van Es/Hulst 1991, 61 ff.

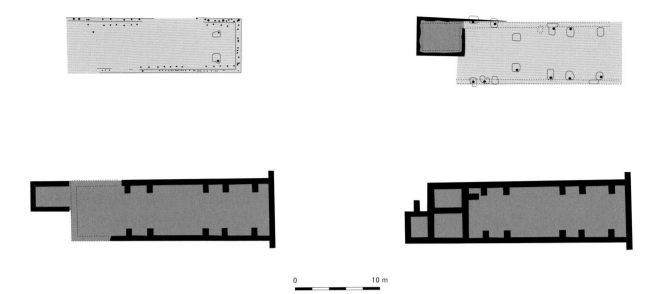

Fig. 3.20. Part of the house development trajectory at Rijswijk-De Bult. First, during the 1st and early 2nd century AD, traditional post-built houses were built here. Then, probably between 130 and 150 AD, a small section on stone foundations was added
to a traditional house. Around 200 AD, a long-rectangular house on stone foundations was constructed at the same location. The
post-built phases are in light grey, phases with stone foundations are in dark grey.

house (26 m long) displayed walls consisting of square greywacke footings. The authors argue that the
inner house space was likely to have been divided into several rooms and that the roof was covered
with tiles. In addition, fragments of painted wall plaster were found there. The presence of a smaller
secondary building, a 16-post granary and some other small buildings and granaries indicate that this
house was part of a rural settlement.

At Rijswijk-De Bult,[174] houses were built in the traditional fashion throughout the 1st and earlier
part of the 2nd century (fig. 3.20). The only house found to be extended with an annex on stone
foundations dated from the period 130-150 AD (house 18/19) and was located on the northeastern
compound within the settlement. Subsequently, around 200 AD, the remainder of this house was
rebuilt on stone foundations. The three small rooms, one of which was heated by means of a hypocaust, connected to this rectangular part on the west side. It should be mentioned that this house on
stone foundations closely resembled the spatial structure of a three-aisled traditional house, the internal
buttresses echoing the internal roof supporting posts. A hearth is situated within the hall. An internal
byre seems to be lacking, however.

The only accurately excavated rural settlement in the German part of the northern sand and clay
regions is that of Weeze-Voorselaer.[175] House 1 of this settlement had a plan comparable to the byre houses known from the Dutch region. House 2 had a somewhat different plan and is associated by the author
with the portico-house of Druten. None of the houses was monumentalised to any extent, however.

In the northern regions, traditional ways of house building remained a dominant practice throughout the Roman period and, in most cases, changes to house building were introduced relatively late.
Although some structures labelled 'portico-houses' were relatively early, like the portico-houses at Oss-
Westerveld and Nistelrode-Zwarte Molen that can be dated in the late 1st or earlier 2nd century AD, the
majority of portico-houses defined by Vos as being 'genuine' dated to the second half of the 2nd cen-

[174] Bloemers 1978, 1980.

[175] Archäologie im Rheinland 2008, 81-83.

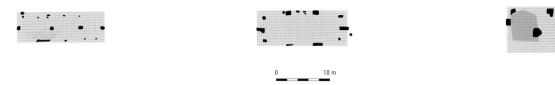

Fig. 3.21. Roman-period houses from the Bruges-Refuge settlement in Flanders.

tury.[176] Another category of changes, the introduction of new foundation technique in traditional post-built houses was documented on three occasions and was dated back to around the first half of the 2nd century AD. At Tiel-Passewaaij (house 3),[177] Houten-Burgermeester-Wallerweg (post-built house, phase 2) and Oss-Westerveld (house 78), one or more roof supporting posts were set on a plank placed inside the posthole. According to Vos, this technique might be of Roman military origin.[178] The introduction of stone foundations was also a fairly late phenomenon in this northernmost region. The house on stone foundations at Druten dated to the second half of the 2nd century, that at Rijswijk to around 200 AD and the one at Houten-Burgermeester-Wallerweg was not constructed before 150/175 AD. Only the house on stone foundations at Hoogeloon, already somewhat further to the south than the examples mentioned above, was probably already built during the first half of the 2nd century.

Finally, I would like to highlight the relationship between the transformation in house building and the changing functionality of the house itself. Vos suggested that portico-houses 9 and 25 at Wijk bij Duurstede-De Horden did not contain internal byres. The same applies to the typical house Druten 12, although it seems that the earlier house 1 still did contain a byre. Similar conclusions can be drawn regarding the stone houses at Rijswijk and Houten-Burgermeester Wallerweg. The fact that houses primarily became residences also implied a change in economic practice within the settlement. This economic dimension will not be further explored here, however.

Flanders

Over recent decades, a considerable amount of knowledge has been acquired in the field of both Roman-period house building and its development in the Flanders region. If we examine the data, it appears that post-built houses remained the norm throughout the Roman period. Although these wooden structures underwent a number of significant changes with regard to construction, no direct Mediterranean architectural elements or influences can be detected. In his synthesis, Wim De Clercq describes the way in which wooden two-aisled Alphen-Ekeren-type houses developed by the replacement of central roof-supporting posts with pairs of posts, set in the walls.[179] This phenomenon is particularly well-documented in this region, but can also be found in a number of settlements in the Dutch sand region, such as Hoogeloon, and in the Belgian Condroz region, including Champion and Hamois.[180]

In settlements like Bruges-Refuge, where the spatial layout paralleled the more southerly well-structured compound settlements, houses continued to be built in a traditional fashion throughout the settlement's existence (see fig. 3.21). There was nothing to indicate the adoption of new techniques, materials, forms and concepts. Only at Antwerpen-Mortsel[181] were changes in house building documented. One of the two excavated houses was a portico-house, resembling that at Druten (house 1). Similarly, inner house space was divided into two parts, likely to have been a byre and a residential section. A cellar constructed using limonite and tiles was connected to the house.

[176] Vos 2009, 250.

[177] Heeren 2006, 214-215.

[178] Vos 2009, 167.

[179] De Clercq 2009, 269-321.

[180] Van Ossel/Defgnee 2001; Chronique de l'archéologie wallone 2000, 195-199; Chronique de l'Archéologie wallone 2001, 200-203; Chronique de l'Archéologie wallone 2002, 240-242.

[181] De Boe 1966; Slofstra 1991, 164.

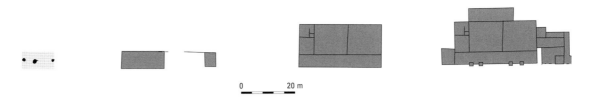

0   20 m

Fig. 3.22. The development trajectory of the main monumental house at Kerkrade-Holzkuil.

The Dutch and German loess region

In the Dutch loess region, house development trajectories can be reconstructed in detail at four sites. At Kerkrade-Holzkuil,[182] the first habitation phase, dated to the late 1st century AD, was characterised by a traditional Alphen-Ekeren-style house with a central row of roof-supporting posts (see fig. 3.22). Next, in the early 2nd century, this house was replaced by a simple hall-type house on stone foundations. Subsequently, around the middle of the 2nd century, a new multi-roomed house on stone foundations was built, consisting of two large and two small rooms, fronted by a portico. At the end of the 2nd century, a new room, a bath section, risalith and two monumental entrances were added, creating an even more impressive and luxurious house.

During the earliest habitation phases of the Voerendaal-Ten Hove settlement small, traditional houses seem to have been predominant. Then, around the middle of the 1st century AD, a simple stone house was constructed, consisting of two identical central rooms, surrounded by several smaller rooms. Around the transition from the 1st to the 2nd century, this house was torn down. Subsequently, a more monumental and organised complex was created, consisting of a new main house, a secondary building, a granary and a bathhouse. The house itself consisted of a central hall with surrounding rooms, fronted by a portico. A later phase saw the buildings linked by a long portico, creating a coherent whole with a monumental, impressive façade. In addition, both the granary and bathhouse were extended.

According to the excavator Brunsting, the first habitation at Kerkrade-Spekholzerheide[183] dated back to between 20 and 70 AD (see fig. 3.23 for the development trajectory). A post-built, probably single-aisled framework structure can be dated to the 1st century AD (12.5 by 7.5 m). However, no plans could be identified of hypothetical older post-built structures. Then, around the end of the 1st century AD, a multi-roomed house on stone foundations was built. In the first phase, the house consisted of a number of rooms fronted by a simple portico. In the second phase, a bath section, a large room at the back of the house and two risaliths were added (the final house measured 52 by 22 m).

At the fourth site, Maasbracht, a house on stone foundations was built around the late 1st century AD.[184] A large hall and some smaller rooms were fronted by a portico-risalith façade. At the end of the 2nd century the existing risaliths were replaced by larger ones with deeper foundations, indicating a tower-like appearance. At the same time a monumental entrance was created at the centre of the portico. This will have boosted the house's monumentality considerably. Many fragments of painted wall plaster can also be dated to this period.

The German region provides more data on house development. Two of the more readily reconstructable trajectories can be found at Jüchen-Neuholz and Pulheim-Brauweiler (for their development trajectories see fig. 3.28a).[185] At Jüchen, the house that was part of the partly enclosed settlement, dated

[182] Tichelman 2005.

[183] This site is also referred to as Kaalheide-Krichelberg. Brunsting 1950; see also Koster/Peterse/Swinkels 2002, 48 ff.

[184] Stuart/De Grooth 1987, 62-63.

[185] Andrikopoulou-Strack *et al.* 2000, 409-488.

 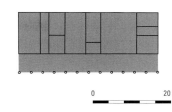 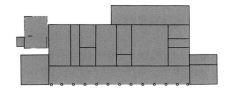

0   20 m

Fig. 3.23. The development trajectory of the house at Kerkrade-Spekholzerheide.

to the Augustan period, was still relatively small and was constructed on horizontal foundation beams. Subsequently, around the middle of the 1st century, two houses of about 20 m in length were built on the first enclosed compound. Although these houses were much larger than their predecessors, their construction seems to have been traditional. This changed with the erection of two new buildings on the same compound, around the late 1st century. These large, single-aisled structures had square and fairly heavy wall posts, serving to support the roof. One of the buildings also had an internal cellar.[186] Then, in the earlier 2nd century AD, a multi-roomed house on stone foundations was built, consisting of a number of rooms, fronted by a portico-risalith façade. In a second phase, several new rooms were attached to the short sides of the existing house. Before the end of the 2nd century, however, this house was destroyed by fire. At Pulheim, the documented traditional houses were likely to have been constructed in the middle of the 1st century AD, using horizontal foundation beams. Around the late 1st century, a new, substantially larger house (28.5 x 13 m) was constructed on the newly created compound. This rectangular house was a single-aisled structure, within which the wall posts, partly set on stone footings, supported the roof. Unlike some other cases, these wall posts were not single square posts, but regular timbers, set in pairs.

In a number of other cases, we also see single-aisled houses with squarish wall posts preceding multi-roomed stone houses. At Broichweiden-Würselen,[187] one such house could be dated back to the 1st century AD, before it was rebuilt as a simple house on stone foundations during the following phase. For the single-aisled house at Neuss-Weckenhoven,[188] the square wall posts could be well documented and reconstructed to have measured between 22 and 30 cm in width, set about 1.5 m apart. This house, 18 by 7.5 m in size, was dated back to the second half of the 1st century AD. During the next phase, a simple house on stone foundations, measuring 32 by 17 m, was constructed. Similar single-aisled houses with heavy walls, dating back to the 1st century AD, were documented at Weisweiler 122.[189] Again, a house on stone foundations replaced them during a subsequent phase.

Similar single-aisled houses, which can be reconstructed as framework hall houses built using new wall and roof construction techniques, were also known to have existed at the settlements Frimmersdorf 49, 131, Hambach 516 and Jüchen-Neuotzenrath. These houses were not replaced by houses on stone foundations, however, as in the examples described above. The wall posts of the rectangular house at Jüchen-Neuotzenrath[190] were set in square postholes with stone packings. In the deeper, down-slope postholes, quartzite blocks were used to anchor and support vertical posts as well as horizontal beams. Fragments of chalk plaster indicate that the outer walls were probably plastered, creating an appearance of smooth white walls. During a later phase, a risalith on stone foundations was connected to one of the corners of the house. The single-aisled house of Frimmersdorf 49[191] was

---

[186] It is this settlement phase that was interpreted as a 'proto-villa' by Frank and Keller (2007).

[187] Bonner Jahrbücher 177, 579.

[188] Haupt 1968, 90-91.

[189] Archäologie im Rheinland 2005, 86-88.

[190] Archäologie im Rheinland 1999, 82-84.

[191] Köhler 2005.

also set on packings of sandstone, tile and ceramic fragments. In addition, it seems to have had a tiled roof. The Frimmersdorf 131[192] house was built in two phases, the first of which has been reconstructed with a single risalith.[193] Only a single post was set on stone material packing, as the roof was likely to have been covered with organic material. Both these houses can be dated to the second half of the 1st century AD. At Hambach 516, the first house, dated around the middle of the 1st century AD, still had round postholes.[194] Unfortunately, however, its plan has only been identified fragmentarily. In the early 2nd century, a single-aisled house was built, with square postholes set on gravel and chalkstone packings. In a next phase, probably also during the earlier or middle 2nd century, two rooms on stone foundations were connected to the existing building, one of which functioned as a risalith, as was the case at Jüchen-Neuotzenrath. A last example is the house of Frimmersdorf 129,[195] where a simple, traditional long-rectangular post-built house (16 by 6 m) was replaced by a squarer house with posts set on packings of gravel, sand, quartzite and tile fragments (18 by 13 m).

At Hambach 512,[196] the two oldest houses, dating back to the second half of the 1st century AD, were post-built, but their plans are only fragmentarily known. One of these houses, containing sandstone, seems to have been comparable to singe-aisled houses with stone footings, such as Jüchen-Neuotzenrath. In the early 2nd century AD, the first house on stone foundations was built, consisting of a large hall and a number of smaller rooms, fronted by a portico-risalith façade. In the next phase, a completely new building with a slightly different orientation was connected to the existing house by means of a tapering section. The new house cut through the settlement ditch and palisade that enclosed the settlement in the second half of the 1st and the first half of the 2nd century AD. Throughout various phases, the house developed into a building containing 15 to 20 rooms, fronted by a portico-risalith façade. A hypothetical bath section was situated in the connecting section between the two houses.

Other phased developments could be found at the settlements of Hambach 59, Cologne-Müngersdorf,[197] Hambach 127[198] and Bad-Neuenahr-Ahrweiler.[199] There was probably a post-built house at Hambach 59[200] in the 1st century AD. Subsequently, during the later 1st century, a basic house on stone foundations was constructed, consisting of a central hall, porticos on three sides, and potentially three non-projecting risaliths. Around the transition from the 2nd to the 3rd century, a bath suite was added on the west side of the existing house. At Hambach 127,[201] the first phase of the basic house on stone foundations (consisting of a larger central hall and a number of smaller rooms, fronted by a portico-risalith façade) can be dated to the second half of the 1st century AD. During the late 1st or early 2nd century, a bath was constructed in the western part of the house. At Cologne-Müngersdorf[202] and Bad-Neuenahr-Ahrweiler,[203] the first basic houses on stone foundations date back to around the middle of the 1st century AD. At the latter site, a bath house was already present during this early habitation phase. In both cases, the first house was replaced by a larger house in the second half of the 1st century. A portico, hypocausts and a bathing section (not until the 3rd century) were added to the house at Müngersdorf during several phases. At Bad-Neuenahr, the new house measured 72 by 18-20 m. In addition, the existing portico was extended towards the separate bathhouse during a later phase. The house at Blankenheim-Hülchrath[204] was already fairly large in its first phase, during the 1st century AD (measuring 48 by 17 m). It also contained 20 rooms: a large hall, surrounded by a

---

[192] Köhler 2005.

[193] Heimberg 2002/2003; Kaszab-Olschewski 2006; Köhler (2005) does not follow this reconstruction, however.

[194] Kaszab-Olschewski 2006, 112-113.

[195] Archäologie im Rheinland 1997, 53-55.

[196] Kaszab-Olschewski 2006, 17-30.

[197] Fremersdorf 1933; Horn 1987, 505.

[198] Archäologie im Rheinland 2000, 73-76.

[199] Fehr 2003.

[200] Hallmann-Preuss 2002/2003.

[201] Archäologie im Rheinland 2000, 73-76.

[202] Fremersdorf 1933; Horn 1987, 505.

[203] Fehr 2003.

[204] Bonner Jahrbücher 123, 210-226.

number of smaller rooms, fronted by two large projecting risaliths. After this house was destroyed by fire around the middle of the 2nd century, it was rebuilt on an even larger scale.

The Belgian loess zone
In the Belgian loess zone, five settlements situated in the region around Tongres were characterised by Alphen-Ekeren-type houses during their early development phases: Vechmaal-Middelpadveld,[205] Lanaken-Smeermaas-Kerkveld,[206] Riemst-Lafelt,[207] Veldwezelt[208] and Neerharen-Rekem.[209] These houses dated back to the later Iron Age or the 1st century AD. And at all these settlements, changes in house building can be documented for the later 1st or 2nd century. At Vechmaal, a two-aisled house was built, probably around the middle of the 1st century, containing a small internal cellar and probably a tiled or partially tiled roof. At Vechmaal, Neerharen, Lanaken and Riemst, a house on stone foundations was built around the later 1st or 2nd century. At the latter two sites, mere fragments of the house were documented, as only the deeper parts, the cellar and hypocaust, were preserved. Only a cellar was documented at Veldwezelt. It can be argued, however, that this cellar was part of a house on horizontal foundation beams or stone foundations that had eroded completely, similarly to Lanaken and Riemst. The Vechmaal house was much better preserved. In the first phase, two rectangular rooms were fronted by a portico-risalith façade. Subsequently, during the late 2nd or early 3rd century, a bath section was built, connected to the existing house by five new rooms. The same applies to the house at Neerharen. In its first phase, during the late 1st century, a portico-risalith façade fronted three smaller rooms. Next, a second portico-risalith façade was added at the back of the house. An apsidal room, which has been interpreted as a *triclinium*, was added behind it. During the last development phase, a bath section was connected to the northeast corner of the house.

Somewhat further to the west, at Wange-Damekot[210] and Erps-Kwerps,[211] Late Iron Age and Early Roman period habitation also consisted of traditional post-built houses. At Wange, there seems to have been a continuous development from the pre-Roman to the Roman period. At some point during the 2nd century, a house on stone foundations was built, consisting of several rooms fronted by a portico-risalith façade and measuring 38 by 15 m. During a second phase, a bath section was added to the west side of the house. At Erps, a stone-built house, measuring 51 by 23 m and placed parallel to the post-built houses, was constructed during the late 1st century AD. Once again, the house consisted of several rooms fronted by a portico. In the 2nd century, the house was likely to have been extended with a portico at the back. Moreover, at Rosmeer-Diepestraat,[212] fragmentary traces of a post-built house were documented. In the second half of the 1st century, a house on stone-foundations was built at the same location. A lack of documentation complicates any attempts to establish the chronological relationship between these building phases, however.

Further to the south, in the Belgian Condroz region, similar development trajectories can be found. At Gesves-Sur le Corria[213] post-built houses characterised the settlement in both the Late Iron Age and the Roman period. During the Roman period at least, these houses were of a two-aisled, Alphen-Ekeren type. The next phase saw the construction of a house on stone foundations, consisting of a large central room and several adjacent rooms, fronted by a portico. A completely new section was added to this existing core in a subsequent phase. A separate bath building was raised south of the house, connected to it by a gallery, constructed later on. The construction of this gallery also involved creating

[205] Vanvinckenroye 1997.

[206] Pauwels/Creemers 2008.

[207] Vanderhoeven/Creemers 2000.

[208] Pauwels 2007.

[209] De Boe 1982, 1985a, 1987.

[210] Lodewijckx 1995.

[211] Verbeeck 1995.

[212] De Boe/Van Impe 1979.

[213] Lefert/Bausier 2006; Lefert 2008.

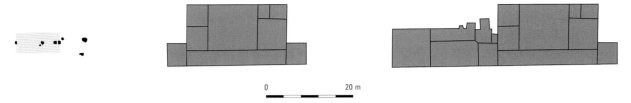

0   20 m

Fig. 3.24. Reconstructed development of the house at Hamois-Le Hody.

a monumental entrance, opening onto the court in front of the main house. The bath house itself was extended to include five bathrooms and three *praefurnia*.

The main house of the Hamois-Le Hody[214] settlement, positioned centrally on the compound, was a post-built, two-aisled structure during its first phase, dated around the middle of the 1st century AD. The following phases saw a house on stone foundations being erected (see fig. 3.24). Hypothetically, the basic, rectangular, bipartite house on stone foundations directly superseding the wooden house represented the first stone phase, but this cannot be established with certainty. A short distance to the east, a house with a large central room and several smaller rooms, fronted by a portico-risalith façade, was built in the late 1st or early 2nd century. After the first extension to the main house towards the west, a bath section was also added. Subsequently, the house was extended two more times, eventually creating a façade approximately 50 m wide.

The axially organised complexes of Haccourt[215] and Meslin-L'Évêque[216] are also characterised by post-built houses in their earliest phases, i.e. the Late Iron Age (as presumed for Haccourt) or Early Roman period (as presumed for Meslin). Although the post-built houses at Meslin were only fragmentarily preserved, one could be identified as an Alpen-Ekeren-type structure. Then, in the later 1st century AD, an axially organised complex was laid out parallel to the existing enclosure ditches and a fairly large house was raised on stone foundations. The next phase saw the main house being expanded to an impressive 117 by 23.5 m. At Haccourt, a Roman-period, post-built structure potentially dated back to the middle of the 1st century AD. Continuity between the pre-Roman and Roman-period habitation certainly seems a possibility.[217] Unfortunately, however, little is known about the building plans of the most ancient houses. The same applies to the new house built around 70 AD, of which only the cellar has been preserved. Several decades later, possibly before the end of the 1st century, a new house was built. This structure consisted of a long rectangular part, comprising several rooms and a bath section at the south end of the building, together creating a structure that was 78.5 m long. In the early 2nd century, a portico connected the house to the bath section. Soon after, the house was torn down to make way for an even bigger house. This building was 103 by 46 m in size and consisted of many rooms and two open courts fronted by a monumental façade with two projecting wings, between which a portico was raised. Again, a separate bathhouse was later connected to the house by means of a porticoed gallery. What is most remarkable about the orientation of this house is the fact that what appears to be the main façade faced away from the settlement complex, reconstructed to have extended towards the southwest. An examination of the relief map suggests that the house was situated on a hill, overlooking the surroundings. This would have been the side of the house most visible to the outside world, which is probably why it boasted such an elaborate façade.

It appears, however, that some monumental, multi-roomed houses did not develop from traditional houses but were built *ex nihilo*. One example is the house at Rochefort-Jemelle. It seems to have been

[214] Chronique de l'Archéologie wallone 2000, 195-9; Chronique de l'Archéologie wallone 2001, 200-3; Chronique de l'Archéologie wallone 2002, 240-242.

[215] De Boe 1973, 1974, 1975, 1976.

[216] Deramaix 2006; Corbiau 1997, 311-314.

[217] De Boe 1974, 43-44.

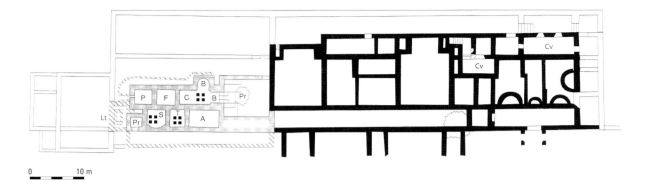

Fig. 3.25. Development of the main building at Rochefort-Jemelle. First phase = black. Second phase = grey. Third phase = shaded. Fourth phase = white. After Brulet 2009, 571.

constructed as a multi-roomed building on stone foundations during the late 1st century without being preceded by a post-built phase. During later phases (see fig. 3.25) several new rooms, a portico and a bath section were added to the existing long, rectangular core. Another potential example is that of Champion-Le Emptinne.[218] Here, the first house, dating back to around the middle of the 1st century AD, was a simple L-shaped structure on stone foundations, containing between five and eight rooms, fronted by a portico. A small, separate bath house was constructed on the northwest side of the house. Subsequently, a new section was built, connected to and partly replacing the previous structure. Around the middle of the 2nd century, the bath section was extended to comprise 15 rooms and was connected to the house by means of a gallery. No pre-monumental building phases were documented for a number of other houses: Merbes-Le-Chateau-Champs de Saint-Eloi,[219] Matagne-la-Petite,[220] Roly,[221] Vodelée[222] and Habay-la-Vieille-Mageroy.[223] Their early monumental phases can be dated back to the second half of the 1st century or first half of the 2nd century AD. The difficulty with this category, however, is that it is not possible to prove that the houses lacked pre-monumental phases. They may have been missed because they were eroded, overbuilt or simply not recognised.

Northwestern France
Compared to the extent of settlement research, relatively little data is available for reconstructing house development trajectories in any detail for this region. We are nevertheless able to shed light on house development for a number of sites.

Parallel to the other regions, traditional house building was predominant during the earliest phases at quite a number of settlements. At Hordain-La Fosse à Loups,[224] the main house was an oval-shaped post-built house, measuring 7.5 by 13 m, which could be dated to the first half of the 1st century AD. A small cellar, lined with planks, was positioned close to the southwestern wall. According to the author, this house was covered with tiles, although the presumed ability of these traditional structures to support such roof-loads is doubtful. Around the middle of the 1st century AD, a basic, rectangular house on stone foundations (18 by 7 m) then superseded this traditional house. Subsequently, during the 3rd century settlement phase, a new, more complex stone building was erected at the same location. A second house on stone foundations, belonging to this latter phase, had a typical plan with a portico-risalith façade.

[218] Van Ossel/Defgnee 2001.
[219] Authom/Paridaens 2007, Chronique de l'Archéologie wallone 15; Authom/Paridaens 2008, 11-16.
[220] Two separate houses; Brulet 2009, 523-524.
[221] Robert 1980.
[222] Rober 1987.
[223] Zeippen/Halbardier 2006.
[224] Séverin *et al.* 2007.

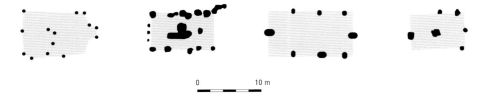

0   10 m

Fig. 3.26. Early post-built houses from the axial settlement complexes of Monchy-le-Preux and Verneuil-en-Halatte and simple compound settlements of Bohain and Hordain (from left to right).

Similar development trajectories were also found at a number of other sites. A traditional, post-built house at Bohain-en-Vermandois,[225] built in the second half of the 1st century AD, was replaced by a single-aisled house during the first half of the 2nd century. This latter house consisted of heavy wall posts on flint packings and an internal stone-lined cellar. The roof seems to have been covered at least partially with tiles. At Seclin-Hauts Clauwiers,[226] the first post-built house with an atypical plan can be dated between the 1st century BC and the 1st century AD. It was subsequently replaced by a simple house on stone foundations in the 1st or 2nd century. And at Hamblain-Les Près,[227] post-built houses, dated to the Late Iron Age and first decades of the 1st century AD, were superseded by a house on stone foundations, measuring 29 by 13 m. At the end of the 1st century AD, the existing house was extended considerably to 65 by 20 m. This house is likely to have contained a bath section as well.

Traditional houses can also be found at the axial complexes, such as Famechon-Le Marais,[228] Verneuil-en-Halatte,[229] Monchy-le-Preux (see fig. 3.26),[230] Beaurieux-Les Grèves,[231] and probably Roye-Le Puits à Marne 1.[232] Consequently, while settlement space was reorganised radically, houses were initially still being built in a traditional manner, giving no indication of the highly monumental residences that succeeded them.

In these axial complexes, the earliest changes in house building can be dated to the Tiberian period. At Famechon, a 12 m-long house was constructed on flint foundations during this period. At the same time, the houses on the working compound were also rebuilt, using chalk and limestone foundations. Changes in house building did not occur until later in the other settlements. Verneuil saw a new house being built during the Tiberian-Claudian period, of which only the cellar, lined with limestone blocks, has been preserved. This house was probably constructed on horizontal foundation beams or shallow stone foundations, and was covered with tiles. At Monchy, a house on stone foundations, measuring 24 by 12 m, was built in the second half of the 1st century AD. It was not until the 2nd century AD that the first stone house was constructed at Roye.

At Saint-Quentin, the earliest documented main house was not of a traditional type. Instead, it was a single-aisled, post-built structure, measuring 10 by 15 m. This building, dated to around the middle of the 1st century AD, is quite similar to the single-aisled structures found within the German loess region. During the late 1st century, the house was rebuilt with limestone foundations, including a stone-lined cellar. This new house was 21.5 by 12.8 m in size.

[225] Archéologie en Picardie 2004 (nr. 28), Bilan scientifique de la région Picardie 2000, 19-20.

[226] Révillion/Bouche/Wozny 1994.

[227] Jacques/Tuffreau-Libre 1984; Carte archéologique de la Gaule 62, 487-489.

[228] Collart 1996, 146-149.

[229] Collart 1996, 124-132; Carte archéologique de la Gaule 60, 491-494.

[230] Gricourt/Jacques 2007.

[231] Haselgrove 1996, 155-161.

[232] Collart 1996, 132-137; Bilan scientifique de la région Picardie 1997, 106-108.

As previously attempted with regard to settlement organisation, I will now attempt to classify houses and their development trajectories. I will describe and present in diagram form the transformation of existing house-building traditions through the introduction of new materials, techniques, forms and concepts, as well as the development of existing monumental houses through time. I will firstly define a number of different house types, initially excluding the diachronic dimension. To begin with, four basic types were defined (fig. 3.27). However, there is considerable variety within each category, especially the fourth.

- Traditional houses: these houses were included in the domain of vernacular architecture. They were built according to local traditions, using local materials and the local workforce. For the northern regions, rectangular two- and three-aisled post-built longhouses were predominant. In most cases, these were byre houses, combining residential functions with a byre section under the same roof. In the south, considerably smaller post-built houses can be found, seemingly lacking internal byres. Houses were constructed using exclusively organic materials and posts were set directly into post holes dug into the ground.

- Romanised traditional houses: these houses were essentially traditional in terms of shape and construction but contained additional elements, representing influences from the Mediterranean architectural lexicon. The best example within this category is the portico-house. A house like Oss-Westerveld was a purely traditional Alphen-Ekeren-type house at its core. The surrounding portico was nevertheless an addition and interpretation of a Mediterranean architectural element and concept. Aside from porticoes, the use of tiles, plaster and natural stone for supporting posts also falls into this category.

- Timber framework houses: these houses represented a new way of building, including new foundation techniques, new wall and roof construction techniques and the use of new materials and concepts. Nevertheless, they did not resemble the multi-roomed houses generally referred to as villas. These houses were single-aisled timber-framework houses, in many cases built on stone footings or packings, as described in the above. Newly constructed, sturdy framework walls took over the function of internal posts supporting the roof. These developments also enabled the roofs of these buildings to be covered with tiles. A façade was created at some of these houses, such as at Jüchen-Neuotzenrath, Hambach 516 and Druten, by constructing a risalith or fronting gallery.

- Multi-roomed houses on stone foundations: these houses are generally referred to as villas in archaeology. They were built on linear stone foundations and their internal space was divided into separate rooms. In most cases, the foundations will have been low walls on which the framework walls were set. This is not to say, however, that walls completely constructed in masonry did not exist. The façade has become a standard and specific part of this category of houses, specifically in the form of a portico or portico-risalith façades. Heterogeneity is particularly marked in this category, which is clearly illustrated in figures 3.27 and 3.28. Houses on stone foundations range from very simple and small, rectangular, hall-like structures containing one or several rooms to exceedingly large residences with over 30 rooms, extended bath sections and monumental façades.

I will now include the diachronic factor, focusing on house development trajectories. Several development trajectories from all parts of the research area are represented in figures 3.28a and b. It should be noted that the scheme includes both concrete and more generalised development trajectories. In

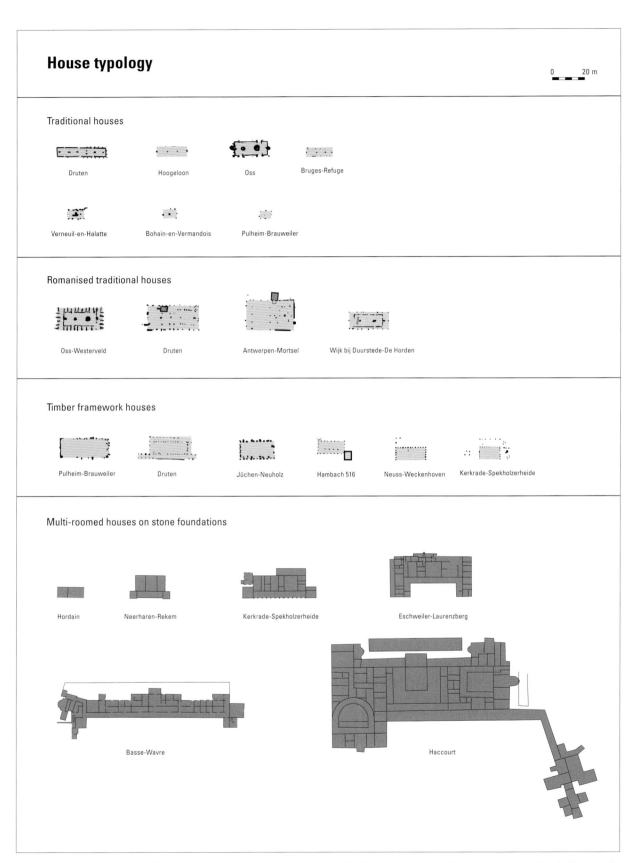

Fig. 3.27. Four basic types of house, as defined in this study. Post-built houses are in grey, houses on stone foundations are in dark grey.

the former, the houses shown are actually part of a coherent development trajectory. In the latter, the relationships between the different houses within the specific settlement are less clear, although general developments can clearly be documented. In some cases, the precise chronological relationship between building phases is unknown as a result of a lack of chronological detail. Six development trajectories are defined:

- Traditional post-built houses that did not undergo significant changes with regard to building techniques, architectural forms and concepts, or the application of building materials. Many such development trajectories are found in the northern sand and clay regions. The settlement of Brugge-Refuge is an example of this category. Over time, central posts were replaced by opposing pairs of roof-supporting posts. However, this constituted an internal development rather than an adoption of Mediterranean architectural techniques.

- Traditional houses developing into romanised traditional houses. Within this category, new architectural elements were added to otherwise traditional houses. Fig. 3.28a shows Oss-Westerveld, Wijk bij Duurstede-De Horden, Antwerpen-Mortsel and Druten. In these cases, traditional houses developed into portico-houses when a wooden portico was constructed around the house. The houses from Druten and Antwerp, dating back to the second half of the 1st century AD, also contained a cellar.

- Traditional houses developing into timber framework houses. Examples include Druten, Jüchen-Neuholz, Pulheim-Brauweiler and Bohain. At Druten, a single-aisled house with a fronting portico was erected in the later first or earlier 2nd century AD. At both Jüchen and Pulheim, the single-aisled framework houses were significantly larger than earlier, more traditional houses. During the 2nd century, the timber-framework house at Hambach 516 was extended to include a single risalith.

- Traditional houses developing into multi-roomed houses on stone foundations. This is a commonly documented development trajectory. Traditional house building was swiftly abandoned, only to be replaced by a completely new way of constructing residences. The diagram shows Hoogeloon, Houten-Burgermeester Wallerweg, Hamois-Le Hody, Monchy-le-Preux, Hordain and Neerharen-Rekem.

- Houses built *ex nihilo*, as multi-roomed houses on stone foundations. No predecessors in vernacular architecture were documented at these sites. One example, shown in the diagram, was the large house at Rochfort-Jemelle. Over time, this house was increasingly extended and monumentalised.

In the above classification, particular emphasis has been placed on the introduction of new materials, techniques, forms and concepts, describing a variety of individual development trajectories in house building. In many cases, quite radical transformations from traditional post-built houses towards multi-roomed houses on stone foundations were reconstructed. It is important to realise that the 'biographies' of these monumental and thus durable houses were much longer than those of their post-built predecessors. As a result, internal developments can often be documented for monumental houses. Here, we will shed some more light on these 'monumental developments'.

In general, three main 'monumental' development trajectories can be defined: development around a simple existing monumental core, development around a large existing monumental core and development involving the complete replacement of the existing monumental core. Again, significant variation may occur within the defined categories.

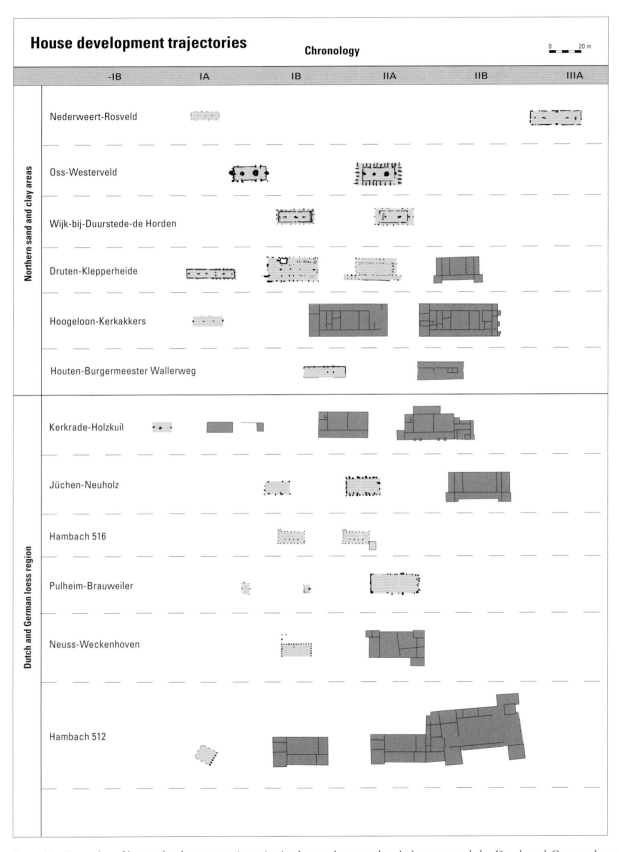

Fig. 3.28a. Examples of house development trajectories in the northern sand and clay areas and the Dutch and German loess region. Post-built houses are in grey, houses on stone foundations are in dark grey.

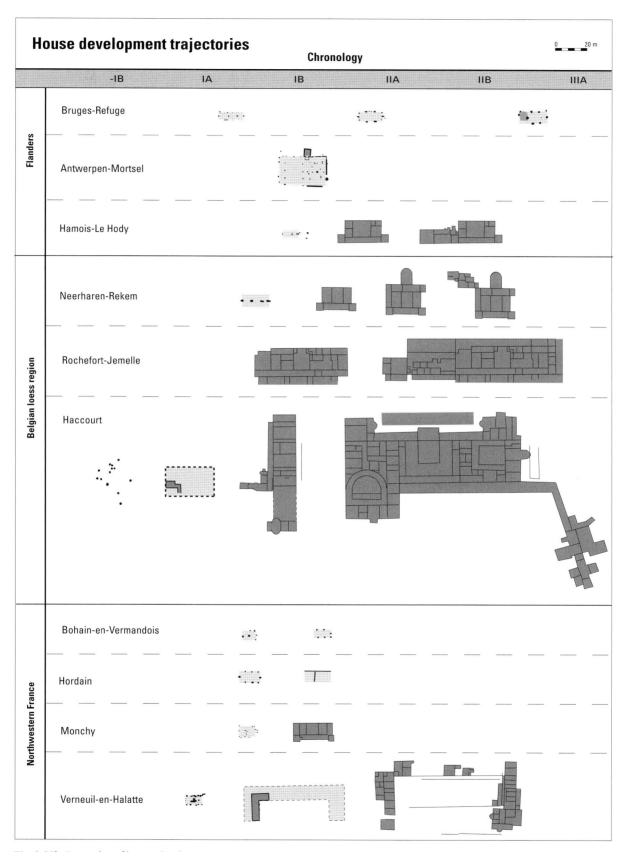

Fig. 3.28b. Examples of house development trajectories in Flanders, the Belgian loess region and northwestern France. Post–built houses are in grey, houses on stone foundations are in dark grey.

Most monumental houses were initially built as fairly small and simple structures, generally not exceeding 30 m in length. Many of these houses consisted of a relatively large central space, a number of smaller rooms and a fronting portico or portico-risalith façade. Examples can be found at Gesves-Sur le Corria, Neerharen-Rekem, Hambach 59, Hamois-Le Hody, Hambach 512, Vodelée, Vechmaal-Middelpadveld, Broekom and probably Merbes-Le-Chateau-Champs de Saint-Eloi during their early phases of monumentalisation (in other words, when a multi-roomed house on stone foundations was built within a settlement for the first time). As the house developed over time, the primary core was generally preserved during the process. Development around this core can be divided into a number of categories. It should nevertheless be stressed that, in most cases, actual house aggrandisement involved a combination of the following:

– the addition of rooms
– the addition or reconstruction of a façade
– the construction of hypocausts and bathing sections
– the addition of a completely new house section.

At Maasbracht, Broekom and Kerkrade-Spekholerheide, the façade was significantly monumentalised. In all three cases, large, projecting risaliths or even wings were added to the existing building, creating a larger and more pronounced façade. Monumentalisation, the wish to create visually impressive architecture, was clearly among the objectives. Another, somewhat less striking example can be found at Kerkrade-Holzkuil, where two entrance points on the existing portico were accentuated by columns, creating a more pronounced façade and entrance to the house. At Vodelée, a new, increasingly monumental façade was also added during a later phase in the 2nd century.

At Gesves, Hambach 512 and Merbes-Le-Chateau-Champs de Saint-Eloi, completely new sections were added. Hambach 512 even saw the erection of an altogether new house (exceeding the size of the existing structure), which was connected to the existing one. The oldest house at Merbes-Le-Chateau was extended by adding complete new sections on both sides, eventually creating a long rectangular building with a fronting façade of about 90 m in length. Such developments were potentially linked to the creation of an actual new house that was possibly inhabited by a new household.[233]

In terms of surface area, it is worth emphasising that some houses increased only slightly in size, while others more than doubled. Examples of this latter category include Broekom and Vechmaal-Middelpadveld; houses incorporating complete new house sections are Gesves, Hambach 512 and Merbes-Le-Chateau-Champs de Saint-Eloi.

Aside from houses that started as small and simple structures, other houses were fairly large from the outset. The house at Rochefort-Jemelle, for example, was around 60 m long during its first phase (fig. 3.28b). In subsequent phases, the house was extended towards one of the sides, reaching a length of over 100 m. It appears that the house of Blankenheim-Hülchrath was also a large structure from the first phase, although its development has not been reconstructed in much detail. Some other houses – Hoogeloon-Kerkakkers, Maasbracht and Champion-Le Emptinne – also measured around 50 m in length when first built.

The third of the three main categories is the total replacement of houses. In this case, the residence did not develop around an existing core that was preserved in the process. Instead, the existing house was actually torn down to allow for the construction of a wholly new, larger one. Two excellent examples of this process can be seen at Eschweiler-Laurenzberg (Siedlung 63) and Voerendaal-Ten

[233] The idea of multiple occupation in monumental villa houses was discussed by J.T. Smith (Smith 1978) among others.

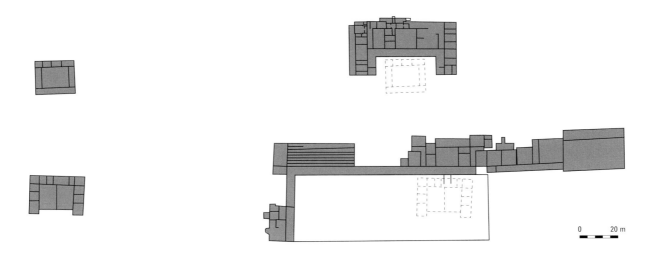

Fig. 3.29. The development trajectories of the monumental houses at Eschweiler-Laurenzberg (top) and Voerendaal-Ten Hove (bottom). In both cases, the first basic house was torn down to allow for the erection of a larger structure directly behind the former residence.

Hove (see fig. 3.29). In both cases, a fairly simple house was torn down to enable the creation of a new one, positioned directly behind the former structure. In the case of Eschweiler, a significantly larger house was built, including projecting wings. At Voerendaal, as described, a coherent, monumental complex was created, including the house, a *horreum* and a bath suite, interconnected by a long portico. Complete reconstruction was also part of the house development trajectories at Haccourt, Kerkrade-Holzkuil and Bad-Neuenahr-Ahrweiler. At Haccourt, the main house was entirely rebuilt on two separate occasions.

3.3.3 ELEMENTS OF CHANGE: MATERIALS, TECHNIQUES, PORTICOES AND FAÇADES, BATHS, CELLARS AND INTERIOR DECORATION

Having explored individual trajectories, I will continue by focusing on specific elements of change in house building, providing additional detail on their charateristics and position within house development trajectories:

— the use of building materials
— new building techniques
— porticoes and façades
— baths
— cellars
— interior decoration: painted wall plaster and mosaics.

The use of building materials
One of the basic and most tangible changes in house building was the use of new building materials. While traditional houses were built exclusively of organic materials from local sources, new developments involved the introduction of natural stone as well as special ceramic building materials such as roof tiles, floor tiles, hypocaust tiles and box flue tiles (*tubuli*). It is important to be aware of the investments made in quarrying and transporting natural stone, as well as producing and transporting specialised ceramic building materials.

73

The most important new building material was natural stone. Within the area researched in this study, a wide variety of stone was used for constructing foundations. An examination of the available data on the use of stone shows that the stone used for the construction of houses was predominantly local. In several cases, sources could be traced to a mere few hundred metres from the building site.[234] In other cases, however, the stone originated from sources that were far more distant. This is certainly the case for the northernmost regions, where natural stone was in fact unavailable. All stone used at these locations had to be transported over significant distances. This is of course a factor that should not be overlooked when assessing the investment involved in building a house on stone foundations.

Limestone quarried at Kunrade, only a few kilometres away, was used for building the monumental houses around Dutch Heerlen. Other kinds of local stone include marl (*mergel*) and various types of sandstone. Slate, tuff and marble, also documented at these sites, were imported from sources further afield – the Ardennes and Eifel. Similarly, readily available flint was used in the construction of foundations at many French and Belgian sites.[235] A comparable pattern emerges for the Picardy region. While flint was used as a building material on the plateaus, chalkstone dominated in the Oise valley.[236] In the German region, greywacke was a popular type of stone that could be quarried in either the northern Eifel or the Ville, just west of Cologne.

During the 1st century AD, the organic roof covering of many houses will have been replaced by ceramic tiles – *tegulae* and *imbrices*.[237] Unfortunately, as these roofs are never excavated, assessing the application of tiles is a difficult task.[238] It nevertheless seems obvious that the use of tiles as roof covering also meant new ways of constructing walls and roofs, as traditional structures were probably incapable of supporting the enormous weight of a tiled roof. For some traditional houses, including those at Lanaken and Hordain, the existence of tiled roofs was suggested by the excavators. A fully tiled roof should not be considered a credible option, however. Perhaps these roofs were only partially tiled, as seems to apply to the portico-house at Oss-Westerveld, where the particularly deeply-set outposts may have supported a tile-covered portico. Tiled roofs have also been suggested for some of the single-aisled framework houses. As we will see below, the new techniques used for building these houses considerably improved their ability to support heavier roof loads, thus allowing the successful construction of a tiled roof. Aside from ceramic roof tiles, slate also seems to have been a popular type of roof covering. The use of slates could be documented at Hambach 512, Frimmersdorf 30, Hambach 59, Cologne-Widdersdorf and Kerkrade-Holzkuil. At the latter two sites, slates were found to contain nail holes, indicating that nails were used to fix them to the roof. Somewhat further south, at Mont-lez-Houffalize-Fin de Ville in the Belgian Ardennes, a complete section of such a slate-covered roof was found, wooden slats included. And at Blankenheim-Hülchrath, a slate-covered roof was reconstructed for the earliest house, dating back to the 1st century AD. Slate was quarried in the Hünsruck or at Eifel and was probably shipped to the north via the Rhine and Mosel.[239]

Ceramic tiles were mass-produced and stamped at production sites. In some cases, such as the Nijmegen-Plasmolen villa, military production is assumed on the basis of the discovery of military tile stamps. In other cases, at a number of Dutch south Limburg settlements for instance, tile stamps like MHF, CEC AFF and AAC seem to be linked to civilian production sites or companies. Other examples include a CISSI stamp from the Belgian Smeermaas site, as well as HAMSIT, ATII, ATIL and ATIS stamps on hypocaust tiles and ATAB and TRPS on roof tiles found at Champion-Le Emptinne.[240]

---

[234] At Gesves-Sur le Corria, 'blocs de dolomie' were quarried only a few hundred metres southwest of the settlement.

[235] For example at Rosmeer-Staberg, Val-Meer-Meerberg, Haccourt, Villers (France) and Famechon (France).

[236] Ben Redjeb/Duvette/Quérel 2005; Haselgrove 1996, 143.

[237] Ben Redjeb/Duvette/Quérel 2005, 143: roof tiles were

used from the Augustan period onwards.

[238] At Kerkrade-Holzkuil, for example, tiles had also been used on walls and floors and sometimes even for constructing stone walls (Tichelman 2005, 258).

[239] Kaszab-Olschewski 2006, 102.

[240] Van Ossel/Defgnee 2001, 172.

New building techniques

The introduction of new building techniques is strongly linked to that of new building materials discussed above. While traditional houses were constructed using wooden posts, set in post-holes, new techniques were adopted from the 1st century AD onwards, including:

– new foundation techniques
– new wall construction techniques
– new roof construction techniques
– new technological systems: hypocaust and bathing systems.

New foundation techniques included a range of ways to create more solid structures, improve the structural support and prevent degradation of the organic parts of the house, significantly increasing its durability (fig. 3.30). The least complicated solution for improving the foundation was filling up post-holes in order to support the wooden post. This filling could be gravel, clay, tiles or, as documented at Oss-Westerveld and Tiel-Passewaaij, a wooden plank. In other cases, actual footings were created with gravel or fragments of natural stone and tile. These footings probably extended somewhat above ground level to prevent contact between the posts they supported and the soil. For some houses, these footings were hewn or sawn stone blocks with holes in them for holding both horizontal and vertical framework construction timbers. The most advanced and frequently documented new foundation technique were linear stone foundations, mostly consisting of a lower foundation of either gravel or rough natural stone fragments and an upper foundation in the form of a generally low masonry wall. A framework structure was then built on the masonry wall to support the roof.[241] Although we should not rule out the existence of walls built entirely of stone, most probably only had stone bases. This limited the need for stone material, but still increased the durability of the structure considerably.

Aside from foundations, changes were also made to the elevation of the houses, as new wall and roof-construction techniques were introduced (see fig. 3.31). Unfortunately, only the lowest foundations have been preserved for the majority of houses, complicating any kind of detailed reconstruction of the aboveground wall and roof construction.[242] Some general ideas can nevertheless be put forward. The walls of the comparatively large single-aisled timber framework houses described earlier seem to have consisted of robust posts that formed the basis of a sturdy framework structure. As there were no central roof-supporting posts, these walls had to support the entire roof load. Cross beams connected the opposite walls, creating the structural coherence of a house and forming an important part of the roof structure at the same time. Fig. 3.31 shows this type of construction. The construction of such new framework walls involved new carpentry techniques for which it seems that nails were also used. The walls and roofs of houses with linear stone foundations were probably built in a similar fashion. Instead of resting on packings or footings, the wooden construction timbers were probably set in holes created in the top of the masonry walls.

Portico and façade

Aside from the introduction of new materials and new techniques, the introduction of new architectural concepts was also very important. One of these new concepts was that of the façade, a phenomenon absent in the vernacular architecture of the traditional house. The façade literally constituted the

---

[241] At Bad-Neuenahr-Ahrweiler, the exceptional state of preservation allowed for the reconstruction of a 1.5 m high masonry base wall. Fehr 2003.

[242] However, there are some interesting exceptions, such

as the exceptionally well-preserved villa house at Bad-Neuenahr-Ahrweiler (Fehr 2003) and the urban site at Amiens-Le Site de la ZAC Cathédrale-Université (Gemehl 2004).

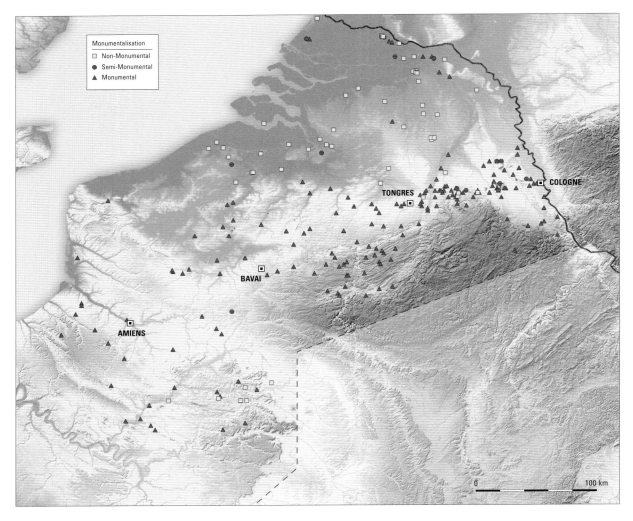

Fig 3.30. Distribution of houses according to three defined degrees of monumentalisation: non-monumental (post-built), semi-monumental (stone material packings and footings) and monumental (linear stone foundations).

'face' of the house, creating an entrance but also conveying a message and impression to the outside world. How was the façade adopted in rural house building within the research area?

The two main elements of the façade were the portico and the risalith. A portico was a colonnaded gallery, covered by a roof and linked to or integrated into buildings, often used in urban, military or rural architecture. A portico had both connecting and buffering purposes. In addition, its characteristic appearance of repetitive columns created a strong visual effect, highly recognisable as a Mediterranean architectural style. The risalith was a square, tower-like corner room, predominantly situated at both front corners of a house, connected by a portico. Because of their position and appearance, they were prominent elements within the residence. Along with the connecting portico, they made up the portico-risalith façade, characteristic of a great number of monumental rural houses in the Roman provinces. Smith, who dedicates no less than two chapters to this phenomenon, defines a threefold purpose for these façades: aesthetic (creating a strong visual, impressive façade), cultural (symbolising a Roman lifestyle) and social (providing additional high-status rooms).[243] He parallels the risalith with

---

[243] Smith 1997, 117-118.

76

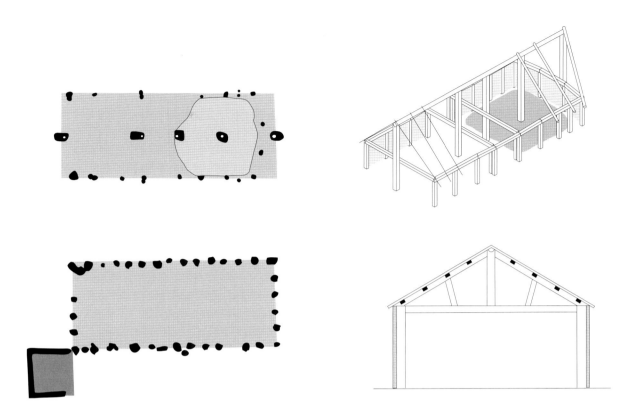

Fig. 3.31. Top: a traditional Alphen-Ekeren house with internal roof supporting posts and its reconstruction. Bottom: a single-aisled timber framework house and its reconstructed cross section. After Hiddink/De Boer 2003; Tichelman 2005, 104.

early modern parlours, as the most private and usually best-appointed rooms used by the master and mistress of the house.[244]

Before discussing these well-known portico-risalith façades further, I will firstly examine other attempts to create residential façades (fig. 3.32). At a number of single-aisled framework houses – Hambach 516, Jüchen-Neuotzenrath and, in all probability, Frimmersdorf 131 – a single risalith was attached to one of the corners. In the first two cases, the risalith was constructed on linear stone foundations, representing later additions. These risaliths will have created and accentuated the façade of the house, as was the case with more elaborate portico-risalith façades. Different examples are a number of houses found in the Dutch sand and clay areas (Druten (house 12), Den Haag-Wateringse Veld (house 107) and Hoogeloon (house 28)). These included impressive façades, created by constructing a wooden portico or porch onto one of the long sides of the fairly basic house. This portico exceeded the length of the house. At Hoogeloon, the house itself could be labelled a traditional two-aisled Alphen-Ekeren type, although posts were in fact set on stone footings. The house at Druten was a single-aisled framework house, however. Fragments of painted wall plaster and a gutter construction inside the house underlined the special character of this particular residence. A similar interpretation applies to the Den Haag house, on the basis of the material culture associated with the house. The façade as a new architectural instrument (even used on traditional houses) thus appears to have been associated with a special social position within the respective settlements. Porticoes like the ones constructed around houses such as Oss-Westerveld were not façades in the strictest sense of the word, as they do not seem

[244] Smith 1997, 118.

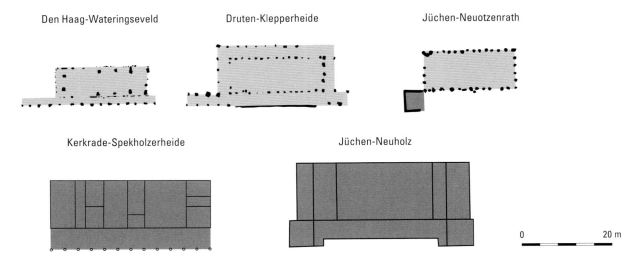

Den Haag-Wateringseveld   Druten-Klepperheide   Jüchen-Neuotzenrath

Kerkrade-Spekholzerheide   Jüchen-Neuholz

0   20 m

Fig. 3.32. Different types of portico on different house types. From top left to bottom right: a fairly traditional three-aisled post-built house with a long wooden portico at Den Haag-Wateringseveld; a single-aisled framework house with a long wooden portico at Druten; a single-aisled framework house with a single risalith at one of the corners at Jüchen-Neuotzenrath; a multi-roomed house on stone foundations with a fronting portico at Kerkrade-Spekholzerheide; a multi-roomed house on stone foundations with a typical portico-risalith façade at Jüchen-Neuholz.

to have accentuated the actual front of the house. Nonetheless, these architectural elements were likely to have had an important socio-symbolic value as well.

The development of the portico-risalith façade can be linked to that of multi-roomed houses on stone foundations. Generally, a portico or portico-risalith façade was already included in the earliest phases of most of these houses (fig. 3.32).[245] As these houses frequently had very basic plans, we could assume that the façade was a vital element. There are, however, also monumental houses that lacked a façade during their earliest phases, such as at Broichweiden-Würselen, Vezin-Namêche, Vodelée, Maubeuge and Kerkrade-Holzkuil. In these cases, a façade was nevertheless constructed during a later development phase. Other houses first displayed a simple portico façade, which was later extended with risaliths, or even projecting wings; Maasbracht, Kerkrade-Spekholzerheide and Kerkrade-Holzkuil fall into this category.

The façade was thus an important feature of the house. The monumentalisation of façades has already been labelled a pivotal objective. In quite a number of cases, such as at Merbes-Le-Chateau, Hamois-Le Hody and Rochefort-Jemelle, the house front was broadened considerably during its development, thereby creating a wider and much more impressive façade. In addition, at Voerendaal, an extremely broad porticoed façade was created, with the intention of integrating the individual buildings of the complex into one coherent and visually impressive whole (see fig 3.33).

Baths
An element in house development that can be directly related to the Mediterranean lifestyle and advanced technological engineering is the bath. The construction of baths demanded a high level of technological expertise that probably involved specialists. In addition, specialised building material and hence substantial financial investment were required. The construction of baths marked an important step in the adoption of an urban-inspired Mediterranean lifestyle.

[245] Good examples include the early monumental houses of Voerendaal-Ten Hove, Neerharen-Rekem, Vechmaal-Middelpadveld, Hamois-Le Hody, Gesves-Sur le Corria and Kerkrade-Spekholzerheide.

Fig. 3.33. Reconstruction of the highly monumental 2nd-century complex at Voerendaal-Ten Hove. A remarkably wide porticoed façade fronted not only the main house, but also the granary, bath house and a secondary building. After Stuart/De Grooth 1987, 4.

Table 3.1 presents an overview of bath sections in rural houses throughout the research region. If we examine this data, we note that most bath sections were later additions to existing monumental houses, dating back to the 2nd or even 3rd century. Only in a minority of cases were baths constructed as early as the second half of the 1st century, as part of the first monumental building phase. Houses with early baths include Haccourt, Champion-Le Emptinne, Ath-Meslin-L'Evêque, Blankenheim and Verneuil-en-Halatte. It is remarkable that all these houses were part of large, axially organised complexes.[246] The early construction of bath buildings in these settlements could underline their direct link to urban centres, the ultimate location of the developing bathing culture within the provinces.[247]

Baths could be or become part of a monumental house in different ways, some of which are presented in fig. 3.34 (for an overview see table 3.1). In quite a number of cases, such as at Neerharen-Rekem (shown), Kerkrade-Holzkuil and Hamoi-Le Hody, bathing sections were attached to an existing house core. Another popular variant was the integration of a bathing suite into the existing house structure, as found at Hoogeloon-Kerkakkers (shown), Eschweiler-Laurenzberg and Hambach 127. In other cases, bath houses were built close to but separate from the house. At Vaals-Lemiers (shown), the bath house remained a separate entity close to the house throughout its occupation. In other cases, such as at Champion-Le Emptinne (shown), Gesves-Sur le Corria (shown) and Voerendaal-Ten Hove, separate baths were later connected to the house by means of a portico. In these cases, the bath section itself was also significantly extended.

With regard to the development of baths, it is interesting to note that the first baths in town houses are older than those in rural villa houses. In the urban centre of Cologne, bathing sections dated back to around 50 AD, while in Bonn they were built around 70 AD.[248] This was somewhat earlier than or contemporary with the earliest baths appearing in rural villa houses. Again, these rural houses with early baths must have had close and direct connections to the urban centres and their culture. The later spread of the bath's popularity within rural house building links back to the rise of a new and more widely adopted villa lifestyle.

[246] The Cologne-Vogelsang villa was situated in close proximity to the town of Cologne, which may explain the early appearance of the bath within the house. Only part of the Eschweiler-Hovermühle complex was excavated, making it impossible to assess the character and dimensions of the settlement.

[247] For their development trajectories see appendix 1.

[248] Dodt 2003, 329.

Site	Bath construction date	Development phase	Position
Kerkrade-Holzkuil	2d	later addition	attached
Neerharen-Rekem	2	later addition	attached
Hamois-Le Hody	post 2a-3a	later addition	attached
Ath-Meslin-l'Evêque	1c	first phase?	separate
Dormagen-Nievenheim	mid 2	later addition	integrated
Verneuil-en-Halatte	2	later addition	separate/attached
Voerendaal-Ten Hove	2a/2A	later addition	separate with connecting portico
Rheinbach-Flerzheim	2d	later addition	attached
Hambach 512	2d	later addition	integrated
Haccourt	1d	early phase	attached /separate
Hambach 59	2d-3a / after 100 AD	later addition	attached
Blankenheim-Hülchrath	1	first phase?	integrated
Champion-Le Emptinne	1B	first phase	separate, later connected
Hoogeloon-Kerkakkers	2A	later addition	integrated
Bad Neuenahr-Ahrweiler-Silberberg	mid 1	first phase	separate with connecting portico
Rochefort-Jemelle	?	later addition	attached
Eschweiler-Laurenzberg-Lürken	2A	early phase	integrated
Bocholtz-Vlengendaal	2a	first phase?	integrated
Valkenburg-Ravensbosch	2a	later addition	attached
Aachen-Süsterfeld	2-3	later addition	separate
Lemiers	1d / 2a	first phase?	separate
Bonn-Friesdorf	2A	first phase?	integrated
Euskirchen-Kreuzweingarten	2d	later addition	attached
Cologne-Müngersdorf	3B?	later addition	attached
Hambach 132	2a	first phase?	integrated (in risalith)
Übach-Palenberg	2	later addition	separate
Hambach 206	2-3	later addition	separate with connecting portico
Schuld	2B	later addition	attached
Hambach 127	1d / 2a	later addition	integrated
Hambach 56	2d?	later addition	integrated
Weisweiler 122	2B	later addition	attached
Neuss-Rommerskirchen	2d /3a	later addition	attached
Verneuil-en-Halatte	1B	later addition?	separate, later attached
Aachen-Stolberg	2a	first phase?	integrated

Table 3.1. Overview of the development of bath sections in rural villa houses. Dates are given. Number: century. Capital A–B: half century. Small letter a–d: quarter century.

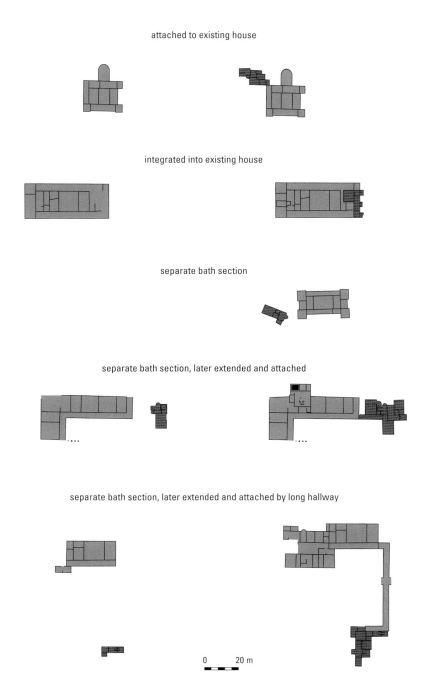

attached to existing house

integrated into existing house

separate bath section

separate bath section, later extended and attached

separate bath section, later extended and attached by long hallway

0   20 m

Fig. 3.34. Visualisation of the various spatial relationships between bath sections and houses. From top to bottom: Neerharen-Rekem, Hoogeloon-Kerkakkers, Vaals-Lemiers, Champion-Le Emptinne and Gesves-Sur le Corria. In the latter two cases, the bath section seems to have been part of the house from its first phase onwards. With regard to the other houses, the bath was constructed during a second development phase.

Cellars

The construction of small cellars is a phenomenon known from pre-Roman house building in the south of the research region. These pre-Roman cellars were small and simply dug into the ground (fig. 3.35). In the northern regions, however, there was no pre-Roman tradition of cellar construction.

Developments in house building were accompanied by changes in cellar construction. Cellars became larger and were now often lined with planks, stone blocks, or even masonry walls. In the

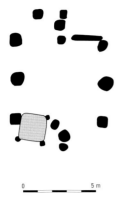

Fig. 3.35. Small cellar (grey) in a traditional house, dating back to the Late Iron Age or Early Roman period.

0 ___ 5 m

Alphen-Ekeren-type house at Vechmaal-Middelpadveld and in the timber framework house at Jüchen-Neuholz, simple cellars were constructed during the second half of the 1st century AD. One of the earliest large cellars, dating back to the Tiberian-Claudian period, was documented at Verneuil-en-Halatte. At Kerkrade-Holzkuil, a cellar was created in the first multi-roomed house on stone foundations that was built around the middle of the 2nd century AD (see fig. 3.36). From the 1st century AD onwards, cellars can also be documented in the sand and clay areas, such as at Druten and Antwerpen-Mortsel. We could perhaps regard cellar construction as an element of traditional house building that became more widespread from the 1st century AD onwards and involved a translation into new forms through the use of new materials and techniques. Cellars had multiple roles, the most obvious of which was the cool storage of perishable foods such as smoked and salted meat, fish and dairy products. This was illustrated, for example, by the *dolia*, dug into the cellar floor of the house at Wange-Damekot.

Interior decoration: wall painting and mosaics

Another important element of Mediterranean house building was interior decoration. Here I will briefly focus on the most prominent features – painted wall plaster and floor mosaics. While the former is a well-documented phenomenon within the research region, the latter is encountered there only rarely.

Again, it is difficult to create a complete overview, as many sites have not been subject to sufficiently detailed publication. For a great many houses we are simply unable to establish whether their walls were decorated or not. Extrapolating from what we do know, however, painted wall plaster seems to have been a fairly standard feature of monumental houses, even the most basic ones. The walls of the simple houses at Rijswijk-De Bult, Houten-Burgermeester Wallerweg and Druten (house 1 and 12) were decorated with painted plaster. At the very early traditional house at Aalter-Langevoorde, dating back to the first half of the 1st century AD, fragments of painted wall plaster were also found. The painted wall plaster found in the villa of Maasbracht, however, was of a different category as it included figurative scenes (fig. 4.14).[249]

The Mediterranean tradition of decorating walls was part of an urban lifestyle before being introduced to rural house building. At Cologne-Margarethenkloster, a simple house on horizontal beam foundations was equipped with plastered walls, decorated with white, red and green spots, and dating back as early as the Augustan period.[250] The first Mediterranean-style house at Tongeren-Kielenstraat also included decorated walls. In a rural context, decorating walls probably only became popular from the middle of the 1st century AD onwards.

The use of mosaics is a relatively rare phenomenon within the research region. Most mosaics are found in the larger monumental houses, such as at Haccourt, Aldenhoven-Schleiden, Euskirchen-Kreuzweingarten, Basse-Wavre and Anthée. There are, however, some indications that simpler houses also contained simple mosaic floors, as was the case at Hambach 59 and 425, where only small fragments were found.

---

[249] Swinkels 1987.

[250] Seiler 2001, 126.

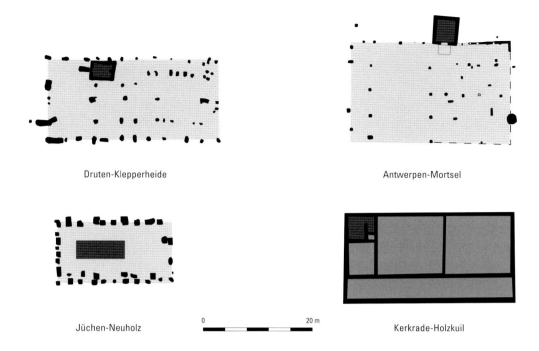

Druten-Klepperheide

Antwerpen-Mortsel

Jüchen-Neuholz

0   20 m

Kerkrade-Holzkuil

Fig. 3.36. Cellars in the houses at Druten (house 1), Antwerpen-Mortsel, Jüchen-Neuholz and Kerkrade-Holzkuil.

3.3.4 DIFFERENTIATION IN HOUSE BUILDING WITHIN SETTLEMENTS: SHEDDING LIGHT ON THE DIFFICULT CATEGORY OF 'SECONDARY HOUSES'

With regard to house building, we have focused so far mainly on houses that underwent the most significant changes through time and thus generally developed into the most monumental houses within their settlements. These houses are often referred to as the main house. Within villa studies, a basic dichotomy is generally created between this main house and a category of secondary buildings. We should be aware, however, that in this latter category we could also expect houses inhabited by other members of the settlement community. If we wish to generate a more complex view on settlement development and the differentiated social relationships within settlements, we should not ignore these 'secondary' houses. I will therefore attempt to shed some light on this rather difficult category of buildings and explore the differentiation in house building and house development trajectories within settlements.

As with secondary buildings in general, it is often difficult to reconstruct functionalities and to identify secondary houses with any degree of certainty. Only in a minority of cases could a direct domestic indicator such as a hearth be documented. In many other instances, the interpretation is more indirect, mainly based on house plans. The focus in this section is on houses as physical structures. In chapter 4 I will also explore them from a social perspective in an attempt to explain the asymmetrical relationships within settlements.

Traditional houses
As described, traditional houses were post-built and constructed according to local traditions. An especially well-studied category of traditional houses is the long-rectangular two-aisled house of the Alphen-Ekeren type. Generally, these houses were associated specifically with the sandy MDS region, but recent research has shown that they were also constructed on the loess soils of the German, Belgian

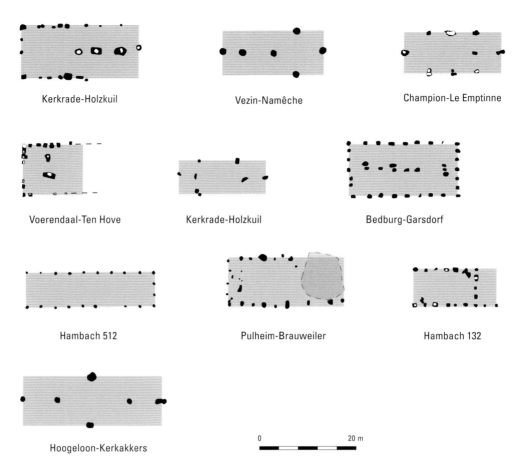

Fig. 3.37. Some examples of post-built houses in settlements throughout the research region.

and seemingly even French parts of our research region.[251] At many sites, the settlement seems to have been dominated by such post-built houses during the early phases of their development, generally the 1st century AD. As I have reconstructed above, one of the houses was often replaced by a new type of house on stone foundations during the second half of the 1st or early 2nd century AD. The other houses within the settlement, however, retained a traditional character in many cases. Fig. 3.37 visualises a number of these post-built houses. For some of them – Hambach 512, Champion and Hoogeloon – the existence of a byre could be suggested. In settlements like Kerkrade, Vezin, Champion, Hamois, Bedburg and Hoogeloon, post-built houses survived after one of the houses was replaced by a monumental building.

Monumentalising secondary houses
Apart from secondary houses that continued to be built in a fairly traditional fashion, we also find secondary houses changing over time. A process of monumentalisation can be documented in many cases. Three general categories have been distinguished: literal monumentalisation, 'extended' monumentalisation and the development of secondary monumental houses with multi-roomed plans and façades quite similar to the main houses.

[251] See sites like Kerkrade-Winckelen, Kerkrade-Holzkuil, Riemst-Lafelt, Neerharen-Rekem, Vechmaal-Middelpadveld, Hamois-Le Hody, Vezin-Namêche, Champion-Le Emptinne, Hambach 512, Bedburg-Garsdorf, Hambach 512 and Kerpen-Sindorf. See also De Clercq/Quérel 2010.

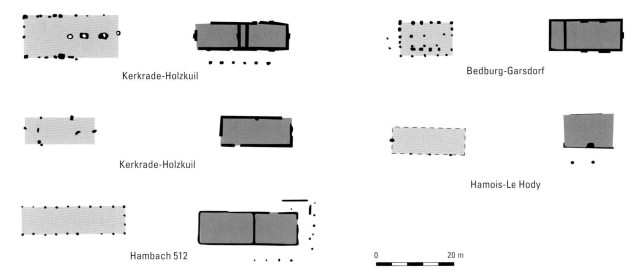

Fig. 3.38. Some examples of the monumentalisation of presumed secondary houses.

Literal monumentalisation involved the rebuilding of post-built houses on stone foundations while adhering to existing plans, measurements and even the exact location. An example is given in fig. 3.38 of the house at Kerkrade-Holzkuil. Further examples can be found at Champion (see fig. 5.4), Vezin and Nuth-Terstraten.

In some other cases, houses were monumentalised rather more extensively. At Kerkrade-Holzkuil, for example, a long-rectangular house was constructed on stone foundations, fronted by a portico and consisting of two equally large sections (see fig. 3.38). And at Hambach 512 a quite similar building, also divided into two spaces, had a portico constructed around one of them. Hypothetically, we could say that this bipartite structure derived from the byre house. In the case of Hambach 512, could the room surrounded by the portico then be interpreted as the residential space? Another hypothetical secondary house with a fronting portico can be found at Hamois. In this category of secondary houses, in addition to new materials and techniques, the new concept of the portico and façade was also adopted in house building. However, the structure of the traditional house still seems to be reflected in these houses. At least for the house at Kerkrade, it can be established that it was monumentalised only after the main house was constructed on stone foundations.

A third category of secondary houses are the multi-roomed dwellings on stone foundations that were quite similar to the plans used for most main houses, even including a portico-risalith façade (fig. 3.39). Traditionally, these houses have been interpreted as the residence of a *vilicus* or a servant family.[252] Good examples of this type were documented at Neerharen-Rekem, Rochefort-Jemelle, Cologne-Müngersdorf, Hambach 403, Rheinbach-Flerzheim and Hambach 127. Such houses can also be found at many axially organised complexes, often positioned on the part of the working compound that was closest to the residential compound (see fig. 3.40).

Thus houses of different architectural character coexisted within a single settlement. While one house was still built in traditional fashion, others were built using stone foundations, were fronted by a portico or were even divided into several rooms. Such intra-settlement differentiation in house building and in house development trajectories goes beyond simplistic dichotomies of main house and secondary buildings.

[252] This seems to characterise the German research tradition
in particular.

0   20 m

Fig. 3.39. Monumental secondary houses at Hambach 127, Neerharen-Rekem and Rochefort-Jemelle.

3.3.5 CHANGES IN RURAL HOUSE BUILDING TRADITIONS IN CONTEXT

As previously suggested, developments in rural house building did not take place in a vacuum. On the contrary, they must be understood within the broader context of the developing Roman provinces. One of the essential features of these provinces was the rise of urban and rural centres with functions of a predominantly administrative, political, economic, social and cultural nature.[253] They were the arenas of power, the locations where the provincial population came into direct contact with the broader empire and its Mediterranean homelands. As such, urban centres were important in the development and spread of new lifestyles.[254] Towns had an important mediating function as places where the provincial people were confronted with new phenomena, concepts, ideas and products rooted in Mediterranean culture. I will now explore architectural developments in these centres, also in relation to rural architectural developments.

Data on house development is available for several urban centres within the research region. At Xanten,[255] Cologne,[256] Bavay[257] and Tongres,[258] traditional house building could be documented for the period around the start of the Common Era. As early as the first decades AD, however, changes in house building appeared as new building techniques were adopted. At both Cologne (the Burgmauer site) and Xanten (the Margarethenkloster site among others), houses with timber framework walls on horizontal foundation beams could be dated to the earliest decades AD.[259] In the house at Xanten, dating back to the Augustan period, walls were even decorated with painted plaster.

During the Tiberian period, multi-roomed houses on stone foundations superseded the wooden houses on horizontal beams at the Cologne-Burgmauer site.[260] A similar development was documented at Cologne-Dome.[261] At Amiens-Palais des Sports, traditional post-built houses, dated between 20 and 50 AD, were replaced in around 60 AD by multi-roomed atrium-type houses with fronting porticoes, white plastered walls and tiled roofs (fig. 3.41).[262] And at Tongres-Kielenstraat,[263] a multi-roomed Mediterranean style house on horizontal foundation beams replaced traditional Alphen-Ekeren-type houses during the Claudio-Neronian period. This house had a U-shaped plan with two wings surrounding an open court. It also had a Mediterranean appearance, including white plastered walls, decorated internal walls and a tiled roof (fig. 3.41). After 69 AD, when the house was demolished, it was rebuilt on stone foundations. At another site in Tongres, Hondstraat,[264] parallel developments were

[253] Vanderhoeven 1996, 224.

[254] It is important to mention, however, that urban centres were certainly not the only contexts in which new lifestyles were developed and spread. We also should not underestimate the importance of military camps, rural santuaries and the early villas. Vanderhoeven 1996, 224.

[255] Brulet 1996, 92.

[256] Hellenkemper 1975; 1980; Brulet 1996.

[257] Brulet 1996, 88.

[258] Vanderhoeven/Vynckier/Vynckier 1991, 1992; Binet

2004.

[259] Seiler 2001, 126, 132; Zieling 2001; for an impression of the construction of such framework houses, see Gemehl 2004.

[260] Seiler 2001, 133.

[261] Excavated by G. Precht in 1969-1970 (Seiler 2001).

[262] Brulet 1996.

[263] Vanderhoeven/Vynckier/Vynckier 1991.

[264] Vanderhoeven/Vynckier/Vynckier 1992.

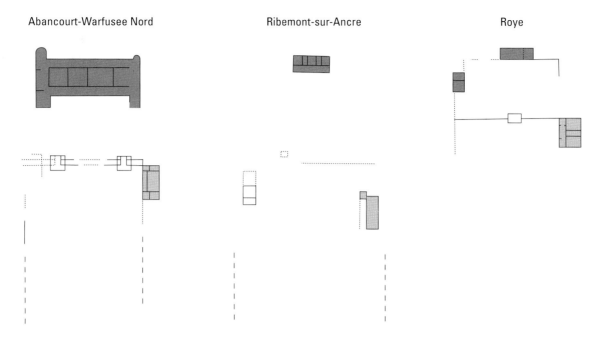

Abancourt-Warfusee Nord   Ribemont-sur-Ancre   Roye

Fig. 3.40. Multi-roomed secondary houses on stone foundations (grey) in the axially organised settlement complex of Abancourt-Warfusee Nord, Ribemont-sur-Ancre and Roye. The main houses are in dark grey.

documented. Here, a still wood-built Mediterranean style, multi-roomed house replaced a number of traditional houses that dated back to the first half of the 1st century AD. Again, the house was rebuilt on stone foundations after 69 AD. Around the middle of the 2nd century, the house was reconstructed once more, now including solid stone walls. This U-shaped house boasted floor mosaics as well as a hypocaust system.

It must be emphasised that these examples do not necessarily represent the earliest architectural developments in urban centres. During the earlier periods of urban developments, Roman-style or Roman-inspired houses may already have existed along the main city roads.[265] It would in fact be reasonable to assume that such early Mediterranean-style houses inspired the further developments in house building examined above.

A unique case that casts light on the earliest phases of urban house building is the Augustan town of Waldgirmes, located east of the Rhine in the German frontier zone. Extensive excavations there have uncovered the early phases of a developing small town, probably founded in anticipation of the complete incorporation of this region into the Roman empire. After Varus' defeat in 9 AD, however, both this plan and the early town were abandoned. One of the most interesting buildings can be found at the centre of the town. Here, a wooden version of an atrium-type house was in all probability constructed around the turn of the millennium, or even somewhat earlier (see fig 3.42). A large monumental complex built on stone foundations superseded this house.[266] This complex can be interpreted as a forum with a long-rectangular basilica, fronted by an open court that was surrounded by a porticoed ambulatory. In relation to the historical situation, this complex should thus be dated

[265] Regarding some of the earliest cases within the research region, houses on stone foundations were built during the second quarter of the 1st century AD. Just south of the research area, in Trier-Irminen, such a Mediterranean-style house could even be dated to the later Augustan period, the earliest example known in this region. Cüppers 1984; Vanderhoeven 1996, 242.

[266] Von Schurbein 2003, Becker 2003.

Fig. 3.41. Reconstructed house development in Tongres-Kielenstraat (left) and Amiens-Palais des Sports (right). Top: houses constructed according to native traditions. Bottom: the first Roman-style houses replacing the traditional dwellings. After Brulet/ Coquelet 2004, 127; Binet 2004, 130.

to before 9 AD. These findings indicate that Mediterranean-style buildings were already being constructed during the earliest provincial and urban phases, while new building techniques and materials, architectural forms and concepts were being introduced. As Waldgirmes is unlikely to be a unique case, we could expect similar early developments in other towns, such as those previously discussed. Destruction during later building activity and the presence of modern towns nevertheless tends to seriously complicate the study of these earliest phases.

Aside from these large urban centres with monumental cores and a regular street grid, many smaller rural centres developed in the countryside. These centres were located at strategic locations along major roads or river crossings. The rise of rural centres also started quite early, and can be linked back to the growth of the road system from the Augustan period onwards.[267] Centres such as Namur[268] and Braives developed from the last decade BC onwards, while the earliest documented phases at Liberchies[269] and Maastricht[270] can be dated to the early 1st century AD. The development of the Grobbendonk centre is exceptionally late, its first phase dating back to the Claudian period.[271] As in urban centres, traditional house building was predominant during the early development phases. At Liberchies, the settlement was first reorganised around the middle of the 1st century AD, by rebuilding the houses close together, their short sides facing the road. Then, in the later 1st and early 2nd century, single-aisled 'strip houses' on stone foundations appeared. During the same phase, a multi-roomed house with a fronting portico was built at Grobbendonk. Its plan was actually similar to simple villa houses

[267] De Boe 1985b.

[268] Plumier 2006.

[269] Demanet 2006.

[270] Panhuysen 1996, 33.

[271] De Boe 1985b.

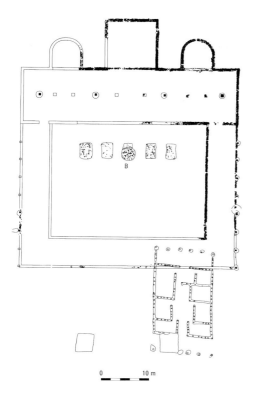

like those found at Hoogeloon and Houten-Burgemeester Wallerweg (fig. 3.43). At this site, houses were rebuilt in stone in the early 2nd century. Even a bath house was built during this period.

3.4 VILLA DEVELOPMENT BETWEEN CONTINUITY AND CHANGE

This chapter has explored changes in rural settlements from a broad and longer-term perspective. The ultimate goal was to gain a greater understanding of the phenomenon of villa development. The perspective chosen in this study highlights the analysis of developments and processes rather than that of static phenomena, such as monumental houses. In general, villa development is understood to be a series of significant transformations in settlement organisation and house building. My approach here has been mainly archae-ological, focusing on spatial organisation and architecture and largely disregarding social or economic interpretations. These will be discussed in subsequent chapters. Examining the data and analyses previously presented, we are able to define villa develop-ment more specifically:

- Villa development was rooted in long-term transformations into discrete, enclosed, stable and well-organised settlement units. The appearance of more durable houses can possibly also be regarded as a longer-term trend.
- Villa development involved new ways of organising settlement space, including spatial structura-tion, segregation and hierarchisation.
- Villa development involved significant changes to house building. New building techniques, materials, forms and concepts were adopted. This was a heterogeneous and phased process with considerable regional and local variation.

As part of longer lines of settlement development, villa development can be situated within the force-field between continuity and change. This forcefield combines long, continuous lines of settlement development (including the above-mentioned trends towards discrete, enclosed, stable and well-organised settlement units), and significant transformations including the reorganisation of settlement space (the introduction of new spatial concepts), monumentalisation and the adoption of Mediter-ranean building styles, breaking with existing traditions. The concept of villa development outlined in this chapter thus goes beyond the traditional 'static' villa definition, with its predominant focus on Roman-style architecture and the use of stone. As a result, villa development can also be associated with settlements that are generally termed 'native' and thus 'non-villa'. Excluding such sites from the study on the basis of a traditional villa definition would restrict our field of vision. Different regions saw different trajectories of villa development, whereby new spatial and architectural concepts were adopted in different ways (see the diagrams presented earlier). The portico is an example of a new

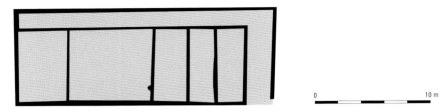

Fig. 3.43. Multi-roomed house on foundation beams from the rural centre at Grobbendonk. Dated to the late 1st century AD.

architectural concept that was adopted in a variety of ways throughout the region. In the northern-most regions, wooden porticoes were added to traditional houses; in the German loess region, single risaliths were added to simple framework houses; and throughout the research region more or less standardised portico-risalith façades were used in multi-roomed houses on stone foundations.

Now that we have explored the various development trajectories in settlement organisation and house building throughout the region, it is time to turn to the question of why. How can these developments be understood in terms of the people inhabiting the settlements and houses?

4　　Exploring the social villa. A human approach to villa development

The preceding chapter explored long-term developments as well as more radical changes and transformations in both the organisation of settlement space and house building, predominantly from a spatio-morphological perspective. Space and time, both essential elements within this analysis, were approached as abstract, measurable entities. However, we should not forget that archaeology should ultimately be about people. After all, it was people who organised settlement space, built houses and broke with existing trends and traditions. In this chapter, I will therefore study villa development from a social or 'human' perspective, making human beings a central element in this chapter's main research question: how can we understand people changing their immediate living environments in often quite radical ways and how can we understand the marked heterogeneity within the research region? People are thus regarded as active and creative agents who actively and consciously changed their immediate living environments. These human agents were continually creating and reproducing society within the constraints of behaviour learnt and understood within that society. Material change, then, should be viewed as an ongoing social discourse that emphasises diversity and the continual reworking of social relations and identities through the material world.[1]

Our key objective is once more to understand changes on the level of the settlement and, consequently, of local communities. However, we cannot and should not attempt to deny the relationships between these local communities and the broader outside world. As Webley argues, '[h]ousehold relations are not insulated from the external world, nor do they respond passively to externally imposed changes. Rather, they can themselves play an important role in maintaining or renegotiating wider social relations'.[2]

Especially in continental studies, villa development has too often been regarded as the logical and unproblematic adoption of new settlement forms and the replacement of simple wooden traditional houses by Roman-style ones. In this chapter, I would like to take a closer look at these developments, studying the backgrounds and implications in more detail and using social theories and models in an attempt to understand more about the complex processes of change in rural settlements within the context of the developing Roman provinces.

Before doing so, I will need to briefly explore some assumptions. Settlement and house (along with semi-fixed and mobile material elements) are both essential elements of the material world that people create directly around themselves, as their immediate living environment. It is within this context that relationships – within families, between families and with the broader outside world – are created and recreated on a day-to-day basis.[3] Settlement and house as material culture are thus indissolubly interwo-

---

[1]　Taylor 2001, 47.

[2]　Webley 2007, 455.

[3]　See also Gerritsen 2007, 155 and Rapoport 1989, XIII. Houses represent close indicators of *habitus*; the very way in which we live in the world, how we view the world, but also how we act. *Habitus* could be viewed as a *modus operandi* (Bourdieu 1977, 79) or, in ontological terms, even as a way of 'being in the world' (Rippengal 1993, 93; Heidegger's concept of 'Dasein'). We should be wary about a separation of people and their environment. As

Lawrence-Zuniga (2001, 171) states: 'Humans tend to experience and live in their immediate environments, in the totality of their material and social, fixed and movable dimensions, as continuous and whole both in use and conception.' People design their immediate environment in relation to environmental factors as well as to take a place in the human world. As such, the built environment as a whole constitutes – and reflects – the social order (DeMarrais 2007, 121-122).

ven with the people that produce it; they are in fact mutually constituting.[4] The house occupies a particularly central position, as it is at the heart of social and cultural life, constituting 'culturally significant space of the highest order'.[5] If we view settlement, house and space as essentially social, it follows that the developments reconstructed in the previous chapter were also highly socially significant.[6] In this chapter we will thus focus on the changing ways in which social relationships were created by means of the reorganisation of settlement and house space, monumentalisation, the creation of new lifestyles, new symbols and new identities in a changing world. In social studies on house and settlement, the general trend has been towards integrated perspectives on the material, social, ideological and political significance of the built environment.[7] In this study we will also attempt to take such an integrated approach.

First of all, I will present a short overview of existing studies on the social dimension of villa settlement and their development as well as positioning the present study within this context. Next, I will discuss the basic 'demographic' scale of rural settlement, exploring how many families lived in the various types of rural settlement. A longer section will then approach the developments reconstructed in the previous chapter from a human perspective. Several themes have been defined: the reorganisation and structuration of space, the break with traditions, monumentalisation and the creation of new lifestyles. And by discussing the anthropological concept of 'peasant', I will also attempt to elucidate the lower echelons of society, which have too often been neglected in villa studies.

4.1   THE SOCIAL STUDY OF VILLAS

The objective of understanding the villa in social terms is by no means new in archaeology. However, insights and approaches have changed considerably over time. As observed in the introduction, the earliest studies reconstructing the development of traditional wooden houses into multi-roomed houses on stone foundations date back to the first half of the 20th century. This discovery first prompted the suggestion that native people lived in these Roman-style houses. From the 1960s in particular, socio-economic approaches to the villa emerged, linked to the growing number of large-scale excavations.[8] Scholars like Rivet and Percival looked at the written evidence from classical authors such as Columella and Varro to examine socio-economic relationships in villas in the provincial countryside.[9] According to this view, the existing agricultural system in the provinces evolved along Italic lines, including the development of *latifundia* and contractual tenure of the Italic type.[10] This approach, labelled the 'Italic model' by Jan Slofstra, was later criticised for transferring the Italic situation to the provinces too simplistically.[11] Instead, Slofstra suggested, anthropological models could help us understand social relationships within what he branded the 'villa system'. His approach demonstrated pronounced neo-Marxist influences and focused on asymmetrical social relationships, thereby also introducing the peasant concept. Asymmetrical relationships and peasants were also discussed by Wightman, in this case on the basis of early medieval Irish law texts.[12]

[4]   Gerritsen 2003, 32; Tilley *et al.* 2006, 440.

[5]   Gerritsen 2003, 31.

[6]   A human perspective will thus be combined with a temporally-sensitive approach, often absent in social studies on house and development (Gerritsen 2003, 37).

[7]   Gerritsen 2007, 155. This kind of approach to the house is rooted in ethnological studies such as that of Claude Levi-Strauss, describing the house as 'a corporate body holding an estate made up from both material and immaterial wealth, which perpetuates itself through the transmission of its name, its goods, and its titles down a

real or imaginary line, considered legitimate as long as this continuity can express itself in the language of kinship or affinity and, most often, of both.' (Levi-Strauss 1982, 174; see also Amerlinck 2001).

[8]   Slofstra 1983, 84.

[9]   Rivet 1969; Percival 1976; Wightman 1978; Drinkwater 1983; Slofstra 1983, 85.

[10]   Wightman 1978, 98.

[11]   Slofstra 1983.

[12]   Wightman 1978.

From the late 1970s, another social approach to the villa arose within British archaeology, initiated by J.T. Smith's 'The villa as a key to social structure'.[13] In this study, Smith attempted to reconstruct social structure on the basis of villa plans, his basic conclusion being that the existing pre-Roman 'Celtic' social structure of the extended family continued into the Roman period, including when new villa houses were built. Although Smith's rather simplistic approach has been criticised, quite a few publications linked to this theme have taken his basic argument further.[14]

The socio-cultural dimension of villas has been a prominent theme in more recent work. Some authors have argued that the villa could best be viewed in terms of changing styles of consumption as people developed a taste for new styles, materials and techniques.[15] Martins emphasised the development not only of new tastes, but also of new, much more conspicuous and individual forms of consumption.[16] Hingley argued that, through the elaboration of spatial form, architectural details, decoration and furniture, the house became the locus for the symbolism of social inequality. Its architecture and elaboration were obsessively concerned with the creation and display of social distinctions, including the complex relationships between master and mistress, slaves and servants, and patron and client.[17] As such, the monumental house represented an architectural statement about identity and aspirations.[18] Unlike in British archaeology, however, such approaches have not really caught on in continental studies.[19]

In general, however, I should emphasise that only a few of these theoretical, interpretational considerations are rooted in continental archaeology or have in fact exercised any influence at all.[20] Many studies on villas and rural settlements have remained at the level of straightforward publications of excavation data, of plans, material culture and chronology. In other cases, the Italic model has been used to make simplistic and generalised interpretations of villa settlements. The processes behind the developments exposed in many large-scale excavations have thus remained unexplored. One of this study's key objectives is to link continental villa study with the theory-based interpretational frameworks of British archaeological studies, architecture studies, material culture studies, anthropology and sociology.

4.2   VARIATION IN SETTLEMENT SCALE

Before discussing social structure, evolving social relationships and community, we first need to ask the basic question about the 'social scale' of rural settlements. How many people were actually living on these settlement compounds and did they belong to one or to several families? And how substantial were the variations in settlements within and between regions?

Unfortunately, although fundamental, this question can be very difficult to answer. First of all, relatively few settlements have been fully excavated to enable a study of each building. Secondly, the functional interpretation of these buildings is generally problematic, as little or nothing can be deduced from their architectural form, interior elements or associated material culture. A hearth, the most straightforward indication of a residential function, is only documented in a minority of cases.

[13]   Smith 1978, 1997.

[14]   Hingley 1989, 1990; Samson 1990a, 1990b; Scott 1990; Rippengal 1993; Clarke 1998, 1999.

[15]   Especially Woolf 1998 and Martins 2005.

[16]   Martins 2005.

[17]   Hingley 2005, 88.

[18]   Mattingly 2006, 373.

[19]   The studies by Courbot-Dewerdt (2004, 2005 and 2006), who has approached French rural settlements using insights from the field of social studies, are an exception here.

[20]   Jan Slofstra's work may be identified as the most influential of these (Slofstra 1983, 1991).

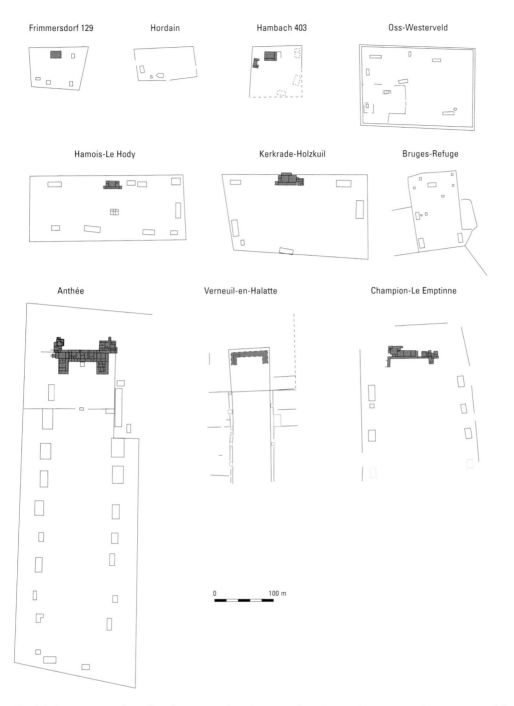

Frimmersdorf 129   Hordain   Hambach 403   Oss-Westerveld

Hamois-Le Hody   Kerkrade-Holzkuil   Bruges-Refuge

Anthée   Verneuil-en-Halatte   Champion-Le Emptinne

0   100 m

Fig. 4.1. Roman-period rural settlements within the research region; variations in settlement size and form. The phases shown can be dated to the later 1st or 2nd century AD. Buildings in grey are the monumentalised main houses.

Nevertheless, several settlements can give us a general idea of their size (fig. 4.1). The first category are the small compound settlements with one or two houses. Here, alongside the most easily identifiable and generally most monumental house, another, less monumental building could sometimes also be interpreted as residential. In many cases, however, these secondary houses remain hypothetical, as functional interpretations are problematic. Examples of settlements in this category include Pulheim-Brauweiler, Hambach 516, Hambach 59, Frimmersdorf 129, Jüchen-Neuholz, Hordain-La Fosse à

Loups, Onnaing-Toyota and Bohain-en-Vermandois. If the interpretations are correct, these small settlements were inhabited by one or two families. At some other settlements – Hambach 66, 69, 127, 403, Rheinbach-Flerzheim, Nideggen-Wollersheim, Neerharen-Rekem, Rochefort-Jemelle and Seclin – the full or partial monumentalisation of a secondary house made the interpretation as a residence easier. With regard to housing and estimating settlement population, we should bear in mind that buildings may have had more than one function, combining residential with agricultural purposes, which makes them more difficult to identify.

For the category of larger settlements, it seems that more families lived on the settlement compound. Apart from the main residence, three to five contemporary houses could be documented at the settlements of Kerkrade-Holzkuil, Hamois-Le Hody and Bruges-Refuge. Settlements in the northern sand and clay areas, such as Oss-Westerveld, Hoogeloon-Kerkakkers and Wijk bij Duurstede-De Horden, also consisted of quite a number of contemporary houses, generally three to seven.

The same applies to the axially organised complexes. At most of these, several houses seem to have been situated on the working compounds, arranged in two opposing rows on both sides of the central axis. At Limé and Famechon-Le Marais, where only part of the working compound was excavated, three or four houses were documented. If these excavated sections are representative, then as many as ten to fifteen houses may have been situated at these large axial complexes. Such a pattern could perhaps also be distinguished at the large complex of Anthée. Unfortunately, no detailed interpretations are available for the secondary buildings there. At the settlement of Champion we find seven Alphen-Ekeren-type structures on the working compound. It seems that some of these had at least a partially residential function, which means that the settlement was inhabited by several, perhaps as many as eight, families.

The population of a few settlements has been estimated in terms of absolute numbers. For the settlement of Hambach 59, for example, Hallmann-Preuss reconstructed an extended family of three generations and a dependent family, bringing the total to 30 to 35 inhabitants.[21] Hinz, studying the German Bergheim region, estimated 35 to 50 people per 100 hectares, which he took as a regular area per settlement.[22] For another small compound settlement of around one hectare, the calculations came to 20 inhabitants.[23] We could expect a larger number, between 50 and 100 people, on axial complexes where the working compounds contained several houses.[24] For the northern regions, a settlement like Tiel-Passewaaij had 20 to 40 inhabitants and Wijk bij Duurstede-De Horden had up to 26 (four houses with an average of 6.5 inhabitants per residence).[25]

4.3 THE REORGANISATION OF SPACE: CONSTRUCTING NEW SOCIAL REALITIES

Domestic space is the central and essential context of the daily routines that shape people's lives. It doesn't simply facilitate these routines, it actually shapes them. This close relationship between dwelling and routine is underlined by the close similarity of the words used for both: 'to inhabit' (*habiter, habitar, wohnen, wonen* in some other languages) and 'habit' (*habitude, hábito, Gewohnheit* and *gewoonte*). As Giddens argues, '[i]t is daily life and its routines that both constrain people within these [social] structures and enable them to either reproduce the existing structure or change it through new behaviour'.[26]

[21] Hallmann-Preuss 2002/2003, 401-402; she also states that 8 to 12 external (seasonal) workers were probably needed at harvest time.

[22] Hinz 1969b.

[23] Hallmann-Preuss 2002/2003, 402.

[24] Roymans/Habermehl 2011.

[25] Heeren 2009, 227; Vos 2009, 213. Vos used an average settlement size of 16 people for his demographic calculations.

[26] Giddens 1984, 25, 50; Jamieson 2002, 14.

As domestic space is so intimately related to people and to how social relationships are created, the major changes in its organisation, as explored in the previous chapter, must have had significant backgrounds and implications. This section will explore how people constructed new social realities by reorganising space, both at settlement and house level. The creation of a new spatial *habitus* will have produced and reinforced new domestic practices and suggested social behaviours that will eventually have been taken for granted as culturally proper and self-evident.[27] Power is a significant aspect. By controlling the organisation and reorganisation of space, it became possible to influence how these social relationships were constructed, thereby also 'fixing' social institutions.

4.3.1 REORGANISING SETTLEMENT SPACE

A principal trend identified in the previous chapter entails the enclosure of settlement space in the northern part of the research region during the 1st century AD and in the southern parts from as early as the later Iron Age. How can we understand this broad move towards the enclosure of settlement space from a social perspective?

Settlement enclosures – ditches in the majority of cases – defined the settlement within the broader landscape. In social terms, they defined a settlement community, simultaneously including and excluding people, by clearly marking the community's boundaries. Viewed in this way, enclosures were both physically functional as well as symbolically significant. As such, they could have played a role in the construction of a collective identity. As Courbot-Dewerdt states, the enclosure was '...one way for Gauls to relate to space and to express their feeling of identity and belonging in different aspects of their life'.[28] In addition, Hingley emphasises that enclosures reflect the '...isolation of the local social group from the wider scale community', and that '... social relations of production are reflected in small-scale, independent social groups which control and appropriate territory independently of one another'.[29] From an anthropological perspective, similar interpretations were made by Thomas, who associated enclosure development with social contraction linked to agricultural intensification and the increasing pressure on land. Social groups started forging links with the land in more concrete ways, striving to preserve it among the local group.[30] A firmer sense of place developed, establishing a lasting association between the family, the house and the land on which the settlement was located. Local communities thus became increasingly closed, as family ties and inheritance became more important ways of gaining access to agricultural land, with sons or daughters remaining in their native household after marriage. It seems plausible that the development of stable and enclosed settlements within the research region reflected such processes. With regard to northern France at least, where the enclosure trend already started during the later Iron Age, agricultural intensification was indeed documented for this period.[31] For the northern regions, these interpretations tie in with Gerritsen's observations regarding the Late Iron Age MDS region, where he reconstructed the reorientation from the wider community towards smaller social entities such as the household or nucleated settlement.[32] Furthermore, botanical studies and the disappearance of the Celtic field system suggest changes in the production system, agricultural intensification and evolving social relationships. In these northern regions, however, settlements were generally not being enclosed until the 1st century AD. In that period,

[27] Robben 1989, 583. 'The patterns of daily life in a rectangular stone-built structure were quite different from those in a round wattle-and-daub house, not to mention the smells, sights and sounds in the two cases.' (Tilley *et al.* 2006, 439).

[28] Courbot-Dewerdt 2005, 56.

[29] Hingley 1984, 25; see also Bowden/McOmish 1987.

[30] Thomas 1997.

[31] Haselgrove 1996.

[32] Gerritsen 2003.

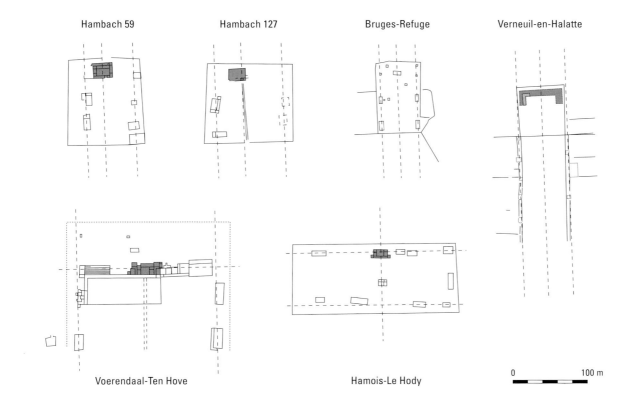

Hambach 59   Hambach 127   Bruges-Refuge   Verneuil-en-Halatte

Voerendaal-Ten Hove   Hamois-Le Hody   0   100 m

Fig. 4.2. Examples of the structuration of settlement space, the use of symmetry and axiality and the control over access, movement and experience. The buildings in grey are the monumentalised main houses.

pre-Roman developments, affecting the way that people settled the landscape, continued and were even significantly amplified by rapidly increasing demographic pressure, large-scale demand for food, increasing pressure on land and changing power relationships and patterns of proprietorship.

This enclosure trend was linked to the reorganisation and increasing structuration of internal settlement space (fig. 4.2). As observed in the previous chapter, many settlements in the northern parts of the research region (but also in the German loess region) consisted of open and loosely structured clusters of buildings during their early phases (up to around the middle of the 1st century AD). Later on, mostly around the middle of the 1st century AD, they were reorganised quite radically, becoming enclosed and relatively well-structured squarish settlement compounds, where the buildings were built along the enclosure ditches and around an open space. In the southern regions, settlements were enclosed as early as the later Iron Age, although internal settlement space was not yet rigidly structured in this period. From the earliest phases of the Roman period and perhaps as early as the latest phase of the pre-Roman period, space at some sites was subject to very radical change, again resulting in well-structured settlements, of which the axial complexes were the best and most striking examples. This spatial reorganisation involved the introduction of new organisational concepts such as geometry, symmetry and axiality, which were not used for the organisation of settlement space during pre-Roman times. The use of these concepts gave rise to well-structured and coherent settlement complexes. This had a number of backgrounds and implications, which I will now continue to explore.

First of all, the reorganisation of settlement space into a coherent, organised whole created some form of spatial hierarchy. Certain houses were placed in prominent positions within the structure of the settlement. At some larger compound settlements, such as Kerkrade-Holzkuil and Hamois-Le Hody, the main house inhabited by the dominant family was situated at a central, prominent position, with its back against the enclosure ditch. As noted before, it is remarkable that this spatial structure already existed before the main house was monumentalised. The reorganisation and structuration of space, and thus the creation of a spatial hierarchy, preceded architectural changes in house building. The same phenomenon can also be found at axially organised complexes such as Verneuil-en-Halatte. The axial layout was created as early as the Augustan period, when the main house, centrally positioned at the top of the main axis, was still constructed in traditional fashion. This use of axiality was a particularly powerful way of creating a hierarchical spatial structure. What is more, in architectural studies axiality is generally associated with authoritarian power, with the 'axis' often leading to the symbol of power. This was certainly the case at the axial complexes where the axis led straight up to the centre of local power – the residence of the dominant family who exercised power over people and production. But axiality and symmetry, as new spatial concepts, were not exclusively used in the very large and rigidly organised axial complexes. At the settlements of Hambach 59, Hambach 127 and Brugge-Refuge, for example, the main residence was located at one end of the settlement compound, while the secondary buildings were organised on both sides of the compound in front, in fact forming a corridor leading up to the residence (see fig. 4.2). This created a spatial layout in which the main residence occupied a prominent and central position. In some cases, hierarchy took an even more concrete shape when a dividing element separated the main house from the rest of the settlement. Again, we find the best example in the large axially organised complexes. In many of these settlements, a wall or ditch separated the main residential compound from the rest of the complex, thereby further increasing and monumentalising the distance between the main residence, the centre of power and the other dwellings where dependent families lived. However, this did not apply to all axially organised settlements. At Champion-Le Emptinne and Monchy-les-Preux, for example, a dividing element was not documented. For the settlements in the most northerly parts of the research region, however, the use of symmetry and axiality for the creation of spatial hierarchies cannot be documented. These settlements were not as rigidly structured as the examples described above. Nevertheless, some of them do suggest the existence of spatial hierarchies as well. As described in the previous chapter, at Oss-Westerveld and Hoogeloon-Kerkakkers, enclosed compounds were created within the settlement, separating a single house from the rest of the settlement. The architectural character of the house in question as well as the material culture with which it was associated underline the special position of its inhabitants. They physically and symbolically created a larger distance between themselves and the rest of the local settlement community. The spatial layout of the settlements of Wijk bij Duurstede-De Horden and Geldermalsen-Hondsgemet could perhaps be interpreted in a similar way. [33]

The use of these organisational concepts also served to control movement and experience. We can imagine the experience of entering a large axial settlement like Anthée at the bottom of the complex and on the central axis. With entering the courtyard, one would see an impressive long courtyard stretching out, characterised by two opposing rows of buildings forming a sort of corridor leading to the far end of the complex where a large monumental house loomed, a wall and gate protecting it from free entry. Movement and vision were clearly directed towards the end of the axis, while dependent families lived and worked on both sides of the field of view. They literally occupied a peripheral position while clearly being physically dominated and controlled by the monumental residence that overlooked the working compound while being physically separated from it. This spatial structure in fact acted as a social metaphor, embodying the asymmetrical relationships of domination and control. [34] But strategies were also used to control movement and experience at some smaller settlements. With the entrance

[33] At Geldermalsen-Hondsgemet, one farmstead with a large house (house 20) was enclosed separately and had an entrance marked by posts, indicating its importance. Furthermore, the material culture associated with this farmstead underlined its special position (Van Renswoude/Van Kerckhove 2009, 467). For the Wijk bij Duurstede-Horden see Vos 2002, 2009.

[34] On socio-spatial metaphors, see Huijbers 2007.

to the settlement positioned opposite the main house, one would immediately be confronted with the monumentality and dominance of this house within the settlement. Paths leading from the entrance straight up the main residence were constructed to direct movement even more specifically. Such paths were documented at for example Hambach 127, Hambach 488 and Voerendaal-Ten Hove (see fig. 4.2).

In conclusion, it is apparent that the adoption of new organisational concepts was not a simple adoption of Roman ideas on organisation but a conscious and active strategy to create and fix new social relationships within the context of the settlement. Such well-structured and coherently organised settlement complexes did not develop organically or gradually. Instead, they were laid out as well-structured, planned settlements, implying centralised power over the organisation of space. This reflects the changed power relationships within the rural sphere. Certain families acquired enough social power to restructure settlement space, create newly structured and coherent settlement complexes and break with existing patterns of settlement organisation. By controlling access, movement and experience and by creating spatial hierarchies as metaphors of dependency and domination, they were able to construct and fix new social relationships within the settlement. These were asymmetrical relationships, whereby the degree of dependency and the character of the relationships, as reflected in the spatial structure of the settlements, seem to have varied considerably. Control is a central concept in this context. Indeed, a leader's status is indicated by his control over others and architecture is an effective way to shape control within the physical context of day-to-day life.[35]

4.3.2 REORGANISING HOUSE SPACE

Domestic space also includes space inside the house. The previous chapter reconstructed a general trend in which traditional post-built houses were transformed into multi-roomed houses on stone foundations, often including baths, hypocausts and rooms decorated with painted walls. This also brought considerable change to the domestic spatial structure. Quintessentially, we see the same trends as with the organisation of settlement space – structuration, hierarchisation and segmentation – albeit on a different scale and in different ways. The construction of multi-roomed houses in fact created a new spatial *habitus*, significantly affecting the daily social practices and routines. Different spaces could relate to different functions, different social meanings, different spheres of live (private or public) or different relations towards the outside world.[36]

Traditional houses included fairly small, multi-purpose living areas lacking physical barriers that subdivided space into functionally or socially differentiated areas. The subdivision of space seems to have been predominantly conceptual. We can gain an impression of such living spaces in well-preserved byre houses at, for example, Ezinge in the north of the Netherlands and in Jutland in Denmark.[37] Only part of the long-rectangular byre house was intended for habitation. The byre was separated from this residential space by an entrance section, generally situated at the centre of the house with entrances on both long sides. The hearth was an important element within the living space, generally occupying a central position. The storage, processing and consumption of food were generally located at the front or rear part of the living space.[38] With regard to Britain, Hingley has reconstructed the use of space in traditional roundhouses according to a structuralist model, defining a basic opposition between the central space around the hearth, where communal domestic life took place, and the peripheral areas of the house associated with more private use, such as storage and sleeping.[39] Perhaps the use of space in traditional houses within the research region could also be understood in these terms.

---

[35] Also see Wilson 1988, 126.

[36] Robben 1989, 582.

[37] Van Giffen 1950; Webley 2007.

[38] Webley 2007, 461-462.

[39] Hingley 1990; Sharples 2010, 182-183; see also Taylor 2001, 49-50.

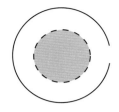 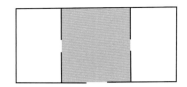

Fig. 4.3. Two models showing the use of space in traditional roundhouses and Roman-period rectangular houses on stone foundations, demonstrating the basic continuity in use of space. Reproduced after Hingley 1989, 131; Taylor 2001, 51. H = Hearth; S = Surface; P = Pit; Hy = Hypocaust; F = Furnace; M = Mosaic; B = Bath; C = Corn drier.

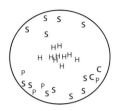 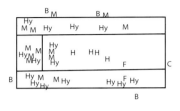

One of the most fundamental issues with regard to developments in house building and domestic spatial structure is that of continuity/discontinuity. Should we regard the development of multi-roomed houses as a break with existing patterns or simply as a translation of existing patterns regarding the use of space into new forms? A major debate on this topic has been raging within British villa studies, initiated by J.T. Smith's influential article 'Villas as a key to social structure'.[40] In short, Smith argued that a basically pre-conquest 'Celtic' society, structured around the extended family, continued to exist behind the Roman-style façades. Following Smith, Hingley also reconstructed basic continuity between the socio-spatial structure of traditional roundhouses and multi-roomed rectangular houses (fig. 4.3).[41] In these latter houses, the central large room or hall contained the hearth and was consequently the place where collective life took place, where people cooked, ate and met. The smaller rooms surrounding this central hall could then be interpreted as sleeping rooms, private guest rooms and storage rooms. According to Hingley, basic existing spatial patterns were thus translated into new forms. Although Smith's study represents a valuable move in a new direction, his views are generally criticised for the unproblematic and simplistic equation of house plans with society, whereby we can simply look at the plans and 'read' the social form.[42] According to Rippengal, Smith fails to examine the relationship between 'society' and 'architecture' itself.[43]

Examining the multi-roomed houses within our research region, we see that hearths, where documented, are also situated within the large central room in the house (see fig 4.4). In line with the discussion above, it seems likely that collective domestic life took place at this spot, centred around the hearth as a source of heat and a place for preparing food. The smaller rooms around the hall had different, potentially more private or specialised purposes.

Nevertheless, even when following Smith's and Hingley's interpretational course emphasising the basic continuity in spatial structure, we should not overlook the fundamental changes also taking place in the organisation of domestic space. To explore these changes, we need to focus on how domestic space was structured, particularly with regard to how social relationships were shaped and maintained within the house and household and between the household and the outside world.

First of all, the creation of separate spaces, physically divided by means of walls, had significant implications for social relationships within the household. The various elements of day-to-day life such as eating, meeting and sleeping could be separated in more distinct ways, while the creation of

---

[40] Smith 1978, 170-172; Rippengal 1993, 80; Clarke 1999.

[41] Hingley 1989, 1990.

[42] Rippengal 1993, 83; Scott 1990.

[43] Rippengal 1993, 83.

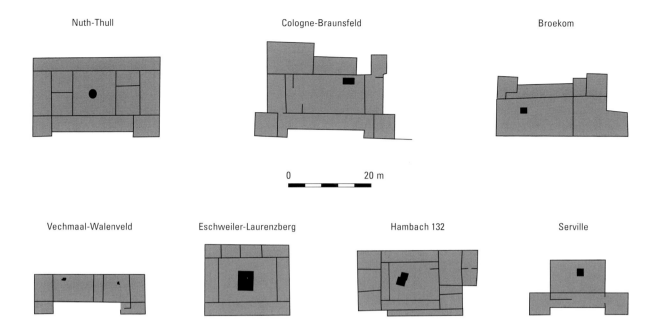

Nuth-Thull   Cologne-Braunsfeld   Broekom

Vechmaal-Walenveld   Eschweiler-Laurenzberg   Hambach 132   Serville

0   20 m

Fig. 4.4. Several multi-roomed houses from the research region with documented hearths in black. Hearths were generally situated in the largest central room or hall of the house. This is where the public life of the household will have taken place.

individual rooms increased possibilities for creating privacy.[44] Taylor regards this development as a shift in discourse towards the spatial segregation of domestic and productive activities.[45] Furthermore, access and exclusion were now more explicitly and monumentally controlled, as the physical and social distance and distinction between people increased.

As the domestic spatial structure became more complex, so too did the symbolic spatial structure. Multi-roomed houses were the locus for the symbolism of social inequality, with domestic space becoming the cultural language of domination.[46] As Hingley states, the architecture and elaboration of these houses were obsessively concerned with the creation and display of distinctions of social rank, including the complex relationships between master and mistress, slaves and servants, and patron and client. Within the house, this symbolic spatial structure was created by means of elements that were fixed (walls, hypocausts), semi-fixed (mosaic and other floors, painted wall plaster) and non-fixed (objects, furniture).[47] In this way, new behavioural patterns, and thus new social realities, were created and fixed within the household.[48] New socially significant patterns of meaning were created through spatial organisation (again, the control over movement and experience), access and exclusion, colours, textures and representations. Certain parts of the house, even particular rooms, were to be seen as high-status and exclusive, allowing access to a select few, while others could be termed more general spaces that were more accessible.

Not only did the distance between the members of the household increase, so too did the distance between the household residing inside the house and the outside world. Some authors have argued that the portico that fronted almost all multi-roomed houses could be interpreted as a barrier between the outside world and the inner house, and that the creation of such porticoes reflected the desire to create

[44] Hingley 2005, 88-89.
[45] Taylor 2001, 50-52.
[46] Hingley 2005, 88.
[47] Rapoport 1994, 460-462.
[48] Hingley 2005, 88-89.

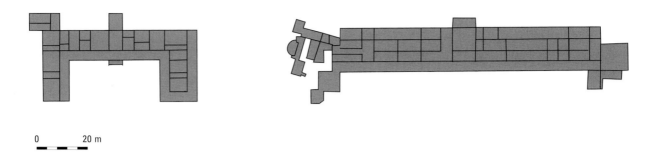

0   20 m

Fig. 4.5. The use of symmetry and axiality in multi-roomed houses. Matagne-La Petite and Basse-Wavre.

a distance between the private home and the public outside world.[49] Scott suggested that this wish could have been a response to a more formal and impersonal economic reality.[50] Rippengal, however, believes that it is more helpful to examine the changing relationships between people within the local community.[51] This latter interpretation can be linked to observations made above about the growing distance between people within the settlement. Just as social relationships within the household were renegotiated by means of space, so too were relationships between the household and the outside world.

Parallel to the reorganisation of settlement space, organisational concepts such as symmetry and axiality were also used for the spatial organisation of the house (fig. 4.5). Again, these were new introductions that did not feature in traditional house building. Symmetry was particularly obvious in the house façades, but also extended to the spatial structures beyond. Especially in the larger houses, symmetry and axiality will have been employed to create a spatial hierarchy within the house, with the position of certain rooms acting as a metaphor for their social importance. Once more, the people with the power to build such houses also had the power to influence the way in which social relationships were constructed, by controlling movement, access and exclusion as well as the symbolic ways in which social messages were communicated and experienced.

The line of reasoning presented here implies that we should not simply regard the size and appearance of these houses as a reflection of the degree of wealth of their inhabitants. In rural houses, not only did the level of luxury vary greatly (the presence or absence of hypocausts, bathing sections, *triclinia* and mosaic floors), but also the degree of complexity in which social relationships were constructed within the household. How large was the distance between the members of the household (fig. 4.6, see also fig. 4.7)? Were they still taking part in collective life in a multi-purpose central room around the hearth or was domestic space more differentiated, strictly separating people from each other by means of different levels of access and limited encounters, facilitated by a differentiated organisation of domestic space and a complex symbolic system? An examination of monumental houses within our dataset shows that, in contrast to the generally uniform way in which traditional residential spaces were organised, the new organisation of domestic space, and thus the way in which people created a new spatial *habitus* and new relationships of power and control, was much more varied in both character and scale. In some cases, houses chiefly consisted of a hall that was still largely multi-functional, lacking segmentation and reflecting a fairly simple socio-spatial structure (such as timber framework houses and simple houses on stone foundations, see fig 4.6). In these houses the household probably was still much like that in the pre-Roman period. The distance between people, physically as well as socially, was probably relatively small. In other cases, we find that small rooms were attached to the central hall. This marked the first step towards a more complex socio-spatial structure, as certain people could potentially distance themselves

[49] On such barriers between the house and street, see Robben 1989, 582 ff.

[50] Scott 1990, 164-165.

[51] Samson 1990b.

102

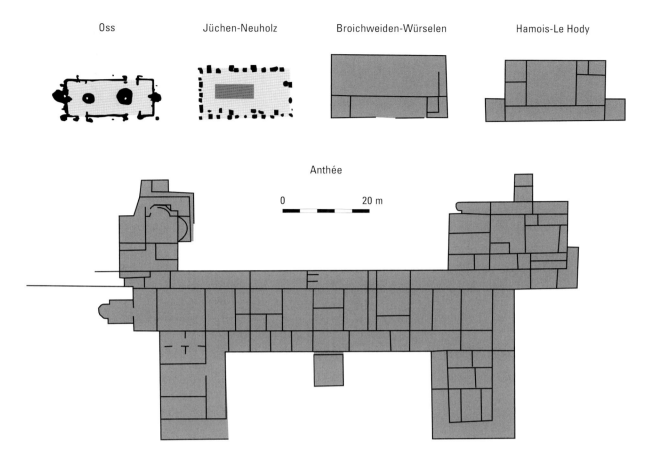

Fig. 4.6. Houses reflecting various degrees of socio-spatial complexity (see also fig. 4.7). From top left to bottom: a traditional two-aisled Alphen-Ekeren house at Oss, a single-aisled framework house at Jüchen-Neuholz, a simple house on stone foundations at Broichweiden-Würselen, a house on stone foundations with a number of separate rooms and a portico-risalith façade at Hamois-Le Hody, and a large, complex and highly differentiated house with projecting wings at Anthée.

from the rest of the household. A much greater variety of rooms and spaces can be found in the larger houses, creating a more pronounced and formal functional as well as social differentiation. Hypocausts, baths, floors, mosaics and painted plaster were in fact instrumental in the creation of this structure. The variety in socio-spatial complexity can probably also be associated with the changing composition of the household. In the larger houses, it is likely that at least several people living there, servants for example, were not members of the actual family household. Consequently, they were kept at a greater distance and social relationships were more formal rather than close and personal.

With regard to the general development from simple multi-functional residential spaces to segregated domestic space, and the appearance of multi-roomed houses, a cross-cultural study by Kent is of particular interest.[52] Kent argues that there was a link between spatial segregation in architecture and the socio-political complexity of the broader society. In this light, it is significant that space in rural houses became increasingly segregated from the 1st century AD onwards, the period during which native communities became integrated into the Roman empire, representing a society and imperial organisation that was socio-politically highly complex, especially when compared to the situation prior to conquest. Certain members of the indigenous communities became directly involved in the

---

[52] Kent 1990.

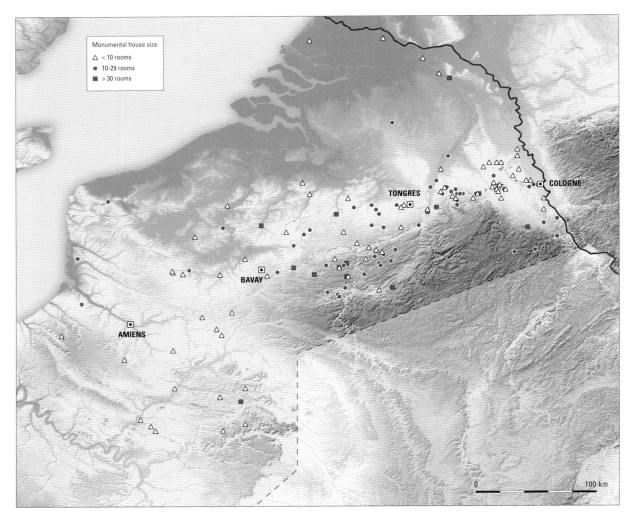

Fig. 4.7. Distribution of monumental houses according to their size, measured in number of rooms.

developing provincial organisation of the empire and thus became integrated into new, complex socio-political networks, eventually affecting social relationships on the level of the local settlement and the individual household. That this development was not typical of the Roman period is well illustrated by a study on the Greek transition from the Early Iron Age to the Archaic period.[53] Cities started to emerge in this period, along with political institutions and markets. Society became much more complex, socially stratified and institutionalised. Different spheres were increasingly spatially separated, eventually affecting families' private residences, which changed from small, simple, multi-functional houses into multi-roomed houses with a courtyard that served as a transitional zone between the inner house and the outside world. In this example we also see that the development of more complex social and economic systems eventually affected the way that people built their houses, structured domestic space, and thus interacted with each other within the context of their house and settlement. Increasing segregation, differentiation and control were prominent in both cases.

Changes in house building could thus be regarded as reflecting changes within both the local community and the household. The house was in fact an active way in which new relationships were

[53] See Lang 2007.

104

created, monumentalised and symbolised, both vertically and horizontally. Vertical relationships were established by connecting to varying degrees with urban lifestyles, provincial administration networks and arenas of power as well as by impressing and dominating people lower on the social ladder. Horizontal relationships came about through links with newly emerging rural elites that formed communities of peers in the provincial countryside.

4.3.3 CONTEXTUALISING CHANGE: THE NORTH AMERICAN CASE

In Roman archaeology, the rise of the 'Roman villa' is sometimes regarded as a specific, if not unique, development. Taking a broader perspective and redefining the theme to changes in settlement origins, house building and consumption within a dynamically changing world, we do indeed find some interesting anachronistic parallels. Could these parallels offer additional insights into the importance of different factors in processes of change or into the changes themselves? The first example, from Greek archaeology, was presented in the previous section. Another interesting case for our purposes is the development of rural habitation in America between the 16th and 20th centuries.

In his overview of American farmstead archaeology, Groover reconstructs both specific and broader trends in the spatial organisation of farmsteads, the construction of houses and the use of mobile material culture, which he links to social and economic trends.[54] The communities inhabiting America prior to the 18th century can be characterised as pre-industrial, with vernacular or folk cultures organised in accordance with tradition. Cultural practices were maintained over relatively long periods of time. The farms within these communities were largely subsistence-oriented, self-sufficient operations, predominantly using human and animal labour and designed to sustain individual farming households. In this period, houses were built in vernacular fashion by means of post-building techniques. At the site of Kingsmill, for example, people from all sectors of the population lived in these post-built houses.[55] In some cases, simple stone foundations were used to support wooden framework structures, lengthening the lifespan of the house structure considerably. While houses built during this period were still fairly traditional, industrially produced items such as glass bottles, tobacco and pipes were already dominating the material culture.[56]

Industrialisation, which took off from the earlier 18th century, brought major changes to people's lives, affecting the material culture used by people in the historic past in profound ways. The development of markets, cities and infrastructure will also have had a significant effect on rural farmstead communities. Industrialisation brought significant social change and had a profound impact on traditional ways of settling and building. During the earlier phases, changes in mobile material culture were the first to become visible. It is not until after the second half of the 1800s that the full extent of industrialisation was reflected in the archaeological record. The rise of consumerism and popular culture was initiated within the upper classes in North America during the Colonial period. Consumer goods were used as status objects that served to set their owners apart from lower and middle segments of colonial society. Many aspects of daily life were affected – domestic architecture, furnishings, dress and food. Nor should we overlook the new food-related activities associated with these changes: drinking tea, smoking tobacco and the many new ways of dining and of consuming wine. From around the later 18th century and continuing into the 19th century, there were some general developments in the organisation and construction of farmsteads and houses. As Groover describes, '[s]patial organisation within many colonial farmhouse lots became structured, standardized, organized,

---

[54] Groover 2008.

[55] Groover 2008, 53.

[56] Groover 2008, 67.

and often symmetrical or balanced. Dwellings were also increasingly built of brick or wood with brick foundations to last longer than the lives of their owners.'[57]

This brief case study demonstrates how a broad, large-scale development such as industrialisation eventually brought significant changes to the farmsteads, houses and, ultimately, the daily lives of people themselves. New consumption patterns were first adopted by the higher social echelons, who profiled themselves against the lower and middle classes. Subsequently, farmsteads were reorganised and new architectural ideas adopted. In several respects these processes of change can be compared to those that we are exploring in this study. New consumption patterns in the Roman period were indeed also linked to some form of industrialisation of production, for example the massive production sites for *terra sigillata* in Gaul. The higher echelons of society were the first to adopt new consumption patterns and lifestyles. And similarly, it was not until a later phase that new architectural ideas were adopted.

4.4 BREAKING WITH THE OLD AND BUILDING THE NEW: SOCIAL STRATEGIES IN A CHANGING WORLD

Having examined the changing ways that social relationships were constructed within the context of the settlement and house by means of the reorganisation of space, I will now continue by focusing on the break with or transformation of existing traditions and the construction of new ones. New building practices developed, new symbols were adopted and new ways of consuming and behaving entered traditional societies. This chapter is chiefly concerned with the question of why people broke so radically with traditions that had existed for centuries. It will also explore how new elements were used to construct new relationships and identities. A number of themes will be discussed:

• the break with traditional ways of building
• the durability and monumentality of the house
• the symbolic construction of the settlement community
• the construction of new lifestyles and symbols.

4.4.1 BREAKING WITH TRADITION: VERNACULAR ARCHITECTURE, CHANGE AND LOCAL COMMUNITY

In the previous chapter we observed that changes in house building involved the adoption of new techniques, materials, forms and concepts. In many cases, traditional post-built houses were replaced by multi-roomed houses on stone foundations in the course of a single generation. How should we understand such a radical break with long-existing traditions and its implications?

House building in accordance with local traditions is generally referred to as vernacular architecture.[58] This architecture is ultimately local, corresponding to local factors, circumstances and choices. Residences found within the research area, like the post-built byre houses and the smaller houses without byres, were built using local materials (wood, loam, thatch), local knowledge (passed down from father to son and transferred through practical learning and imitation) and a local workforce. In other words, house building was deeply embedded in local communities. Created within the commu-

---

[57] Groover 2008, 67.

[58] The study of vernacular architecture has a rich tradition, especially in anthropology, and some important work has been done in recent years. For an overview of the recent developments in the study of vernacular architecture, see Blier 2006. Oliver (1997) has published a three-volume overview of vernacular architecture worldwide.

nity itself, houses probably even acted as symbols for the coherence of community, for the identity of the group.[59] This is underlined by the general uniformity of houses within rural settlements, which is indicative of the traditional character of these communities. These communities tend to be homogeneous, constraining the behaviour, activities and lifestyle of their members. This was achieved through the pressure of social conformity and homogeneity, dedicated to preserving the social order.[60] In other words, these communities were relatively closed, stressing their community identity and tabooing the expression of individual identities in an ostentatious material way.[61] Deviations from standard architecture were not accepted, as the house was the supreme symbol of community membership and continuity between past and present.[62]

As traditional house building was an important and embedded part of the local community, the break with these traditions must have had significant social implications, stimuli and motivations. With regard to changes in house building, the introduction of new building materials firstly involved the use of non-local materials from quarries at various distances and specialised ceramic building materials produced in workshops situated outside local communities. Secondly, the newly adopted architectural forms and concepts did not relate to local traditions but were adopted from external sources, in most cases probably the towns or army camps. Thirdly, building multi-roomed houses on stone foundations will have required specialist knowledge and a specialist workforce, which again came from outside the local community. It is unlikely that the knowledge and craftsmanship needed to construct the technologically advanced stone foundations, framework walls, roofs, hypocaust and bath systems were available within local communities themselves. Instead, building these kinds of houses required formally trained specialists, who were probably town-based. House building thus moved into the realm of formal architecture, created by educated specialist architects and builders and was no longer deeply embedded within the local community.[63] The families building such a new house actually broke with tradition, with existing cultural rules and with the ethic of uniformity and collectivism within their traditional communities.

Developments in house building, which are part of broader changes in consumption patterns, could thus be associated with significantly changing relationships, both within local communities and between them and the broader outside world. In general, a trend can be reconstructed away from highlighting collectivity and communality and towards an emphasis on the individual or individual family. This latter type of consumption involved luxury enjoyed by a few and experienced in private, and was aimed at emphasising difference and superiority in a conspicuous way.[64] From the 1st century AD onwards, within the context of the developing Roman provinces, some members of traditional communities were able to break with collectivist ideologies of indigenous society; they became more independent, less interdependent, and could justify their privileged and ostentatious lifestyle.[65] This process of diminishing interdependency within local communities was also reconstructed by Wilk in a study on the Kekchi Indians.[66] Wilk identified the integration of this community into a cash-based economy as the main cause of this development. Cash cropping created new goals that were not linked to traditional economic patterns, predominantly focused on the inner community.[67] In the process, the ethic of collectivism and cohesion – and thus communal consumption standards – weakened and there was less emphasis on uniformity and the taboo surrounding the expression of individual identities. Consequently, the house became an important symbol in the developing economic and social competi-

---

59 Rapoport 1989, XVIII.

60 Oliver 1997, 121.

61 Wilk 1990, 38.

62 Wilk 1990, 38; Rapoport 1989, XVIII.

63 For some thoughts on vernacular versus industrial building practices, see Roberts 1996, 70.

64 See also Martins 2005, 134, Rodman 1985, 271: 'The

meaning attached to the house serves as an important indicator of central structuring relations and of the shift from collectivism to individualism, one of the most fundamental social transformations in history'.

65 Martins 2005, 134.

66 Wilk 1990.

67 Schindlbeck 1990.

tion.[68] Interestingly, Wilk's study illustrates that during the primary phases of integration, wealth was mainly invested in personal adornment and the consumption of mobile material culture. It was not until later that wealth, once above a certain economic threshold, was invested in the house.[69] A similar pattern could also be demonstrated for the Roman period, where it is possible to pinpoint changes to the mobile material culture before changes in house building became apparent. How the collection of personal wealth could alter existing social relationships within communities is also illustrated by an example provided by Cohen.[70] In Pueblo communities, the wealthy (*los ricos*) and those bearing the honorific title Don were regarded as perverting the egalitarian social order by means of their ambitions and were symbolically placed outside the community: 'He is not one of 'us'.'[71]

Knowing the characteristics and implications of these changes in house building nevertheless fails to explain the processes that caused them. It is generally safe to assume that a substantial set of factors will have been involved, including economic, social, political and cultural. New market relations, new political relationships, an administrative structure, the introduction of law, increasing demand for agricultural products, taxation, evolving patterns of proprietorship and a growing connectivity and mobility brought considerable changes to the world in which local communities lived. It is this changing world that undermined existing community boundaries, making communities increasingly subject to influences from outside, resulting in significant change.[72]

4.4.2 DURABILITY, MONUMENTALITY AND REPRESENTATIVENESS: CREATING NEW SYMBOLS AND NEW SOCIAL REALITIES

Some important aspects that have been neglected until now are the increased durability, monumentality and representativeness of the house. Unlike the ephemeral and non-monumental post-built structures, houses on stone foundations existed for several generations, sometimes even spanning centuries. They also developed a certain monumentality, designed to communicate symbolic messages to the outside world. I will now explore the backgrounds and implications of these developments further. A central consideration is whether the increasing structural durability and monumentality should be regarded as a secondary consequence of the adoption of Mediterranean-style architecture or as a much more conscious decision to build more durable and monumental houses, related to new social strategies developed by particular groups within the rapidly changing Roman provinces.

The structural character of the house can be viewed in relation to the social system in which it exists.[73] Ephemeral structures are generally associated with egalitarian, sharing forms of heritage. They could be pulled down and rebuilt elsewhere. The fact that this was an actual practice was illustrated by Gerritsen's study on settlement dynamics in the Meuse-Demer-Scheldt region.[74] A different story can be told with regard to perennial structures, built and restored to stand the test of time. These houses were to be passed on to a single heir, thus symbolising the uninterrupted continuity of the landowners' lineage.[75] If we examine villa development, the use of new building materials may in fact reveal a considerable change in the values attached to the house itself.

Above, we reconstructed a trend towards the increasing locational stability of settlements. Interpreting this phenomenon, Gerritsen has pointed out the possibility of a developing 'ideal of permanence'.[76]

---

[68] Wilk 1990, 38.

[69] Wilk 1990, 37; Rapoport (1994, 467) states that non-fixed and semi-fixed elements respond more easily and quickly to social and cultural changes.

[70] Cohen 1985, 113.

[71] Cohen 1985, 113.

[72] Cohen 1985, 44.

[73] Oliver 1997, 117-120.

[74] Gerritsen 2003.

[75] Oliver 1997, 117-120.

[76] Gerritsen 2003, 2007.

The rebuilding of houses on the same locations could be regarded as 'mnemonic bridging', a strategy that serves to maintain links with previous generations.[77] This allowed the residents to construct narratives of a permanent social group with a fixed place in the world and in time.[78] These developments can also be related to the changing ways in which the farming population thought about resources and wealth. Whereas in the Early and Middle Iron Age resources were largely considered the collective property of a local community, during the Late Iron Age families seem to have developed strategies to collect resources and wealth and pass these on from generation to generation.[79] The growing locational continuity and durability of houses reflected the increasingly permanent investment of land rights in family groups. In addition to the increasing locational continuity of settlement and house, houses themselves seem to have become more durable as well. The appearance of the sturdy Alphen-Ekeren-type house is seen as part of this development.[80] And as we reconstructed in the previous chapter, from around the middle of the 1st century AD, houses were built as even more durable structures through the use of stone material foundations, sturdy framework wall constructions and tiled roofs. The emergence of these ultimately durable houses could possibly be viewed as creating a durable 'social house', physically symbolising the lasting relationship between the family or family group and the land they were settling on. The appearance of these durable houses could then be understood as part of a longer-term development.

As physically durable houses, built to last, stone-built houses thus became structures with a historical dimension reaching far beyond a single generation. These houses were passed down from the ancestors and in fact became 'lieux de mémoire', monuments that symbolised the continuity of the community living in these houses, and perhaps even represented the broader settlement community. They created a tangible link between the past and the present. In fact, linked to a fixed location within the landscape, they could act as a means of fixing history.[81] Monumentality is an important phenomenon in this regard. Monuments '….provide stability and a degree of permanence through the collective remembering of an event, person…' and '…are powerful because they appear to be permanent markers of memory and history and because they do so both iconically and indexically, i.e. they can evoke feelings through their materiality and form as well as symbolise social narratives...'.[82]

In addition to this durability and monumentality, houses developed into more representative structures, communicating to the outside world in more elaborate, visible and conscious ways, simply by being impressive and visible. One of the ways in which this was achieved involved the white plastered walls and red tiled roofs that were a feature of most monumental houses. Even from larger distances, they will have been visible within the landscape. It is also interesting to return to the façade, discussed in the previous chapter. Unlike traditional post-built houses, houses on stone foundations commonly boasted façades that literally acted as the face of the house. The evolving façades can be linked to the changing purpose and significance of the house. Houses became a factor in the creation and maintenance of social relationships, in social competition, and thus developed a character that was considerably more focused on communicating with the outside world. The façades of many houses were extended and monumentalised over time. For example, at Kerkrade-Spekholzerheide and Maasbracht, an existing simple rectangular house was extended by the addition of two risaliths during a later phase. As a result, the façades of these houses became increasingly monumental and impressive (see fig. 4.8). Also at Broekom, a new, broad portico-risalith façade was added during the third monumental building phase, increasing the monumentality of the house considerably (see fig. 4.8). A fourth and most impressive example is the settlement of Voerendaal-Ten Hove. As described earlier, a very monumental façade was created there by connecting several buildings by means of a long portico. In many other

---

[77] Gerritsen 2007, 163.

[78] Gerritsen 2007, 163.

[79] Gerritsen 2007, 167–168.

[80] Gerritsen 2003; Slofstra 1991.

[81] Rowlands/Tilley 2006, 500.

[82] Rowlands/Tilley 2006, 500.

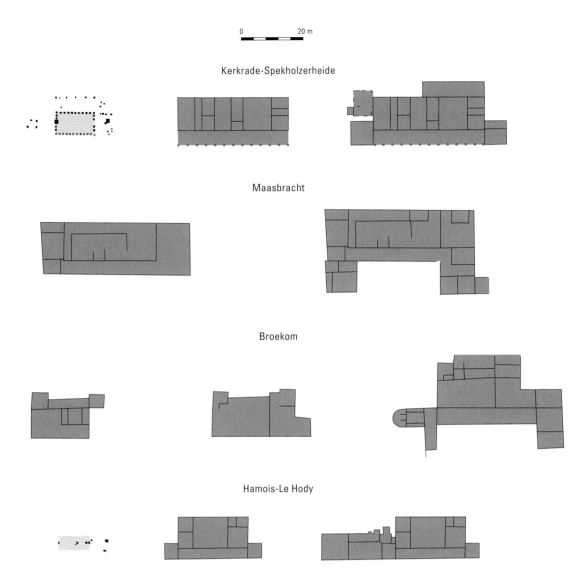

Fig. 4.8. Aggrandisement of the houses at Kerkrade-Spekholzerheide, Maasbracht, Broekom and Hamois-Le Hody.

cases, house façades were extended over the years as new house sections were added to the existing core (e.g. at Hamois-Le Hody (fig. 4.8), Rochefort-Jemelle, Merbes-Le-Chateau-Champs de Saint-Eloi and Hambach 512). In many cases, increasing the width and monumentality of the house's façade seems to have been a key objective.

Such developments could be identified by means of the 'aggrandisement' concept, involving the act of increasing the wealth or power of something, physically as well as socially. Constructing larger, more impressive and monumental façades increased the wealth and power of the house, its representativeness − it was aggrandised. Consequently, the monumental façade constituted a crucial element in house building. It can be regarded as an important symbolic instrument for constructing, communicating and fixing asymmetrical social relationships within local communities. The fact that the façade concept was in fact of broader significance and not confined to the well-known portico-risalith type is illustrated by the simple framework houses at Jüchen–Neuotzenrath and Druten, where the construction of façades was also documented.

Fig. 4.9. Three images of monumental houses: a sculptural model from Fontoy (France), a relief on the inside of the Simpelveld sarcophagus and a painted image from Trier. After Gebus/Klag 1990, 88; Rijksmuseum van Oudheden, Leiden; Fischer 2001, 83.

With the house evolving into a monumental and durable structure in which people were willing to invest, the ideology of the household and house seems to have intensified.[83] As mentioned above, the house became a monument symbolically holding the memory and expressing the social status and continuity of a specific person or family line and indirectly also relating to claims on land, social power and possession.[84] At the same time, the house also became a significant theme in representations, as found in sculptures, wall paintings and iconographic depictions (see fig. 4.9).[85] For the Mediterranean regions, the practice of depicting villas in wall paintings is interpreted by Bodel as prefiguring the enshrinement of the house in the literary record, a few decades later. 'Both developments reflect the increasingly important symbolic function that villas came to acquire during the early Empire as architectural entities worthy of artistic commemoration in their own right.'[86] On the basis of the examples mentioned above it seems plausible to suggest that a similar development took place in the provinces.

Viewed from the perspectives discussed in the previous section, the developments in house building reconstructed in chapter 3 should not be regarded as the passive adoption of Mediterranean architectural forms and building practices, but rather as an active social strategy to create new symbols of power and continuity in a changing world. The people building these monumental houses were in fact denying the realities of change, attempting to create and fix new social realities both by linking them to history and their ancestors and by creating durable, highly visible and representative symbols that were instrumental in the creation of new social relationships within local communities as well as between these communities and the broader outside world. The monumentalisation of the house can be interpreted as a strategy used in a period when positions of pre-eminence needed to be maintained and family estates had to be consolidated. Alternatively, according to Gerritsen, the development of durable houses can be viewed as a social strategy serving to gain control over material and immaterial wealth.[87]

Now that we have introduced the symbolic dimension of the monumental house, let us look somewhat more closely at symbolism and meaning. In general, objects, including architecture, are invested with meaning by a culture and they function within that culture as signs used in a dynamic relationship to articulate cognitive information.[88] All manner of social information is communicated to people in symbolic ways by means of cues and markers, reminding them of appropriate conduct.[89] These reminders define boundaries, which often serve to establish, define and maintain group identity.[90] Cues can take

[83] Wilk 1990, 40.

[84] Bodel 1997. Bodel (1997, 10) demonstrates that a villa could be so intimately connected with a specific person that it was demolished in the event of a *damnatio memoriae*.

[85] See also Wickham 2005, 467.

[86] Bodel 1997, 17.

[87] Gerritsen 2007, 169.

[88] Jamieson 2002, 12.

[89] In other words, environments are mnemonic (Rapoport 1982, 56).

[90] Rapoport 1994, 493.

various forms, all of which tend to be highly culture-specific, for example colour schemes, texture, size, landscaping, fences, walls, enclosures, the height of the wood pile, indoor plumbing or furnace heating.[91] Within the environment in which these cues and markers are employed, the settlement and house, interdependencies and collective relationships are materialised. Breaking with existing building traditions also denoted a defiance of traditional symbolism. As argued above, such symbols predominantly served to underline the coherence of local communities. Developments in house building consequently also implied a significant shift in the symbolic world of local communities. New cues were 'created' for the construction and communication of social identities, within local communities as well as to the outside world. Apart from the house, traditional symbolic systems were particularly prone to breaking down rapidly with regard to mobile material culture.[92] While older generations still adhered to time-honoured objects with their customary meanings, the younger generation found it much easier to break with traditions and adopt a new range of objects with a new system of meanings. At the same time, they regarded the traditional objects as old-fashioned and backward.[93] Similar processes might have applied to the Roman period as well. New generations were born into a rapidly changing world that they would handle very differently to older generations who were closer to their traditional roots. It seems plausible that the fairly rapid transformation from traditional housing to new, non-traditional multi-roomed houses on stone foundations could also be interpreted in this fashion. New generations adopted new practices and symbols with considerable ease, discarding the old, which they possibly even regarded as backward.

It should once more be emphasised, however, that it was the upper social groups that were most likely to determine the use, symbolic meaning and shape of mobile material culture and domestic space.[94] They were the first to adopt new lifestyles and the first to be able to construct new material and social realities.[95] Anthropological studies suggest that objects used to reinforce hierarchical relationships are often intricate and eye-catching, employ scarce material or include exotic origins.[96] It is therefore not surprising that Mediterranean goods and forms were used for this particular purpose within the rural settlements of the research region. Socially prominent individuals created new symbolic systems first by using mobile material culture, later also by means of house building. With regard to villa development, important symbols include the use of the façade with its visually prominent portico and risaliths, the presence of a bathing suite as a clear symbol of an urban lifestyle, and

---

[91] Rapoport 1982, 34.

[92] Self-evidently, non-fixed and semi-fixed elements are easily moved and changed; as such, they also respond to social and cultural changes more quickly and more easily (Rapoport 1994, 467).

[93] Lutkehaus *et al.* 1990, 246-247.

[94] Donley-Reid 1990.

[95] In anthropological studies around the globe, the adoption of new symbols of architecture and housing is a fairly well-documented phenomenon. In India, the construction of European-style bungalows and western domestic furniture and equipment was a clear indication of status. Among the first to do this were the elites, marking themselves and creating a distinction between themselves and others. The European styles they adopted symbolised changing values and attitudes; they were markers of a particular group membership (Rapoport 1982, 142). In the Greek town of Eressos, status came to be expressed through the degree of modernisation, rather than through a well-defined hier-

archical system of size and features that had persisted in previous periods (Pavlides/Hesser 1989, 365). In addition, in a study on Swahili culture, elaborate stone houses were regarded as active loci through which elites sought to symbolically neutralise fears concerning their position within an increasingly competitive and divided society (Fleisher/LaViolette 2007, 175). This constituted an attempt to position themselves as a separate social class. In a final example, research on modernisation in 20th-century Portugal established that the construction of modern bathrooms and kitchens played an important role in the construction and communication of new ideas, norms and identities, although these new elements were not always used the way they should be (Lawrence-Zuniga 2001, 192-193). This example makes it clear that the adoption of kitchens and bathrooms was more symbolic of the adoption of new lifestyles than simply involving innovative comfort technologies.

[96] Demarrais 2007.

the characteristic and impressive appearance of the house with its white plastered walls and red tiled roof. As previously stressed, new symbolic systems were also constructed within the house's interior, including painted wall plaster, mosaic floors, furniture and the use of luxury materials such as marble.

So far we have focused on how people constructed, symbolised and communicated identities and social relationships in relation to one another. However, we should not overlook the significance of the construction of the self, particularly as social identities also need to be internalised. A number of authors have related this phenomenon of self-construction to domestic architecture, viewing domestic architecture as reinforcing the notion of the legitimate social position for the inhabitants of these houses themselves.[97] In their study on the development of Swahili stone houses, Fleisher and LaViolette argue that the emergence of elaborate private spaces facilitated the construction of elite subjectivity and that it was part of a process in which elites attempted to convince themselves of the validity of their status and the soundness of their house, especially as it was under siege in rapidly changing political and economic circumstances.[98] 'Some of the social work of stone houses may be processes of self-construction', they state.[99] In this light, we could claim that the villa was also an important element in the self-construction of rural elites. By building villa houses, they strove among other things to legitimise their new roles in administrative and political positions and their dominant roles in any links with the Roman authorities and in taxation. By establishing new rural lifestyles, involving new material culture, values and behaviour, elites both communicated new identities to the outside world and legitimised their new positions to themselves. In relation to the symbolic way in which new identities were constructed, Martins argues that villa development was more about creating a persona than about a changing type of construction or a change in function.[100]

4.4.3 SYMBOLICALLY CONSTRUCTING LOCAL COMMUNITY

Aside from considering personal social identities, we cannot disregard the fact that the people who were cohabiting in a settlement compound formed a social collective, a local or settlement community. Were such collective identities also constructed and communicated within the context of the settlement?

Following Cohen, we could say that communities were constituted in symbolic ways, especially by marking their boundaries.[101] The community concept is primarily a symbolic construct and consists not so much of social structures or 'performing' social behaviour, but rather of thinking about it.[102] Viewed from this perspective, we could argue that the settlement was not just how a community created its physical place in the world, but was also part of how a community was constituted symbolically. I will now focus on elements within settlements that may have held significance in this symbolic constitution of settlement communities.

Earlier, it was argued that settlement enclosures defined both settlement space and settlement community. The enclosures held a symbolic significance; they marked the boundaries of the settlement community physically as well as symbolically and in that way helped to bring about this community, both inwardly and vis-à-vis the outside world. The existence of palisades, earthen ramparts or vegetation[103] along the ditched enclosure would have reinforced the message even further, creating a promi-

[97] Thams 1990, 67.

[98] Fleisher/LaViolette 2007, 179.

[99] Fleisher/LaViolette 2007, 179.

[100] Martins 2005, 134.

[101] Cohen 1985.

[102] Cohen 1985, 98.

[103] Vegetation was suggested for settlements in northern France by Courbot-Dewerdt (2005, 50-51) and for the botanically reconstructed settlement of Hambach 59 (Hallmann-Preuss 2002/2003). Palisades were found in quite a number of Hambach settlements, including Hambach 403, 512, 516 and Jüchen-Neuholz.

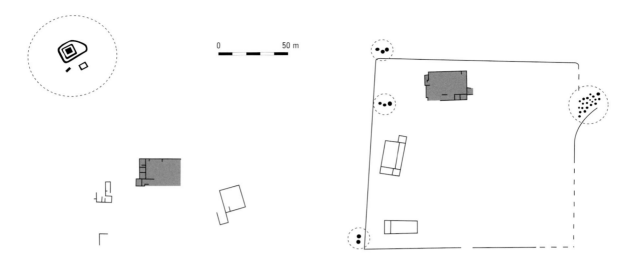

Fig. 4.10. Two examples of the direct association between graves and the settlement. Left: Nideggen-Wollersheim. Foundations of what was probably a monumental grave pillar near the settlement compound (indicated by the dotted circle). Right: Hambach 127. Clusters of simple cremation graves (black dots) around the settlement enclosures (indicated by the dotted circle).

nent visual symbol within the landscape as well as a 'place' within 'space'.[104] Enclosures can thus be regarded as important elements in the active creation of well-defined communities within the rural landscapes of the research region and therefore within wider society.

Another element that potentially played a role in the symbolic construction of the settlement community was the monumental house itself. As the most eye-catching element in the settlement, it might have served, aside from symbolising the wealth and status of the family inhabiting the house, as a symbolic marker for the settlement community as well. We can assume that, on a certain level, people experienced their social position as belonging to a settlement community – to a particular villa – and that the monumental house acted as an eye-catching and representative symbol, possibly even creating a sense of belonging.[105] In that sense, the monumental house may have unified as much as it expressed social divisions.

A third element that I would like to highlight is graves. In quite a number of settlements, basic cremation graves were situated at the outer edges, often directly along the enclosure ditches.[106] The liminal position of these graves is particularly significant as liminal space often carried a special ritual significance and tended to be marked by ritual depositions. The clusters of graves found here associated the community of the dead, the ancestors, with the community of the living. In this way, the relationship between the community and the settlement was symbolically strengthened, thereby also adding historical depth. These basic graves were not in any sense monumental, however, and thus did not function as visually significant markers or monuments, whereas another category of graves did. These latter graves, which include *tumuli* and pillars, were much more monumental and powerful symbolic markers, prominent within the landscape. They are likely to have played a part in symbolically constituting the settlement community. The association of such monumental graves and settlements is well documented in some cases (see fig. 4.10).[107] In essence, they symbolise ancestral claims on land and the continuity of the community itself.

[104] Courbot-Dewerdt 2005.

[105] See also Bodel 1997.

[106] Good examples are Hambach 127, 403, 512, 516 and Jüchen-Neuholz. See Gaitzsch 1993.

[107] Foundations of a monumental grave pillar were documented near the villa settlements of Nideggen-Wollersheim, Duppach and Newel (the latter two outside the research region). Smaller, but nevertheless monumental

The development of settlement enclosures, monumental houses and (monumental) graves directly associated with the settlement clearly shows that settlement communities were symbolically constructed in increasingly explicit and visible ways. As a consequence, the settlement community developed into a more distinct, perhaps even tightly-knit entity. Looking from a longer-term perspective, we see people moving from a focus on a broader community during the Iron Age, sharing grave fields and agricultural land, towards smaller social entities, families and family groups, living in separate, stable and enclosed settlements and defining themselves in a more pronounced manner.[108]

4.4.4 CONSTRUCTING NEW LIFESTYLES, CREATING NEW NETWORKS

So far we have mainly explored villa development on the basis of the organisation of settlement space and house building. However, we should not forget that this went beyond the spatial and architectural, involving a much broader creation of new lifestyles among the upper social groups in the provincial countryside. Lifestyle could be viewed as a useful overarching and integrative concept, encompassing the way in which people construct their lives (and thus their place in the world) in relation to themselves, each other and their surroundings through the practice of living and through behaviour, ideas, values, world views (cognitive), food, material possessions, form and style (material).[109] New value systems define what is and what is not considered proper, correct and civilised within a certain lifestyle. Indeed, lifestyles are intrinsically social; they play a role in the creation of social bonds, or in distinguishing oneself from others. As Daloz states, '…especially when it comes to asserting oneself over others, external signs prove to be crucial resources.'[110]

Returning to the Roman provinces, we can interpret the construction of new lifestyles as a way to create a new place in a changing world. As we saw earlier, urban lifestyles were expressed in domestic architecture by means of baths, monumental façades and other features. The widespread appearance of these elements in house building underlined their important position within developing lifestyles. Besides domestic architecture, however, grave assemblages, iconography, mobile material culture and wall paintings can also shed an interesting light on newly developing lifestyles. In this section we will briefly explore how new lifestyles emerged during the 1st century AD, while other, traditional lifestyles were abandoned. This involves examining a select number of aspects and elements, including bathing and bath suites, dining and the *triclinium*, wall paintings and gardens.

An important theme touched upon in the previous chapter is that of bath suites and the practice of bathing. We saw that in the majority of existing monumental houses, bath suites were not added until a later development phase. In my view, this phenomenon could be seen as part of an emerging new rural lifestyle. We also saw, however, that some houses were equipped with bath suites in their first building phases, generally around the middle or the second half of the 1st century AD. I argued that the inhabitants of these houses were most directly connected with urban centres and therefore with urban lifestyles. Public bathing was an integral part of urban life and wealthy house owners also built private bath suites in their urban houses. It was probably the people most closely involved in urban life who first integrated a bathing section into their rural residences. However, it was not until later that bathing came to be an integral and more common part of a new rural lifestyle, as the bath suite became a general feature of monumental houses in the countryside. The fact that the idea and practice of bathing and bodily care assumed ever-greater importance within the newly developing lifestyles was also reflected in richer grave assemblages (fig. 4.11), that often include *strigiles*, used for scraping

graves were also documented at Hambach 127, 132, 133 and possibly at Voerendaal and Druten. See also Crowley in prep.

[108] See also Gerritsen 2003.

[109] Rapoport 1994, 476; Rapoport 1989, XVI.

[110] Daloz 2010, 61.

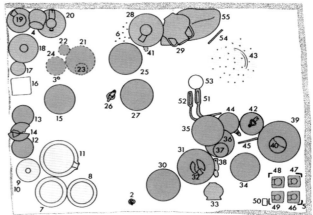

Fig. 4.11. Rich grave assemblies from Bocholtz (the Netherlands) and Helshoven (Belgium). After: De Groot 2006; Massart 2006, 81.

oily skin, and *balsamaria*, containing oil, relating to Mediterranean bathing practices.[111] These graves can probably be linked to the people residing in the monumental houses with baths. It thus becomes clear that new ideas and practices concerning bodily care were adopted by upper social groups in the countryside from around the middle of the 1st century AD.

Dining and drinking were another aspect for which changing ideas and practices were documented. Like bathing, they can be associated with Mediterranean-style ideas and practices that probably also first arose within the context of provincial urban culture. One crucial concept is the *symposium*, a dining and drinking party, and more specifically a fairly ritualised practice, whereby people reclined on couches for dinner, generally in specialised rooms called *triclinia*. From a social perspective, the symposium represents an important social institution in relation to patron–client relationships. It was where social relationships were ritualised and thereby shaped, strengthened and reconstituted.[112] Those invited into *triclinia* were enveloped in an atmosphere created by the host, in which he tacitly asserted his identity and position.[113]

Several elements of this symposium could be identified in the archaeological records. First of all, sets of dining and drinking ware in grave assemblages are often associated with the symposium.[114] Compared to pre-Roman graves, a clear shift can be documented, from the dominance of cooking pots to the use of sets of individual plates and bowls as well as bottles and flagons, indicating meals at which people ate from individual plates, similar to the Mediterranean symposium. This would suggest that, apart from the obvious material changes that occurred during this time, dining practices actually changed during the Roman period as well.

Other objects relating to dining, couches and tables are not generally found in the archaeological record, although some wooden table legs are known to have survived.[115] These legs were decorated with lion heads and, when preserved, the feet generally resembled a lion's claw. Marble tables with these legs are known from excavations at Pompeii and Herculaneum. However, these tables and couches are found much more often in iconography. One good example is the Simpelveld cinerary, in which the 'lady of Simpelveld', depicted on one side of the coffin, is reclining on a low couch

[111] For a detailed discussion on grave assemblages and their interpretation, see Crowley in prep.

[112] Slofstra 1995, 81; Dunbabin 1996.

[113] Lynch 2007, 249.

[114] De Groot 2006.

[115] Liversridge 1950; Fellmann 2009, 85 ff.; see also an example from Oberaden (Horn 1987, 179, fig. 113).

Fig. 4.12. Indications for symposia within the research region. The sarcophagus of Simpelveld and a tombstone from Dodewaard. After Rijksmuseum van Oudheden, Leiden (photo); Leemans 1875.

with high armrests. The other side depicts a typical three-legged table with lion heads (see fig 4.12). Both the couch and table are elements also found on many grave steles (see fig 4.12). Dressed in a toga, the deceased reclines on a couch with the table bearing food and drink placed in front of him. These scenes demonstrate that people in the countryside were at least familiar with these new dining practices as well as the material culture with which it was associated. Furthermore, it appears that the symposium was an important theme in the self-representation of people in the higher echelons of rural society. To what degree, however, did this phenomenon relate to actual practice? Were symposia like the ones depicted actually held in specialised *triclinia* inside the monumental houses as previously presented in this study?

The basic *triclinium*, as found for example in Pompeii, featured a rectangular arrangement of three couches with a round table at the centre.[116] Slofstra, who studied the larger and most luxurious villas, also identified a range of examples in the western provinces. These apsidal rooms occupied a prominent position within the house and were generally situated on the central axis. The fact that they were actually used for symposia was underlined by the patterns found on their mosaic floors. However, the examples presented by Slofstra are all situated south of our research area and all constitute part of houses organised around a *peristylium*, a house type generally not found in the more northerly regions. Furthermore, mosaic floors are found only rarely in the latter regions. As a result, room shape, along with position, remains the most significant indication for identifying hypothetical *triclinia* within our own dataset.

The *triclinium* should be regarded as a fairly private space; it was not used as a public reception space or for communal domestic life, and only those invited had access to the room. In multi-roomed houses within the research region, the central hall is most frequently interpreted as public and communal space. In the smaller category of houses, this space will have been used for cooking and eating as well as receiving guests. It was probably only the larger, more complex and luxurious villa houses that contained specialised, more private dining rooms, similar to the *triclinium*. In large houses such as Haccourt, Nennig, Basse-Wavre, Maillen-Ronchinne and Aldenhoven-Schleiden (which included a special multi-apsidal room), both the central reception hall and the more private dining room could be identified with a degree of certainty (fig 4.13). Interestingly, in the cases of Haccourt and Nennig,

[116] Slofstra 1995, 80.

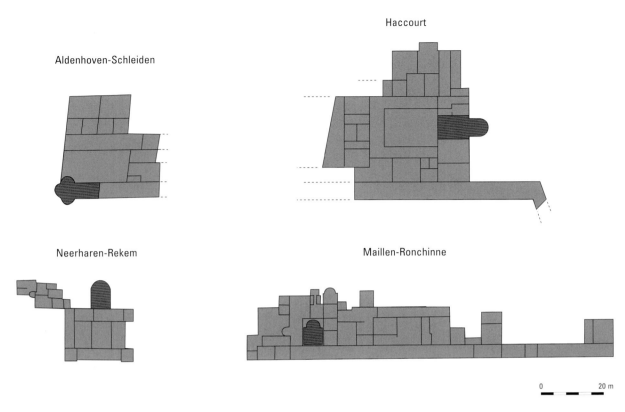

Aldenhoven-Schleiden

Haccourt

Neerharen-Rekem

Maillen-Ronchinne

0   20 m

Fig. 4.13. Indications for symposia within the research region. Hypothetical *triclinia* (dark grey) in the houses of Aldenhoven-Schleiden, Haccourt, Neerharen-Rekem and Maillen-Ronchinne.

these rooms were situated on an open court, similar to *triclinia* in Mediterranean houses that were situated on the *peristylium*.

Hypothetical *triclinia* were also identified elsewhere.[117] At Neerharen-Rekem, the apsidal room that was added to the back of the existing house during a later building phase has been interpreted as a *triclinium*. This position at the back of the house further underlines an interpretation as a more private dining room (see fig 4.13). At Vechmaal-Middelpadveld and Broekom, apsidal spaces were also added during secondary building phases. These may perhaps also be identified as private dining rooms.

For our region, it might be productive to take a somewhat broader approach and go beyond looking for typical *triclinia* similar to those in villas in the Mediterranean and the south of the research region.[118] Special rooms heated by a hypocaust were created in many monumental houses within the research region, generally during later development phases. Quite a few of these rooms also had *opus signinum* floors. We should perhaps regard such rooms as prominent spaces that were solely available to a select number of household members and invited guests. However, it cannot be established whether they were also used for dining in ways equivalent to the Mediterranean symposium. The fact that they were heated might nevertheless underline such a purpose, as heating would be needed when hosting dinners and these smaller rooms seem to have lacked a fireplace. An example can be found at Champion-Le Emptinne, where a large square room was constructed within an existing house, heated by a hypocaust

[117] Besides the ones mentioned, hypothetical *triclinia* were identified in the monumental houses at Maillen-d'Al Sauveniére, Maillen-Ronchinne, Matagne-la-Petite, Bad-Neuenahr-Ahrweiler and Euskirchen-Kreuzweingarten.

[118] As Lynch emphasises for the Greek Andron, it should be thought of as a conceptual space, not necessarily as an architecturally distinct space (Lynch 2007).

Fig. 4.14. Reconstructed scene of the wall paintings found in the house at Maasbracht. After Stuart/De Grooth 1987, 72.

and characterised by an *opus signinum* floor. Could we regard this room as a privileged dining or reception room? Similar developments could also be documented at Hoogeloon, Vodelée and elsewhere.

New ideas and practices were also expressed in decorations such as wall paintings. However, little figurative wall decoration has been documented within the research region. One of the best examples can be found at Maasbracht, where a *bestiarius*, an individual who fought wild beasts in an amphitheatre, is depicted in one of the reconstructed figurative scenes (fig. 4.14). This scene may be linked to the games organised by the villa owner in the urban centre and may therefore symbolise his important position in and relation to the urban sphere. By creating such scenes in his house, the owner displayed his wealth and euergetism. Another person in the scene is depicted holding a writing tablet and a *stylus*. This expresses the act of writing as a symbol of civilisation, and possibly of belonging to the administrative world of those in power. Some of the ideas and ideals of the villa inhabitants were thus expressed on the wall paintings at Maasbracht.[119] Similar themes appeared in other rural houses, as in the mosaic floors at the large house of Nennig.

A final lifestyle element that I will mention here concerns the gardens that have sometimes been documented in front of monumental villa houses. Especially in the larger, most monumental complexes, such as the axial complexes known from Belgium and France, gardens were probably created in front of the main residences. These gardens were actually an extension of the representative structure of the house. They were also about controlling spatial organisation and movement and even symbolising control over nature. Because gardens are generally difficult to excavate, reconstructions remain fairly hypothetical. Nonetheless, how we could imagine such gardens is illustrated by the famous villa of Fishbourne and the axial complex at Dietikon, both situated outside the research region (fig. 4.15).[120] Here, ditches for plants were documented, demonstrating that a well-structured garden existed in front of the house. Often, water basins will also have been part of gardens. Such water basins were found at a larger number of settlements, such as Verneuil-en-Halatte, Mercin-et-Vaux and Anthée, but also at smaller villas at for instance Neerharen-Rekem and Simpelveld-Bocholtz-Vaesrade.

The urban connection has already been touched upon a number of times. New bathing and dining practices seem to have been adopted and developed first in urban centres. This is not at all surprising if we consider that these urban centres were the arenas of power with fairly close connections to the core of the empire. It was there that traditional societies, especially those people with dominant social positions, managed to connect with these new urban and Mediterranean lifestyles for the first time.

[119] Swinkels 1987.

[120] Cunliffe 1971; Ebnöther 1995.

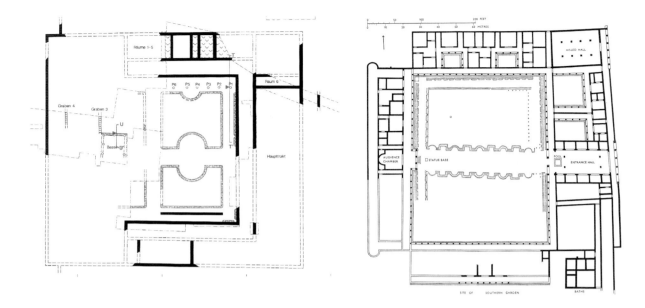

Fig. 4.15. Documented gardens at Dietikon (left) and Fishbourne (right), both outside the research region. After Ebnöther 1995, 32; Cunliffe 1971, 75.

These people were part of indigenous societies and as such were still connected with the countryside, where their social, cultural, economic and ancestral roots lay. They interacted with each other in these urban centres, resulting in a new social group, a community of peers if you like, with a specific urban-inspired lifestyle. Thus urban centres actually functioned as mediators between Mediterranean lifestyles and the countryside, where traditional lifestyles still dominated during the earlier 1st century AD.

In all probability, a fairly small group of people had already created a direct link to the urban world and developed urban lifestyles at an early stage of the development of the provinces. They were subsequently the first to introduce urban lifestyles to the countryside. As part of a potential second phase, the newly introduced lifestyle further evolved in this rural sphere, reaching those who had less direct links to the urban centres. However, there is no convincing evidence that a significantly early villa development genuinely existed, and particularly little regarding the northerly regions. Unfortunately, the fine dynamics of such a process have become lost in the fairly low chronological resolution associated with the difficulty of providing absolute datings for development phases.

Taking up new lifestyles was therefore not a simple and unconscious adoption of new ways, materials and ideas because they were intrinsically better or resulted in increased comfort. Instead, it was much more about the creation of new social networks, about taking part in them to forge a position within the changing realities of the developing Roman provinces. In this light, and to emphasise the active role of the agent, we chose the word 'constructing' in the above. Constructing a lifestyle was about establishing your place in the world. New relationships were created vertically as well as horizontally. On the one hand, the adoption of Roman-Mediterranean lifestyles involved forging links with the world of the powerful at the upper end and differentiating oneself from lower social echelons adhering to more traditional lifestyles at the bottom end. On the other hand, a new rural community of peers developed along with the creation of a new rural lifestyle. Increased mobility and related globalisation processes expanded knowledge about the marks of superiority of other elites.[121]

[121] See Daloz 2010, 135-136.

This probably increased intra-elite competition and facilitated the development and spread of certain lifestyles, which would explain the widespread appearance of certain elements in house building and mobile material culture.

As well as attempts by existing elites to maintain their power by adopting new lifestyles, the break with traditional lifestyles and the development of new ones probably also offered interesting opportunities for new aspiring elites.[122] These people now had an opportunity to distinguish themselves by connecting with newly emerging elite lifestyles, without being rooted in established elite families and their respective lifestyles.

4.5 LOCAL AND REGIONAL HETEROGENEITY AND THE NATURE OF ASYMMETRICAL SOCIAL RELATIONSHIPS WITHIN SETTLEMENTS

In this chapter I have chiefly focused on the ways in which asymmetrical relationships were created by the reorganisation of domestic space, the break with tradition, the creation of new symbols and monuments and the construction of new lifestyles. Now it is time to look more closely at the nature of these asymmetrical relationships and at the people involved in them. The dependent parties in these relationships have tended to be ignored in existing studies of the countryside, those of the villa in particular. These people were less directly linked to urban centres, new lifestyles and new building practices and consequently lived lives that were less Roman, and at the same time less archaeologically visible. However, in order to gain a proper understanding of the basic character of villa development, we must also study these less visible non-elite people. Furthermore, we need to explore the different ways in which relationships were created within different types of settlements across the research region. First, however, I will examine local and regional heterogeneity from a social perspective.

4.5.1 UNDERSTANDING LOCAL AND REGIONAL HETEROGENEITY

An important objective of the broad approach taken in this study is to discuss the enormous heterogeneity within the dataset. This heterogeneity developed from the 1st century AD onwards in particular. As explored in the third chapter, some settlements remained small and barely monumentalised, while others developed into larger and sometimes very substantial, strictly organised and highly monumentalised complexes. Size, spatial organisation, monumentalisation and degree of luxury varied considerably, both between regions and within a single locality.

In the previous chapter, some general regional patterns were reconstructed. We established that axially-organised complexes were especially dominant in northern France and the Belgian loess region. We also saw that the northern sand and clay regions were characterised by less rigidly organised multi-farmstead settlements. Here, houses showed influences from the Mediterranean architectural lexicon and were monumentalised only in a minority of cases. The German loess plain was particularly characterised by relatively small compound settlements with modest monumental houses. How can these general regional differences in settlement form be understood? Can we learn more about the factors behind this differentiation? To understand more about this regionality, it is important to focus on the broader context of the settlements: the specific characteristics of the region during the Roman period (the specific way in which the region developed into part of the Roman province) as well as the Iron Age background.

---

[122] See Daloz 2010, 128 ff.

Starting in the Iron Age, an important pastoral tradition in the northernmost regions saw people inhabiting byre houses together with their livestock.[123] Generally, no spatially coherent and organised settlement compounds existed; settlement was organised on the level of the individual farmstead. Nor is there much indication of the existence of a social hierarchy; no asymmetrical relationships seem to have been created within the context of these settlements. During the Roman period, the Rhine region became an important military zone, with early military camps situated at Nijmegen, Velsen and Vechten. Subsequently, a military-controlled corridor – the *limes* – developed along the Rhine. This dominant military presence will have had a significant influence on the rural areas of this region.[124] Urbanisation, on the other hand, remained at a fairly low level. The centres of Ulpia Noviomagus and Forum Hadriani were limited in size, while the centre of Xanten, located in modern-day Germany, was much larger. Furthermore, sand and clay soils were not suitable for the large-scale production of wheat, the crop demanded by the urban and military population in sizeable quantities. And in relation to house building, we should not ignore the availability – or lack – of building material. Natural stone was not available in these northern regions and therefore had to be transported from distant sources, generally by river. As previously argued, the generally late date of the stone houses known from these northern regions might be linked to the large-scale transportation of building stone to these regions for the monumentalisation of the army camps along the *limes*.[125] The cultural background of the people in the northern regions is another explanation given for the lower numbers of monumental, Mediterranean-style houses and hence greater continuity.[126] According to Roymans, those with pastoral lifestyles and values were less susceptible to the influences that caused significant change in the more southerly regions, which were predominantly more focused on agriculture. Nevertheless, we should remember that significant changes did in fact take place in the settlements within this region. The reorganisation of space, segregation and changes in house building can be understood in relation to changing relationships within the settlements, changing patterns of control and production and changing relationships with the outside world. For these regions, the role of veterans has often been emphasised. Veterans may have served as 'cultural mediators', as they had lived in army camps where they were confronted with Mediterranean culture for several years before returning to their home settlements.[127] It is also likely that veterans had increased access to social and economic networks outside the local settlement. By building portico-houses as found in several settlements, they expressed their connection to the Roman world as well as their prominent position within the settlement.[128]

A different situation is recorded in more southerly regions, which were less militarised and more urbanised. Important urban centres, including Tongres, Cologne, Bavay and Amiens, as well as many smaller rural centres, will have significantly affected social, economic and cultural relations. Furthermore, a well-developed infrastructure connected larger and smaller centres, underlining their importance as centres, while secondary roads linked rural settlements to the main routes. In these regions, settlements generally developed into well-organised compounds with one or more buildings being rebuilt on stone foundations over time. They were transformed into monumental, Mediterranean-style houses that were both durable and prestigious. As previously argued, these houses representing a specific lifestyle developed in close association with the urban world. Consequently, the greater impact of urban culture in these regions may have influenced the way in which settlements developed there. However, wealth was a precondition for creating such settlements and houses. Loess soils were suit-

---

[123] Roymans 1996.

[124] Roymans 2010.

[125] Glasbergen 1967; Haalebos *et al.* 2000; Polak/Klooster-man/Niemeijer 2004.

[126] See Roymans 1996.

[127] This role of veterans has been explored by Derks/Roy-

mans 2006, Nicolay 2005, Roymans 2010 and others.

[128] For the discussion on veteran houses, see Vos 2009. The problem with the term 'veteran house' is its inherent social interpretation. The term portico-house instead takes the morphological character of the house as its point of departure.

able for the large-scale production of wheat. Indeed, it seems logical to connect surplus production of this crop with the accumulation of wealth. Furthermore, building stone for the construction of stone foundations was locally available in most cases.[129]

Again focusing on the pre-Roman background, it is remarkable that, as explored in chapter 3, the distribution of Roman-period axially-organised settlements seems to generally coincide with the region in which settlements were already being enclosed during the pre-Roman period. A possible explanation is that a more complex settlement system had already developed in the southern regions during the pre-Roman period. As we saw in the model created by Malrain, Matterne and Méniel, some settlements were already organised in a more hierarchical manner, seemingly reflecting direct asymmetrical social relationships and the prominent position of a single family able to control others (see section 3.2.3).[130] It is perhaps these families that were able to control even more families from the Roman period onwards, expressing and fixing this control in newly structured, axially-organised settlement complexes.

Examining the above in more detail, we are able to list some important factors that could explain regional differentiation in rural landscapes. Singling out one of these factors is a hazardous undertaking, however, as the reality is likely to be more complex. Here I would like to emphasise the following:

- Existing (pre-Roman) lifestyles, traditions in house building and settlement organisation, and societal structures. Within the research region there was a marked differentiation in the way settlements were organised and houses were constructed, as well as in the degree of socio-political complexity. Further, there are regions that were not inhabited in pre-Roman times. These varied backgrounds are an important factor in the differentiated development dynamics.

- Existing agrarian regimes. In general terms, it is possible to distinguish between agrarian regimes focusing on arable farming on the loess soils and those focusing on pastoral farming on the sand and clay soils of the north.[131] How communities lived and worked will have helped determine how they created a new place in the changing world.

- The physical substrate. This factor is closely related to the previous one, as the character and quality of the physical substrate largely determined its agricultural use and potential and, indirectly, also how people organised their settlements, built their houses and became integrated into the Roman empire.

- The degree of urbanisation. As market and consumer centres, towns provided an important economic stimulus. They were also the places where new lifestyles developed and where inhabitants of the countryside took part in the social arena of the town, thus connecting with new lifestyles. Urban culture influenced rural culture, and hence villa development, in important ways. In non-urbanised regions, more traditional, tribal forms of organisation remained intact for longer. Here, elites were deprived of a way to create direct links with the Roman administration, religious structures and associated urban lifestyles.

- The availability of building material. A lack of stone might have been a limiting factor in house development. In the sand and clay regions, where fairly few houses were rebuilt on stone foundations, natural stone could not be quarried locally, but had to be transported from more distant sources. It is therefore important to realise that the investment required to build a house on stone foundations is likely to have been significantly higher in this region.

---

[129] And, as demonstrated in chapter 3, basic building stone was indeed quarried locally in the majority of cases.

[130] Malrain/Matterne/Méniel 2002, 137 ff.

[131] See Roymans 1996.

- Infrastructure. Roads were vital for the integration of rural settlements and their communities into the wider economy and social networks, and thus for the diffusion of new materials, forms and ideas. Especially high-potential areas, such as the loess region, were opened up through good-quality infrastructural networks, influencing the development of the rural settlements there in important ways. Other regions that were not opened up as much, such as the core of the sandy MDS region, remained peripheral. Only little change can be documented there.

Some general patterns of regional differentiation were sketched above. Looking more closely, however, we see that rural settlement could also vary significantly within the same locality or micro-region. How should we interpret from a social point of view the local coexistence of very large, monumental complexes, simple compound settlements with a monumental main house, and loosely organised settlements with traditional houses? Alternatively, viewed from a development perspective, why do some settlements develop into large, monumental and Mediterranean-style complexes, while others remain essentially small and traditional? Several interpretations and key factors can again be advanced.

First of all, it is important to take a brief look at a few examples from our dataset. What kind of rural settlements are situated within the same locality? One interesting and well-researched area can be found in the western part of the German Rhineland west of Cologne, not far from the Dutch border (fig. 4.16). At Aldenhoven-Schleiden and Eschweiler-Laurenzberg (situated about 10 km apart), two very large monumental houses were documented, each with over 30 rooms. Settlements with much simpler monumental houses were located not far from these houses, for example at Alsdorf-Hoengen and Broichweiden-Würselen. The latter house essentially consisted of a simple hall and a fronting portico with risaliths. Its façade did not exceed 20 m. Similar situations can be found on the Belgian loess. Only 2 km from the large monumental axial complex of Anthée was a simple house consisting of a hall fronted by a portico-risalith façade. And simple houses were also documented near the large complexes of Saint-Gerard-Try Hallot and Mettet-Bauselenne.[132] Interestingly, recent excavations on the loess have revealed even simpler settlement forms, dominated by post-built houses, near and alongside monumentalised settlement complexes. Examples are Kesselt, Heerlen-Trilandis, Arras-Delta 3 and Onnaing-Toyota.

The broader factors listed previously are less relevant when it comes to interpreting local differentiation. Here, we need to explore a number of other factors. Traditionally, wealth has been regarded as a key factor. Some people were able to acquire more wealth than others and were consequently able to build bigger houses. While this appears to be essentially true, the situation is in fact more complex. Why were these people able to acquire more wealth? And what does the variation in settlement form suggest about the relationships between the inhabitants of these settlements?

Slofstra, in a study of the development of the rural settlement system in the first centuries AD, emphasises the fact that the differential access to the various sources of power, which evolved during the period of closer relations with the Roman authorities, led to increasing socio-political hierarchisation within the tribal societies of the MDS area.[133] This in turn led to social interdependencies other than the kinship relations that were dominant in tribal societies. Examples of these clientship and tenancy relations have already been mentioned. With regard to the settlement system, this hierarchisation and the development of new forms of social interdependencies clearly affected settlement development as reconstructed in the previous chapter. According to Slofstra, the emergence of fairly large enclosed settlements in the northern regions, such as those at Hoogeloon and Oss-Westerveld, was 'the spatial expression of organisation of local communities under elite control'.[134] In small, open rural settlements, however, no indications for such a hierarchy can be identified.

---

[132] See Brulet 2009, 547-551.

[133] Slofstra 1991, 177.

[134] Slofstra 1991, 177.

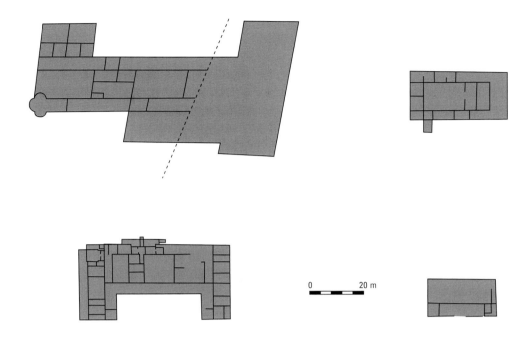

Fig. 4.16. Four houses situated within a relatively small area, near Aachen, Germany. How should we understand this significant differentiation in social terms? From top left to bottom right: Aldenhoven-Schleiden, Alsdorf-Hoengen, Eschweiler-Laurenzberg and Broichweiden-Würselen.

Other authors have suggested a kind of domain-structured, dendritic settlement model for other regions. Examining the middle Aare valley in Switzerland, Schucany defined three villa categories: large complexes (over 5 ha), middle-sized villas (up to 3 ha) and small farmsteads (up to 1 ha). She then went on to reconstruct a landscape consisting of domains (termed *fundi* in Latin), centred around the large, mostly axially-organised complexes and controlling between one and three medium-sized villas and a similar number of small farmsteads.[135] A domain comprised between 150 and 200 people. Quite a number of workers lived on the working compound of the main complexes. The remainder inhabited smaller settlements within the domain. The existence of similar domain-structured landscapes has also been suggested in other studies, such as Wickham's.[136] If these did indeed exist, can large complexes like Anthée, Saint-Gerard-Try Hallot and Mettet-Bauselenne mentioned above then be interpreted as centres of such a domain? In this model, the appearance of settlements and houses is directly related to the social position of their inhabitants. People lower down the social hierarchy, who were probably controlled by landowners living in luxurious villas, were considerably less wealthy. In addition, these people had less access to urban centres and markets and exercised less or no control over the workforce (production) and consumption. Some authors, however, have argued for a less direct association of appearance and social position and have emphasised the agency of people who become consumers.[137]

The following section explores dependency relationships in more detail and lists factors relating to social differentiation. These factors are intimately linked to the way that settlements developed and thus to local differentiation in rural settlements. For example, the degree of control over land and workforce can be associated with the way that domestic space was organised. The same can be said for access to the urban world and markets. Access to urban centres meant access to decision-making arenas, to new urban lifestyles and to urban markets. People who were able to forge links with the

[135] Schucany 2011.
[136] Wickham 2005, 465 ff.
[137] Martins 2005.

urban world at an early stage were able to improve and fix their social status in the countryside, at the same time introducing new lifestyles. Many other rural inhabitants will not have connected with the urban world and urban lifestyles until later.

4.5.2 ELITES AND PEASANTS: EXPLORING THE CHARACTER OF SOCIAL DIF-FERENTIATION AND ASYMMETRICAL RELATIONSHIPS

Both the reorganisation of settlement space and the increasing heterogeneity within the settlement system, discussed in the previous section, have been associated with the development of new, more complex asymmetrical relationships within society, and thus with the process of hierarchisation. This section aims to explore the character and background of this hierarchisation and focus on the asymmetrical relationships that were constructed in this process. I will focus explicitly on the dependent parties within these relationships, as they are the ones who are often overlooked because of their poor material culture and archaeological visibility. Their houses, graves and material culture were generally less monumental, less durable, less luxurious and less conspicuous than those belonging to upper social groups. I would here like to focus on the less visible people: where and how did they live, and what was their relationship to the elites?

Within the context of the significantly changing socio-politics of the developing Roman provinces, new relationships developed between native elites and Roman authorities as well as within native communities. Slofstra made a general distinction between patron-client relationships and tenancy relationships. In his view, patron-client relationships were relatively informal and personal. Wightman has demonstrated, however, that considerable variety was likely within the category of clients. Studying early medieval Welsh and Irish legal texts, she made a distinction between free clients and base (or semi-free) clients.[138] While the group of free clients held land of their own (though still owing renders and services), base clients did not own land and probably lived on the lord's property. Free clients, then, might have had the potential to prosper modestly. According to Wightman, they could buy or rent land and even take offices such as service in the auxiliary forces.[139] Tenancy relationships were more formal, impersonal and perhaps even contractual. Tenants worked the lord's lands and had to pay rent in produce or money. Certain well-known iconographic scenes were interpreted as depicting such situations, whereby tenants were paying their landlords.[140] In general it is important to realise that dependency relationships could take various forms and may also have varied considerably within and between different settlements. The spectrum could range from basically unfree dependants who were very directly controlled and had no free choice with regard to production and consumption, to basically free farmers who paid their landlord money or part of the produce in return for the use of land or some form of help or protection. As Whittaker summarises, '[d]ependence is never a single status but a spectrum between freedom and slavery.'[141]

As stated, the aim here is to shed more light on the dependent parties within the asymmetrical relationships: the clients, tenants and possibly even slaves. Compared to the higher echelons of society, these groups were less mobile, less wealthy, and had limited or no access to the urban world and new lifestyles. One interesting concept used for approaching such people, especially within the disciplines of sociology and anthropology, is that of 'peasant'. Peasants are traditional farmers in complex state societies who are generally subject to the demands and sanctions of power-holders outside their social

---

[138] Wightman 1978.

[139] Wightman 1978, 103.

[140] For a different view, see Drinkwater (1981) who interprets these scenes as workers being paid by their land-lords.

[141] Whittaker 1980, 83.

stratum.[142] They are distinguished from tribal farmers on the one hand and citizen farmers, agrarian entrepreneurs highly integrated into a market economy on the other. Although they function within a state system, peasants are integrated into that system only to a limited degree, lacking full or direct access to the centralised systems of decision-making and the market economy.[143]

Both Wolf and Wickham contrast peasant societies with 'primitive' or 'tribal societies'.[144] In primitive societies, production is decentralised, local and familial. Producers control the means of production, including their own labour, exchanging their labour and its products for the culturally defined equivalent goods and services of others. With the rise of peasant societies, however, control of the means of production passes into the hands of groups who do not carry out the productive processes themselves. The surplus produced by peasants is transferred to a dominant group of rulers, who use it both to underwrite their own standard of living and to distribute the remainder to groups in society who do not farm but must be fed, in return for the specific goods and services these people have to offer. To peasants, exchange has become indirect. Slofstra terms this development 'peasantisation', involving the integration of tribal societies into a state system.[145]

This integration into a state system involved the development of much more profiled and complex asymmetrical social relationships. However, it would be a mistake to assume a simple conceptual dichotomy between elite and peasant. As previously argued, there may still have been considerable variation within the category of dependent peasants – clients – with respect to personal freedom, the ability to possess land and acquire wealth in particular.[146] Families owning land could still be directly involved in agricultural production and could thus be regarded as peasants. In all probability, they were themselves free clients, while at the same time they could, as patrons, control people below them on the social ladder. Smaller villa settlements may perhaps be interpreted in this way. As free clients, these people were able to acquire wealth that they eventually invested in their house. As Woolf has argued, it is unlikely that a tenant who did not own the house he inhabited would invest in monumentalisation.[147]

In short, it appears that we should look beyond a simple binary opposition of elite and non-elite, or elite and peasant. Both social differentiation and the way that asymmetrical relationships were constructed were much more complex. Several significant factors can be identified regarding this differentiation:

- Access to a centralised system of decision making; access to social networks of power
- Access to markets
- Control over workforce and production
- Access to new agricultural and other technologies
- Mobility
- Control of exchange
- Legal position/status (under Roman law).

With these factors in mind, we can define some general categories within society. As emphasised earlier, the most powerful people in the countryside were mobile and had direct access to urban centres and thus to the centralised system of decision making, markets and new urban lifestyles. Such people seem to have been able to control the workforce, production and exchange. It is highly plausible that they even spent part of the year living in urban centres. Other groups only had indirect access to urban

[142] Slofstra 1983, 80; Wolf 1966, 11; see Wolf 1966 for a full discussion.

[143] Slofstra 1983, 80.

[144] Wolf 1966; Wickham 2005.

[145] This hypothesis is inspired by Norbert Elias' state forma-

tion theory (Elias 1982) and Eric Wolf's 'Europe and the People Without History' (Wolf 1982). Slofstra 1983, 75–82.

[146] Wightman 1978.

[147] Woolf 1998, 163-164.

centres, systems of decision making, markets and new lifestyles, probably by means of patron–client relationships. They lived in the countryside permanently and were probably directly involved in agricultural activities; they could more or less control their own production, although they were subject to rent payment. Yet another category of people were mobile to only a very limited degree, did not control their own production as they were directly controlled by others and did not have access to the urban world, new lifestyles or markets. The cadasters from Orange are an interesting illustration of the level of disparity between the positions of different people, revealing that only eleven people rented approximately 70% of the municipal land and a single person rented as much as 12%.[148]

So is it possible to locate these different categories of people within the settlements explored in this study? And how do the different types of settlement reflect their social position and the way in which asymmetrical social relations were being created? This exploration concerns both how asymmetrical social relationships were constituted spatially, by means of the organisation of settlement space, as well as how new, urban-inspired lifestyles were adopted and integrated. Three data categories will be discussed:

- Settlement compounds with a monumental main residence and secondary houses (villa settlements)
- Non-monumental settlements (non-villa settlements)
- Non-monumental graves (simple cremation graves).

A logical first step would be to identify the dependants in the settlements discussed in the previous chapter. In the section on secondary houses (section 3.3.4), we identified a variety of houses inhabited by people who evidently occupied a more or less dependent relationship to the inhabitants of the main house. In many settlements, post-built houses were documented on the compounds, associated with fairly traditional ways of house building and lifestyles. Here, we need to emphasise that the main monumental residence had generally evolved from a traditional house. This suggests that a single family was able to connect with new lifestyles first, while the other families could not, or not until a later phase. In settlements such as Hamois-Le Hody, Kerkrade-Holzkuil, Vezin-Namêche, Champion-Le Emptinne and some in the hinterland of Cologne, traditional houses were still being built, while one house had already been rebuilt as a monumental structure with characteristics adopted from the Mediterranean architectural lexicon. Some of these traditional secondary houses were fully or partially monumentalised during a later phase, generally expressing new lifestyles only to a limited extent, while still clearly adhering to traditional ideas of house building, more so than in the case of the main residences that represented a more radical break with tradition (see the semi-monumentalised secondary houses at for example Hamois-Le Hody, Kerkrade-Holzkuil, Vezin-Namêche and Champion-Le Emptinne).

How then can the relationship between the people living in the main monumental residences and those living in the more traditional secondary houses be characterised in terms of the varied spatial organisation of settlement complexes? As previously argued, asymmetrical relationships were constructed and symbolised particularly rigidly in axially-organised complexes. The peasants living on the working compound were physically separated from the people inhabiting the main residence, who literally and visually controlled those who were directly dependent on them. Control was direct and clearly integrated into the design of such complexes, while the distance – both physical and symbolic – between the people in the main residence and those on the working compound was substantial. Furthermore, apart from the organisational uniformity of the complexes (with houses neatly lined up on both sides of a courtyard), strict morphological uniformity of such houses may also be identified in quite a few cases. In settlements such as Famechon-Le Marais, but especially in axial complexes south of our research region (e.g. at Reinheim, Dietikon, Oberentfelden and Neftenbach), uniform

---

[148] Whittaker 1980, 76.

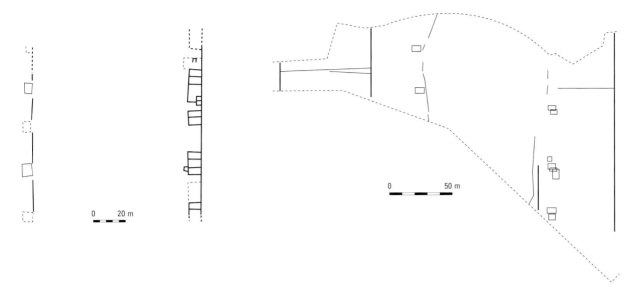

Fig. 4.17. Houses on the working compound of large axial complexes at Famechon-Le Marais (left: two phases) and Juvincourt-et-Damary (right).

and basic residential units – in fact barracks – on stone foundations were situated on the rigidly organised working compound (fig. 4.17).[149] These barracks were an integral part of a well-designed plan carried out under the supervision of the proprietor and thus reflected strong and direct control from above. Dependent families were therefore living in residences that they probably did not build or own. Furthermore, they were integrated into a spatial structure that strongly embodied their dependency and the landlord's control. Examining these arguments, it seems that the relationship between the owner of the complex and the people living on the working compound was quite distant, formal and probably impersonal. As they were directly controlled, these people seem to have occupied a direct dependent relationship to the landlord, probably as a type of base client. Exactly how dependent they were is difficult to say. The existence of slavery has been suggested by some scholars, especially with regard to the type of standardised axial complex previously described.[150] However, direct indications for or against are not available.[151] In general, Whittaker suggests a minimal change in labour relations, arguing in favour of continuity in dependency relationships and labour organisation between the pre-Roman and Roman periods.[152] According to Whittaker, complexes such as Anthée suggest that 'the evidence is just as consistent with rural production carried out by traditional clients as it is with a slave system.'[153] More recent work combines various sources to argue that slavery relationships could indeed have existed within rural settlements in the provincial countryside.[154] Epigraphy and the presence of leg irons provide the most convincing evidence. However, the best documented cases are found south of our research region.

The situation at compound settlements, where the distance between the main residence and other houses was much smaller, on both a physical and symbolic level, was quite different from that at the axial complexes previously discussed. The houses in these settlements were organised around a shared compound and the main house was not separated from the other houses by a wall. Furthermore,

[149] See also Gaston 2008 on standardisation of secondary buildings.
[150] Whittaker 1980. For the debate on rural slavery, see also Samson 1989; Webster 2005, 2008 and 2010.
[151] See Roymans/Zandstra 2011; Whittaker (1980) states

that is impossible to prove extensive chattel slavery.
[152] Whittaker 1980, 90.
[153] Whittaker 1980, 79.
[154] Roymans/Zandstra 2011.

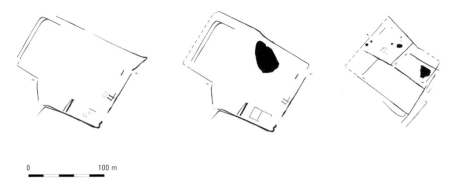

0   100 m

Fig. 4.18. Simple non-monumental enclosed settlements within the 'villa landscape' at Onnaing. After Clotuche 2009, 54.

housing was generally less uniform and it appears that the inhabitants were themselves involved in building their houses. Some of these secondary houses were monumentalised over time, in most cases probably only after the rebuilding of the main house as a multi-roomed house on stone foundations. A secondary house at Kerkrade-Holzkuil was rebuilt as a two-roomed house with a fronting portico. And at several settlements, a secondary house had a plan similar to the well-known portico-risalith façaded houses. On the basis of the spatial character of these types of settlement, I would like to argue that these asymmetrical relationships were relatively informal, personal and direct. Indeed, it seems plausible that the families living together on the compound were biologically related, possibly even representing different generations of the same extended family.[155] Traditionally, however, monumentalised secondary houses have often been interpreted as the residence of a *vilicus* (bailiff) or servant family (*Gesinde* in German), especially within German villa studies. Such interpretations fit in with the Italic model mentioned earlier in this chapter, and would imply more formal relationships between the inhabitants. In my view, this model is somewhat far-fetched for this type of settlement and I therefore choose not to follow such interpretations. This is not to say, however, that they could not apply to other types of settlements, such as axially-organised complexes.

Yet another category of settlements, rather neglected until now, are the small, non-monumental settlements (fig. 4.18). Unlike the larger villa settlements, these are not strictly organised and do not contain monumentalised houses influenced by Mediterranean-style architecture. They may have existed on a fairly large scale within 'villa landscapes', but until recently have received no archaeological attention. At both Onnaing and Arras, mentioned earlier, larger parts of the landscape were excavated, demonstrating the presence of these small, non-monumental settlements. In recent years, similar non-monumental settlements were also discovered at Veldwezelt, Kesselt and Heerlen-Trilandis in Dutch southern Limburg and Belgian Limburg, telling us much more about the real differentiation in rural settlement in the provincial countryside. The families inhabiting these settlements can clearly be regarded as peasants, as they were directly involved in agricultural practice. With regard to their social position we could possibly regard them as tenants living on their lord's land. Using the dendritic model previously discussed, these settlements were at the bottom of the settlement hierarchy within the domain, which was probably controlled by the landlord, residing in a large monumental, potentially axially-organised settlement complex. Unlike the dependent families living on the working compounds of these large complexes, however, the families living in the small rural settlements were probably relatively free in the sense that they were not directly or physically controlled. It is highly likely that their obligations towards their landlords took the form of rent in kind and seasonal work on his land. Nevertheless, they controlled their own production and consumption and were relatively autonomous.

[155] See also Wightman 1978.

An attempt to interpret the dataset leads us to suspect a social reality – both between and within settlements – that is more complex than we are able to reconstruct archaeologically. Some settlement categories may have been inhabited by a range of people of different social status. In other words, their dependent relationships towards their patrons or landlords were essentially different. Some people were living on the rigidly-organised axial complexes themselves, and were highly dependent, directly controlled and possibly even unfree. However, we might also suspect social differentiation within this category of people living on the working compounds of such complexes.[156] In many cases, a larger, monumentalised house at the top of the working compound, close to the residential compound, was probably inhabited by someone of higher social standing, related to the proprietor in a closer, more personal way (see fig 3.40). This person, possibly a *libertus* (freedman), may have been responsible for coordinating the settlement's production. In the literature, such an individual is generally referred to as a *vilicus*. Once again, a different dependency relationship can be suspected for people living in the most basic post-built settlements near the larger monumentalised settlements. These people were subjected to a more indirect level of control.

Another data category that may tell us more about the peasants living in the settlements is that of graves. For Germany in particular, graves are documented in direct association with the settlement compound, clustered around the settlement enclosure ditches in most cases. As described above, these were simple cremation graves with no apparent monumental markers above ground, no luxurious containers for the ashes and no extensive sets of grave goods. No themes were expressed such as we found in the elite graves, touched upon previously. They therefore reflected different lifestyles. We can assume that the people interred in these small grave clusters belonged to the lower echelons of society, living their local lives on the settlement compounds, probably in dependent relationship to a dominant family. This is also reflected in the position of the simple grave clusters in relation to the richer graves that are sometimes found. In a number of cases, separately enclosed graveyards were documented (Hambach 34, 230, 303 and 503), which can probably be associated with the prominent family within the settlement. At Hambach 303, it could even be anthropologically established that the walled graveyard (7 by 6.6 m) contained a family grave.[157] In other cases, rich graves were spatially separated from the simple grave clusters (e.g. at Cologne-Müngersdorf and Hambach 69). These observations underline the social position of the people interred in the simple graves in relation to the more prominent people buried in richer and more monumental ones.

4.6   SOME CONCLUDING THOUGHTS

This chapter has attempted to explore villa development from a human perspective. I have argued that the reorganisation of settlement space and the transformation of or break with house-building traditions were an integral part of changing social relationships in the provincial countryside. Existing structures were actively and creatively manipulated on the level of the rural settlement, within the context of the changing world of the developing Roman provinces. Within this evolving, socio-politically and economically much more complex world, new social identities and new asymmetrical relationships were created, communicated and fixed in the built environment and through the adoption of new lifestyles. Villa development was thus a way of settling in a changing world – a social strategy to create and fix new social, economic and cultural relationships within the local settlement communities as well as within broader society.

For the sake of clarity I will summarise this chapter's key points:

---

[156] Whittaker 1980, 83, 89.   [157] Gaitzsch 1993, 25-26.

- The enclosure of settlements may generally be linked to developments in agriculture, intensification of production and increasing pressure on land. As early as the pre-Roman period, pressure on land intensified, seemingly in the southern part of the research region in particular, where settlements were already enclosed during the pre-Roman period. In the northern parts, settlements were not enclosed until the 1st century AD, probably also as a result of growing pressure on land.

- Communities became well-defined and highly fixed within the landscape, both physically and symbolically, reflecting stable and continuous claims on land. Settlement communities evolved to become fairly closed entities.

- Breaking with tradition denoted a break with existing structures rather than the logical and passive adoption of new forms. It was an active way of creating new social realities and a new place within a changing world.

- The increasing socio-political complexity in communities is evident at various levels. On a household level, social space within multi-roomed houses on stone foundations was organised in more complex ways, segmenting space and creating new ways to differentiate space symbolically by means of decoration and furniture. At the level of the settlement, space was also more rigidly organised and hierarchised, indicating centralised control over design and consequently over access and exclusion, movement and experience. On a higher level, it is evident that a significant differentiation in rural settlements developed in the countryside, which could be interpreted as reflecting asymmetrical relationships between settlement communities.

- The creation of more durable and monumental houses implied changing ways in which people related to the past. Settlement and house in fact became ancestral objects and symbols for the continuity of the family and perhaps even the settlement community. In this light, the monumentalisation of the house could be regarded as a strategy to construct stable family lines and emphasise continuity and existing claims rooted in the past.

- In the countryside, the concentration of power and control increased. The settlement and house were instrumental in the creation of asymmetrical relationships of control over people and produce. While some people gained power and control and could take advantage of new opportunities, others became increasingly dependent and their opportunities were curtailed. When exploring these relationships, it is important to think beyond basic dichotomies between elites and peasants. Within rural communities throughout the research region there is considerable differentiation in the degree of control over production and exchange, of mobility, and of access to the urban world with its administrative and political institutions and new lifestyles. The character of asymmetrical relationships is also differentiated.

- New ways of house building were part of the broader development of new lifestyles. These lifestyles, strongly influenced by the urban sphere, were actively 'created' as strategies to construct new social identities. Dining and bathing also constituted an important part of villa lifestyles, reflected in houses, graves and iconographic representations.

- In some regions, socio-political complexity seems to have increased more than in others. Large axial complexes, typical of the southern parts of the research region, were highly hierarchised, differentiated and segmented (both symbolically and physically). In the northern regions, settlement organisation and house building were transformed to a significantly lesser degree, probably reflecting a lower level of socio-political complexity.

5 Villa development and the organisation of production

This study has so far paid little attention to an important dimension of villa development – agricultural production. This chapter will therefore attempt to elucidate this economic dimension and explore developments in both production and the way it was organised. Once more, the settlement is taken as the main level of analysis. How did the agricultural orientation and organisation of settlements throughout the research region develop over time, also in relation to the organisation of settlement space, building practices and changing social relationships?

From the 1960s in particular, when a growing number of settlements were excavated on a larger scale, the villa was viewed as a production unit, functioning within the newly developing Roman market economy. Slofstra even spoke of an economic 'villa system', with villas producing within a specific 'villa mode of production'.[1] This model views the villa as a specific market-oriented farm, based on a form of dependent labour and focusing on the production of a surplus for sale in the urban market.[2] The thesis of a specific mode of production has played an important part in our understanding of the villa and hence its conceptual definition. Moreover, it has often been linked to the adoption of effective methods to boost productivity, as rationality and efficiency are introduced into production, similar to capitalist production.[3] As emphasised in the previous chapter, studies later moved towards more consumption-oriented approaches, focusing on concepts such as material culture, globalisation and consumerism.

This chapter will once again look at developments in rural settlements between the later Iron Age and the late empire. This time, however, the central theme will be both production and its physical and social organisation. Is it possible to shed light on longer-term developments as well as more radical changes in agricultural production, and how should these changes be understood within the context of the developing Roman provinces? In addition, to what degree can the villa be regarded as a production form, imported from or influenced by the Italic region?[4]

I will attempt to answer these questions by first of all exploring some of the significant broader economic developments that took place within the Roman provinces and that had a dramatic impact on the countryside and its settlements. I will then examine production activities in rural settlements in greater detail, using both archaeobotanical and archaeozoological data. Is it in fact possible to reconstruct changes in production between the pre-Roman period and Roman period and to distinguish more specific changes to patterns of production within individual settlements and between regions? The focus will then shift to analysing the organisation of production, by looking at both individual buildings – in this case secondary buildings – and the development of a functional working compound, where part of the agricultural activities will have been carried out. The granary, used for storing crops, will be studied in particular detail as it lends itself well to reconstructing both qualitative and quantitative changes in production, storage, and control over production.

[1] Slofstra 1991.

[2] Slofstra 1991, 161, 179.

[3] Becker 2007.

[4] Peters 1994, 41.

5.1 THE WIDER CONTEXT OF ECONOMIC DEVELOPMENTS IN THE COUNTRYSIDE

Before focusing on developments in production on the level of the settlement, I will assess some of the significant broader economic developments that took place within the context of the Roman provinces. Here, I will predominantly focus on the rise of regional markets, monetisation, the army as consumer, the town as consumer, infrastructural developments and increased mobility.

5.1.1 THE DEVELOPMENT OF REGIONAL MARKETS

One of the basic economic changes within the research region was the rise of a new 'economic infrastructure', a market system. In such a system, economic agents (individuals or groups) are connected within networks of exchange in which markets can function as central points.[5] The growth of such a network gives rise not just to horizontal ties, but to complex vertical ties, enabling goods to pass from the countryside to towns, towns to cities, cities to seaports and from seaports to overseas markets.[6] This allows peasants working the land to become involved in a market system with many levels of ever- widening scope.

Physical markets are places where the economic exchange of goods and money concentrate and where producers, consumers, middlemen, tradesmen and officials can meet to exchange and trade. In an important study on markets in the Roman empire, Luc de Ligt has examined rural and urban markets in the western Roman provinces, mainly on the basis of toponyms and archaeological sources, as written sources on this topic are lacking.[7] The market functions of quite a few towns can be deduced from their names. Forum Hadriani and Ulpia Noviomagus in the northernmost part of the research area are particularly good examples. It is highly likely that both towns had regional market functions, possibly already from the earlier Roman period, although it was not until later that they started evolving into urbanised centres. Noviomagus was granted the *ius nundinarum* (market right) by Emperor Trajan, potentially in order to stimulate the economy. However, the many other large and small centres within the research region will also have had important market functions.

These observations underline the link between the emergence of a market system and that of a network of urban and rural centres from the earliest Roman period onwards. These centres were located at strategic locations and were well-connected by high-quality roads. They seem to have served as important nodes in the economic system that developed during the Roman period, attracting produce from the surrounding countryside, both for their own inhabitants and for further distribution. Central markets combined with a quality infrastructure are essential for the development of a more complex economic system.

5.1.2 MONETISATION AND THE NATURE OF EXCHANGE

Closely related to the development of a new economic infrastructure is the emergence of new practices of exchange, with the process of monetisation as a key aspect. This process involves the use of coins for impersonal exchange. This is not to say, however, that coins could not have been used in other spheres, such as ritual and religious domains.[8]

[5] On markets in peasant societies, see Wolf 1966, 40 ff.

[6] Wolf 1966, 42.

[7] De Ligt 1993, 117.

[8] For a discussion on coins and monetisation, see Aarts 2005.

Coins are not a Roman-period innovation; they are also known and were widely used in Late Iron Age societies within the research region. However, we observe a shift in the use of money that was highly embedded in social relationships of a personal nature to increasing use within commodity exchange and market situations, mainly involving impersonal exchanges.[9] In this situation, money, in the form of coins, had its true economic meaning as a portable and standardised means of exchange and payment. This shift in the use of coins is clearly linked to broader changes in production. Traditional communities were largely self-sufficient and exchange was personal and highly embedded in small-scale social structures. The significant changes in the economic reality of the developing provinces with their taxation system, large-scale military presence, emerging urban centres and markets eventually led to the integration of rural settlements into much wider spheres of exchange, reaching far beyond the local community and existing personal social relationships. Viewed in this light, the increasing use of money can be understood as an economic means of exchange. Once again, however, parallel to this kind of monetised exchange, more socially embedded modes of exchange continued to exist.

Similar patterns are identified in an anthropological model of exchange created by Bloch and Parry, who defined a short-term and a longer-term sphere of exchange.[10] The short-term sphere relates back to exchange in the domain of the individual, where social relations play a limited part, and where acquisition is paramount.[11] This form of exchange occurs mostly between independent actors and strangers. Conversely, the long-term sphere of exchange is about reproduction of the social and cosmic order. This is the domain of social structure that transcends the individual. Aarts argues that this model could be used to explain change in the Roman provinces. He does so by thinking in terms of shifting patterns in the ways these two spheres interacted with one another, rather than the progression from one mode of exchange to another, as is the case in the economic-historic model.[12] As previously argued, the short-term sphere of exchange will have gained particular importance during the first centuries AD. It was suggested in the previous chapter that this could also have had a significant effect on relationships within local communities. The interdependence of members of local communities weakened as they began participating in commercial cash-based economies, increasing the importance of wealth for the individual at the expense of producing for the continuity of the local community.

For the northern regions, Roymans argues that a key stimulus for monetisation and the commercialisation of exchange was actually the Roman army, by means of the commercial transactions made by native groups and payments to local auxiliary troops.[13] This caused a fundamental change in the significance of cattle, as the emphasis came to lie on their subsistence value.[14] Traditional economy, with its traditional values, initially seems to have been predominantly transformed by outsiders from Italy or southern Gaul, as they were not embedded in local values of exchange and were prepared to purchase and supply goods at markets in exchange for cash.[15] In doing so they broke the traditional barriers between the exchange of different categories of objects in the native world, and thus changed patterns of short-term and long-term exchange.

5.1.3 THE ARMY AS A CONSUMER

As already pointed out, an important aspect of the rapidly changing economic circumstances was the large-scale presence of the Roman army in the research region, especially in the northernmost parts where the heavily manned *limes* developed as a stable frontier from around the middle of the 1st

[9] Scheidel 2005.

[10] Aarts 2005; Bloch/Parry 1989.

[11] Aarts 2005, 13.

[12] Aarts 2005, 13-14.

[13] See Roymans 1996, 59.

[14] Roymans 1996, 59.

[15] Roymans 1996, 60.

Fig. 5.1. The Woerden grain ship during its excavation in 1978. Although the ship was not completely excavated, it could be established that it had contained a cargo of grain. After Haalebos 1997, 76.

century AD.[16] Already from the earliest Roman period, however, the army will have required considerable amounts of goods such as grain, hides, textiles or wool, wine and pottery for its soldiers. In terms of grain, the southern loess regions were probably the most important wheat suppliers. The fact that this wheat was actually transported to the Rhine *limes* is illustrated by the well-preserved ship of Woerden (Woerden ship 1; fig. 5.1), containing part of an original stock of grain.[17] Weeds found among the grains point to the loess region as the source of this cargo. The ship probably travelled the Rhine from Mainz and Cologne or via the Meuse to supply the *castella* along the *limes*.

Another source that sheds light on grain supply to the army are the votive stones that mention *negotiatores frumentarii* (grain traders) and *nautae* (shipsmen). A *frumentarius* was a grain trader in the service of the army or of a private entrepreneur. Carreras Monfort argues that *frumentarii* were used especially when supplies came from faraway regions.[18] An altar stone from Nijmegen (fig. 5.2) mentions a *negotiator frumentarius* from the *civitas* of the Nervii, situated in the fertile loess region around Bavay. This *frumentarius* is likely to have been involved in supplying army camps with grain.[19] Another inscription refers to the *nautae* from the *civitas* of the Tungri, of which Tongres was the capital. These shipmen may also have played a role in supplying the army companies with food from the fertile soils in their region of origin.

If we consider that the army was a substantial consumer, can this demand for grain be quantified? An initial calculation concerns the average quantity of grain per soldier per day. Anderson estimates this at between 0.9 and 1.36 kg.[20] Estimations based on ancient written sources result in essentially the same quantities. Anderson prefers to use the lower limit of 0.9 kg per day, as army companies were stationary, in contrast to expedition companies that would have needed more food. Assuming a figure of 0.9 kg, auxiliary forts like the ones found along the Lower Rhine *limes* would have required a total quantity of grain of around 432 kg per day, or 157.7 ton per year. Calculated for the Dutch river area,

[16] For a discussion on the economic impact of the army, see Roymans 1996; Groot *et al.* 2009; Stallibrass/Thomas 2008.

[17] Pals/Hakbijl 1992; Haalebos 1997.

[18] Carreras Monfort 2002, 776.

[19] Van Enckevort/Haalebos/Thijssen 2000, 51.

[20] Anderson 1992, 99.

Fig. 5.2. Two votive altars. The altar on the left is from Vechten, the one on the right from Nijmegen. After Hessing *et al.* 1997, 66 and Willems 1990, 68.

and assuming twenty auxiliary camps and one legionary camp,[21] a total supply of 14 ton per day or 5124.6 ton per year was required. For the entire Lower Rhine area, Roymans employs the figure of 42,000 soldiers at the time of Tiberius and a grain quota per soldier per year of between 200 and 496.4 kg.[22] This puts the demand at 8,400 to 21,000 tons of grain annually.

It is important to realise that this calculation is only a general indication of the army's demand for grain. In fact, if we were to include the need to feed livestock – chiefly horses – and the needs of civilians living in or just outside the camps, such as immediate family and perhaps even slaves, we would be talking about much higher quantities. Also missing from these calculations are military personnel stationed at smaller posts or moving from place to place.

If we link these findings to logistical requirements, assuming an estimated capacity of 50 to 70 tons for a ship like that of Woerden,[23] 73 to 102 ships fully laden with grain will have been needed each year to supply the army in the Dutch part of the *limes*. Significantly more grain and ships would have been required for the entire Lower Rhine *limes*.

5.1.4 THE TOWN AS A CONSUMER

Aside from the army, the growing numbers of non-agrarian civilians living in urban centres also formed a large consumer market. Unfortunately, it is difficult to find out how towns were supplied. A significant portion of this supply seems to have been dominated by an urban elite made up at least partly of large landowners from the surrounding countryside, controlling production by means of tenancy relationships and/or a directly dependent labour force.[24] Wealthy grain traders could sometimes

---

[21] Such a legionary camp was situated at Nijmegen between 70 and 105 AD. A total of 6000 men is generally assumed for these camps.

[22] Roymans 1996, 59.

[23] Mees/Pferdehirt 2002, 34.

[24] De Ligt 1993, 211-212.

also play a role in urban supply. However, Roman law tried to prevent the accumulation of large stocks by large landowners and traders.[25] Nor should the role of small farmers be underestimated. Literary sources suggest that urban supply could be severely disrupted if these farmers stayed away from the market for some reason.[26] As these sources originate from the eastern Roman empire, however, it is difficult to assess whether this situation also applied to the research region relevant to this study. Large landowners probably focused chiefly on large-scale grain production, while smaller farmers also supplied towns with products such as eggs, milk and wool.

5.1.5 THE INTRODUCTION OF A SYSTEM OF TAXATION

A formal system of direct taxation was introduced in the research region under the reign of Augustus. According to Hopkins, this system stimulated the development of complex interprovincial networks of trade and encouraged agrarian production, resulting in commercialisation and monetisation of various sectors of the native economies. This particularly applied to those controlled by native elites via traditional mechanisms for the centralisation of an agrarian surplus. Hopkins consequently argues that taxation was the key mechanism boosting a market-oriented agrarian production.[27]

Roymans, however, emphasises that Hopkins underestimates the free selling of agrarian surplus at urban and military markets for money.[28] He argues that it is this free selling that seems to have formed the financial basis of urban and rural building activities. He also argues that in a number of regions, especially in the north, taxation took the form of the supply of auxiliary troops. Other regions probably also supplied soldiers, supplemented by grain or pastoral products, depending on the regional economic focus. The tribes in the southwest part of Gallia Belgica were primarily taxed in wheat. In conclusion we can say that the general impact of the 1st-century AD Roman taxation system on the native agrarian economies was not that it generated new regional patterns, but that it strengthened already existing regional differences.[29]

5.2 MARKET ORIENTATION AND DEVELOPMENTS IN AGRARIAN PRODUCTION

Having explored a number of broader economic developments, I will now focus on agricultural production at the level of the rural settlement. Again, the reconstruction and understanding of development and change are a central objective, and I have once again opted for a longer-term approach. Below I will discuss developments in crop and animal spectra, exploring both general development trends and more radical transformations. Can we identify general processes of specialisation, intensification, the introduction of new crops and breeds? Is it possible to elucidate the economic development trajectories of individual settlements?

[25] De Ligt 1993, 211-212.

[26] De Ligt 1993, 212.

[27] See Roymans 1996; Hopkins 1980.

[28] Roymans 1996, 87.

[29] Roymans 1996, 87.

More so than architecture, agricultural practice is intimately related to the rural settlement's immediate environment. As a result, we should be cautious about generalising within the extensive and geographically highly diverse research region. For the sake of clarity, however, a general geographical distinction is maintained between the northern sand and clay soils (covering the Dutch region and Flanders) and the more southerly loess soils.

A general picture can be painted of pre-Roman agricultural practice. On the northern sand and clay soils the crop spectrum was dominated by barley, emmer wheat, oats and millet.[30] Traces of spelt wheat, linseed and gold-of-pleasure are also documented there, but these seem to have been marginal crops. On the loess soils, emmer wheat and hulled barley dominated, followed by spelt wheat and millet, resulting in a picture quite similar to the sand and clay regions.[31] Bread wheat was known in this period, but did not become a major crop until the Roman period.

As early as the Late Iron Age, some significant developments in agriculture and the crop spectrum can be pinpointed, including a rise in the number of crops and the growing importance of spelt wheat. For the German Rhineland, a clear increase in agricultural activity can be reconstructed from around 300 BC.[32] The high percentage of narrowleaf plantain indicates land that has been ploughed frequently. Changing patterns of land use could also be documented on the basis of pollen diagrams.[33] Forest coverage had clearly declined in comparison to earlier periods. For the Late Iron Age, we can reconstruct an almost entirely deforested, open landscape with intensive agriculture and scattered remainders of oak forest.[34] Looking at the crop spectrum, we find that at the settlements of Hambach 382 and Eschweiler-Laurenzberg, dated to the 1st century BC, barley and emmer wheat were still the dominant crops, while millet had lost its importance. Spelt wheat and naked barley were also grown, but were marginal within the spectrum.[35]

In the Roman period, both continuities and significant changes can be documented with regard to arable farming. In the northern sandy regions, there seems to have been little significant change. At the settlement of Oss-Westerveld barley, emmer wheat, spelt wheat and millet were grown, as well as flax and turnip.[36] At Wijk bij Duurstede and Tiel in the Dutch River area, hulled barley and emmer wheat remained the most important crops throughout the Roman period, while at Houten-Tiellandt, threshing waste, dated to the 1st century AD, consisted of a mixture of oats, barley and wheat.[37] Van Beurden states that a continuous line can be reconstructed with regard to arable farming in the MDS region. Barley generally remained the dominant crop and, on the basis of botanical studies, no agricultural intensification was documented.[38] A similar conclusion can be drawn for the Menapian region in sandy Flanders. At Bruges-Refuge the crop spectrum was similar to the pre-Roman spectrum, with emmer wheat, spelt wheat, millet and oats being grown there.[39] For this region in general, there are no indications that arable farming aimed to produce a considerable surplus.[40]

[30] Van Wijngaarden-Bakker/Brinkkemper 2005, 507 (table 22.5); Van Hoof 2007; Roymans 1996, 49-50.

[31] At the well-documented site of Maasbracht, wild barley, emmer wheat, millet, gold-of-pleasure and also lentil, oats, rye and wheat were documented for the Late Iron Age/Early Roman period (Kooistra 1996, 253 ff.). For Late Iron Age agrarian production, see also Roymans 1996, 49-50.

[32] Meurers-Balke/Kalis 2006, 274-275.

[33] Meurers-Balke/Kalis 2006, 267-276.

[34] Bunnik 1995. It has also been established for more south-

erly regions, like the Saar-Mosel region, that large-scale deforestation associated with intensified land use started as early as the Iron Age. During the Roman period, no significant increase in the use of agricultural land could be documented (Wiethold 2000).

[35] Meurers-Balke/Kalis 2006, 275.

[36] Wesselingh 2000, 71-169.

[37] Groot *et al.* 2009; Kooistra 1996, 119, 300-306.

[38] Van Beurden 2002, 305.

[39] Cooremans/Desender/Ervynck/Schelvis 1997-1998.

[40] De Clercq/Van Dierendonck 2008, 12.

On the loess soils, the story is somewhat different. At Pulheim-Brauweiler, spelt wheat had already secured an important position within the crop spectrum during the Early Roman period.[41] During this early period, however, crops such as millet and gold-of-pleasure, typical of the pre-Roman period, also continued as part of the spectrum. During the following period, though, their proportions declined significantly. The still dominant position of barley in combination with the small quantities of emmer wheat, millet and gold-of-pleasure indicate a transitional situation, characterised by a crop spectrum that had Late Iron Age characteristics but also showed clear indications of change. This latter observation implies that agricultural developments were a gradual rather than radical transformation. In general, spelt wheat increasingly became the focus during the Roman period, as it could be produced efficiently in large quantities. As the newly introduced grain species were more efficient, millet, oats and rye disappeared.[42] This is a clear sign of the specialisation and intensification of production, especially from the second half of the 1st century AD onwards. This observation is underlined by the Cerealia curve peaking between 50 and 220 AD.[43]

One of the settlements where these processes of intensification and specialisation can be reconstructed is Voerendaal-Ten Hove. While wheat had already become the predominant crop during the second half of the 1st century AD, further specialisation in spelt wheat can be documented for the 2nd century.[44] Regarding this latter period, the presence of a large threshing floor, the construction of a large *horreum* and clear signs of soil erosion also indicate the intensification of arable farming. Similar specialisation in spelt wheat can be documented for the settlement of Kerkrade-Holzkuil, not far from Voerendaal.

Nevertheless, there are also indications that we should not overestimate changes in the crop spectrum, especially during the 1st century AD. In Early Roman Tongres, there are no clear signs suggesting changes in the Iron Age crop spectrum. The same applies to the Aisne valley.[45] And in the more southerly Saar-Mosel region, little new land was taken into agricultural production, suggesting only negligible changes to the crop spectrum and the nature of production.[46]

Aside from arable farming, livestock farming was also a vital part of the rural economy. I will now explore archaeozoological data to discuss the character and relative importance of animal husbandry through time and throughout the research region. Unfortunately, both sand and loess soils – and thus the majority of the research region – are generally unsuitable for the good conservation of bone material, limiting the extent and usability of the dataset.

In both the pre-Roman and Roman periods, the most important members of the animal spectrum were cattle, pigs, sheep or goats, horses and dogs. Chickens, donkeys and cats seem to have been introduced during the Roman period. As was the case with arable farming, however, there was considerable differentiation across the research region.

During the pre-Roman period, the cattle element was especially dominant in the northern regions, with sheep, goats and pigs occupying subordinate positions within the animal spectrum.[47] The predominance of livestock farming within these northern economies is clearly illustrated by the presence of byre houses, where people and animals – as an essential part of the economic subsistence basis – lived under one roof.[48] In the southerly loess regions, the pattern may have been somewhat different.

[41] Andrikopoulou-Strack *et al.* 2000.

[42] Eck 2004, 427 ff.

[43] Bunnik 1995, 337.

[44] Kooistra 1996, 181-182.

[45] Cooremans/Desender/Ervynck/Schelvis 2002, 217.

[46] Wiethold 2000.

[47] Lauwerier 1988; Laarman 1996. Roymans mentions a relative figure for cattle of 50% to 90% of the animal spectrum (Roymans 1996, 51).

[48] Even clearer specialisation in animal husbandry can be found in the Dutch peat areas. In the other cases, settlements had mixed economies, combining agriculture and animal husbandry (Van Wijngaarden-Bakker/Brinkkemper 2005, 507 ff.). For a discussion on the importance of livestock and cattle in particular, see Roymans 1996.

At the Late Iron Age settlement at Haccourt, sheep predominated, with pigs occupying second place and cattle only third in the spectrum.[49] The significant position of sheep within the spectrum was also suggested for pre-Roman settlements in the French region.[50]

Regarding the Roman period, it is possible to reconstruct some developments with regard to livestock farming. A few of the best archaeozoologically studied settlements are those in the northernmost part of the research region: Tiel, Wijk bij Duurstede, Houten and Geldermalsen.[51] Bone is especially well preserved in the clay soils on which these settlements were situated.[52] During the first half of the 1st century AD, the animal spectrum at Wijk bij Duurstede consisted predominantly of cattle, small percentages of sheep or goats, horses and pigs. From the second half of that century onwards, however, the percentage of horses rose dramatically (up to a third of the animal spectrum), probably indicating specialist horse breeding. Such specialisation can be associated with the Roman army, which would have required over a thousand replacement horses every year (calculated for the military in Germania Inferior). Specialised production could also be identified at Tiel, in this case in sheep for wool, dated to the 1st century and first half of the 2nd century AD. Sheep seem to have already been kept during pre-Roman times. The settlement specialised in sheep breeding for wool production, probably as a result of the military demand for wool. After around 150 AD, however, the decline of sheep and the increasing number of horse bones seems to indicate a shift in economic focus from wool production to horse breeding.[53] Both Wijk bij Duurstede and Tiel may also have produced surplus cattle, although Groot emphasises that no specialised production of beef was needed to meet the demand.[54]

Compared to these northern regions, animal husbandry seems to have been less important in the loess regions. Studying the Cologne hinterland, Eck even stated that animal husbandry did not go beyond subsistence level.[55] Pollen diagrams give relatively little indication of the presence of open grassland or meadows. Nevertheless, a number of changes to the animal spectrum can be noted. As early as the early 1st century AD, cattle became more prominent in the animal spectrum. In the Cologne region, they were responsible for up to 90% of meat supply.[56] In another study, King presents figures for Gallia Belgica and Germania Inferior, putting the relative importance of cattle at 65% and 60% or more respectively.[57] This trend is also evident at a number of individual settlements. At Broekom, a comparison of the Late Iron Age with the Flavian period documented a clear jump in cattle numbers and a decline in sheep or goat numbers.[58] And in the more southerly Rhine-Danube region, cattle also rose in importance during the Roman period. Peters links this increase to the military's growing need for meat, milk and cowhides.[59] A somewhat different picture emerges from Cologne-Müngersdorf, one of the earliest archaeozoologically researched villa settlements. According to Fremersdorf, pigs and sheep were especially important there. The interpretation of secondary buildings as separate byres for cattle, sheep, pigs and horses underlines the supposed importance of animal husbandry within this settlement.[60] However, the interpretation of both the archaeozoological data and the buildings should at least be critically reassessed.

Horses were not generally a frequently documented species in the settlements of the loess region. Eck argues, however, that they may have been bred in larger numbers in the Eifel region.[61] Furthermore, the position of pigs within the animal spectrum remained stable, although they were slaughtered at a younger age, which may indicate that they were increasingly being kept for meat. It is remarkable

[49] López Bayón 1997.

[50] Malrain/Matterne/Méniel 2002, 112.

[51] Groot et al. 2009; Kooistra 1996, 291.

[52] Groot et al. 2009; Groot 2007.

[53] Groot 2007, 190.

[54] Groot 2007, 91.

[55] Eck 2004, 431.

[56] Becker 2007, 137.

[57] King 2001.

[58] Vanvinckenroye 1988, 37-42.

[59] Peters 1994, 39.

[60] Fremersdorf 1933, 122 ff.

[61] In this context, he discusses a veterinarian from Blankenheim (Eck 2004, 430).

that at Voerendaal, Maasbracht, Kerkrade and Broekom the proportion of pigs exceeded that of sheep and goats (although cattle always remained dominant).[62] Perhaps this was associated with changing tastes in food, as pork was the meat of choice in the Roman world. High percentages of pork were also associated with rich houses in the urban centre of Tongres.[63] With regard to sheep, it is interesting that they seem to have been the dominant species in the most southerly part of the research region. This can probably be explained in the light of the important textile industry that characterised the region.[64]

Detailed bone studies also demonstrate that animals themselves changed over time. While indigenous cattle had a height of around 100-115 cm, from the Early Roman period onwards we find cattle up to 140 cm high.[65] Over the 1st century AD, the number of larger cattle increased considerably and, by the 2nd century, larger species had almost completely replaced their smaller counterparts.[66] In the Lower Rhine region, however, this process was somewhat less far-reaching, with the percentage of larger species not exceeding 50%.[67] The fact that not only cattle, but also sheep, goats and pigs increased in size during the Roman period has been demonstrated with regard to northern France by Lepetz.[68]

5.2.2 ECONOMIC DEVELOPMENT TRAJECTORIES OF INDIVIDUAL SETTLEMENTS

It is possible to reconstruct specific economic development trajectories for some settlements. Those at Tiel-Passewaaij and Wijk bij Duurstede-De Horden have already been mentioned. The former specialised in sheep breeding for wool production during the 1st and first half of the 2nd century AD, before shifting its focus to horse breeding. The settlement at Wijk bij Duurstede focused on horse breeding from as early as the 1st century AD. Economic reorientation could also be suggested for the settlement of Hambach 512. During the earliest settlement phase, the presence of two or three byres, probably byre houses combining residential with byre functions, indicated an important role for livestock farming. In the second settlement phase, however, the number of byres declined and the size of the granary grew, indicating a shift from stock farming to arable farming, according to Kaszab-Olschewski; at the same time, the settlement compound became smaller, as fewer animals were kept.[69]

An all-round style of farming was practised at Voerendaal-Ten Hove before the end of the 1st century AD.[70] From the early 2nd century onwards, however, there is evidence of an increasing emphasis on arable farming, with a particular focus on the growing of spelt wheat. Apart from this specialisation, intensification is indicated by increased erosion, the construction of a large *horreum* and a threshing floor.

For the settlement of Champion-Le Emptinne, a focus on beef production (cattle breeding) was reconstructed for the period up until the second half of the 2nd century. From the late 2nd century onwards, however, this emphasis seems to have shifted towards sheep breeding and then wool production.[71] Unfortunately, little is known about arable farming for this settlement, so the relative importance of stock farming remains unclear; however, the fairly large number of byre houses could be indicative. In this light it is interesting to note that similar types of house were also found in several villa settlements near Champion – Hamois-Le Hody and Vezin. Did stock farming also play a fairly major role in these settlements? If so, this relative importance of stock farming may have been char-

[62] Kooistra 1996, 253 ff; Tichelman 2005, 305.

[63] Pigière/Ervynck/Van Neer 2006, 40-43.

[64] See Agache 1978, 358-359.

[65] Peters 1994.

[66] See Hegewisch (2007, 138-139) for an overview of this process in the German Rhineland; Eck 2004, 427 ff.

[67] Becker 2007, 133-143.

[68] Lepetz 1996.

[69] Kaszab-Olschewski 2006, 108, 222.

[70] Kooistra 1996, 182.

[71] Van Ossel/Defgnee 2001, 177-178.

acteristic of the Condroz region where these settlements were situated. Compared to the loess plains, the stronger relief and less fertile soils would have favoured a more mixed production, increasing the importance of stock farming at the expense of arable farming.

5.2.3 QUANTIFYING PRODUCTION: ESTIMATES OF SURPLUS SIZE

With developments identified on a qualitative level, is it possible to quantify changes in production and shed some light on the potential production of surpluses?

Kooistra has constructed quantitative production models for a number of villa settlements in the Dutch and German loess region. Examining the size of byres and granaries, she concluded that byres in German villa settlements could hold an average of 24 head of cattle. In addition, granaries (with an average surface area of 56 m^2) could store 15,400 kg of spelt wheat, 12,208 kg of emmer wheat, or 17,472 kg of barley (produced on 50 ha of land). This capacity exceeded the settlements' own demand by over five times.[72] The 36 m^2 granary at the axially organised settlement of Champion is calculated to have had a capacity of 10 tons.[73] For the villas in the Dutch loess region, Kooistra states that the seven villa settlements in the Heerlen valley had a production capacity to feed 700 to 2,800 people.[74]

From another perspective, the land's yield ratio (i.e. how much sowing yields how much grain) is a key factor. Kooistra presents an example of Canadian pioneers who used 200 kg of grain to sow one hectare of land, yielding 1000 kg of grain and resulting in a yield ratio of 5. Eck states that the yield ratio could be between 4 and 15, depending on the quality of the soil. This figure implies a yield of between 0.4 and 3.6 tons of grains per hectare. The annual production potential of the Cologne territory, with a land area of around 400,000 hectares, about half of which was probably not used for grain production, will therefore have been between 80,000 and 720,000 tons of grain. From a demand perspective, employing figures of one kg of grain per person per day and a population of 150,000 for the Cologne territory, including the army, it is clear that production will certainly have considerably exceeded the regional subsistence level.[75] Despite the uncertainties associated with such calculations, we may conclude that this region was probably quite capable of producing large surpluses for export. The fact that grain production did in fact take place on a large scale is underlined by the already mentioned Cerealia curve, peaking between 50 and 220 AD, exactly the period when the *colonia* at Cologne flourished.[76]

5.3 EXPLORING THE SPATIAL ARCHITECTURAL AND SOCIAL DIMENSIONS OF PRODUCTION

Having focused on rural production in general terms, I will now turn my attention to the theme of production within the context of the settlement. This section will attempt to shed light on the organisation of production, both on a spatial architectural and a social level. The focus of study will be the category of secondary buildings, which has so far been little discussed. In addition to the houses explored above, these buildings were an integral and essential part of rural settlements. Thus in order to gain a better understanding of how rural settlements functioned, we also need to explore this category.

First of all, we will attempt to shed some light on this elusive category of secondary buildings with economic functions, as well as on the development of 'economic compounds'. Secondly, the specific

---

[72] Kooistra 1996, 101.

[73] Van Ossel/Defgnee 2001, 232 (note 102).

[74] Kooistra 1996, 126-127.

[75] Eck 2004, 428.

[76] Bunnik 1995, 337.

group of storage buildings generally referred to as granaries or *horrea* will be discussed. Unlike the general category of secondary buildings, these storage buildings are fairly readily identifiable and can help elucidate both developments in production and production organisation. Once again the development perspective is the central approach of this section. How are new production strategies, new objectives and techniques developed and integrated within the settlement by creating new structures of production (involving both the reorganisation of settlement space and the creation of new buildings)?

5.3.1 SECONDARY BUILDINGS AND THE ECONOMIC COMPOUND

The creation of a simple dichotomy between the main house and secondary buildings is common practice within villa studies. Secondary buildings are assumed to have been important elements in the rural settlements as an agricultural unit. As was established in the third chapter, however, interpretational problems are paramount, making it difficult to reconstruct the purposes of individual buildings and settlements as a whole. In many cases, buildings that could (hypothetically) be interpreted as houses are also included in the broad category of secondary buildings.[77] Furthermore, it seems likely that some buildings will have had both residential and production functions. We will focus here on secondary buildings with production purposes.

Rural settlements were locations of production. Land was worked, sown and harvested outside the settlement compound, while crops were predominantly processed and stored within the compound. Animals could be kept in byres, let loose on the compound or herded out in the fields or on the fallow lands. It is likely that milk, meat and dung were processed on the compound as well. Artisan production, such as the manufacture and repair of tools, also took place within the settlement. Is it possible to identify these activities within settlements as reflected in the structure of an 'economic compound'? Also, how did this economic compound evolve in relation to the developments previously reconstructed?

During the later Iron Age and earliest Roman period, settlements seem to have been mainly organised on the level of the individual farmstead. These farmsteads consisted of a house and a number of secondary structures. As already mentioned several times, byres in the northern regions tended to be integrated into the house, with quite a few small four- or six-post structures also often found outside the house. These are generally referred to as granaries (*spiekers* in Dutch or *Speichers* in German), and are assumed to have been used for the storage of crops.[78] It is nevertheless possible that morphologically similar structures may have served a variety of purposes; they might in fact have been multifunctional.[79] The somewhat larger post-built structures are even more difficult to interpret. For example, should two buildings at Frimmersdorf 129, with floor areas of 24 and 35 m² respectively (see fig 5.3), be interpreted as byres, sheds, large granaries or even simple residences? Pion has argued that the only credible functional distinction for such buildings is that between small structures with four to nine posts and larger structures with more posts and much more varied plans.[80]

Thus for the pre-Roman and Early Roman periods, buildings with economic functions were simple, small and probably at least partly multi-functional. Throughout the research region crops were stored in small granaries situated close to each house. Economic practice thus seems to have been

---

[77] See for example Heimberg 2002/2003.

[78] Such small structures were found in most pre-Roman and Early Roman-period rural settlements throughout the research region, including Hambach 412, Frimmersdorf 129, Hordain, Verneuil-en-Halatte, Tiel-Passewaaij, Beauvais-Le Brin de Glaine, Wijk bij Duurstede-De

Horden, Jüchen-Neuholz and Pulheim-Brauweiler.

[79] At Pulheim-Brauweiler, two simple post-built structures (9 and 13 m² floor area respectively) were interpreted as byres or sheds (Andrikopoulou-Strack *et al.* 2000).

[80] Pion 1996, 90.

small-scale, predominantly based on the level of the individual farmstead and the individual family. Each family seems to have kept livestock and grown and harvested crops that they stored in their own small storage buildings.

From the 1st century AD onwards, however, both the organisation of settlement space and house building changed considerably. In the previous chapter, these developments were linked to significant changes in the social relationships between people within the household, local community and broader society. If we now focus on production and secondary buildings, how did both these buildings and the 'economic compound' develop over time?

The excavation of secondary buildings within villa settlements is a relatively recent phenomenon. An exception here is the excavation at Cologne-Müngersdorf, where a complete settlement compound including all its secondary buildings was unearthed in the 1920s.[81] As mentioned earlier, excavator Fremersdorf attempted to make sense of the complete settlement, where agricultural activities had evidently taken place, on the basis of the form of these secondary buildings, combined with the outcomes of the archaeozoological study carried out there. Interpretations of secondary buildings within the many more recently excavated settlements tend to be somewhat less bold. In many cases, no functional interpretations are made at all. Here, I would like to present a short overview of the variety of secondary buildings and their possible functions. This is by no means intended as an exhaustive review. Its key goal is to gain some insight into general trends with regard to secondary buildings.

Heimberg has produced a useful overview of secondary buildings (*Wirtschaftsgebäude*) between the Rhine and Meuse.[82] Although she focused on buildings with economic functions, a number of secondary houses with at least partially domestic functions were also included (such as those at Hambach 512). The typological overview makes a distinction between post-built structures, post-built structures with partly stone foundations, stone-built structures and granaries. The category of post-built structures included small four-, six- and nine-post structures and a category of larger rectangular buildings, partly with internal posts (often around 20 m in length or even more). More likely in some cases than in others, this latter category could be interpreted as houses or byre houses. Belonging to another category, the plans of buildings with partial stone foundations could generally not be reconstructed in detail. Heimberg suggests a byre function for such buildings. Alternatively, in some cases it could be argued that the sections on stone foundations may be reconstructed as residences and the post-built sections as byres, but this remains highly hypothetical. The secondary buildings on stone foundations were generally rectangular or squarish, while their degree of internal segregation varied substantially. One special category is that of long-rectangular buildings (around 20 m or even larger) on stone foundations with protruding buttresses.[83] The precise location of these buttresses ranges from exclusively on the inside of the wall, to exclusively on the outside and on both the inside and outside. It remains unclear, however, whether this phenomenon can be associated with the building's function. Although a storage function has been suggested for many of these buildings, other functions were documented as well. At Voerendaal, a rectangular building with buttresses was associated with iron working and in some other cases byre functions have been suggested. Buttresses can also be found in houses, such as at Cologne-Braunsfeld, Jüchen-Neuholz, Hambach 23 and Rijswijk-De Bult. And when a development trajectory could be reconstructed, it appears that buttresses were situated at the places where support-

[81] Fremersdorf 1933. Other, highly monumental complexes, such as those at Anthée and Blankenheim had also been fully excavated, but no economic interpretations were made.

[82] Heimberg 2002/2003, 110 ff.

[83] Fig. 5.3 presents examples from Hambach 132 and Voerendaal, but similar buildings were also documented at quite a few sites, including Hambach 133, Seclin, Cologne-Müngersdorf, Kerkrade-Holzkuil, Saint-Gerard-Try Hallot, Nivelles, Jüchen-Neuholz and Champion-Le Emptinne.

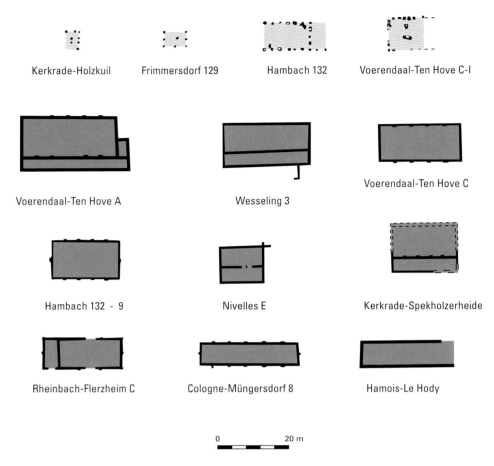

Kerkrade-Holzkuil   Frimmersdorf 129   Hambach 132   Voerendaal-Ten Hove C-I

Voerendaal-Ten Hove A   Wesseling 3   Voerendaal-Ten Hove C

Hambach 132 - 9   Nivelles E   Kerkrade-Spekholzerheide

Rheinbach-Flerzheim C   Cologne-Müngersdorf 8   Hamois-Le Hody

0   20 m

Fig. 5.3. A selection of secondary buildings from rural settlement throughout the research region. The wooden buildings in the top row can be dated to the 1st century AD. The other buildings, on stone foundations, can be dated to the 2nd century AD.

ing posts stood when the building was still constructed with posts set in postholes (see fig. 5.4). It thus seems that these buildings in fact represented the translation of a traditional type of building into a new technique.[84] The opposing pairs of supporting posts were no longer set in postholes; instead, they were set on stone buttresses, connected by a low foundation wall. Viewed from this perspective, the use of buttresses seems a more general building technique, applied in a range of buildings with probably different functions rather than being related to a specific building function.

Another, rather varied category of buildings is interpreted as byres by their excavators. Quite comparable buildings were found at Voerendaal (building A) and Wesseling (building 3; see fig 5.3), characterised by a long narrow space fronting a larger rectangular room. Also similar is the building at Kerkrade-Spekholzerheide, for which no function was reconstructed. For two other, consecutive buildings from Voerendaal (buildings C-I (1st century) and C (2nd century); see fig. 5.3) a byre function was also suggested. With the rebuilding of the post-built structure, the dimensions were preserved in the stone foundations with buttresses (quite parallel to what was documented for one of the buildings at Champion-Le Emptinne; see fig. 5.4). Two different, remarkably long, rectangular and narrow buildings, documented at Cologne-Müngersdorf and Hamois-Le Hody, have been identified as sheep

[84] See also the developments of the house at Rijswijk-De
Bult (see section 3.3.1) and the building at Bocholtz
(Hiddink/De Boer 2003).

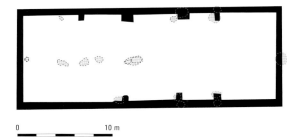

Fig. 5.4. Two phases of one of the secondary buildings at Champion-Le Emptinne. The building on stone foundations is a literal translation of the wooden structure, whereby the exact dimensions were preserved. Unlike the two-aisled post-built structure, the building on stone foundations is single-aisled.

0   10 m

byres. Perhaps the similar building at Lez-Roux-Les Fosses could also be interpreted as such.

Although typological studies like that of Heimberg are useful, they ignore the factor of time and the theme of development. Reconstructing the development of secondary buildings may shed more light on the variety of secondary buildings as well as on changes in production and its organisation. Unfortunately, less detailed data on developments is available for these secondary buildings than for the houses explored in the third chapter. We can nevertheless shed light on their development in some cases.

In the two well-excavated settlements of Jüchen-Neuholz and Pulheim-Brauweiler, small four- and six-post structures functioned as secondary buildings with economic functions during the Early Roman period. When an enclosed compound was created at Jüchen in around the middle of the 1st century AD, these types of secondary structures were still being built. Thus when two larger rectangular buildings were constructed in the second half of the 1st century, it is unclear whether one should be interpreted as a secondary building with economic functions or whether we should regard both as multi-functional or domestic structures. In the larger 2nd-century compound settlement, apart from the main house, two larger rectangular buildings were constructed, one of the well-known type with stone foundations and buttresses, the other post-built. A function as shed is suggested for the latter.[85] At Pulheim, at least two larger secondary buildings were constructed when the settlement was reorganised as a compound settlement in the early 2nd century. One of these buildings could possibly be interpreted as a shed or garage for a cart.[86] For some settlements, it could be established that the development of post-built secondary buildings into structures on stone foundations took place in a phase after the initial monumentalisation of the main house. At Voerendaal-Ten Hove, for example, the main house was built in stone around the middle of the 1st century AD, while the secondary buildings were rebuilt with stone foundations during the large-scale reorganisation of the complex in the early 2nd century. And at Kerkrade-Holzkuil, it was not until the late 2nd or early 3rd century that the secondary buildings were rebuilt on stone foundations.[87]

Examining the dataset, we see considerable variation in secondary buildings in rural settlements. The secondary buildings of some settlements developed into rather complex and monumental structures, while those of others remained fairly basic and traditional. This variation can potentially be linked to the degree of specialisation and intensification of production at these settlements. While the secondary buildings remained simple at Champion-Le Emptinne, Hamois-Le Hody and many smaller German compound settlements, at settlements such as Voerendaal and Blankenheim they were rebuilt as more complex and new types of buildings on stone foundations.

Apart from this variation, however, we observe a general trend towards differentiation and speciali- sation in activities. The range of secondary buildings increased significantly and activities that were

[85] Andrikopoulou-Strack *et al.* 1999, 156.

[86] Andrikopoulou-Strack *et al.* 2000, 431-432.

[87] A number of simple post-built granaries and a 10 m long two-aisled building interpreted as a shed (building 5; see Tichelman 2005, 114-116).

probably carried out in or around the house in earlier times were now housed in special buildings. It seems that animals kept outside during earlier periods now tended to be kept in byres. And if the interpretation is correct, specialised byres were built for cattle, horses, pigs and sheep. At Tiel-Passewaaij and Wijk bij Duurstede-De Horden, a number of buildings representing new types were interpreted as horse byres.[88] And at Hoogeloon, a wooden corral for keeping cattle or horses can probably be associated with the monumental house.[89] These developments are probably connected with the breeding of animals for the market in more coordinated and specialised ways, while some other structures may be associated with the storage of growing numbers of agricultural tools and even carts.

Another factor is centralisation. Organised compound settlements seem to have been coherent economic units. Production was organised at the level of the compound that potentially contained several houses and secondary buildings. The large storage buildings and specialised byres found in these settlements were not connected with separate farms but were part of a single economic compound controlled by the dominant family living in the often monumental residence. In the northern regions, the situation tended to be somewhat different. Generally, production there still seems to have been organised on the level of the farmstead. In fact, no real coherent compound settlements arose within this particular area.

5.3.2 DEVELOPMENTS IN STORAGE FACILITIES AS AN INDICATOR OF ECONOMIC CHANGE

One category of secondary buildings that lends itself well to study is that of storage structures. These can be quite directly linked to arable production, as they contained the harvested crops. This section will focus on these buildings and their development and position within rural settlements in particular.

Grain especially needs to be stored in dry, airy and cool places (below 15 degrees celsius), away from any vermin. As already described, traditional granaries tended to be the small four- or six-post structures, reconstructed by archaeologists as supporting a raised platform with walls and roof, found in almost all pre-Roman and early Roman rural settlements. The often sizeable number of granaries documented near farms indicates that it is likely that they were frequently rebuilt.

Besides the already explored developments in settlement organisation and house building, it is also apparent that storage buildings were often subject to considerable change. This may be associated with changing production strategies, changing storage practices and evolving socio-economic relationships within the settlements. Figures 5.5a and b present a selection of storage structures within the research region. For some sites, it was possible to reconstruct a development trajectory. In general, pre-Roman and Early Roman period settlements boasted simple four- or six-post granaries. This is the case not only at northern settlements like Tiel-Passewaaij, Oss-Westerveld and Rijswijk-De Bult, but also at for instance Verneuil and Seclin, settlements situated in the southern regions that would later develop into larger, highly organised complexes. Throughout the research area, new types of storage buildings were constructed from around the middle of the 1st century AD onwards. In the northern sand and clay region, new types of wooden storage buildings emerged. These consisted of a core of posts, set in either post-holes or ditches, with an ambulatory of posts around it. Such structures can be found at for example Oss-Westerveld, Houten-Tiellandt and Tiel-Passewaaij (see fig. 5.5a).[90] Some scholars have suggested a military influence behind this new type of granary.[91] A somewhat different type of storage

[88] Heeren 2009, 172-173; Vos 2009, 85-86; Groot 2008, 83-84; Groot et al. 2009, 250; Groot in press.

[89] Jeneson 2004.

[90] Such a structure can probably also be identified at Hoo-

geloon. It was originally interpreted as part of a house, but clearly resembles storage buildings like those of Houten and Oss.

[91] Heeren 2009, 237.

Fig. 5.5a. Examples of storage building development trajectories within the research region.

building evolved on one of the farmsteads within the settlement of Rijswijk–De Bult (fig. 5.5a). During the 1st and early 2nd century AD, a traditional type of granary existed, consisting of two rows of posts (four and five posts respectively). Larger and sturdier buildings were constructed in subsequent development phases. The first consisted of three parallel ditches in which posts were set. An even larger one was then built, the now four parallel ditches being filled with stone material, potentially to support horizontal construction beams. The youngest structure, consisting of a core structure and an

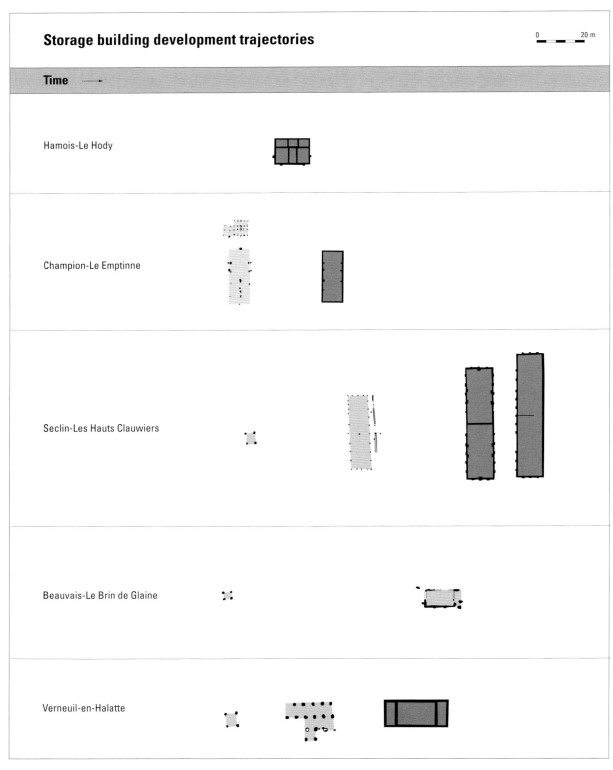

Fig. 5.5b. Examples of storage building development trajectories within the research region.

ambulatory of posts, was originally interpreted as a temple by the author. However, its similarities to other granaries have led others to suggest that it served as a granary instead.[92]

---

[92]   Derks 1998, Heeren 2009.

The monumentalisation of storage buildings went even further in settlements in the loess region. At Hambach 512, a granary with parallel foundation ditches, in which the reconstruction suggests that horizontal foundations beams were placed, was dated to the first half of the 2nd century.[93] Then, in the second half of the 2nd century, a multi-roomed storage building on stone foundations was built on the same location (fig. 5.5a). This building had a surface area four times larger than the post-built structure. Relatively similar multi-roomed storage buildings on stone foundations were also documented at Hamois-Le Hody and Hambach 132. The one at Hamois has not been dated, while that at Hambach 132 was imprecisely dated between the late 1st and early 3rd century AD.[94] This specific type of building can even be found outside the research region, notably in France and Switzerland.[95]

Another type of storage buildings on stone foundations are those with rectangular plans, such as the ones documented at Hambach 127, Jülich-Kirchberg, Voerendaal-Ten Hove and Verneuil-en-Halatte (figs 5.5a and b). In the first three cases, internal supports were documented that carried the raised floor needed to protect the stored crops from moisture and vermin. The building at Jülich was divided into two identical rooms. In the other cases, the buildings had one large and one or two smaller rooms. A development trajectory could be reconstructed for Verneuil (see fig. 5.5b). In the earliest, Augustan-Tiberian phases of the settlement, granaries were small and post-built. Then in the Claudian period, a very large post-built storage building was erected on the working compound. Subsequently, during the Flavian period, a long-rectangular building on stone foundations was built at the same location.

At Kerkrade-Holzkuil, a number of smaller post-built structures dated to the earlier settlement phases can be interpreted as granaries. For the later phase, a large rectangular, single-aisled building (building 1), constructed on square stone material footings, may possibly be identified as a granary.[96]

At Seclin, a large post-built structure has been identified for no clear reason as a storage building.[97] During a later phase, two larger buildings with buttresses were constructed on stone foundations. These buildings together provide a remarkably larger storage capacity that cannot be explained in terms of the nature and size of the settlement. Perhaps we should be cautious about interpreting these two buildings as granaries.

Some of the storage buildings had buttresses protruding from their walls. As mentioned previously, buttresses have often been associated with storage functions. One possibility is that they were used to support an overhanging roof that kept the walls of the building dry and thus guaranteed dry storage conditions for crops.[98] Another interpretation as reinforcements to cope with the horizontal pressure created by stored crops also suggests a potential storage function for these buildings.[99] And thirdly, internal buttresses may even have facilitated the construction of a raised floor, as these buildings generally lacked internal supports.

By examining some of the development trajectories discussed above, we discover that storage buildings increased considerably in size and capacity over time. Table 5.1 offers an overview of the development of storage building surface areas. For some settlements, the earliest granaries dated back to the earlier 1st century or even the Late Iron Age. These simple four- or six-post structures only had a limited surface area and thus limited storage capacity. Subsequently, generally in the second half of

[93] Kaszab-Olschewski 2006, 35.

[94] For the settlement phasing of the Hambach 132 settlement, see Brüggler 2009, 280 ff.

[95] Although a function as granary can be presumed for many cases, these buildings also seem to have been used as houses in some cases, for example at the axial complex of Port-sur-Saône (see Gaston 2008). The distribution of these buildings over a considerable geographical region has led Gaston (2008) to suggest standardisation.

[96] Tichelman 2005, 100-103.

[97] Révillion/Bouche/Wozny 1994, 109-110.

[98] Hallmann-Preuss 2002/2003, 330.

[99] Gentry (1976, 15, 62 ff.) stated that buttresses can be found at many storage buildings in Britain, which prompts the conclusion that they served to create a sturdy structure that could cope with the immense horizontal pressure.

Site	Surface in m2 (dating)	Surface in m2 (dating)	Surface in m2 (dating)	Surface in m2 (dating)
Tiel-Passewaaij	5-15 (1)	80 (1d-2A)	64 (3A)	
Houten-Tiellandt		67 (2A)		
Rijswijk-De Bult	13 (1d-2a)	29 (2b)	123 and 93 (2d-3a)	119 and 64 (3)
Hambach 512		44 (2A)	160 (2B)	
Verneuil-en-Halatte	9-25 (1a)	240 (1b)	250 (1B-2)	
Seclin	9 m2 (LIA)	182 (1)	650 and 370 (1-2)	600 and 625 (2-3)
Voerendaal-Ten Hove		430 (2a)		
Jülich-Kirchberg		400		

Table 5.1. Overview of the surface area in square metres of storage structures and their dating. Dates are given between brackets. Number: century. Capital A-B: half century. Small letter a-d: quarter century. LIA = Late Iron Age.

the 1st or first half of the 2nd century AD, much larger granaries were built, in most cases multiplying the storage capacity several times. Some more general observations have been made for a number of regions and settlements. Around the Dutch town of Oss, Iron Age granaries had a floor area of between 2 and 18 m^2, with an average of around 6.5 m^2. During the Roman period, this average increased substantially to 28 m^2, the largest being over 80 m^2. This suggests either an increase in the amount of grain grown and stored or a change in storage strategies, whereby storage was concentrated in fewer granaries.[100] During the first half of the 1st century AD, every household at Tiel and Wijk bij Duurstede-De Horden had several small granaries. In the second half of the 1st century, the average surface area of the Wijk bij Duurstede settlement was 17 m^2, while Tiel's was 9.9 m^2. At this latter site, however, a large granary offered storage capacity for more than one household. During the first half of the 2nd century, each house still had several associated granaries. At the same time, several larger granaries were built as well. At Tiel, the average surface area of the storage buildings increased at the expense of the number of structures. One of the larger granaries was a new type. It had a storage capacity of 45.6 m^2, exceeding the local needs by almost 100%. These post-built examples are nevertheless fairly small compared to some of the granaries on stone foundations found in the more southerly loess regions. The granaries at Voerendaal-Ten Hove and Jülich-Kirchberg were both around 400 m^2 in floor area and the very large buildings at Seclin, if correctly interpreted as storage buildings, even measured around 600 m^2.

With regard to the chronology of the development of storage buildings, the available data is unfortunately limited. From some dated cases, it is nevertheless possible to obtain a general impression. The relatively late development of larger storage buildings on stone foundations is particularly remarkable. At both Voerendaal and Hambach 512, such larger buildings were not constructed until the 2nd century, well after the main house had been rebuilt on stone foundations. This phenomenon may be linked to the increasing specialisation of production at these settlements. As previously described, the settlement at Voerendaal developed from mixed, more or less all-round type of production during the 1st century AD, into much more specialised and intensive production during the 2nd century.[101] Control over production may also have increased, symbolised by these large storage buildings that may even have been actively used to create and communicate positions of control. This particular theme will now be discussed.

[100] Gerritsen 2003, 71-72.   [101] See Kooistra 1996.

Granaries not only reflect developments in storage practice and production, they also shed light on changes in the organisation of production and thus on changing socio-economic relationships within settlements. As Given states: 'Assuming proper identification, changes in social and economic relationships can be charted by means of changing storage patterns'.[102] In order to study these storage patterns, granaries need to be placed in their settlement context. How does the position and character of storage buildings within the settlements reflect socio-economic relationships? And how could they have been actively used to construct new socio-economic relationships and new patterns of control over production?

Control over production and storage is essential for those wanting to acquire social power in a complex society. According to Purcell, storage control was one of the principal ingredients of the very formation and maintenance of elites in Mediterranean history.[103] Containing the agricultural wealth that was essential to the survival of the community, storage buildings were both functionally and symbolically important, communicating control over surplus, storage and exchange. As a consequence, they could be employed in the creation and maintenance of socio-economic relationships. After all, in the Roman tradition, storage buildings were intended to impress.[104]

In a study on the control over surplus in colonial situations, Given found that the ability to produce and control agricultural surplus became critical, particularly when surplus was required for tax payment. Dependency relationships were often economically shaped by the extraction of a proportion of people's grain or dairy produce by others. They were literally made dependent by partly removing self-subsistence and autonomy; they no longer controlled their own risk buffering.[105] Storage was instrumental in this process. As Given states, '[s]tored food is a concrete expression of people's role in society. It can embody a head of household's prudence and care, or the power of an elite over its subjects, or the proud memory of a family's hard work during the harvest.'[106]

Having said that, how can these processes be identified within our dataset? First of all, the increasing storage capacity of granaries could be related to the centralisation of storage and thus the centralisation of control over production and surplus. Instead of every farmstead and household having its own small granaries, storage was now centrally organised and controlled. Such processes were identified at several settlements described above. In a number of cases, a development could be documented from several small four- or six-post granaries to a single large storage building, often constructed on stone foundations. These larger storage buildings were found in many settlements. The other houses on the compound do not seem to have had their own granaries. Parallel processes were also identified in the northern regions. At Tiel-Passewaaij, the average floor area of the storage structures increased at the expense of their number and at several other rural settlements new, fairly large storage buildings developed.[107] These larger storage buildings clearly exceeded the personal needs of the household.

Secondly, the specific spatial relationship between the large storage building and the main house was significant. Examining the dataset, we see that the close association of the main house with a large granary is well-documented. Control over production and surplus was spatially symbolised in this way. At Hamois, the storage building was situated directly in front of the main house (fig. 5.6). A similar situation was documented at Eschweiler-Laurenzberg. At Cologne-Müngersdorf, Hambach 132, Le Roux-lez-Fosse, Hambach 512, Rheinbach-Flerzheim and Rijswijk-De Bult and elsewhere,[108]

---

[102]   Given 2004, 36.

[103]   Purcell 1995, 169.

[104]   Purcell 1995, 169.

[105]   Given 2004, 29-30.

[106]   Given 2004, 36.

[107]   Groot *et al.* 2009.

[108]   Bloemers interpreted this non-residential structure as a temple, but Derks (1998, 152, note 96) and Heeren (2009, 217) have argued that it should be re-interpreted as a large *horreum*.

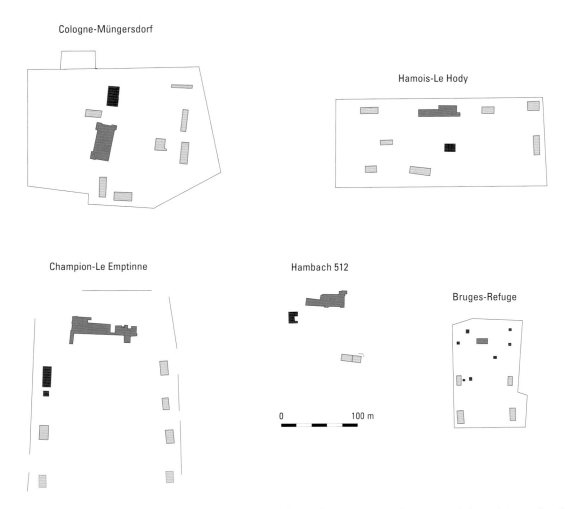

Fig. 5.6. Examples of the spatial association between monumental main houses (grey) and granaries (dark grey). Secondary buildings are indicated in light grey.

storage buildings were situated right next to the main house (see fig. 5.6 for examples). At Voerendaal-Ten Hove, the granary was even connected to the main house by means of a portico. In addition, the storage buildings at the axially organised complexes of Verneuil-en-Halatte and Champion-Le Emptinne were situated on the working compound but, remarkably, at a location closest to the residential compound. A somewhat different situation is found at Bruges-Refuge and Neerharen-Rekem. In both settlements, an Alphen-Ekeren type house was directly associated with a cluster of seemingly contemporary granaries. At Bruges, the house in question occupied the most prominent position within the settlement and at Neerharen-Rekem, the house was replaced by a multi-roomed house on stone foundations during the late 1st century AD. We could therefore suspect that the inhabitants of these houses had a prominent position within the settlement communities and that their apparent control over production was symbolised and communicated through the construction of several granaries in direct association with their residence. As the houses themselves were still non-monumental traditional buildings, this was a clear way of symbolising control, wealth and power. Apparently, changes in patterns of control were not necessarily related to the construction of new and larger types of storage building.

A third factor concerns the monumentalisation of storage buildings, resulting in their increased durability and prestige. As described, many storage buildings evolved from fairly small and inconspicuous structures into quite large and rather monumental buildings, potentially furnished with white-washed walls and red-tiled roofs, comparable to monumental houses. This monumentalisation might have played a role in the creation, communication and fixation of new socio-economic relationships. As conspicuous and durable structures, they were now ultimately suited to symbolising the lasting prominence of the dominant family, within the settlement and possibly even in the wider society.

All in all, storage buildings were actively used in the creation, communication and fixation of new socio-economic relationships, of new patterns of control over production. As large, durable and conspicuous structures, spatially associated with the main house and containing surpluses extracted from dependent workers, they symbolised the control and lasting prominence of a single family. Constructing such buildings helped the construction and maintenance of dependency relationships.

The situation in the northernmost region might be somewhat different, however. As discussed earlier, recent studies have elucidated changing economic relationships within settlements in this region.[109] In an interesting paper, Groot has looked at economic differentiation on a household level and discovered that interesting patterns could in fact be identified.[110] While some households specialised in their production, others maintained traditional patterns. Groot demonstrates that the farmsteads of these specialised households were often characterised by prominent houses (relatively large houses or portico-houses (sometimes termed 'veteran houses')),[111] special material culture (*militaria*, keys, seal boxes), specialised horse stables and rather large granaries.[112] Similar patterns have also been documented at other settlements. At Den Haag-Wateringse Veld, for example, the house with a long fronting portico was also associated with *militaria*.[113]

It is likely that these phenomena were associated with veterans returning to their settlements. With their knowledge of the army and its needs, their contacts and their financial position, they would have been able to specialise production, probably targeting the military market. In addition, veterans may have had a prominent social status within the communities to which they returned. The involvement of returning veterans may be suspected in more settlements in these northern regions. At Oss-Westerveld, the inhabitant of the portico-house on the separate compound could well have been a veteran, specialising production and acquiring wealth and status. The same could be true of the inhabitant of the monumental house at Hoogeloon, where the find of a military diploma further underlines such an interpretation. In this latter case, the corral associated with the house could be seen as marking the importance of livestock and, at the same time, as symbolising the prominent economic position of the family in question.[114]

At these northern settlements, it seems that production continued to be organised at farmstead level, without being centralised through the creation of relationships of dependency within the local community. It appears that socially and economically prominent people within these communities, such as veterans, were able to specialise and intensify production without directly controlling other families in asymmetrical dependency relationships. According to Groot, these other families appear to have continued to produce in traditional ways. This lack of direct dependency relationships is also reflected in the settlement layout, which was spatially and architecturally hierarchised to a lesser degree than their southern counterparts.

[109] On Tiel-Passewaaij and Wijk bij Duurstede-De Horden, see Heeren 2009 and Vos 2009. An economic analysis of these settlements was carried out in Groot *et al.* 2009 and Groot in press.

[110] Groot in press.

[111] See Vos 2009.

[112] Examples are house 20 at Geldermalsen-Hondsgemet and House 3 at Tiel-Passewaaij.

[113] Siemons/Lanzing 2009, 275-276, 376-372.

[114] See Jeneson 2004, 46-48.

5.4 REGIONAL DIFFERENTIATION: NUANCING THE 'VILLA MODE OF PRODUCTION'

One of the prominent elements in the definition of 'the villa' has been its economic function as a production unit. Slofstra even defined a specific 'villa mode of production'.[115] From this perspective, the villa is regarded as the centre of a landholding exploited by controlling the labour of others. Production was intensive, aimed at producing surpluses for the market and using asymmetrical social relationships to control production.[116] Studied from a broader, less essentialist approach, which is the aim in the present study, this economic interpretation of 'the villa' also needs to be reassessed. Especially in view of the new insights into the economic developments within settlements in the northern regions, it could be argued how typical this 'villa mode of production' actually was. The production of a surplus and increased control over production and workforce were mentioned as important aspects. However, it seems that these processes can also be identified for several northern settlements generally characterised as non-villa and 'indigenous'. Here, we also find changes in production orientation and specialisation, in production relationships and in the physical dimension of production (buildings with economic functions and their location). These processes are at least partly comparable to those found in the southern regions, albeit in a somewhat different form.

I would therefore like to argue for a broader approach to developments relating to production. Once more, it is clear that the definition of 'villa' should not be considered in essentialist terms. Processes of change, also with regard to agricultural production, can be identified throughout the research region, although with regional emphases. Production and the organisation of production, including the social relationships involved, certainly changed, but a more nuanced approach is needed for analysing and understanding these developments. Parallel to the earlier conclusions of this study, it could be stated that the concept of the 'villa mode of production' is a too essentialist tool for doing that.

---

[115] Slofstra 1991.
[116] Slofstra 1991, 161, 179.

6   Settling in a changing world: a synthesis

This final chapter aims to provide a synthesis of the preceding study. On the one hand, the central phenomenon of 'villa development' is discussed in an integrated way, combining insights from the analyses and hopefully reaching a better understanding of these processes. On the other hand, the reconstructed processes are viewed from a wider perspective, embedding them in their broader context of the profound developments that accompanied the integration of this region into the Roman empire.

As elaborated in the introduction to this study, two main objectives can be identified. The first involves reconstructing, visualising and analysing development trajectories in settlement organisation and house building. The second is understanding these developments from a dimensional perspective, combining the short and the long term, local and global as well as social and economic perspectives and focusing on both structure and agency. The diachronic dimension is crucial, especially if we wish to shed light on processes of social and economic change within the context of the settlement and house. It is in this way that archaeology can greatly contribute to studies of the Roman past in ways that other disciplines cannot.

In this chapter I will review the results of these two objectives. The first part focuses on the variety in settlement development within the research region. The following section will present a coherent view on how we could interpret these developments socially. I then discuss in brief how villa development relates to processes of 'becoming Roman' that have been reconstructed in recent studies on the Roman provinces. Lastly, I will present some recommendations for future research.

Before starting, I should emphasise that the present study has set out to explore villa *development*. This takes it beyond the study of 'the villa' in a traditional sense, which is defined as a monumental house with strong Roman architectural influences or a settlement with such a main house. Taking a broader perspective, this study explores the complex of development processes within the rural settlements of the provincial countryside.

6.1   RECONSTRUCTING DEVELOPMENT TRAJECTORIES

Over the decades, large-scale excavations of rural settlement have led to a marked rise in settlement data, providing new potential for studying the organisation of wider settlement complexes and the diachronic dimension of both settlements and individual houses. This data sheds new light on the developments taking place in the countryside of the northern provinces during the first centuries AD.

The development process itself is the key object of this analysis rather than the final results of these developments, which were generally highly structured settlements with buildings that were monumentalised to a greater or lesser degree. For shedding light on this process, a range of development trajectories in settlement organisation and house building have been reconstructed.

Using the five regions distinguished within this study, we will briefly recapitulate the variety of developments within the broad research region. In the northern regions during the later Iron Age and into the Roman period, a trend can be identified of farmsteads becoming increasingly clustered and spatially stable. Increasingly, houses were rebuilt at the same location. This trend continued into the Roman period, when settlements were being fixed within the landscape by means of their ditch enclosures, simultaneously defining and structuring settlement space. Houses were often rebuilt within the enclosures and in many cases even on exactly the same spot. This trend towards stability can also be seen in house building itself. Around the Early Roman period, a new type of post-built house emerged that was sturdier than its predecessors. From the second half of the 1st century, houses in some settlements were founded on stone footings, which significantly increased their durability. Most frequently, however, the existing tradition of building two-aisled post-built houses remained the norm in this northern region. In some cases, new elements were adopted in house building, although traditional ways of building seem to have remained dominant. The post-built houses extended by a portico are particularly interesting. In some cases, the creation of such a portico was associated with the use of new building materials and construction techniques. Multi-roomed houses on stone foundations were relatively rare in this region. In the coastal region and central river area, it seems that such houses were only built from the second half of the 2nd century onwards. This may have been linked to the monumentalisation of the military camps along the *limes* in this region, from around 160 AD. However, the monumental houses documented around Nijmegen appear to have been constructed somewhat earlier. The same applies to Hoogeloon.

For the Dutch, German and Belgian loess regions, the pre-Roman and earliest Roman habitation of the countryside remains difficult to reconstruct. In Germany, clusters of post-built structures have been documented at a number of sites. These seem to have been loosely structured settlements, consisting of one or more contemporary farmsteads. In the German region, these do not appear to have been enclosed by ditches in the pre-Roman period. However, pre-Roman enclosures have in fact been documented in several cases within the Belgian region. This can be linked to the region of northern France, where pre-Roman enclosed settlements are a well-documented phenomenon.

In the German region, it can be established that from around the middle of the 1st century AD settlements were organised as rectangular, well-structured compound settlements, with the buildings arranged along the enclosure ditches and surrounding an open space. The development from loosely structured farmstead(s) to a well-structured compound could be documented at a number of sites (Pulheim-Brauweiler, Hambach 412 and Frimmersdorf 129). Also with regard to the many other compound settlements in this region, it is important to be cautious when interpreting them as colonial units, planted in the landscape in a planned manner. As sites like Pulheim and Jüchen have demonstrated, development phases may have existed that were earlier than previously thought. In quite a few structured settlements, houses were still post-built during the early phase of development; it was not until much later that they were monumentalised. Some houses were rebuilt as rectangular hall-like single-aisled houses, constructed with posts set on stone footings. At other sites, post-built houses were replaced by the well-known type of multi-roomed houses on stone foundations.

Within the Belgian region, a development trajectory from post-built settlements to well-structured and monumentalised settlements can also be documented. At Meslin-L'Evêque an enclosed settlement with simple post-built houses was replaced by a highly monumental and axially organised settlement in the late 1st century AD. This complex is situated at exactly the same location, adhering to the existing orientation. At many other sites, post-built houses dating back to the Late Iron Age or earlier Roman period were documented, pre-dating the construction of multi-roomed houses on stone foundations.

In northern France, existing settlements enclosed by curvilinear ditch systems were replaced by much more rigidly organised settlement compounds, often rectangular in shape. Some settlements seem to have been replaced quite rapidly by highly structured and axially organised settlement complexes. In other cases, rectangular compound settlements developed. A new way of organising settlement space is apparent, creating a clear spatial hierarchy by means of organisation and axiality as well as segregating space by means of walls and ditches.

A variety of development trajectories were also reconstructed with regard to house building. In many settlements in the northern sand and clay region, house building continued in traditional ways, with two-aisled post-built byre houses. In some settlements, however, interesting changes to house building could be documented. The first category concerns traditional houses that were extended by a new architectural element – the portico. Quite a few houses in this region have been interpreted – though not always entirely convincingly – as portico-houses, which were more or less traditional houses surrounded by a wooden portico. In other cases, the construction of the house itself also changed. Central roof-supporting posts were replaced by heavy wall structures supporting the roof. These houses, many of which included wall posts on stone footings, can also be also found in the German loess region (Hambach 516, Jüchen-Neuotzenrath, Frimmersdorf 131). One such house, located at Druten, had a long fronting wooden portico, acting as a façade. At Jüchen and Hambach 516, a façade was created by adding a single risalith to the hall-like house. These houses were still essentially traditional structures or remarkably close to it. The category of multi-roomed houses on stone foundations, however, represented more of a break with tradition. These houses were built using new materials, techniques, forms and concepts, such as the portico-risalith façade, and they had a different domestic spatial organisation with several rooms. This move from traditional houses to multi-roomed houses on stone foundations could be documented throughout the research region, from Druten in the northernmost part to Verneuil-en-Halatte in the south.

Besides houses, buildings associated with production also evolved over time. The 1st and 2nd centuries AD saw the emergence of a variety of relatively large buildings whose precise function is generally difficult to reconstruct. The category of storage buildings, which are easier to identify, were generally rebuilt as larger buildings, often constructed on stone foundations. In terms of the spatial structure of the settlement, it is interesting to note that these conspicuous storage structures were often spatially associated with the main monumental houses.

If we focus on development processes, moving beyond differentiation in eventual form, we can identify some general trends in settlement organisation and house building:

- A long-term trend towards increasing stability of settlement: over time, settlements became stable and well-defined, enclosed units within the landscape.

- Increasingly structured, differentiated and complex organisation of domestic space: spatial segregation, organisational concepts (like symmetry and axiality), monumentalisation and a more complex symbolic structure (especially inside the house through the use of decorative elements and furniture) were ways in which more socio-politically complex and asymmetrical relationships were created in both settlements and houses.

- Increasing durability: houses became more durable structures through the use of new materials and techniques.

- Increasing differentiation of house building: some houses developed into larger, monumentalised and spatially complex structures, while others remained more or less traditional.

- Larger, more specialised buildings with economic functions: these reflected and were probably actively used in the creation of new production relationships. In several settlements, it could be established that control over surplus was symbolised by the spatial association of a monumental storage building with a monumental house.

- Increasing differentiation in the settlement landscape: some settlements developed into large, highly monumental settlements while others remained small, simple and barely monumentalised.

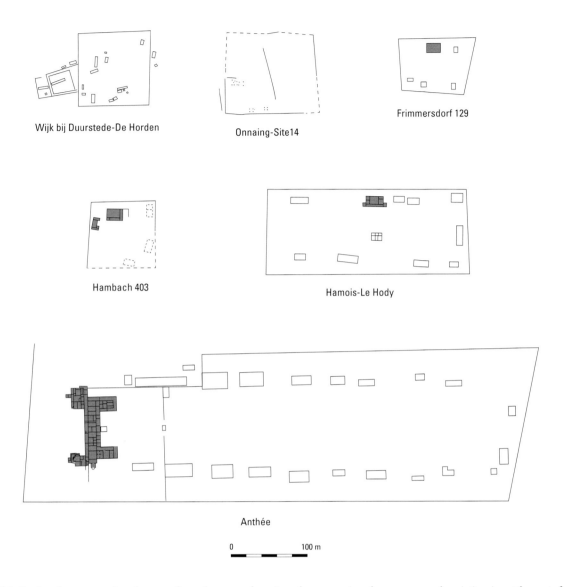

Wijk bij Duurstede-De Horden

Onnaing-Site14

Frimmersdorf 129

Hambach 403

Hamois-Le Hody

Anthée

0   100 m

Fig. 6.1. Enclosed compound settlements from the research region, demonstrating the pronounced variation in settlement, form, size and character.

As the above descriptions show, these general developments did not occur in uniform fashion across the research region, nor even within the same region or locality. While in some cases the reorganisation of domestic space and the transformation of architecture remained limited, in others, new, highly structured, complex and luxurious settlement forms emerged. With regard to the different ways in which these developments took place, a number of settlement and house types can be defined (see fig. 6.1):

- Multiple-farmstead settlements: these settlements continued to be organised as a cluster of individual farmsteads, although a common ditch enclosure was created. A strict organisation is lacking, however. In some cases, one of the houses changed, with new concepts, techniques, materials or forms being introduced. Generally, however, there is only little differentiation between houses in the settlement.

- Compound settlements with one or more houses: houses and settlement were more differentiated, structured and monumentalised.

- Axial complexes: houses and settlement were highly structured and differentiated.

- Simple, small and little structured and differentiated settlements with post-built structures in villa-dominated landscapes.

6.2 INTERPRETING DEVELOPMENT TRAJECTORIES FROM A MULTI-DIMENSIONAL APPROACH

To understand the complex implications and backgrounds of the developments sketched here, a multi-dimensional approach has been suggested, combining social, cultural and economic perspectives, both short and long term, global and local. The focus is also on both the agency of individuals and the effect of institutional developments (i.e. structure). This is a reminder not to focus solely on current theoretical issues but to find a balanced theoretical approach.

The concept of villa development used in this study relates to how people constructed within their immediate living environment (settlement and house) a new place in the changing world of the developing Roman provinces. Over time, most aspects of the lives of the majority of people inhabiting the provincial countryside will have been affected. However, there were geographical and social differences in how people responded to these developments, the precise forms these changes took and how profound they were. Generally speaking, new social and economic realities were created by reorganising space, breaking with traditions and changing patterns of consumption and production. Relationships both within local communities and between communities or individuals and the outside world were redefined and redesigned within the local settlements of the provincial countryside. The basic research question, then, is how new social and economic realities were constructed within the context of the rural settlement between the Late Iron Age and Roman period.

Firstly I will focus on the reorganisation of domestic space as a means of creating new social and economic relationships. This involved increasing spatial structuration and segregation and thus increasing control over access and exclusion, movement and experience, on the level of both the settlement compound and the house. With this a new spatial hierarchy as a metaphor for social centrality, prominence and control was created. The location of monumental houses in prominent locations, segregation by means of ditches and walls, the spatial association with large granaries and the creation of paths to guide movement were all instrumental in this proces. In general, the more complex and differentiated way that space was organised can be understood as reflecting an increasing socio-political complexity. The fact that settlement complexes were laid out as planned units, as well as their spatial structure, indicate significantly shifting patterns of power and control. It was in this new spatial structure of their immediate living environment that people interacted on a day-to-day basis, thus highly structuring their social behaviour and relationships.

A second important process was monumentalisation, for which two dimensions should be highlighted. On the one hand monumentalisation involved the increasing objective of communicating social distinction to the outside world, as illustrated by the creation of impressive façades as well as the basic visual character of the house with its white walls and red roof. On the other hand, it involved the increasing physical durability of the house, making it a monument derived from the past. Associated with past generations, the house became an enduring monumental symbol for the continuity of the family line and its social and economic prominence. The introduction of new building materials should therefore not be regarded as a passive adoption of Roman forms or ways, but as an active way of creating a new and enduring symbol of power and continuity.

Another aspect of house building developments was the act of breaking with existing traditions. The construction of houses on stone foundations involved the introduction of new techniques, materials, forms and concepts from outside the local communities. Knowledge and labour were also brought in from outside. By breaking with local practices rooted in history, social relationships were redefined and new positions created. Viewed from a broader perspective, developments in house building were part of a broader break with existing lifestyles and the construction of new ones. This redefined existing relationships and created new ones, both within the sphere of emerging rural elites and vis-à-vis the arenas of administrative and political power, located in the urban centres.

Obviously, some people had the opportunity to redefine social relationships and to create, strengthen, fix and communicate their prominent and dominant position. However, that is only part of the story: as some people became more powerful, others must have become increasingly powerless and dependent. It is this latter group who tend to be neglected because they are generally less visible archaeologically and their material culture is regarded as less interesting. Here, we have attempted to shed more light on the broader social range in the countryside. In general, we distinguish between the higher social groups, the middle classes and the lower social groups. The higher classes include those who took advantage of the opportunities emerging in the context of the provincialisation of the research region. They managed to improve, renew or strengthen their power positions within society and to successfully relate to the new institutions of power created by the Roman authorities. The old elite, new elite and veterans all fall into this category.

The middle classes of society included those with no immediate links to new institutions and arenas of power but who managed to make a good living by owning smaller plots of land or being successful tenants. They invested in their housing and partly adopted newly emerging lifestyles in the countryside, probably indirectly inspired by urban lifestyles and more directly by the large rural villa complexes.

The lower social groups included people who became increasingly powerless and dependent as some groups gained in power. As we have seen, they were controlled in different ways. There was still considerable variation within this category, however, ranging from small free tenants to slaves or people who were controlled so closely that they were practically unfree.

Different development trajectories can in some ways be linked to the different social classes described above. Because different people responded to changes in different ways, they constructed their place in the new world in different ways. We can probably assume that there was a 'fashion for the foreign' among the highest social groups. They welcomed new forms, materials, objects and ideas to redefine themselves and distinguish themselves from others.[1] They were the ones who first started consuming in new ways and who first adopted new, urban lifestyles, bringing them to the countryside. Another response is adaptation, borrowing piecemeal in order to incorporate the pieces into a traditional structure.[2] Cultural adaption involves de-contextualisation and re-contextualisation, lifting an item out of its original setting and modifying it to fit its new environment.[3]

Focusing more explicitly on the multi-dimensional approach, we should ask what this approach has actually contributed to understanding processes of change. Looking at both long-term and short-term development has certainly increased our understanding of development processes. Changes in settlement organisation, the economy and possibly also social changes began in the pre-Roman period and continued into the Roman period. More radical transformations were taking place during the Roman period, but it seems that these should be placed within the longer lines of development. It has therefore been argued that villa development should be viewed as a process in the forcefield between continuity and change. Villa development is not just a radical break from existing traditions; in some ways, it is also a continuation of existing trends.

[1]   On different responses to cultural encounter and exchange, see Burke 2009, 72 ff.

[2]   Burke 2009, 93; a phenomenon termed 'bricolage' by Levi-Strauss.

[3]   Burke 2009, 93-94.

With regard to local and global, this study has mainly focused on the local in the sense that the settlement and house were central objects of study. However, we cannot understand changes at this local level if we disregard more global developments on the level of the *civitas*, province or even empire. Changes at 'global' level eventually influenced people at the 'local' level of their settlements and houses, the setting of their daily lives. The rise of an increasingly market-oriented economy (because for the first time in this region large groups were not directly involved in agricultural production) significantly influenced how production was organised, and the related process of monetisation affected the spheres of exchange, leading to the growing importance of short-term exchange. This eventually had an impact on how settlements were organised and how people interacted. Something similar could be said for the political–administrative system that the Romans introduced to administer the provinces. This highly institutionalised and socio–politically complex system eventually gave rise to more complex and asymmetrical relationships in the countryside. These relationships were reflected in the reorganisation of domestic space at the level of both settlement and house. From a rather different perspective, the elites no longer focused on the local when redefining their social position, but increasingly adopted 'global' lifestyles, referring to sources and using elements, forms and ideas from outside the local community. As emphasised earlier, these more 'global' lifestyles developed mainly in the urban centres.

Finally, with regard to agency and structure, or the cultural and institutional dimension as Slofstra terms it, this study has focused on creative individuals who actively restructured existing relationships by choosing to reorganise settlement space and to break with existing ways of house building. This was an active strategy to define, communicate and fix new relationships. However, another important part of villa development was the institutionalisation that took place on a broader level. Power was now increasingly organised in institutions and some people in the countryside became part of such institutions. Relationships within rural settlements also seem to have been formalised in some cases. Especially in the most rigidly organised axial complexes, it seems likely that relationships between the proprietor living on the main residential compound and workers on the working compound were quite formal and probably organised in the form of contractual tenancy. It is these people who probably lost individual freedom (agency) compared to the pre-Roman situation. Another important institutionalising factor with regard to villa development was the creation of a taxation system: by being taxed, rural inhabitants became connected to Roman law systems and therefore part of Roman institutions.

6.3 INTERPRETING VILLA DEVELOPMENT AS A PROCESS OF CHANGE: 'BECOMING ROMAN'?

The adoption of Roman materials, objects and symbols is often associated with the adoption of Roman culture and is viewed as a process of 'becoming Roman'.[4] But does this correctly represent what was going on? Were people who used new materials, techniques and forms in fact becoming Roman? Did they want to display a Roman identity?

In his influential study, Cohen showed how influences of an intruding power can be employed in the service of indigenous symbolic systems. As emphasised above, the adoption of new objects and forms involved incorporating them into a traditional structure.[5] This study has also argued that rather than a passive adoption of Roman forms, villa development is much more about the creative and active use of new forms to forge new social and economic realities. It is therefore vital to exercise caution when relating the adoption of new forms, objects and concepts to an intentional desire to 'become

[4] Woolf 1998.

[5] Burke 2009, 93.

Roman' or communicate a Roman identity, even though the objects themselves may have been of Roman origin or inspired by Roman forms. New ways of organising and building were less about explicitly creating a new Roman identity and more about creating a system of internal social differentiation. Inhabitants reinterpreted Roman culture to fit their circumstances and because it was useful and necessary.[6] It was necessary because adherence to Roman values and lifestyle meant participation in the ruling strata of the empire, and useful because it gave them a secure place within the new order and access to the broader horizon of imperial life.[7] Viewed in this way, were people who built villas 'exploiting a medium of alien origin for the conceptualisation and expression of essentially indigenous ideas'?[8] 'Roman' should in most cases be understood in relative terms, as 'Roman' villas were adapted to the colder climate and also seem to have incorporated native ideas on house building. This makes them new, hybrid creations rather than straightforward copies of Roman forms. It was not about being Roman or native, but about creating new and much more complex identities in a changing world through the creative manipulation of material culture.[9] Meaning and perception are other key themes. Were certain 'Roman' styles indeed associated with Roman-ness or were they too embedded in local systems of meaning? The adoption of styles can be part of conscious social strategies (e.g. to connect with arenas of decision making and power), without having a direct relationship to the cultures that archaeologists generally associate with these styles.

With this in mind, we should perhaps distinguish between the first generations of locals who were confronted with Roman culture and later generations who grew up in a Roman province. While the former group may indeed have associated certain forms with the newly arrived Roman culture, for the latter these Roman objects had blended into local cultures and were no longer specifically associated with Roman-ness.

6.4 AVENUES FOR FUTURE RESEARCH

At the heart of this study are specific choices about data use and research themes that have both shaped and confined it. I will mention some of these limitations once again, as they represent potential avenues for further research.

The spatial organisation of rural settlements and the house have been key objects of research in the present study. As a result, mobile material culture has received little attention, although this category could have been used to explore themes addressed here. A decision was also taken to approach reconstructed patterns and processes from a mainly archaeological-anthropological perspective. The intersection between archaeological and historical sources, however, has not been explored.

I would like to conclude this study with a few recommendations for future research into rural settlements. Although existing studies have produced an enormous amount of data on rural settlements, the quality of both excavations and publications often remains problematic, making it difficult to answer more detailed research questions. Completely and integrally excavated complexes for which the constituent elements are described and discussed in detail are particularly vital (e.g. Kerkrade-Holzkuil, Hambach 59, 512 and 516). Such research could answer questions that cannot be answered by the multitude of fragmentarily excavated settlements. Specific recommendations for more detailed settlement research include:

[6] Trow/James/Moore 2009, 67; see also Tilley 2004: 'Roman forms were not imposed from the outside, but grew up [....] as a combination of local types and materials with long histories with outside influences, from both Mediterranean culture and neighbouring Gaul.'

[7] Trow/James/Moore 2009, 67.

[8] Cohen 1985, 76.

[9] See Taylor 2001.

- More detailed study of secondary buildings. This could greatly improve our understanding of the social structure and economic functioning of settlements. Analyses to identify building functions could include detailed botanical research in and around the building, artefact and micro-artefact studies in and around the building, phosphate analysis and attempts to find a hearth place. Identifying secondary houses should be an important objective.

- The detailed phasing of settlement features is essential if we wish to gain a better understanding of the developments taking place in rural settlements.

- Research should focus not only on the settlement compound and its buildings, but should include associated graves, ditch systems and roads, and if possible, the relationship between the development of these structures and the settlement. Graves themselves should also be studied in more detail, including physical-anthropological analyses of the cremated remains.

- Micro-regional studies could increase our knowledge of the social settlement hierarchy and the relationships between settlements. It would be particularly interesting to search for non-monumental settlements within the landscapes dominated by monumental villa settlements.

References

Aarts, J.G., 2005: Coins, money and exchange in the Roman world, *Archaeological Dialogues* 12 (1), 1–28.

Agache, R., 1978: *La Somme Pré-Romaine et Romaine d'après les prospections aériennes à basse altitude*, Amiens.

Agache, R., 1983: Typologie et devenir des villae antiques dans les grandes plaines de la Gaule septentrionale, in W. Janssen/D. Lohrmann (eds), *Villa-Curtis-Grangia. Landwirtschaft zwischen Loire und Rhein von der Römerzeit zum Hochmittelalter*, München, 17-29.

Allison, P., 2004: *Pompeian Households. An analysis of the Material Culture*, Los Angeles.

Allison, P. (ed.), 1999: *The Archaeology of Household Activities*, London.

Amerlinck, M.-J. (ed.), 2001: *Architectural Anthropology*, Westport.

Anderson, J. D., 1992: *Roman Military Supply in North-East England: An Analysis of and Alternative to the Piecebridge Formula*, Oxford (British Archaeological Reports 224).

Andrikopoulou-Strack, J.-N. *et al.*, 1999: Eine frührömische Siedlung in Jüchen-Neuholz. Überlegungen zur Siedlungskontinuität in der Lößbörde, *Bonner Jahrbücher* 199, 141-180.

Andrikopoulou-Strack, J.-N. *et al.*, 2000: Der frührömische und kaiserzeitliche Siedlungsplatz in Pulheim-Brauweiler, *Bonner Jahrbücher°* 200, 409-488.

Andrikopoulou-Strack, J.-N., 2001: Eburonen – und was dann?, in G. Brands *et al.* (eds), *Rom und die Provinzen. Gedenkschrift für Hanns Gabelmann*, Bonn (Beihefte der Bonner Jahrbücher 53), 163-172.

Andrikopoulou-Strack, J.-A., 2007: Römische Strassen in den Nordwest-provinzen des Imperium Romanum, in M. Hegewisch (ed.) *Krieg und Frieden. Kelten, Römer, Germanen*, Bonn/Darmstadt, 239-242.

Authom, N./N. Paridaens, 2008: La villa Gallo-Romaine du 'Champ de Saint-Eloi' à Merbes-Les-Château. Seconde campagne de fouilles (2007), in W. De Clercq *et al.* (eds), *Journée d'Archéologie Romaine 2008 - Romeinendag 2008*, Brussels, 11-16.

Bakels, C.C., 2009: *The Western European Loess Belt, Agrarian History, 5300 BC - AD 1000*, Dordrecht.

Barrett, J.C., 1997: Romanization: a critical comment, in D.J. Mattingly (ed.), *Dialogues in Roman imperialism*, Portsmouth, Rhode Island (International Roman Archaeology Conference Series; Journal of Roman Archaeology supplementary series 23), 51-64.

Bauchhenss, G., 1983: *Archäologie in den rheinischen Lössborden. Beitrage zur Siedlungsgeschichte im Rheinland*, Cologne (Rheinische Ausgrabungen 24).

Bausier, K./S. Lefert/I. Nachtergael, 2000: La villa gallo-romaine du Hody (Champion), in J. Plumier-Torffs/S. Duhaut (eds), *Huitieme Journée d'archéologie namuroise, Rochefort, 25 et 26 février 2000*, Rochefort, 59-66.

Bayard, D., 1996: La romanisation des campagnes en Picardie à la lumière des fouilles récentes: problèmes d'échelles et de critères, in D. Bayard/J.-L. Collart (eds), *De la ferme indigène à la villa romaine*, Amiens, 157-184.

Bayard, D./J.-L. Collart (eds), 1996: *De la ferme indigène à la villa romaine. La romanisation des campagnes de la Gaule*, Amiens (Revue Archéologique de Picardie, special 11).

Bayard, D./N. Mahéo (eds), 2004: *La marque de Rome. Samarobriva et les villes du nord de la Gaule*, Amiens.

Becker, A., 2003: Lahnau-Waldgirmes. Eine augusteische Stadtgründung in Hessen, *Historia* 52, 337-350.

Beckers, O.M., 1928: Beschrijving der vondsten uit Stein, *Oudheidkundige Mededelingen uit het Rijksmuseum van Oudheden te Leiden* 9, 20-47.

Bedoyere, G. de la, 1994: Roman Villas and the Countryside, *The classical review* 44-2, 419 ff.

Bender, H./H. Wolff (eds), 1994: *Ländliche Besiedlung und Landwirtschaft in den Rhein-Donau-Provinzen des Römischen Reiches*, Espelkamp.

Bentmann, R./M. Müller, 1990: Die villa als Herrschaftsarchitektur, in F. Reutti (ed.) *Die römische villa*, Darmstadt, 389-440.

Ben Redjeb, T./L. Duvette/P. Quérel, 2005: Les campagnes antiques: Bilans et perspectives, *Revue Archéologique de Picardie* 3-4, 177-222.

Berendsen, H.J.A., 1997: *Landschappelijk Nederland*, Assen.

Binet, E., 2004: Un quartier d'habitations à Amiens. Le site du Palis des Sports/Coliseum, in D. Bayard/N. Mahéo (eds), *La marque de Rome. Samarobriva et les villes du nord de la Gaule*, Amiens, 128-130.

Birkenhagen, B., 2004: *Die römische Villa Borg. Ein Begleiter durch die Anlage*, Merzig.

Blake, E., 2004: Space, Spatiality, and Archaeology, in L. Meskell/R.W. Preucel (eds), *A Companion to Social Archaeology*, Oxford, 230-254.

Blancquaert, G./G. Prilaux, 2003: Exceptionnels vestiges de la conquête romaine, *Archéologia* 404, 13-25.

Blanton, R.E., 1994: *Houses and Households. A Comparative Study*, New York.

Bloch, M./J. Parry (eds), 1989: *Money and the morality of exchange*, Cambridge.

Bloemers, J.H.F., 1978: *Rijswijk (Z-H) 'De Bult': Eine Siedlung der Cananefaten*, Amersfoort (Nederlandse Oudheden 8).

Bloemers, J.H.F., 1980: Rijswijk (Z.H.) 'De Bult', een nederzetting van de Cananefaten, *Hermeneus* 52, 95-106.

Blom, E./L.M.B. van der Feijst/H.A.P. Veldman (eds), 2012: *Plangebied Keizershoeve I. Archeologisch onderzoek op 'De grote Aalst' te Ewijk (gemeente Beuningen)*, Amersfoort (ADC rapport 2000).

Bodel, J., 1997: Monumental Villas and Villa Monuments, *Journal of Roman Archaeology* 10, 5-35.

Bogaers, J.E., 1959: Houten, *Bulletin & Nieuwsbulletin van de Nederlandse Oudheidkundige Bond* 6-12, 83 ff.

Bogaers, J.E., 1986: Villa of praetorium?, in *Munsters in de Maasgouw. Archeologie en Kerkgeschiedenis in Limburg*, Maastricht, 50-55.

Bosman, A.V.A.J., 2001: Romeinen te Beegden. Waarnemingen in een waterleidingsleuf, *Archeologie in Limburg* 89, 2-13.

Bott, S./P. Cattelain, 1997: Viroinval/Treignes: recherches récentes dans la villa gallo-romaine des 'Bruyères', *Chronique de l'Archéologie wallonne* 4-5, 185-186.

Bott, S./P. Cattelain, 2000: Viroinval/Treignes: la villa gallo-romaine des Bruyères. Achèvement des recherches dans le bâtiment principal, *Chronique de l'Archéologie wallonne* 8, 197-199.

Bouten, W. *et al.*, 1985: Ontstaan en erosie van de lössleemgronden in Zuid-Limburg *K.N.A.G. Geografisch Tijdschrift* 19- 3, 192-208.

Bowden, M.C.B./D. McOmish, 1987: The required barrier, *Scottish Archaeological Review* 4, 76-84.

Bowen, H.C., 1969: The Celtic Background, in A.L.F. Rivet (ed.), *The Roman Villa in Britain*, London.

Braat, W.C., 1934: Nieuwe opgravingen van Romeinsche villae, *Oudheidkundige Mededelingen uit het Rijksmuseum van Oudheden te Leiden* 15, 4-38.

Braat, W.C., 1941: Nieuwe opgravingen van Romeinsche villa's in Limburg *Oudheidkundige Mededelingen uit het Rijksmuseum van Oudheden te Leiden* 22, 39-51.

Braat, W.C., 1953: De grote Romeinse villa van Voerendaal, *Oudheidkundige Mededelingen uit het Rijksmuseum van Oudheden te Leiden* 34, 48-79.

Braekeleer, R. de, 1994: Ath/Meslin-l'Evêque: tombe à incirération, *Chronique de l'Archéologie wallonne* 2, 44.

Branigan, K./D. Miles (eds), 1989: *Villa Economies: The economies of Romano-British villas*, Sheffield.

Braund, D., 1984: *Rome and the Friendly King: The Character of Client Kingship*, London.

Bridger, C., 2001: Zur römischen Besiedlung im Umland der *Colonia Ulpia Traiana/Tricensimae*, in T. Grünewald (ed.) *Germania Inferior. Besiedlung, Gesellschaft und Wirtschaft an der Grenze der römisch-germanischen Welt*, Berlin, 185-211.

Bridger, C., 2006: Veteran settlement in the Lower Rhineland: the evidence from the civitas Traianensis, *Journal of Roman Archaeology* 19, 137-149.

Brüggler, M., 2009: *Villa rustica, Glashütte und Gräberfeld. Die kaiserzeitliche und spätantike Siedlungsstelle HA 132 im Hambacher Forst*, Mainz (Rheinische Ausgrabungen 63).

Brulet, R., 1970: La villa romaine du Try-Halot à Saint-Gérard. Étude topographique, in Cl. Levie *et al.* (eds), *Recherches d'archéologie et d'histoire de l'art (antiquité)*, Leuven, 63-80.

Brulet, R., 1996: La maison urbaine en Gaule Belgique et en Germanie Inferieure, in P. Gros (ed.), *La maison urbaine d'époque romaine en Gaule narbonnaise et dans les provinces voisines*, Avignon, 73-97.

Brulet, R./C. Coquelet, 2004: Les maisons privées, in D. Bayard/N. Mahéo (eds), *La marque de Rome. Samarobriva et les villes du nord de la Gaule*, Amiens, 122-127.

Brulet, R. (ed.), 2009: *Les Romains en Wallonie*, Brussels.

Brunsting, H., 1950: Verslag van de opgraving van een Romeinse villa te Kerkrade (Krichelberg-Kaalheide), *Berichten van de Rijksdienst voor het Oudheidkundig Bodemonderzoek* 1-13, 31-32.

Buchli, V. (ed.) 2002: *The Material Culture Reader*, Oxford/New York.

Buchli, V., 2004: Material Culture: Current Problems, in L. Meskell/R.W. Preucel (eds), *A Companion to Social Archaeology*, Oxford, 179-194.

Bunnik, F.P.M., 1995: Pollenanalytische Ergebnisse zur Vegetations- und Landwirtschtsgeschichte der Jülischer Lössbörde, *Bonner Jahrbücher* 195, 313-349.

Bunnik, F.P.M. *et al.*, 1995: Archäopalynologische Betrachtungen zum Kulturwandel in den Jahrhunderten um Christi Geburt, *Archäologische Nachrichten* 18-2, 169-185.

Burke, P., 2009: *Cultural Hybridity*, Cambridge.

Carreras Monfort, C., 2002: The Roman Military Supply during the Principate. Transportation and Staples, in P. Erdkamp (ed.), *The Roman Army and the Economy*, Amsterdam, 70-87.

Carroll, M., 2003: The genesis of Roman towns on the lower Rhine, in P. Wilson (ed.), *The Archaeology of Roman Towns*, Oxford.

Carsten, J./S. Hugh-Jones, 1995: *About the House. Lévi-Strauss and beyond*, Cambridge.

Clarke, S., 1990: The Social Significance of Villa Architecture in Celtic North West Europe, *Oxford Journal of Archaeology* 9-3, 337-53.

Clarke, S., 1998: Social Change and Architectural Diversity in Roman Period Britain, in C. Forcey/J. Hawthorne/R. Witcher (eds), *TRAC 97. Proceedings of the Seventh Annual Theoretical Conference, Nottingham 1997*, 28-41.

Clarke, S., 1999: Architectural and social change during the Roman period, in A. Leslie (ed.), *Theoretical Roman Archaeology and Architecture. The Third Conference Proceedings*, Glasgow, 111-121.

Close, F., 1993: Bassenge/Wonck: villa romaine, *Chronique de l'Archéologie wallonne* 1, 62.

Close, F., 1997: Bassenge, Eben-Emael. Un sauvetage archéologique et la découverte d'occupations anciennes à 'Int' les Deux Voyes', dans la carrière CBR du Romont, in M.-H. Corbiau (ed.), *Le patrimoine archéologique de Wallonie*, Namur, 345-347.

Close, F., 1997: La villa gallo-romaine de Wonck, in *Richesses archéologiques de la Basse-Meuse Liégeoise*, Visé, 117.

Close, F., 1997: La villa romaine de Bassenge, in *Richesses archéologiques de la Basse-Meuse Liégeoise*, Visé, 38.

Clotuche, R., 2009: The Scheldt Valley Commercial Activity Zone: 350 Hectares of the Gallo-Roman Landscape, *Britannia* 90, 41-64.

Cohen, A.P., 1985: *The symbolic construction of Community*, London/New York.

Collart, J.-L., 1996: La naissance de la *villa* en Picardie: la ferme gallo-romaine précoce, in D. Bayard/J.-L. Collart (eds), *De la ferme indigène à la villa romaine*, Amiens, 121-156.

Colleredo-Mansfeld, R., 1994: Architectural Conspicuous Consumption and Economic Change in the Andes, *American Anthropologist* 96-4, 845-865.

Collingwood, R.G./I.A. Richmond, 1969: *The Archaeology of Roman Britain*, London.

Compagnon, E. *et al.*, 1995: La villa gallo-romaine de Somain, *Revue du Nord* 77, 159-168.

Cooremans, B./K. Desender/A. Ervynck/J. Schelvis, 2002: Onderzoek van plantaardige en dierlijke resten uit een Romeinse waterput van de vindplaats 'Refuge' te Sint-Andries, Brugge (prov. West-Vlaanderen): economie en ecologie, *Archeologie in Vlaanderen* VI, 209-229.

Corbiau, M.-H. (ed.) 1997: *Le patrimoine archéologique de Wallonie*, Namur.

Corrigan, P., 1997: *The Sociology of Consumption*, London.

Courbot, C., 2004: *L'évolution des établissements ruraux entre la fin de l'Âge du fer et la mise en place du système de villae dans le quart nord-ouest de la France, Ier siècle avant - IIe siècle après J.-C.*, Paris (dissertation University of Paris).

Courbot-Dewerdt, C., 2005: 'Mending Gauls' fences with the Romans': spatial identities from farmsteads to sacred places in northern Gaul, in D. Hofmann/J. Mills/A. Cochrane (eds), *Elements of being. Mentalities, Identities and Movements*, Oxford (British Archaeological Reports International Series 1437), 50-56.

Courbot-Dewerdt, C., 2006: An alleged Far West? The Romanisation of the countryside in western Gaul, in B. Croxford *et al.* (eds), *TRAC 2005. Proceedings of the 15th Annual Theretical Roman Archaeogical Conference, Birmingham 2005*, Oxford, 73-82.

Crowley, L., 2011: The role of mortuary ritual in the construction of social boundaries by privileged social groups within villa landscapes, in N. Roymans/T. Derks (eds), *Villa Landscapes in the Roman North. Economy, Culture and Lifestyles*, Amsterdam, 195-209.

Crowley, L., in prep.: *Dying in a Material World. Self-representation and its implications in mortuary contexts in the villa landscapes between Bavay and Cologne*, Amsterdam (unpublished dissertation VU University Amsterdam).

Cunliffe, B., 1971: *Fishbourne. A Roman Palace and its Garden*, London.

Cüppers, H., 1984: Frührömische Siedlungsreste und Funde aus dem Stadtgebiet von Trier, in *Trier. Augustusstadt der Treverer. Stadt und Land in vor- und frührömischer Zeit*, Mainz, 48-51.

Cüppers, H. (ed.) 1990: *Die Römer in Rheinland-Pfalz*, Stuttgart.

Cuyt, C., 1983: Gallo-Romeinse en Middeleeuwse bewoningssporen te Wijnegem, *Archaeologia Belgica* 253, 61-64.

Cuyt, C., 1991: Een inheemse nederzetting uit de vroeg-Romeinse tijd te Wijnegem, *Archeologie in Vlaanderen* 1, 85-106.

Daloz, J.-P., 2010: *The sociology of elite distinction. From theoretical to comparative perspectives*, Basingstoke.

De Boe, G., 1966: *De Gallo-Romeinse nederzetting op de Steenakker te Mortsel (Antwerpen)*, Mortsel.

De Boe, G., 1971: *De Romeinse villa op de Meerberg te Val-Meer (Limburg)*, Leuven (Acta Archaeologica Lovaniensia 4).

De Boe, G., 1971: *De Romeinse villa's in Gallië en Germanie*, Leuven (thesis Universiteit Leuven).

De Boe, G., 1973: De landelijke bewoning in de Romeinse tijd, *Het oude land van Loon* 28, 85-114.

De Boe, G., 1974: Haccourt I. Vestiges d'habitat pré-romain et prémières périodes de la villa romaine, *Archaeologia Belgica* 168.

De Boe, G., 1975: Haccourt II. Le corps de logis de la grande villa, *Archeologia Belgica* 174.

De Boe, G., 1976: Haccourt III. Les bains de la grande villa, *Archeologia Belgica* 182.

De Boe, G., 1982: Meer dan 1500 jaar bewoning rond de Romeinse villa te Neerharen-Rekem, *Archaeologia Belgica* 247 (Conspectus 1981), 70-74.

De Boe, G., 1984: De Romeinse vicus te Grobbendonk: de houtbouwfase, *Archaeologia Belgica* 258, 69-73.

De Boe, G., 1984: De Romeinse vicus te Grobbendonk: de steenbouwfase, *Archaeologia Belgica* 258, 74-78.

De Boe, G., 1984: Romeinse nederzetting en begraafplaats te Donk, *Archaeologia Belgica* 258, 69-82.

De Boe, G., 1985a: De opgravingscampagne 1984 te Neerharen-Rekem, *Archaeologia Belgica* I-2, 53-62.

De Boe, G., 1985b: Het ontstaan en de ontwikkeling van de Romeinse 'vicus' te Grobbendonk, *Acta Archaeologica Lovaniensia* 24, 101-108.

De Boe, G., 1987: Bewoning rond de villa te Neerharen-Rekem (B), in P. Stuart/M.E.Th. de Grooth (eds), *Langs de weg*, Heerlen/Maastricht, 51-54.

De Boe G./F. Lauwers, 1979: Een inheemse nederzetting uit de Romeinse tijd te Oelegem, *Archaeologia Belgica* 213 (Conspectus 1978), Brussels, 83-87.

De Boe, G. /F. Lauwers, 1980: Een inheemse nederzetting uit de Romeinse tijd te Oelegem, *Archaeologia Belgica* 228, 82-87.

De Boe, G. /L. Van Impe, 1979: Nederzetting uit de ijzertijd en Romeinse villa te Rosmeer, *Archeologia Belgica* 216.

De Clercq, W., 2003: L'habitat gallo-romain en Flandre orientale (Belgique). Recherches 1990-2001 dans les civitates Menapiorum et Nerviorum, *Revue du Nord* 85- 353, 161-179.

De Clercq, W./R. van Dierendonck, 2008: Extrema Galliarum. Zeeland en Noordwest-Vlaanderen in het Imperium Romanum, *Romeins Erfgoed, Zeeuws Tijdschrift* 58-3, 5-34.

De Clercq, W., 2009: *Lokale gemeenschappen in het Imperium Romanum. Transformaties in rurale bewoningsstructuur en materiële cultuur in de landschappen van het noordelijk deel van de civitas Menapiorum (provincie Gallia-Belgica, ca. 100 v. Chr. – 400 n. Chr.)*, Gent (unpublished dissertation University of Ghent).

De Clercq, W./S. Mortier, 2002: Aalter, industrieterrein Langevoorde. Grootschalig noodonderzoek van een meerperiodenvindplaats., *Monumentenzorg en Cultuurpatrimonium. Jaarverslag van de provincie Oost-Vlaanderen 2001*, 146-154.

De Clercq, W./C. Quérel, 2010: Les paysages dits de 'non-villa' et les maisons-étables du Nord-Ouest de la Gaule, in *'Y a-t-il vraiment une villa gallo-romaine dans le Nord-Pas-de-Calais, pré-actes colloque*, Villeneuve d'Ascq, 29 janvier 2010.

Delaruelle, S./C. Verbeek/W. de Clercq, 2004: Wonen en leven op het HSL-traject in de Romeinse tijd (circa 50 v.Chr.-476 na Chr.), in C. Verbeeck/S. Delaruelle/J. Bungeneers (eds), *Verloren voorwerpen. Archeologisch onderzoek op het HSL-traject in de provincie Antwerpen*, Antwerpen.

De Ligt, L., 1993: *Fairs and markets in the Roman Empire. Economic and social aspects of periodic trade in a pre-industrial society*, Amsterdam.

Delmaire, R. (ed.), 1994: *Le Pas-de-Calais*, Paris (Carte archéologique de la Gaule 62/1).

Delmaire, R. (ed.), 1996: *Le Nord*, Paris (Carte archéologique de la Gaule 59).

Demanet, J.-C, 2006: L'agglomération semi-urbaine de Liberchies, *Dossiers Archéologie et sciences des origines* 315 *(La Belgique Romaine)*, 48-51.

DeMarrais, E., 2007: Settings and symbols: Assessing complexity in two pre-Hispanic polities, in S. Kohring/S. Wynne-Jones (eds), *Socialising complexity: Approaches to power and interaction in the archaeological record*, Oxford, 118–139.

Denis, J. (ed.) 1992: *Geografie van België*, Brussels.

Deramaix, I./P.-P. Sartieaux, 1994: Ath/Meslin-l'Evêque: sauvetage d'une villa romaine inédite dans un zoning industriel, *Chronique de l'Archéologie wallonne* 2, 42-43.

Deramaix, I., 2006: Meslin-l'Évêque. Imposante villa hainuyère, *Dossiers Archéologie et sciences des origines* 315 *(La Belgique Romaine)*, 64-67.

Deramaix, I., 2010: Synthèse des occupations romaines de la ZAE de Ghislenghien/Meslin-L'Evêque (Ath), in A. Bosman *et al.*, *Romeinendag. Jaarlijks Belgisch congres voor Romeinse archeologie. Louvain-la-Neuve 24-04-2010*, Louvain-la-Neuve, 47-52.

Derks, T., 1998: *Gods, temples and ritual practices. The transformation of religious ideas and values in Roman Gaul*, Amsterdam (Amsterdam Archaeological Studies 2).

Derks, T./N. Roymans, 2006: Returning auxiliary veterans in the Roman empire: some methodological considerations, *Journal of Roman Archaeology* 19, 121-135.

Destexhe, G., 1973: La villa belgo-romaine de Warfée (commune de St. Georges), *Les chercheurs de la Wallonie* 22, 63-211.

Devillers, L., 1971: La villa romaine de Wancennes, *Annales de la Société archéologique de Namur* 56, 97-132.

Provoost, A., 1982: *Het bodemarchief van Oost-Brabant. Le sous-sol archéologique du Brabant oriental*, Leuven.

Dijkstra, J., 1997: *Aanvullend Archeologisch Onderzoek (AAO), vindplaats Kerkrade-Winckelen, verkaveling Maar-West*, Amersfoort (Rapportage Archeologische Monumentenzorg 51).

Dodt, M.A., 2003: *Die Thermen von Zülpich und die römischen Badeanlagen der Provinz Germania inferior*, Bonn.

Donley-Reid, L., 1990: A structuring structure: The Swahili house, in S. Kent (ed.), *Domestic architecture and the use of space*, Cambridge, 114-127.

Doorselaer, A. van, 1995: Neue Ergebnisse zur Anwesenheit von Römerzeitlichen Villae im Scheldetal (Belgien), in S.K. Palágyi (ed.) *Balácai Közlemények III. 1994*, Veszprem, 124-133.

Doppelfeld, O., 1961: Das Diatretglas aus dem Gräberbezirk des römischen Gutshofs von Köln-Braunsfeld, *Kölner Jahrbuch für vor- und frühgeschichte* 5, 7-35.

Doyen, J.-M., 1985: La villa gallo-romaine de Treignes: campagnes 1984-1985, *Amphora* 42, 18-25.

Doyen, J.-M., 1987: Villa romaine à Treignes, in A. Cahen-Delhaye/C. de Lichtervelde/F. Leuxe (eds), *L'archéologie en Wallonie 1980-1985*, Namur, 266-271.

Drinkwater, J.F., 1981: Money-rents and food-renders in Gallic funerary reliefs, in A. King/M. Henig (eds), *The Roman West in the Third Century*, Oxford, 215-233.

Drinkwater, J.F., 1987: Urbanization in Italy and the Western Empire, in J. Wacher (ed.), *The Urbanization in Italy and the Western Empire Roman World*, London, 345-387.

Dunbabin, K.M.D., 1991: Triclinium and stibadium, in W.J. Slater (ed.), *Dining in a classical context*, Ann Arbor, 121-148.

Dunbabin, K.M.D., 1996: Convivial spaces: dining and entertainment in the Roman villa, *Journal of Roman Archaeology* 9, 66-80.

Duncan, J.S., 1982: *Housing and Identity. Cross-cultural perspectives*, London.

Duurland, M., 2000: *Romeinse vindplaatsen in het landelijke gebied tussen Tongeren en Maastricht: een inventarisatie en periodisering*, Amsterdam (unpublished thesis University of Amsterdam).

Dyson, S., 2003: *The Roman Countryside*, London.

Ebnöther, C., 1995: *Der römische Gutshof in Dietikon*, Zürich/Egg (Monographien der Kantonsarchäologie Zürich 25).

Eck, W., 2004: *Geschichte der Stadt Köln. Köln in römischer Zeit*, Cologne.

Elias, N., 1982: *The Civilizing Process: State Formation and Civilization*, Oxford.

Erdkamp, P., 2002: The Corn Supply of the Roman Armies during the Principate (27 BC - 235 AD), in P. Erdkamp (ed.), *The Roman Army and the Economy*, Amsterdam, 46-69.

Eriksen, T.H., 1995: *Small Places, Large Issues: An Introduction to Social and Cultural Anthropology (Anthropology, Culture and Society)*, London.

Fehr, H., 2003: *Römervilla. Führer durch die Ausgrabungen und Ausstellung am Silberberg Bad Neuenahr-Ahrweiler*, Koblenz.

Fellmann, R. 2009, *Römische Kleinfunde aus Holz aus dem Legionslager Vindonissa*, Brugg (Veröffentlichungen der Gesellschaft Pro Vindonissa 20).

Fischer, T., 2001: *Die Römer in Deutschland*, Stuttgart.

Fleisher, J.B./A. LaViolette, 2007: The Changing Power of Swahili Houses, Fourteenth to Nineteenth Centuries A.D., In R.A. Beck jr. (ed.), *The Durable House: House Society Models in Archaeology*, Carbondale.

Fokkens, H./R. Jansen (eds), 2002: *2000 jaar bewoningsdynamiek. Brons- en ijzertijdbewoning in het Maas-Demer-Scheldegebied*, Leiden.

Frank, K., 2007: Zur 'einheimischen' Bevölkerung in frühromischer Zeit, in M. Hegewisch (ed.), *Krieg und Frieden. Kelten, Römer, Germanen*, Bonn/Darmstadt, 258-261.

Frank, K./C. Keller, 2007: Jüchen-Neuholz. Vom eisenzeitlichen Gehöft zur Villa rustica, in M. Hegewisch (ed.), *Krieg und Frieden. Kelten, Römer, Germanen*, Bonn/Darmstadt, 316-324.

Frébutte, C., 1997: Chièvres/Ladeuze: hameau laténien et vestiges gallo-romains, *Chronique de l'Archéologie wallonne* 4-5, 60.

Freeman, P.W.M., 1993: 'Romanisation' and Roman Material Culture. Review of M. Millett's The Romanization of Roman Britain. An Essay in Archaeological Interpretation, *Journal of Roman Archaeology* 6, 438-445.

Freeman, P.W.M., 1997: Mommsen to Haverfield: the origins of studies of Romanization in late 19th-c. Britain, in D.J. Mattingly (ed.), *Dialogues in Roman imperialism*, Portsmouth/Rhode Island (International Roman Archaeology Conference Series, Journal of Roman Archaeology supplementary series 23), 24-50.

Fremersdorf, F., 1933: *Der Romische Gutshof Köln-Müngersdorf*, Berlin/Leipzig (Römisch-Germanischen Forschungen 6).

Gaitzsch, W., 1983: Römische Siedlungsplatze im Verlauf der antiken Strasse von Köln nach Jülich, in G. Bauchhenss (ed.), *Archaologie in den rheinischen Lossborden. Beitrage zur Siedlungsgeschichte im Rheinland*, Cologne (Rheinische Ausgrabungen 24), 347-361.

Gaitzsch, W., 1986: Grundformen Römischer Landsiedlungen im Westen der CCAA, *Bonner Jahrbücher* 186, 397-427.

Gaitzsch, W., 1990: Der Römische Gutshof im 'Gewahrhau' bei Niederzier. Modell einer Landsiedlung in der Germania Inferior, in H. Hellenkemper *et al.* (ed.), *Archäologie in Nordrhein-Westfalen*, Mainz, 235-241.

Gaitzsch, W., 1993: Brand und Körpergraber in römischen Landsiedlungen der Jülicher Lossborde, in M. Struck (ed.) *Römerzeitliche Gräber als Quellen zu Religion, Bevolkungsstruktur und Sozialgeschichte*, Mainz, 17ff.

Gaitzsch, W., 2004: Die *Via Belgica* zwischen Elsdorf und Jülich. Aufschlüsse im Vorfeld des Braunkohlentagebaus Hambach, in H. Koschik (ed.), *"Alle Wege führen nach Rom...". Internationales Römerstrassenkolloquium Bonn*, Pulheim Brauweiler (Materialen zur Bodendenkmalpflege im Rheinland 16), 175-196.

Gaitzsch, W., 2010: Römische Siedlungsgrabungen im rheinischen Braunkohlenrevier. Forschungsschwerpunkte und Ergebnisse, in J. Kunow (ed.), *Braunkohlenarchaologie im Rheinland. Entwicklung von Kultur, Umwelt und Landschaft, Kolloquium der Stiftung zur Forderung der Archaologie im rheinischen Braunkohlenrevier vom 5.-6. Oktober 2006*, Weilerswist.

Garnsey, P. (ed.), 1980: *Non-slave labour in the Greco-Roman world*, Cambridge.

Gaston, C., 2008: Bâtiments 'standardisés' dans la pars rustica des villae: deux exemples récemment découverts en Franche-Comté, *Revue archéologique de l'Est* 57, URL: http://rae.revues.org/index3123.html. Consulté le 04 août 2010.

Gebus, L./T. Klag, 1990: Fontoy, in J. Baudoux *et al.*, *La Lorraine Antique. Villes et villages*, Metz, 88.

Gechter, M., 1990: Der romische Gutshof von Rheinbach-Flerzheim, in H. Hellenkemper *et al.* (ed.) *Archäologie in Nordrhein-Westfalen*, Mainz, 251-255.

Gechter, M./J. Kunow, 1986: Zur ländlichen Besiedlung des Rheinlandes in römischer Zeit, *Bonner Jahrbücher* 186, 375-396.

Gemehl, D., 2004: Découverte d'un faubourg d'Amiens. Le site de la ZAC Cathédrale – Université, in D. Bayard/N. Mahéo (eds), *La marque de Rome. Samarobriva et les villes du nord de la Gaule*, Amiens, 131-137.

Gerritsen, F., 2003: *Local Identities: Landscape and Community in the Late Prehistoric Meuse-Demer-Scheldt Region*, Amsterdam (Amsterdam Archaeological Studies 9).

Gerritsen, F.A., 2004: Archaeological Perspectives on Local Communities, in J. Bintliff (ed.), *Blackwell Companion to Archaeology*, Oxford, 141-154.

Gerritsen, F.A., 2007: Relocating the house. Social transformations in late prehistoric Northern Europe, in R.A. Beck (ed.), *The Durable House. House Society Models in Archaeology*, Carbondale, 154-174.

Giddens, A., 1984: *The constitution of society: Outline of the theory of structuration*, Cambridge.

Giffen, A.E. van, 1950: *Inheemse en Romeinse terpen. Opgravingen in de dorpswierde te Ezinge en de Romeinse terpen van Utrecht, Valkenburg (Z.H.) en Vechten*, Den Haag.

Given, M. 2004: *The Archaeology of the Colonized*. London.

Glasbergen, W., 1967: *De Romeinse castella te Valkenburg Z.H. De opgravingen in de dorpsheuvel in 1962*, Groningen.

Glaudemans, M., 2000: *Amsterdams Arcadia. De ontdekking van het achterland*, Nijmegen.

Goossens, W./J.H. Holwerda/N.J. Krom, 1908: Opgravingen bij het Ravenbosch bij Valkenburg, *Oudheidkundige Mededelingen uit het Rijksmuseum van Oudheden te Leiden* 2, 25-44.

Goossens, W., 1916: Die Römische Villa bei Vlengendaal, *Bijblad der Nederlandse Anthropologische Ver-eeniging* (Internationales Archiv fur Ethnographie 24), 19-40.

Gosden, C./C. Knowles, 2001: *Collecting Colonialism. Material Culture and Colonial Change*, Oxford/New York.

Gosden, C./Y. Marshall 1999: The cultural biography of objects, *World archaeology* 31, 169-178.

Grahame, M., 1998: Redefining Romanization: material culture and the question of social continuity in Roman Britain, in C. Forcey/J. Hawthorne/R. Witcher (eds), *TRAC 1997. Proceedings of the Seventh Annual Theoretical Roman Archaeology Conference*, Exeter, 1-10.

Greene, K., 1986: *The Archaeology of the Roman Economy*, London.

Gricourt, D./A. Jacques, 2007: Le mobilier de la villa gallo-romaine de Monchy-le-Preux (Pas-de-Calais), *Revue du Nord* 89 (nr. 373), 173-196.

Groot, T. de, 2001: *Brandend zand. Een inheems-Romeinse nederzetting te Brandevoort (gemeente Helmond)*, (unpublished thesis VU University Amsterdam).

Groot, T. de, 2005: *De Romeinse villa Meerssen-Onderste Herkenberg. de resultaten van het waardestellend archeologisch onderzoek in 2003 in relatie tot de onderzoeksgeschiedenis en landschappelijke context van het villacomplex*, Amersfoort (Rapportage Archeologische Monumentenzorg 125).

Groot, T. de, 2006: *Resultaten van de opgraving van een Romeins tumulusgraf in Bocholtz (gem. Simpelveld)*, Amersfoort (Rapportage Archeologische Monumentenzorg 127).

Groot, T. de, 2006: Roman Villae in the Loess Area of the Dutch Province of Limburg: an Analysis of their Number, Distribution and Preservation, *Berichten van de Rijksdienst voor het Oudheidkundig Bodemonderzoek* 46, 275-301.

Groot, M., 2008: *Animals in ritual and economy in a Roman frontier community. Excavations in Tiel-Passe-waaij*, Amsterdam (Amsterdam Archaeological Studies 12).

Groot, M., in press: Household specialisation in horse breeding: the role of returning veterans in the Batavian river area, *Proceedings of Fines imperii, imperium sine fine?*, Osnabrück.

Groot, M./S. Heeren/L.I. Kooistra/W.K. Vos, 2009: Surplus production for the market? The agrar-ian economy in the non-villa landscapes of Germania Inferior, *Journal of Roman Archaeology* 22-1, 231-253.

Groover, M.D., 2008: *The archaeology of North American Farmsteads*, Gainesville.

Haalebos, J.K., 1997: Een Romeins graanschip in Woerden, in R. van der Eerden *et al.* (ed.), *47-1997. 1950 jaar Romeinen in Utrecht*, Utrecht, 67-96.

Haalebos *et al.*, 2000: *Alphen aan den Rijn – Albaniana 1998-1999. Opgravingen in de Julianastraat, de Castellumstraat, op Het eiland en onder het St.-Jorisplein*, Nijmegen.

Habermehl, D., 2011: Exploring villa development in the northern provinces of the Roman empire, in N. Roymans/T. Derks (eds), *Villa Landscapes in the Roman North. Economy, Culture and Lifestyles*, Amsterdam, 61-82.

Habets, J., 1871: Exploration d'une villa Belgo-Romaine au Herkenberg à Meerssen, *Publications de la Société Historique et Archéologique dans le Limbourg* 8, 379-428.

Habets, J., 1895: Uit de nagelaten geschriften van de wijlen Zeer Eerw. Heer Jos Habets over Wegen en Gebouwen uit het Romeinsch tijdperk, in het Hertogdom Limburg, *Publications de la Société Historique et Archéologique dans le Limbourg* 32, 257-296.

Hales, S., 2003: *The Roman House and social identity*, Cambridge.

Hallmann-Preuss, B., 2002/2003: Die villa rustica Hambach 59, *Saalburg Jahrbuch* 52/53, 287-537.

Harsema, O., 2005: Boerderijen tussen de raatakkers. Nederzettingen op de noordelijke zandgronden, in L.P. Louwe Kooijmans *et al.* (eds), *Nederland in de prehistorie*, Amsterdam, 543-555.

Haselgrove, C., 1990: The Romanization of Belgic Gaul: some archaeological perspectives, in T. Blagg/M. Millett (eds), *The Early Roman empire in the West*, Oxford, 45-71.

Haselgrove, C., 1995: Social and symbolic order in the origins and layout of Roman villas in Northern Gaul, in J. Metzler *et al.* (eds), *Integration in the Early Roman West. The role of Culture and Ideology*, Luxembourg (Dossiers d'Archeologie du Musee National d'Histoire et d'Art 4), 65-75.

Haselgrove, C., 1996: Roman impact on rural settlement and society in southern Picardy, in N. Roymans (ed.) *From the Sword to the Plough*, Amsterdam (Amsterdam Archaeological Studies 1), 127-187.

Haselgrove, C., 2007: The age of enclosure: Later Iron Age settlement and society in northern France, in C. Haselgrove/T. Moore (eds), *The later Iron Age in Britain and beyond*, Oxford, 492-522.

Haselgrove, C./T. Moore (eds), 2007: *The later Iron Age in Britain and beyond*, Oxford.

Haupt, D., 1968: Die Kleinfunde eines römischen Landhauses aus Neuss-Weckhoven, in L.H. Barfield *et al.* (eds), *Beitrage zur Archäologie des römischen Rheinlands*, Düsseldorf (Rheinische Ausgrabungen 3), 153-165.

Haverfield F., 1905-1906: The Romanization of Roman Britain, *Proceedings of the British Academy* 2, 185-217.

Hazee, H., 1969: Notes au sujet de la Villa gallo-romaine de Strud (Haltinne), *Bulletin du Cercle Archaéologique Hesbaye-Condroz* 9, 75-78.

Heeren, S., 2006: *Opgravingen bij Tiel-Passewaaij 1. De nederzetting aan de Passewaaijse Hogeweg*, Amsterdam (Zuidnederlandse Archeologische Rapporten 29).

Heeren, S., 2009: *Romanisering van rurale gemeenschappen in de civitas Batavorum. De casus Tiel-Passewaaij*, Amersfoort (Nederlandse Archeologische Rapporten 36).

Hegewisch, M. (ed.) 2007: *Krieg und Frieden. Kelten, Römer, Germanen*, Bonn/Darmstadt.

Heimberg, U., 2002/2003: Römische Villen an Rhein und Maas, *Bonner Jahrbücher* 202/203, 57-148.

Hellenkemper, H. *et al.* (ed.) 1990: *Archäologie in Nordrhein-Westfalen*, Mainz.

Hendon, J.A., 2004: Living and Working at Home: The Social Archaeology of Household Production and Social Relations, in L. Meskell/R.W. Preucel (eds), *A Companion to Social Archaeology*, Oxford, 272-286.

Hessing, W. *et al.*, 1997: *Romeinen langs de snelweg, bouwstenen voor Vechtens verleden*, Abcoude.

Hiddink, H.A., 1991: Rural centres in the Roman settlement system of Northern Gallia Belgica and Germania inferior, in N. Roymans/F. Theuws (eds), *Images of the Past. Studies on ancient societies in northwestern Europe*, Amsterdam, 201-233.

Hiddink, H.A., 2004: *Een grafmonument uit de Romeinse tijd in Nieuwenhagen, gemeente Landgraaf*, Amsterdam (Zuidnederlandse Archeologische Rapporten 17).

Hiddink, H.A. (ed.), 2005a: *Archeologisch onderzoek aan de Beekseweg te Lieshout*, Amsterdam (Zuidnederlandse Archeologische Rapporten 18).

Hiddink, H.A., 2005b: *Opgravingen op het Rosveld bij Nederweert 1. Landschap en bewoning in de IJzertijd, Romeinse tijd en Middeleeuwen*, Amsterdam (Zuidnederlandse Archeologische Rapporten 22).

Hiddink, H.A., 2008: *Archeologisch onderzoek op de Groot Bottelsche Akker bij Deurne. Bewoning uit de Steentijd, IJzertijd, Romeinse tijd, Vroege en Volle Middeleeuwen op de Groot Bottelsche Akker bij Deurne*, Amsterdam (Zuidnederlandse Archeologische Rapporten 33).

Hiddink, H.A./E. de Boer, 2003: *Archeologische opgravingen tussen Schinnen en Bocholtz in het tracé van de 36 inch gastransportleiding van NV Nederlandse Gasunie*, Amsterdam (Zuidnederlandse Archeologische Rapporten 10).

Hillier, B./J. Hanson, 1984: *The Social Logic of Space*, Cambridge.

Hingley, R., 1984: The Archaeology of Settlement and the Social Significance of Space, *Scottish Archaeological Review* 3, 22-26.

Hingley, R., 1989: *Rural Settlement in Roman Britain*, London.

Hingley, R., 1990: Domestic Organisation and Gender Relations in Iron Age and Romano-British Households, in R. Samson (ed.), *The Social Archaeology of Houses*, Edinburgh, 125-147.

Hingley, R., 1996: The 'legacy' of Rome: the rise, decline, and fall of the theory of Romanisation, in J. Webster/N.J. Cooper (eds), *Roman imperialism: Post-colonial perspectives*, Leicester (Leicester Archaeology Monographs 3), 35-48.

Hingley, R., 2000: *Roman Officers and English Gentlemen*, London.

Hingley, R., 2005: *Globalizing Roman culture. Unity, diversity and empire*, Abingdon/New York.

Hingley, R., 2008: *The Recovery of Roman Britain 1586 to 1910: A Colony so Fertile*, Oxford.

Hinz, H., 1969a: *Die Ausgrabungen auf dem Kirchberg in Morken, Kreis Bergheim (Erft). Von der Steinzeit bis ins Mittelalter*, Düsseldorf (Rheinische Ausgrabungen 7).

Hinz, H., 1969b: *Kreis Bergheim*, Düsseldorf (Archäologische Funde und Denkmaler des Rheinlandes 2).

Hodder, I.R. (ed.), 1989: *The meanings of things. Material culture and symbolic expression*, London.

Hodder, I.R., 2004: The 'Social' in Archaeological Theory: An Historical and Contemporary Perspective, in L. Meskell/R.W. Preucel (eds), *A Companion to Social Archaeology*, Oxford, 23-42.

Holwerda, J.H./W. Goossens, 1907: De Romeinsche hoeve bij den Heihof bij Valkenburg, *Oudheidkundige Mededelingen uit het Rijksmuseum van Oudheden te Leiden* 1, 10 ff.

Holwerda, J.H./A.E. Remouchamps/O.M. Beckers, 1928: Nederzettingen bij Stein aan de Maas, *Oudheidkundige Mededelingen uit het Rijksmuseum van Oudheden te Leiden* 9, 3-60.

Hoorne, J. *et al.*, 2008: Voorlopige resultaten van het preventief archeologisch onderzoek te Sint-Denijs-Westrem - Flanders Expo (Stad Gent, provincie Oost-Vlaanderen): drie Gallo-Romeinse erven, in W. De Clercq *et al.* (eds), *Journée d'Archéologie Romaine 2008 - Romeinendag 2008*, Brussels, 67-72.

Hopkins, K., 1980: Taxes and trade in the Roman Empire (200 BC-AD 400), *Journal of Roman Studies* 70, 101-25.

Horn, H.G., 1987: *Die Römer in Nordrhein-Westfalen*, Stuttgart.

Horn, H.G. (ed.), 1990: *Archäologie in Nordrhein-Westfalen*, Stuttgart.

Houbrachts, D./J.-M. Zambon, 1994: Ath/Meslin-l'Evêque: analyse dendrochronologique d'échantillons provenant de la fouille d'une villa romaine, *Chronique de l'Archéologie wallonne* 2, 43 ff.

Hulst, R.S., 1978: Druten-Klepperhei, Vorbericht der Ausgrabungen einer römischen Villa, *Berichten van de Rijksdienst voor het Oudheidkundig Bodemonderzoek* 28, 133-151.

Hulst, R.S., 1980: Een Romeinse villa bij Druten, *Hermeneus* 52, 117-127.

Huijbers, A.M.J.H., 2007: *Metaforisering in beweging. Boeren en hun gebouwde omgeving in de Volle Middeleeuwen in het Maas-Demer-Scheldegebied*, Amsterdam (unpublished dissertation University of Amsterdam).

In 't Ven, I./W. De Clercq (eds), 2005: *Een lijn door het landschap. Archeologie en het vTn-project 1997-1998*, Brussels.

Ingold, T. (ed.), 1994: *Companion Encyclopedia of Anthropology. Humanity, Culture and Social Life*, London/New York.

Jacques, A./G. Prilaux, 2005: Les fouilles d'Actiparc à Arras (Pas-de-Calais, France). Aspects méthodologiques et prémiers résultats, in J.-M. Léotard (ed.) *Actes des Journées d'archéologie en Wallonie 2004*, Liège, 61-79.

Jacques, A./M. Tuffreau-Libre, 1984: La villa gallo-romaine d'Hamblain-les-Près. Les états du Ier siècle, *Revue du Nord* 66, 181-205.

Jamieson, R.W., 2002: *Domestic architecture and power. The historical archaeology of colonial Ecuador*, New York.

Jansen, R./H. Fokkens, 1999: *Bouwen aan het verleden. 25 jaar archeologisch onderzoek in de gemeente Oss*, Leiden.

Jansen, R., 2008: *Bewoningsdynamiek op de Maashorst. Bewoningsgeschiedenis van Nistelrode van laat-neolithicum tot en met volle middeleeuwen*, Leiden (Archol Rapport 48).

Jeneson, C.F., 2004: *Terug naar Hoogeloon. Een nieuwe kijk op de Romeinse nederzetting rond de villa op de Kerkakkers*, Amsterdam (unpublished Master's thesis VU University).

Jeneson, K., 2011: Evaluating settlement patterns and settlement densities in the villa landscapes between Tongres and Cologne, in N. Roymans/T. Derks (eds), *Villa Landscapes in the Roman North. Economy, Culture and Lifestyles*, Amsterdam, 259-273.

Jeneson, K., in prep.: *Exploring the Roman villa world between Tongres and Cologne. A landscape archaeology approach*, Amsterdam (unpublished dissertation VU University).

Joachim, H.-E., 2006: Die Eisenzeit im nördlichen Rheinland in der Grenzzone von Kulturgruppen, in J. Kunow/H.H. Wegner (eds), *Urgeschichte im Rheinland*, Köln, 241-253.

Kaszab-Olschewski, T., 2006: *Siedlungsgenese Im Bereich Des Hambacher Forstes 1.-4. Jh. N. Chr. - Hambach 512 und Hambach 516*, Oxford (British Archaeological Reports International Series 1585).

Keay, S./N. Terrenato (eds) 2001: *Italy and the West: Comparative Issues in Romanization*, Oxford.

Kent, S., 1990: *Domestic architecture and the use of space. An interdisciplinary cross-cultural study*, Cambridge.

King, A., 2001: The Romanization of Diet in the Western Empire: Comparative archaeozoological studies, in S. Keay /N. Terrenato (eds) *Italy and the West: Comparative Issues in Romanization*, Oxford, 210-223.

Knörzer, K.-H., 1984: Veränderungen der Unkrautvegetation auf rheinischen Bauernhöfen seit der Römerzeit, *Bonner Jahrbücher* 184, 479-503.

Knörzer, K.H./J. Meurers-Balke, 1990: Die Wirtschafts- und Nützungsflachen eines römischen Gutshofes. Eine Rekonstruktion auf grund des botanischen Befundes, in H. Hellenkemper *et al.* (ed.), *Archäologie in Nordrhein-Westfalen*, Mainz, 242-246.

Köhler, B., 2005: *Villa rustica Frimmersdorf 49 und Villa rustica Frimmersdorf 131. Studien zur römischen Besiedlung im Braunkohlentagebaugebiet Garzweiler I*, Cologne.

Kohring, S./S. Wynne-Jones (eds), 2007: *Socialising Complexity. Structure, Interaction and Power in Archaeological Discourse*, Oxford.

Kooistra, L.I., 1991: *Arable farming in the heyday of the Roman villa at Voerendaal (Limburg, The Netherlands)* Amersfoort (Rijksdienst voor het Oudheidkundig Bodemonderzoek prints 409).

Kooistra, L.I., 1996: *Borderland farming. Possibilities and limitations of farming in the Roman Period and Early Middle Ages between the Rhine and Meuse*, Assen.

Koot, C.W./R. Berkvens (eds), 2004: *Bredase akkers eeuwen oud. 4000 jaar bewoningsgeschiedenis op de rand van zand en klei*, Amersfoort/Breda (Rapportage Archeologische Monumentenzorg 102/Erfgoedstudies Breda 1).

Koschik, H. (ed.) 2004: *"Alle Wege führen nach Rom...". Internationales Römerstrassenkolloquium Bonn*, Pulheim Brauweiler (Materialen zur Bodendenkmalpflege im Rheinland 16).

Koster, A./K. Peterse/L. Swinkels, 2002: *Romeins Nijmegen boven het maaiveld*, Nijmegen.

Kouwen, C.P.J. van, 1978: De Romeinse villa van Winssen. De geschiedenis van het verzonken klooster van Winssen of hoe een Romeinse villa ontdekt werd, *Westerheem* 27, 207-213.

Kunow, J., 1994: Die Ländliche Besiedlung im Südlichen Teil von Niedergermanien, in H. Bender/H. Wolff (eds), *Ländliche Besiedlung und Landwirtschaft in den Rhein-Donau-Provinzen des Römischen Reiches*, Espelkamp, 141-197.

Kunow, J./H.H. Wegner (eds), 2006: *Urgeschichte im Rheinland*, Köln.

Laloo, P. *et al.* 2008: Grootschalig nederzettingsonderzoek in een inheems-Romeins landschap. Resultaten 2006-2007 en voorlopig bilan van het preventief archeologisch onderzoek 'Kluizendok' in de Gentse haven, in W. De Clercq *et al.* (eds), *Journée d'Archéologie Romaine 2008 - Romeinendag 2008*, Brussels, 73-84.

Lambert, H., 1971: Vestiges superposés d'une villa gallo-romaine en matériaux durs et d'une habitation en bois à Velaines-Popuelles, *Archaeologia Belgica* 133, 5-14.

Laarman, F.J., 1996: Zoological material of the Bronze Age, Iron Age and Roman period from Wijk bij Duurstede-De Horden, in L.I. Kooistra, *Borderland farming. Possibilities and limitations of farming in the Roman period and Early Middle Ages between the Rhine and the Meuse*, Assen/Amersfoort, 369-380.

Lang, F., 2007: House-community-settlement. The new concept of living in Archaic Greece, in R. Westgate/N. Fisher/J. Whitley (eds), 2007: *Building communities. House, settlement and society in the Aegean and beyond*, London, 183-193.

Lauwerier, R.C.G.M., 1988: *Animals in Roman times in the Dutch eastern river area*, 's-Gravenhage/Amersfoort

Lawrence-Zuniga, D., 2001: From Bourgeois to Modern: Transforming houses and family life in rural Portugal, in M.-J. Amerlinck (ed.), *Architectural Anthropology*, Westport, 171-200.

Leemans, C., 1875: *Het Romeinsch grafteeken van Dodewaard*, Amsterdam.

Lefert, S., 2002: Ohey/Haillot: le corps de logis et les bains de la villa de Matagne, *Chronique de l'Archéologie wallonne* 10, 243-245.

Lefert, S., 2008: La villa Gallo-Romaine du Corria à Gesves, in W. De Clercq *et al.* (eds), *Journée d'Archéologie Romaine 2008 - Romeinendag 2008*, Brussels, 85-92.

Lefert, S./K. Bausier, 2006: Gesves/Gesves: la galerie orientale du logis de la villa gallo-romaine du Corria, *Chronique de l'Archéologie wallonne* 13, 234-236.

Lefert, S./K. Bausier/I. Nachtergael, 2000: Hamois: la villa gallo-romaine 'Sur le Hody', *Chronique de l'Archéologie wallonne* 8, 195-197.

Lefert, S./K. Bausier/I. Nachtergael, 2001: Hamois/Hamois: la villa gallo-romaine 'Sur le Hody', *Chronique de l'Archéologie wallonne* 9, 200-203.

Lefert, S./K. Bausier/I. Nachtergael, 2002: Hamois/Hamois: la villa 'Sur le Hody', quatre nouveaux bâtiments annexes, *Chronique de l'Archéologie wallonne* 10, 240-243.

Lensen, J.-P., 1987: Site protohistorique et Gallo-Romaine de Haccourt 'Froidmont', in A. Cahen-Delhaye/C. de Lichtervelde/F. Leuxe (eds), *L'archéologie en Wallonie,* Namur, 159-160.

Lenz, K.H., 1998: Villae rusticae. Zur Entstehung dieser Siedlungsform in den Nordwestprovinzen des Römischen Reiches, *Kölner Jahrbuch für vor- und frühgeschichte* 31, 49-70.

Lenz, K.H., 1999: *Siedlungen der Römische Kaiserzeit auf der Aldenhovener Platte*, Frankfurt.

Lenz, K.H., 2006: Veteranen der römischen Armee im Siedlungsbild einer früh- und mittelhaiserzeitlichen Koloniestadt und deren Hinterland. Das Beispiel der Colonia Claudia Ara Agrippinensium (Köln), *Germania* 84, 61-91.

Lepetz, S., 1996: Effets de la romainisation sur l'élévage dans établissements ruraux du nord de la Gaule. L'exemple de l'augmentation de la stature des animaux domestiques, in D. Bayard/J.-L. Collart, *De la ferme indigène à la villa romaine. La romanisation des campagnes de la Gaule*, Amiens (Revue Archéologique de Picardie, special 11), 317-324.

Levi-Strauss, C., 1982: *The way of the masks*, Seattle.

Liversridge, J., 1950: Tables in Roman Britain, *Antiquity* 24, 5-29.

Lodewijckx, M., 1995: *Eine Römervilla im Wange (Brabant, Belgien) mit Depot von bronzenem Pferdegeschirr-Ein vorläufiger Bericht*, in S.K. Palágyi (ed.), *Balácai Közlemények III. 1994*, Veszprem, 143-150.

López Bayón, I., 1997: Étude archéozoologique du gisement de Haccourt (âge du fer), *Bulletin des Chercheurs de la Wallonie* 37, 175-185.

Louwe Kooijmans, L.P. *et al.* (eds), 2005: *Nederland in de prehistorie*, Amsterdam.

Low, S.M./E. Chambers, 1989: *Housing, culture, and design: a comparative perspective*, Philadelphia.

Lutkehaus, N. *et al.* (eds), 1990: *Sepik Heritage. Tradition and change in Papua New Guinea*, Durham.

Lynch, K.M., 2007: More thoughts on the space of the symposium, in Westgate, R./N. Fisher/J. Whitley (eds), *Building communities. House, settlement and society in the Aegean and beyond*, London, 243-249.

Maas, J.C., 2007: *Druten-Klepperheide revisited. Een inheems-Romeinse nederzetting in de civitas Batavorum*, Amsterdam (unpublished thesis VU University).

Maeyer, R. de, 1937: *De Romeinsche villa's in België: een archeologische studie*, Antwerpen.

Maeyer, R. de, 1940: *De overblijfselen der Romeinsche Villa's in België*, Antwerpen.

Malrain, F./V. Matterne/P. Méniel, 2002, *Les paysans Gaulois (IIIe siècle − 52 av. J.-C.)*, Paris.

Martins, C.B., 2005: *Becoming Consumers: Looking beyond Wealth as an Explanation of Villa Variability. Perspectives from the East of England*, Oxford (British Archaeological Reports British Series 403).

Massart, C., 2006: Sépultures privilégiées sous grands tumulus, *Dossiers Archéologie et sciences des origines* 315 *(La Belgique Romaine)*, 78-85.

Materne, D., 1969: Notes au sujet de la villa belgo-romaine de Miecret (province de Namur), *Bulletin du Cercle Archéologique Hesbaye-Condroz* 9, 79-81.

Matthys, A., 1973: *La villa gallo-romaine de Jette*, Brussels (Archeologia Belgica 152).

Matthys, A., 1974: *La villa romaine de Vesqueville*, Brussels (Archeologia Belgica 159).

Mattingly, D.J., 1997: Dialogues of power and experience in the Roman Empire. In D.J. Mattingly (ed.), *Dialogues in Roman Imperialism. Power, discourse and discrepant experience in the Roman Empire*, Portsmouth/Rhode Island (Journal of Roman Archaeology, supplementary series 23), 7-20.

Mattingly, D.J., 2004: Being Roman: expressing identity in a provincial setting, *Journal of Roman Archaeology* 17, 5-25.

Mattingly, D.J., 2006: *An Imperial Possession: Britain in the Roman Empire*, London.

Mees, A./B. Pferdehirt, 2002: *Romerzeitliche Schiffsfunde in der datenbank 'Navis I'*, Mainz (Kataloge Vor- und Frühgeschichtlicher Altertummer, band 29).

Meskell, L./R.W. Preucel (eds), 2004: *A Companion to Social Archaeology*, Oxford.

Meunier, M., 1964: *La villa belgo-romaine de 'Fin-de-Ville' (commune de Mont-Lez-Houffalize)*, *Archaeologia Belgica* 78.

Meurers-Balke, J./A.J. Kalis, 2006: Landwirtschaft und Landnutzung in der Bronze- und Eisenzeit, in J. Kunow/H.H. Wegner (eds), *Urgeschichte im Rheinland*, Köln, 267-276.

Mignot, P., 1988: *Les bâtiments gallo-romains de Halloy*, Ciney.

Mignot, P., 1996: La villa romaine de Malagne à Rochefort/Jemelle, in J. Plumier (ed.), *Cinq années d'archéologie en province de Namur 1990-1995*, Namur (Etudes et documents. Fouilles 3), 29-34.

Mignot, P., 1997: Rochefort/Jemelle: la villa romaine, *Chronique de l'Archéologie wallonne* 4-5, 183-185.

Mignot, P., 2006: La villa de Jemelle à Rochefort, *Dossiers Archéologie et sciences des origines* 315 *(La Belgique Romaine)*, 72-75.

Millett, M., 1990: *The Romanization of Roman Britain. An Essay in Archaeological Interpretation*, Cambridge.

Millett, M., 1990: Romanization: historical issues and archaeological interpretation, in T. Blagg/M. Millett (eds), *The early Roman empire in the West*, Oxford, 35-41.

Millett, M./N. Roymans/J. Slofstra, 1995: Integration, culture and ideology in the early Roman west, in J. Metzler *et al.* (eds), *Integration in the early Roman west. The role of culture and ideology*, Luxembourg (Dossiers d'Archéologie du Musée National d'Histoire et d'Art 4), 1-5.

Mommsen, T., 1886: *The Provinces of the Roman Empire: from Caesar to Diocletian*, London.

Mücher, H.J., 1973: Enkele aspecten van Loess en zijn noordelijke begrenzing, in het bijzonder in Belgisch en Nederlands Limburg en het daaraan grenzende gebied in Duitsland, *K.N.A.G. Geografisch Tijdschrift* 7- 4, 259-276.

Müller, A./J. van Doesburg, 2008: *Fruit van rijke bodem, veldonderzoek (februari 2007) in het kader van handhaving op het monument Cothen-De Zemelen*, Amersfoort (Rapportage Archeologische Monumentenzorg 168).

Müller-Wille, M., 1970: Die landwirtschaftliche Grundlage der Villae rusticae, in H. Hinz (ed.) *Germania Romana. Römisches leben auf germanischem Boden*, Heidelberg (Gymnasium Beihefte 7), 26-42.

Nicolay, J., 2005: *Gewapende Bataven. Gebruik en betekenis van wapen- en paardentuig uit niet-militaire contexten in de Rijndelta (50 voor tot 450 na Chr.)*, Amsterdam.

Oelmann, F., 1916: Die römische Villa bei Blankenheim in der Eifel, *Bonner Jahrbücher* 123, 210-226.

Oelmann F, 1921: Die Villa rustica bei Stahl und Verwandtes, *Germania* 5, 64-73.

Oelmann, F., 1928: Ein galloromischer Bauernhof bei Mayen, *Bonner Jahrbücher* 133, 51-140.

Oliver, P. (ed.), 1997: *Encyclopedia of Vernacular Architecture of the World*, Cambridge.

Otte, M., 1990: *Les Fouilles de la place Saint-Lambert à Liège 3*, Liège.

Pals, J.P./T. Hakbijl, 1992: Weed and insect infestation of a grain cargo in a ship at the Roman fort of Laurium in Woerden (Province of Zuid-Holland), *Review of Palaeobotany and Palynology* 73, 287-300.

Paepe, P. de/L. van Impe, 1991: Donk, in *Archeologie in Vlaanderen*, 1991-1, 148.

Panhuysen, T.A.S.M, 1996: *Romeins Maastricht en zijn beelden*, Assen.

Parker Pearson, M. /C. Richards, 1994: *Architecture and Order. Approaches to Social Space*, London/New York

Pauwels, D. 2007: Veldwezelt tussen protohistorie en Tachtigjarige Oorlog, *Archeologie in Limburg* 106, 14-23.

Pauwels, D./G. Creemers, 2006: Een Romeinse landelijke nederzetting te Smeermaas (Lanaken, prov. Limburg), *Relicta* 2, 49-118.

Pauwels, D./A. Vanderhoeven/G. Vynckier, 2000: Lafelt (Riemst): Nederzetting uit de ijzertijd en bijgebouwen van een Romeinse villa, in A. Vanderhoeven/G. Creemers (eds), *Archeologische Kroniek Limburg 1999*, Tongeren.

Pavlides, E./J.E. Hesser, 1989: Vernacular Architecture as an Expression of Its Social Context in Eressos, Greece, in S. Low/E. Chambers (eds), *Housing, Culture and Design, a Comparative Perspective.* Philadelphia, 357-374.

Pekáry, T., 1994: Die römischen Agrarschriftsteller und die nördlichen Provinzen, in H. Bender/H. Wolff (eds), *Ländliche Besiedlung und Landwirtschaft in den Rhein-Donau-Provinzen des Römischen Reiches*, Espelkamp, 65-72.

Percival, J., 1976: *The Roman Villa, a Historical Introduction*, London.

Peters, P., 1922: Romeinsche Villa bij Overstenhof, Schaesberg, *Publications de la Société Historique et Archéologique dans le Limbourg* 58, 102-118.

Peters, P., 1930: Romeinsche villa te Bovenste Caumer, Heerlen, *Publications de la Société Historique et Archéologique dans le Limbourg* 66, 189-199.

Peters, J., 1994: Nutztiere in den westlichen Rhein-Donau-Provinzen während der römischen Kaiserzeit, in H. Bender/H. Wolff (eds), *Ländliche Besiedlung und Landwirtschaft in den Rhein-Donau-Provinzen des Römischen Reiches*, Espelkamp, 37-63.

Piepers, W., 1959: Römischer Gutshof und späteisenzeitliche Siedlungsspuren bei Garsdorf, Ldkr. Bergheim (Erft), *Germania* 37, 296 ff.

Pigière, F. *et al.*, 2001: Etude archéozoologique de la villa romaine de Bruyelle, *Chronique de l'Archéologie wallonne* 9, 42-43.

Pion P., 1996: Les établissements ruraux dans la vallée de l'Aisne, de la fin du second Age du Fer au début du Haut Empire romain (IIIème siècle av. J.-C./Ier siècle apr. J.-C.): bilan provisoire des données et esquisse de synthèse, in D. Bayard/J.-L. Collart, *De la ferme indigène à la villa romaine. La romanisation des campagnes de la Gaule*, Amiens (Revue Archéologique de Picardie, special 11), 55-107.

Pitts, M., 2008: Globalizing the local in Roman Britain: An anthropological approach to social change, *Journal of Anthropological Archaeology* 27, 493-506.

Plumier, J., 1984: La villa Gallo-Romaine des 'Grandes Pièces' a Latinne, in P. van Ossel/J. Plumier/ P.J. Claeys (eds), *Archeolo-J. 15 années, 15 chantiers*, Rixensart, 69-87.

Plumier, J., 1987: Structures gallo-romaines à Bieure, Matgne-la-Petite (comm. de Doische), *Archaeologia Belgica* 3, 145-152.

Plumier, J., 2006: Namur. Un *vicus* fluvial, *Dossiers Archéologie et sciences des origines* 315 *(La Belgique Romaine)*, 44-47.

Polak, M./R.P.J. Kloosterman/R.A.J. Niemeijer, 2004: *Alphen aan den Rijn - Albaniana 2001-2002. Opgravingen tussen de Castellumstraat, het Omloopkanaal en de Oude Rijn*, Nijmegen.

Pope, R., 2003: *Prehistoric Dwelling: Circular structures in North and Central Britain c 2500 BC–AD 500*, Durham (unpublished dissertation University of Durham).

Precht, G./N. Zieling (eds), 2001: *Genese, Struktur und Entwicklung römischer Städte im 1. Jahrhundert n. Chr. in Nieder- und Obergermanien. Kolloquim vom 17. bis 19. Februar 1998 im Regionalmuseum Xanten*, Mainz (Xantener Berichte 9).

Preston Blier, S., 2008: Vernacular Architecture, in C. Tilley *et al.* (eds), *Handbook of Material Culture*, London, 230-253.

Purcell, N., 1987: Town in country and country in town, in E.B. MacDouggall (ed.) *Ancient Roman Villa Gardens*, Washington DC, 187-203.

Purcell, N., 1995: The Roman *villa* and the landscape of production, in T. Cornell /K. Lomas (eds), *Urban Society in Roman Italy*, London, 151-179.

Quérel, P./M. Feugère, 2001: Des traces antiques exceptionelles: le recyclage du bronze, *Archéologia* 374, 42-48.

Rapoport, A., 1982: *The Meaning of the Built Environment: A Nonverbal Communication Approach*, Beverly Hills

Rapoport, A., 1989: Foreword, in S.M. Low/E. Chambers, *Housing, culture, and design: a comparative perspective*, Philadelphia, XIII.

Rapoport, A., 1994: Spatial Organization and the Built Environment. In T. Ingold (ed.), *Companion Encyclopedia of Anthropology: Humanity, Culture and Social Life*, London, 460–502.

Rech, M., 1980: Eine Villa rustica im Hambacher Forst, Kr. Düren, *Bonner Jahrbücher* 180, 461-491.

Rech, M., 1983: Eine Villa rustica bei Niederzier-Hambach, Kreis Düren (Hambach 66), in G. Bauchhenss (ed.) *Archäologie in den rheinischen Lössbörden: Beiträge zur Siedlungsgeschichte im Rheinland*, Köln (Rheinische Ausgrabungen 24).

Remouchamps, A.E., 1925: Opgravingen van een Romeinse villa in het Ravensbosch, *Oudheidkundige Mededelingen uit het Rijksmuseum van Oudheden te Leiden* 6, 6-77.

Remouchamps, A.E., 1928: Opgravingen van Romeinsche gebouwen te Stein (L.), *Oudheidkundige Mededelingen uit het Rijksmuseum van Oudheden te Leiden* 9, 4-14.

Renes, J., 1988: *De geschiedenis van het Zuidlimburgse Cultuurlandschap*, Assen/Maastricht.

Révillion, S./K. Bouche/L. Wozny, 1994: La partie agricole d'une grande exploitation rurale d'époque romaine: le gisement des 'Hauts de Clauwiers', Seclin (Nord), *Revue du Nord. Archéologie* 76, 99-146.

Rippengal, R., 1993: 'Villas as a Key to Social Structure'? Some Comments on Recent Approaches to the Romano-British Villa and Some Suggestions Toward an Alternative, in E. Scott (ed.) *Theoretical Roman Archaeology: First Conference Proceedings*, Aldershot, 79-101.

Rivet, A.L.F. (ed.), 1969: *The villa in Roman Britain*, London.

Robben, A.C.G.M., 1989: Habits of the home. Spatial hegemony and the structuration of house and society in Brazil, *American Anthropologist* 91-3, 570-588.

Rober, A., 1980: Sanctuaire et villa à Matagne-la-petite, *Archeologia Belgica* 223.

Rober, A., 1984: La villa gallo-romaine de Matagne-la-Petite, *Archeologia Belgica* 258.

Rober, A., 1987: Une villa gallo-romaine à Vodelée (comm. de Doische), *Archaeologia Belgica* 3, 153-164.

Robinet, C., 2004: Villa romaine de Vezin-Namêche, *Annales de la Société archéologique de Namur* 78, 95-140.

Roger, D./I. Catteddu, 2002: Onnaing-Toyota: Bilan Archéologique, *Archéologia* 386, 43-51.

Roosens, H., 1955: Une villa romaine à Bourcy, *Archaeologia Belgica* 27.

Rowlands, M./C. Tilley, 2006: Monuments and Memorials, in C. Tilley *et al.*, *Handbook of material culture*, London, 500-514.

Roymans, N., 1990: *Tribal societies in Northern Gaul. An Anthropological Perspective*, Amsterdam (Cingula 12).

Roymans, N. (ed.) 1995: *Opgravingen in de Molenakker te Weert. Campagne 1994*, Amsterdam (Zuidnederlandse Archeologische Rapporten 1).

Roymans, N., 1996: The sword or the plough. Regional dynamics in the romanisation of Belgic Gaul and the Rhineland area, in N. Roymans (ed.) *From the sword to the plough*, Amsterdam (Amsterdam Archaeological Studies 1), 9-126.

Roymans, N. 2004: *Ethnic identity and imperial power. The Batavians in the Early Roman Empire*, Amsterdam (Amsterdam Archaeological Studies 10).

Roymans, N./F. Theuws (eds), 1991: *Images of the Past: studies on ancient societies in Northwestern Europe*, Amsterdam.

Roymans, N./A. Tol (eds), 1996: *Opgravingen in Kampershoek en de Molenakker te Weert. Campagne 1995*, Amsterdam (Zuidnederlandse Archeologische Rapporten 4).

Roymans, N./A. Tol/H.A. Hiddink (eds), 1998: *Opgravingen in Kampershoek en de Molenakker te Weert. Campagne 1996-1998*, Amsterdam (Zuidnederlandse Archeologische Rapporten 5).

Roymans, N./F. Theuws, 1999: Long-term perspectives on land and people in the Meuse-Demer-Scheldt region (1100 BC-1500 AD). An introduction, in F. Theuws/N. Roymans (eds), *Land and Ancestors*, Amsterdam, 1-32.

Roymans, N./T. Derks 2006: Returning auxiliary veterans: some methodological considerations, *Journal of Roman Archaeology* 19, 121-135.

Roymans, N./T. Derks (eds), 2011: *Villa Landscapes in the Roman North. Economy, Culture and Lifestyles*, Amsterdam (Amsterdam Archaeological Studies 17).

Roymans, N./T. Derks, 2011: Studying Roman villa landscapes in the 21st century. A multi-dimensional approach, in N. Roymans/T. Derks (eds), *Villa Landscapes in the Roman North. Economy, Culture and Lifestyles*, Amsterdam, 1-44.

Roymans, N./D. Habermehl, 2011: On the origin and development of axial villas with double courtyards in the Latin West, in N. Roymans/T. Derks (eds), *Villa Landscapes in the Roman North. Economy, Culture and Lifestyles*, Amsterdam, 83-105.

Roymans, N./M. Zandstra, 2011: Indications for rural slavery in the northern provinces, in N. Roymans/T. Derks (eds), *Villa Landscapes in the Roman North. Economy, Culture and Lifestyles*, Amsterdam, 161-177.

Samson, R., 1989: Rural Slavery, Inscriptions, Archaeology and Marx: A Response to Ramsay Macmullen's 'Late Roman Slavery', *Historia* 38, 99-110.

Samson, R. (ed.), 1990a: *The Social Archaeology of Houses*, Edinburgh.

Samson, R., 1990b: Comment on Eleanor Scott's Romano-British villas and the social construction of space, in R. Samson (ed.), *The Social Archaeology of Houses*, Edinburgh, 173-180.

Scheidel, W., 2005: From monetization to culture change, *Archaeological Dialogues* 12-1, 35–37.

Schinkel, C., 1994. *Zwervende erven. Bewoningssporen in Oss-Ussen uit Bronstijd, IJzertijd en Romeinse tijd. Opgravingen 1976-1986*, Leiden (dissertation Leiden University).

Schindlbeck, M., 1990: Tradition and Change in Kwanga Villages, in N. Lutkehaus *et al.* (eds), *Sepik Heritage*, Bathurst.

Schinkel, K., 2005: Buurtschappen in beweging. Nederzettingen in Zuid- en Midden-Nederland, in L.P. Louwe Kooijmans *et al.* (eds), *Nederland in de prehistorie*, Amsterdam, 519-541.

Schnurbein, S. von, 2003: Augustus in Germania and his new 'town' at Waldgirmes east of the Rhine, *Journal of Roman Archaeology* 16, 93-108.

Scholl, G., 1987: Fouilles de la Villa de 'La Coulbrie' à Soignies, in A. Cahen-Delhaye/C. de Lichtervelde/F. Leuxe (eds), *L'archéologie en Wallonie 1980-1981*, Namur, 93-95.

Schucany, C. 2011: A villa landscape and its chronological dimension. The middle Aare valley on the south foot of the Jura range (CH), in N. Roymans/T. Derks (eds), *Villa Landscapes in the Roman North. Economy, Culture and Lifestyles*, Amsterdam, 275-283.

Schuermans, H., 1867: Exploration de villas belgo-romaines outre Meuse, *Bulletin des Commissions royales d'art et d'archéologie* 6, 229-303.

Schuler, A., 2000: Abschlußgrabung in Hochneukirch: von der «Protovilla» zur villa rustiqua, *Archäologie im Rheinland* 2000, 69 ff.

Scott, E., 1990: Romano-British Villas and the Social Construction of Space, in R. Samson (ed.), *The Social Archaeology of Houses*, Edinburgh, 149-172.

Scott, E., 1993: *A Gazetteer of Roman Villas in Britain*, Leicester.

Seiler, S., 2001: Vorcolonialzeitliche Siedlungsspuren im Norden des römischen Köln, in G. Precht/N. Zieling (eds), *Genese, Struktur und Entwicklung römischer Städte im 1. Jahrhundert n. Chr. in Nieder- und Obergermanien. Kolloquim vom 17. bis 19. Februar 1998 im Regionalmuseum Xanten*, Mainz (Xantener Berichte 9), 123-134.

Séverin, C. *et al.*, 2007: *Archéologie en Nord-Pas-de-Calais. La Fosse à Loups, ZAC Hordain-Hainaut*, Villeneuve d'Ascq.

Siemons, H./J.J. Lanzing (eds), 2009: *Bewoningssporen uit de Romeinse tijd in het Wateringse Veld*, Den Haag (Haagse Oudheidkundige Publicaties 11).

Sier, M.M./C.W. Koot (eds), 2001: *Kesteren-De Woerd, bewoningssporen uit de IJzertijd en de Romeinse tijd*, Utrecht (Rapportage Archeologische Monumentenzorg 82).

Sier, M.M., 2003: *Ellewoutsdijk in de Romeinse tijd*, Bunschoten.

Sharples, N., 2010: *Social relations in later prehistory. Wessex in the first Millennium BC*, Oxford.

Slofstra, J., 1983: An anthropological approach to the study of romanization processes, in R. Brandt/J. Slofstra (eds), *Roman and native in the Low Countries. Spheres of interaction*, Oxford (British Archaeological Reports International Series 184), 71-104.

Slofstra, J., 1987: Een nederzetting uit de Romeinse tijd bij Hoogeloon, in W.C.M. van Nuenen (ed.) *Drie dorpen een gemeente. Een bijdrage aan de geschiedenis van Hoogeloon, Hapert en Casteren*, Hapert, 51-86.

Slofstra, J., 1991: Changing settlement systems in the Meuse-Demer-Scheldt area during the Early Roman period, in N. Roymans/F. Theuws (eds), *Images of the past. Studies on ancient societies in northwestern Europe*, Amsterdam (Studies in pre- en protohistorie 7), 131-199.

Slofstra, J., 1995: The villa in the Roman West: space, decoration and ideology, in J. Metzler *et al.* (eds), *Integration in the Early Roman West. The role of Culture and Ideology*, Luxembourg (dossiers d'archéologie du musée national d'histoire et d'art 4), 77-90.

Slofstra, J., 2002: Batavians and Romans on the Lower Rhine. The Romanisation of a frontier area, *Archaeological Dialogues* 9-1, 16–38.

Slofstra, J., 2003: *Een Romeins villa-systeem ten noorden van de löss?*, Amsterdam (unpublished paper, held at the Archaeological Centre of the Free University, Amsterdam, May 22nd, 2003).

Slofstra, J., 2004: Rome en de Anderen, *Tijdschrift voor Mediterrane Archeologie* 32, 52–57.

Smith, J.T., 1978: Villas as a key to social structure, in M. Todd (ed.), *Studies in the Romano-British Villa*, Leicester, 149-185.

Smith, J.T., 1997: *Roman villas. A study in social structure*, London.

Spiegel, E.M., 2002: Ausgrabungen in einem römischen Siedlungsplatz mit zwei spätantiken burgi in Köln-Widdersdorf, *Kölner Jahrbuch* 35, 699 ff.

Sprokholt, H.J., 1992: *Romeinse bewoning in en om het Maasdal. Catalogus van villaterreinen in Limburg en delen van Noord-Brabant en Gelderland*, Amersfoort (unpublished thesis).

Stallibrass, S./R. Thomas (eds), 2008: *Feeding the Roman army: the archaeology of production and supply in NW Europe*, Oxford.

Stuart, P./M.E.Th. de Grooth, 1987: *Langs de weg*, Maastricht.

Swinkels, L.J.F., 1987: A *gladiatorum munus* depicted in a Roman villa at Maasbracht, in *Pictores per provincias*, Avenches (Cahiers d'archéologie romande 43), 191-195.

Swoboda KM, 1919: *Römische und Romanische Paläste. Eine architektur-geschichtliche Untersuchung*, Wien.

Taylor, J., 2001: Rural society in Roman Britain, in S. James/M. Millett (ed.) *Britons and Romans: advancing an archaeological agenda*, Walmgate (CBA research report 125), 46-59.

Theuws, F./N. Roymans, 1999: *Land and Ancestors*, Amsterdam (Amsterdam Archaeological Studies 4).

Thomas, R., 1997: Land, Kinship Relations and the Rise of Enclosed Settlement in First Millenium B.C. Britain, *Oxford Journal of Archaeology* 16 (2), 211–218.

Tichelman, G., 2005: *Het villacomplex Kerkrade-Holzkuil*, Amersfoort (Archeologisch Diensten Centrum Rapport 155).

Tichelman, G., in prep.: *Heerlen-Trilandis*, Weert (RAAP-rapport).

Tietze, W. *et al.* (eds), 1990: *Geographie Deutschlands*, Berlin/Stuttgart.

Tilley, C. *et al.* (eds), 2006: *Handbook of material culture*, London.

Trow, S./S. James/T. Moore, 2009: *Becoming Roman, being Gallic, staying British. Research and Excavations at Ditches 'Hillfort' and Villa 1984-2006*, Oxford.

Van Beurden, L., 2002: Botanisch onderzoek in het Maas-Demer-Schelde gebied. De Romeinse en vroegmiddeleeuwse periode, in H. Fokkens/R. Jansen (eds), *2000 jaar bewoningsdynamiek. Brons- en ijzertijdbewoning in het Maas-Demer-Scheldegebied*, Leiden.

Van den Broeke, P., 2002: *Vindplaatsen in vogelvlucht. Beknopt overzicht van het archeologische onderzoek in de Waalsprong 1996-2001*, Nijmegen.

Van der Sanden, W.A.B., 1990: Een nederzetting uit de Romeinse tijd te Oss (Zaltbommelseweg), *Brabants Heem* 42, 95-102.

Van der Velde, H. (ed.), 2008: *Cananefaten en Friezen aan de monding van de Rijn. Tien jaar archeologisch onderzoek op de Zanderij-Westerbaan te Katwijk (1996-2006)*, Amersfoort, (Archeologisch Diensten Centrum monografie/Rapport 1456).

Van Dockum, S.G., 1990: Houten in the roman period, part I: a stone building in Burgemeester Wallerweg, *Berichten van de Rijksdienst voor het Oudheidkundig Bodemonderzoek* 40, 297-321.

Van Enckevort, H., 2001: Bemerkungen zum Besiedlungssystem in den südöstlichen Niederlanden während der späten vorrömischen Eisenzeit und der römischen Kaiserzeit, in T. Grünewald (ed.), *Germania Inferior. Besiedlung, Gesellschaft un Wirtschaft an der Grenze der römisch-germanischen Welt*, Berlin, 336-395.

Van Enckevort, H./J.K. Haalebos/J. Thijssen, 2000: *Nijmegen. legerplaats en stad in het achterland van de Romeinse limes*, Abcoude/Nijmegen (Archeologische Berichten Nijmegen 3).

Van Es, W.A., 1981³: *De Romeinen in Nederland*, Haarlem.

Van Es, W.A./R.S. Hulst, 1991: *Das merowingische Gräberfeld von Lent*, Amersfoort (Nederlandse Oudheden 14/Project Oostelijk Rivierengebied 2).

Van Hoof, L., 2007: *Evaluatie van het onderzoek naar de late prehistorie in Limburg sinds 1995*, http://limburg.nl/upload/pdf/KEC_CE_Late%20Prehistorie.pdf.

Van Hoof, L.G.L./I.M. van Wijk, 2007: *Romeinen aan de Ring. Een villa-terrein aan de binnenring te Landgraaf?*, Leiden (Archol Rapport 66).

Van Impe, L., 1983: Het oudheidkundig bodemonderzoek in Donk (Gem. Herk-de-Stad) 1977-1982, *Archaeologia Belgica* 255, 65-94.

Van Impe, L., 1984: Romeinse nederzetting en begraafplaats te Donk: het onderzoek in 1983, *Archaeologia Belgica* 258, 79-82.

Van Impe, L./P. Strobbe/P. Vynckier, 1984: Romeinse nederzetting en begraafplaats te Donk: het onderzoek in 1983, *Archaeologia Belgica* 258 (Conspectus MCMLXXXIII), 79-82.

Van Impe, L./P. Strobbe/P. Vynckier, 1985: Het bodemonderzoek in Donk in 1984, *Archaeologia Belgica* I (Conspectus MCMLXXXIV), 51-52.

Van Impe, L. *et al.*, 2002: De Keltische goudschat van Beringen (prov. Limburg), *Archeologie in Vlaanderen* 6, 9-132.

Van Ossel, P., 1983: L'établisement romain de Löen à Lixhe et l'occupation rurale au Bas-Empire dans hesbaye Liégeoise, *Helinium* 23, 9-27.

Van Ossel, P., 1984: La villa belgo-romaine du Leckbosch à L'Ecluse, in P. van Ossel/J. Plumier/P.J. Claeys (eds), *Archeolo-J. 15 années, 15 chantiers*, Rixensart, 5-9.

Van Ossel, P./J. Plumier/P.J. Claeys (eds), 1984: *Archeolo-J. 15 années, 15 chantiers*, Rixensart.

Van Ossel, P./A. Defgnee, 2001: *Champion, Hamois: une villa romaine chez les Condruses: archéologie, environment et économique d'une exploitation agricole antique de la Moyenne Belgique*, Namur.

Van Renswoude, J./J. Van Kerckhove, 2009: *Opgravingen in Geldermalsen-Hondsgemet. Een inheemse nederzetting uit de Late IJzertijd en Romeinse tijd*, Amsterdam (Zuidnederlandse Archeologische Rapporten 35).

Van Wijngaarden-Bakker, L./O. Brinkkemper, 2005: Het veelzijdige boerenbedrijf. De voedselproductie in de metaaltijden, in L.P. Louwe Kooijmans *et al.* (eds), *Nederland in de prehistorie*, Amsterdam, 491-512.

Vanderhoeven, A., 1996: The earliest urbanisation in Northern Gaul. Some implications of recent research in Tongres, in N. Roymans (ed.), *From the sword to the plough*, Amsterdam (Amsterdam Archaeological Studies 1), 189-260.

Vanderhoeven, A./G. Creemers (eds), 2000: *Archeologische Kroniek Limburg 1999*, Tongeren.

Vanderhoeven, A. *et al.*, 2006: Veldwezelt. Vues socio-économiques nouvelles sur les campagnes, *Dossiers Archéologie et sciences des origines* 315 *(La Belgique Romaine)*, 60-63.

Vanderhoeven, A./G. Vynckier/P. Vynckier, 1991: Het oudheidkundig bodemonderzoek aan de Kielenstraat te Tongeren, Interimverslag 1987, *Archeologie in Vlaanderen* 1, 107-124.

Vanderhoeven, A./G. Vynckier/ P. Vynckier, 1992: Het oudheidkundig bodemonderzoek aan de Hondstraat te Tongeren (prov. Limburg). Interimverslag 1989, *Archeologie in Vlaanderen* 2, 65-85.

Vanvinckenroye, W., 1988: *De Romeinse villa op de Sassenbroekberg te Broekom*, Tongeren (Publicaties van het Provinciaal Gallo-Romeins Museum Tongeren 38).

Vanvinckenroye, W., 1990: *De Romeinse villa's van Piringen ('Mulkenveld') en Vechmaal ('Walenveld')*, Tongeren (Publicaties van het Provinciaal Gallo-Romeinse Museum Tongeren 42).

Vanvinckenroye, W. 1997: De Romeinse villa in het 'Middelpadveld' te Vechmaal (Heers), *Limburg –Het Oude land van Loon* 76, 179-192.

Verbeek, C./S. Delaruelle/J. Bungeneers (eds), 2004: *Verloren voorwerpen. Archeologisch onderzoek op het HSL-traject in de provincie Antwerpen,* Antwerpen.

Verbeeck, M. 1995: Eine Römervilla in Erps-Kwerps (Kortenberg-Belgien) mit merowingerzeitlichem Gräberfeld, in S.K. Palágyi (ed.), *Balácai Közlemények III. 1994*, Veszprem, 151-158.

Verbrugge, A./G. De Doncker/Cherrett, 2008: Een inheems-Romeins landelijke nederzetting aan de Posthoornstraat in Machelen (gem. Zulte, prov. Oost-Vlaanderen), in W. De Clercq *et al.* (eds), *Journée d'Archéologie Romaine 2008 - Romeinendag 2008*, Brussels 139-140.

Vermeulen, F., *et al.*, 1998: Romeinse rurale nederzettingsstructuren in Sint-Gillis-Waas, *Romeinendag 4e editie,* Brussels, 10-12.

Vermeulen-Bekkering, A.M., 2006: *Een Romeinse villa langs de Maas bij Afferden, gemeente Bergen (Limburg)*, Amersfoort (Rapportage Archeologische Monumentenzorg 116).

Versluys, M.J., 2004: An idea at the back of it? Romanisering als cultuurhistorisch fenomeen, *Tijdschrift voor Mediterrane Archeologie 32*, 37-43.

Verwers, W.J.H., 1998: *North Brabant in Roman and Early Medieval Times. Habitation History*, Amersfoort.

Verwers, W.J.H./L.I. Kooistra, 1990: Native house plans from the Roman period in Boxtel and Oosterhout, *Berichten van de Rijksdienst voor het Oudheidkundig Bodemonderzoek 40*, 251-284.

Vonder, I. van den, 2008: Een Gallo-Romeinse villa met grafveld te Merchtem-Dooren (Vlaams Brabant), in W. De Clercq *et al.* (eds), *Journée d'Archéologie Romaine 2008 - Romeinendag 2008*, Brussels, 115-9.

Von Petrikovits, H., 1956: Neue Forschungen zur römerzeitlichen Besiedlung der Nordeifel, *Germania 34*, 99-125.

Vos, W.K., 2002: *De inheems-Romeinse huisplattegronden van De Horden te Wijk bij Duurstede*, Amersfoort (Rapportage Archeologische Monumentenzorg 96).

Vos, W.K., 2003: *Archeologisch onderzoek in Beneden Leeuwen - vindplaats 'De Ret', gemeente West Maas en Waal*, Bunschoten (Archeologisch Diensten Centrum Rapport 153).

Vos, W.K., 2009: *Bataafs platteland: Het Romeinse nederzettingslandschap in het Nederlandse Kromme-Rijngebied*, Amersfoort (Nederlandse Archeologische Rapporten 34).

Vossen, I.M.J., 1997: *Riethoven-Heesmortel. Een inheems-Romeinse nederzetting in de Brabantse Kempen*, Amsterdam (unpublished thesis VU University Amsterdam).

Webley, L., 2007: Households and social change in Jutland, 500 BC-AD 200, in C. Haselgrove/T. Moore (eds), *The later iron age in Britain and beyond*, Oxford, 454-467.

Webster, J./N.J. Cooper (eds), 1996: *Roman imperialism: Post-colonial perspectives*, Leicester (Leicester Archaeology Monographs 3).

Webster, J., 1996: Roman imperialism and the 'post imperial age', in J. Webster/N.J. Cooper (eds), *Roman imperialism: Post-colonial perspectives*, Leicester (Leicester Archaeology Monographs 3), 1-17.

Webster, J., 2005: Archaeologies of slavery and servitude: bringing 'New World' perspectives to Roman Britain, *Journal of Roman Archaeology 18(1)*, 161-179.

Webster, J., 2008: Less beloved. Roman archaeology, slavery and the failure to compare, *Archaeological Dialogues 15(2)*, 103-149.

Webster, J., 2010: Routes to slavery in the Roman World: a comparative perspective on the archaeology of forced migration, in H. Eckardt (ed.), *Roman Diasporas: Archaeological Approaches to Mobility and diversity in the Roman Empire*, Portsmouth, Rhode Island (Journal of Roman Archaeology Supplementary Series 78), 45-65.

Wegner, H.H., 1985: Die römische Villa von Ahrweiler, *Archäologie in Deutschland 1*, 4-5.

Wesselingh, D.A., 2000: *Native neighbours. Local settlement system and social structure in the Roman period at Oss (The Netherlands)*, Leiden (Analecta Praehistorica Leidensia 32).

Westgate, R./N. Fisher/J. Whitley (eds), 2007: *Building communities. House, settlement and society in the Aegean and beyond*, London (British School at Athens Studies 15).

Wetzels, E.P.G., 2001: IJzerhandel versus IJzertijd. Een noodopgraving met bewoningssporen uit de Vroege IJzertijd en de Romeinse tijd te Sittard-Nusterweg, *Archeologie in Limburg 88*, 16-23.

Whittaker, C.R., 1980: Rural labour in three Roman provinces, in P. Garnsey (ed.), *Non-slave labour in the Greco-Roman world*, Cambridge, 73-99.

Wickham, C., 2005: *Framing the Early Middle Ages: Europe and the Mediterranean, 400–800*, Oxford.

Wiethold, J., 2000: Kontinuität und Wandel in der landwirtschaftlichen Produktion und Nahrungsmittelversorgung zwischen Spätlatènezeit und Gallo-römischer Epoche. Archäobotanische Analysen in der römischen Grossvillenanlage von Borg, Kr. Merzig-Wadern, in A. Haffner/S. von Schnurbein (eds), *Kelten, Germanen, Römer im Mittelgebirgsraum zwischen Luxemburg und Thüringen. Akten des Internationalen Kolloquiums zum DFG-Schwerpunktprogramm "Romanisierung" in Trier vom 28. bis 30. September 1998,* Bonn (Kolloquien zur Vor- und Frühgeschichte 5), 147-159.

Wightman, E.M., 1978: Peasants and Potentates in Roman Gaul, *American Journal of Ancient History* 3, 43-63.

Wightman, E.M., 1985: *Gallia Belgica*, London.

Wilk R R./W.L. Rathje, 1982: Household archaeology, *American Behavioral Scientist* 25-6, 617-640.

Wilk, R.R., 1990: The Built Environment and Consumer Decisions, in S. Kent (ed.), *Domestic Architecture and the Use of Space*, Cambridge, 34-42.

Willems, W.J.H., 1981: Romans and Batavians, a regional study in the Dutch eastern river area I, *Berichten van de Rijksdienst voor het Oudheidkundig Bodemonderzoek* 31, 7-217.

Willems, W.J.H., 1984: Romans and Batavians: a regional study in the Dutch eastern river area II, *Berichten van de Rijksdienst voor het Oudheidkundig Bodemonderzoek* 34, 39-331 (491).

Willems, W.J.H., 1986: De Romeinse villa te Voerendaal: opgraving 1985, *Archeologie in Limburg* 28, 143-150.

Willems, W.J.H./L.I. Kooistra 1987: De Romeinse villa te Voerendaal: opgraving 1986, *Archeologie in Limburg* 32, 29-38.

Willems, W.J.H./L.I. Kooistra 1988: De Romeinse villa te Voerendaal: opgraving 1987, *Archeologie in Limburg* 37, 137-147.

Wilson, P. J. 1988: *The Domestication of the Human Species*, New Haven.

Wolf, E.R., 1966: *Peasants*, Englewood Cliffs.

Wolf, E., 1982: *Europe and the People Without History,* Los Angeles/Berkeley.

Woolf, G., 1992: The unity and diversity of Romanisation, *Journal of Roman Archaeology* 5, 349-52.

Woolf, G., 1997: Beyond Roman and natives, *World archaeology* 28, 339-50.

Woolf, G., 1998: *Becoming Roman. The Origins of Provincial Civilization in Gaul*, Cambridge.

Zeippen L./B. Halbardier, 2006: La villa de Mageroy et la pisciculture, *Dossiers Archéologie et sciences des origines* 315 *(La Belgique Romaine)*, 76-77.

Zieling, N., 2001: Konstruktionstypen vorcoloniazeitlicher Gebäude auf dem Areal der Colonia Ulpia Traiana, G. Precht/N. Zieling (eds), *Genese, Struktur und Entwicklung römischer Städte im 1. Jahrhundert n. Chr. in Nieder- und Obergermanien. Kolloquim vom 17. bis 19. Februar 1998 im Regionalmuseum Xanten*, Mainz (Xantener Berichte 9), 27-36.

Appendix 1. Site catalogue

In this appendix, the data that is at the basis of this study is catalogued and briefly described per site. Sites are organised per subregion[1] and in alphabetical order. Per site record, the following characteristics are described:

- site number
- location and toponym
- scale of research
- period of research
- short description of the site: character, development, chronology and special elements
- reference

The site location is generally defined by means of a general location, in most cases a municipality, combined with a toponym, generally a street name, field name or the name of the development (project) related to the research. Scale of research is defined by rating letters A, B, C or D. The category of A-sites comprises large-scale excavations whereby complete settlements were excavated. Overall, good-quality chronological data on developments in settlement organisation and house building is available for these sites. The B-category contains partially excavated settlements. Here, excavation reaches beyond the level of the individual building, but the entire settlement complex is not documented. Sites classified in category C include settlements where only the main house was excavated. In many cases, the development trajectory of house building could be reconstructed. Lastly, category-D sites are fragmentarily excavated sites that nonetheless provide useful data on settlement morphology, chronology or development.

With regard to the period of research, a research period has been determined for each site, divided into three chronological groups: before 1950, 1950 to 1979, and after 1980. In the short description, some basic characteristics are described, especially focussing on basic morphology and development trajectories in settlement organisation and house building. Special elements could include bath sections, (monumental) graves or elements with a possible ritual function. Lastly, per site the main references are presented.

---

[1] The subregional division used is introduced in chapter 2.

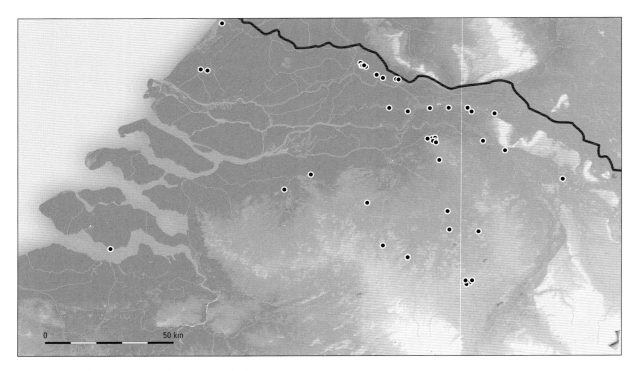

Distribution of sites in the northern sand and clay areas.

001 Beneden-Leeuwen, D, 2000s, periphery of a hypothetical villa settlement. Several traditional post-built houses could be dated between the first half of the 1st century AD and the Late Roman period. Special material culture included military equipment, import objects, tiles and *tubuli* as well as painted wall plaster. No structural traces of monumental house building were found, however, Vos 2003.

002 Breda-Steenakker/Huifakker, A, 2000s, two well-excavated settlement cores. At the Huifakker-site, several post-built houses could be dated to the 1st century AD. They were not inhabited simultaneously, however. One of the houses has a wooden ambulatory that could possibly be interpreted as a portico (Koot/Berkvens 2004, 380). Long ditches organise settlement space and surrounding lands during this phase, although no coherent settlement compound seems to have been created. In the 3rd century, the site is re-occupied with five probably contemporary houses, situated relatively close to one another. The Steenakker site was occupied from the Late Iron Age until the 4th century AD. Two or three houses could be dated to each settlement phase, except for the 2nd century AD. In the Roman period, large ditches seem to have drained the area. Settlement space was not organised by a common ditch system, Koot/Berkvens 2004.

003 Cothen-De Zemelen, D, 2000s, simple building on stone foundations (26 x 9.5 m) This building had a plan similar to a byre house, but was constructed on stone foundations, Müller/Doesburg 2008; Vos 2009, 51-52.

004 Den Haag-Wateringseveld, A, 1990s-2000s, around the middle of the 1st century AD, a small settlement with several farmsteads was founded on a levee. In the second half of the 1st and early

2nd century, the settlement consisted of two or three contemporary farmsteads. Then, in the second quarter of the 2nd century, a large ditch system was created, organising both settlement space and the surrounding landscape. This system was laid out according to a Roman measure system. During the 2nd and early 3rd century the settlement remained the same size. In this period, a portico-house (with a long fronting façade) similar to Druten house 12 and Hoogeloon house 28 was built, which is interpreted as a veteran house by the authors. The settlement was abandoned in the early 3rd century AD, Siemons/Lanzing 2009.

005 Deurne-Groot Bottelsche Akker, B, 2000s, open multiple-farmstead settlement, dated between the first half of the 1st century AD and the middle of the 3rd century. Over time, two or three contemporary farmsteads existed. Houses were rebuilt within the same locality but shifted in location over short distances, Hiddink 2008.

006 Druten-Klepperheide, A, 1970s, in the first half of the 1st century AD, an open settlement with probably two contemporary farmsteads existed. In the second half of the 1st century one farmstead was probably enclosed. The house on this enclosed compound could be reconstructed as a kind of portico-house with an internal cellar or room, partly constructed with stone. Fragments of painted wall plaster were found here (for a discussion on the interpretational difficulties see Heeren 2009, 203-205). Maas, who recently restudied the 1970s excavation, also dates the hypothetical round grave monument and bath house in this phase, although, according to Heeren, this latter structure should be dated much later. In the late 1st and first half of the 2nd century, several single-aisled houses formed a structured settlement, seemingly enclosed and organised by ditches. One of the houses had a long fronting portico, an internal gutter made of tiles and plastered walls. In the second half of the 2nd century, a house on stone foundations was constructed. Although it cannot be proven, it seems plausible that the small bath house could be associated with this stone house. Besides the stone house, a number of post-built houses were part of the settlement during this later phase. The settlement was abandoned somewhere in the 3rd century, Hulst 1978; Maas 2007; Heeren 2009, 203-205.

007 Ellewoutsdijk, B, 2000s, a settlement consisting of an open cluster of contemporary farmsteads (with a distance of 50-100 m between the farmsteads). The houses were traditional post-built structures. Habitation could be dated between around the middle of the 1st and the middle of the 2nd century AD. Per habitation phase, two to four farms will have been inhabited. Houses were rebuilt in the same location or shifted over short distances, Sier 2003.

008 Ewijk-De Grote Aalst, B, 2000s, enclosed, organised compound settlement with several buildings excavated, except for the monumental main house. The settlement started around the middle of the 1st century AD and consisted of wooden two-aisled houses during this early phase. Later on, during the 2nd and 3rd century, elements of Mediterranean architecture were also adopted, probably including the use of tiles for roof covering. Blom/Van der Feijst/Veldman 2012.

009 Geldermalsen-Hondsgemet, A, 2000s, habitation on this site started already in the 2nd century BC, with a small number of farmsteads situated along an old river arm. Farmstead shifted over short distances during this early period and the settlement was enclosed nor organised by a common ditch system. During the early 1st century AD, the settlement consisted of three farmsteads that were each individually enclosed by a ditch. In the second half of the 1st century, the larger settlement was enclosed by a ditch system. One farmstead seemed to take a special position within this enclosed settlement, as indicated by the entrance to the farmstead's compound and fragments of military equipment found here. In the phase between 120 until 270 AD a new enclosure system was constructed, measuring 208 x 73 m. Houses within this system were rebuilt at the same location several times. After this phase, the settlement declined and only a single farmstead remained on the enclosed settlement compound, Van Renswoude/Van Kerckhove 2009.

010 Helmond-Mierlo-Hout-Brandevoort, B, 1990s, multiple-farmstead settlement without enclosure. This settlement was founded around 200 AD, and comprised two habitation phases with two or three contemporary farmsteads. Remarkable features were two rows of granaries that would have provided significant storage capacity. Habitation was probably limited to the first half of the 3rd century AD, De Groot 2001.

011 Hoogeloon-Kerkakkers, A, 1980s, enclosed multiple-farmstead settlement that was inhabited during the first three centuries AD. The settlement was founded as an enclosed settlement during the first half of the 1st century AD. All houses, of which up to seven could have existed simultaneously, were traditional post-built Alphen-Ekeren type constructions. One of the houses (number VII/VIII) had a prominent position on a slightly higher part of the settlement terrain. In combination with the early imports found here, Slofstra argues that this house was the residence of a prominent member of the settlement community. In the 2nd century, a house on stone foundations was constructed within the existing settlement and on the exact location of the houses VII/VIII (51.5 x 19 m). This stone house was situated on a separate compound (49 x 71 m), enclosed by means of a palisade. During this phase, the traditional houses within the settlement were all situated well outside this separate compound (according to Slofstra seven or eight houses existed during this phase). Later in the 2nd century, a hypocausted room and a small bath section were constructed within the existing stone house. These were also decorated with painted wall plaster, Slofstra 1987; Jeneson 2004.

012 Houten-Burgemeester Wallerweg, D, 1950s, two consecutive traditional post-built houses could be dated between 50/75 AD and 150/175 AD. The second house was associated with Roman-style imported objects. During a subsequent phase, after 175 AD, a house on stone foundations, measuring 27.75 x 11.35 m, was constructed at the same location. The fragmentarily documented house consisted of a number of rooms, fronted by a portico, Van Dockum 1990; Vos 2009, 164-174.

013 Houten-Doornkade, B, 1980s, at this site, several farmsteads could be dated to the Late Iron Age or Early Roman Period. Possibly, the settlement was partly organised by ditches, comparable to the Wijk bij Duurstede-De Horden settlement. During the Flavian period, a large ditch system was created within which farmsteads were situated. At one of the farmsteads, large 12- and 15-post granaries were documented. The settlement was occupied until around the middle of the 2nd century, Vos 2009, 118-127.

014 Houten-Molenzoom, C, 1990s, multi-phased farmstead that during a first phase consisted of a traditional two-aisled house dated to the second half of the 1st century BC or first half of the 1st century AD. During a later period, probably starting in the first half of the 2nd century, four consecutive or partly contemporary houses of a single-aisled type were constructed. Two of these were post-built, two others were constructed with footings of tile fragments, brick and fragments of wall painting (the youngest house), Vos 2009, 174-182.

015 Houten-Overdam (Terrein 8A), B, 1990s, dispersed cluster of farmsteads, enclosed around the middle of the 1st century AD (possibly, in a primary phase only a single farmstead was enclosed). In the Flavian period, a ditch system was constructed. Like at some nearby settlements, ditches continued into the surrounding landscape. Probably, a maximum of two contemporary farmsteads existed at this site. The settlement could be dated to at least the 1st and 2nd century AD, Vos 2009, 148-156.

016 Houten-Tiellandt, B, 1980s, enclosed multiple-farmstead settlement. Remarkable is a large *horreum*. The house associated with this *horreum* had an ambulatory of wooden posts and was interpreted as a veteran farm by Vos (see Vos 2009, 238). The phasing of this settlement is not clear; no absolute chronology is available, Vos 2009, 133-141.

017 Houten-Wulven, B, 1990s, enclosed multiple-farmstead settlement with two or three contemporary farmsteads, including a portico-house. The geometrical settlement enclosure was probably constructed during the Flavian period, parallel to Wijk bij Duurstede-De Horden. There are some fragmentary and non-confirmed indications for monumental building at this site (stone foundations). The settlement traces were not well dated but can probably be placed within the 1st and 2nd century AD, Vos 2009, 127-133.

018 Katwijk-Zanderij-Westerbaan, B, 2000s, at this site, a relatively small-scale ditch system (with a width of less than 100 m) enclosed and organised settlement space. Through time, the settlement consisted of two contemporary houses. One of these houses was rebuilt at exactly the same location a number of times. The other shifted in location over short distances. From the early 2nd century onwards, the ditches seem to have been replaced by a palisade. Occupation was dated between the middle of the 1st century and the middle of the 3rd century AD. During the second half of the 1st century AD, a relatively large granary was part of the settlement, Van der Velde 2008.

019 Lent, 1980s, C, at the site of a Merovingian grave field, some Roman period traces of habitation were documented. Remarkable is the find of a large rectangular hall-like building with squarish footings in all four walls (made out of greywacke fragments). The building measured around 26 x 9,5 m. The authors argue that the inner house space was probably divided into several rooms and that the roof was covered with tiles. Fragments of painted wall plaster were also found. The building as such could not be directly dated. A well near the house, however, was dated between 70 and 150 AD. Besides this large building, a smaller secondary building, a 16-post granary (4.25 x 3.20 m) and some other small buildings and granaries were documented, Van Es/Hulst 1991, 61 ff.

020 Lieshout-Beekseweg, B, 2000s, open multiple-farmstead settlement with between two and four contemporary farmsteads, founded in the last decades BC and occupied until the late 2nd century AD, Hiddink 2005a.

021 Moergestel, B, 1980s, open multiple-farmstead settlement consisting of four adjacent farmsteads. At two of the farmsteads, the house was rebuilt twice, on the others rebuilding took place three times. At least three farmsteads were inhabited simultaneously, Verwers 1998, 66-67.

022 Mook-Plasmolen-Sint Jansberg, C, 1930s, large monumental house on stone foundations (20 x 83 m). The house was probably not constructed before 125 AD and was abandoned during the 3rd century. It consisted of a long stretched middle part with two porticoes/hallways at the front and back and wings on both sides. The house can be reconstructed with 41 rooms, Braat 1934; Koster/Peterse/Swinkels 2002, 41 ff.

023 Nistelrode-Loo, B, 2000s, this settlement probably had roots in the Late Iron Age, although this settlement phase could not be well documented. Two consecutive post-built houses were dated to the earlier Roman period, Jansen 2008, 152-153.

024 Nistelrode-Zwarte molen, B, 2000s, rural settlement, developing between around 70 and the 3rd century AD. Earliest habitation, around 70 AD, consisted of a large portico-house (26 x 12 m) and a small hypothetical enclosed sanctuary (ritual compound). During a second phase, the late 1st century AD, four wells formed a perfect square with sides of 180 feet long, and a surface of 1 *iugerum*. The author suspects the use of a *groma* and the involvement of military land surveyors. Around the early 2nd century AD, three post-built buildings and two granaries existed. Two houses and an enclosure ditch could be dated in the period between 120 and 130 AD. They were possibly part of a well-structured settlement compound. Around the middle of the 2nd century, several other post-built buildings were constructed. Again, the authors suggest that this settlement was structured according to geometrical principles; probably with the help of land surveyors and their *groma* (see Jansen 2008, 140-141). A post-built house and a circular ditch were the only structures that could be dated to the 3rd century, Jansen 2008.

025 Oosterhout-Muldersteeg B, 1980s, three post-built houses that were part of a settlement. Two of these houses were inhabited simultaneously between around 160/170 and 190 AD. One of the houses had a wooden portico constructed around the traditional core, Verwers/Kooistra 1990.

026 Oosterhout-Van Boetzelaerstraat, A, 1990s-2000s, enclosed multiple-farmstead settlement covering a surface of around 4.5 hectares. The settlement had a long-stretched layout, along a water-carrying channel. All houses were traditional post-built constructions. Habitation could be dated between the early 1st century AD until the middle of the 3rd century. Each phase will have consisted of a maximum of five or six contemporary farmhouses, Van den Broeke 2002, 12-18.

027 Oss-Horzak, B, 1990s-2000s, at this site, a long settlement history could be documented. Four houses of an Oss-Ussen type with double wall-posts could be dated to the Late Iron Age. A ditch possibly separated farmsteads from each other and the surrounding landscape. During this period the settlement became increasingly stabile, consisting of more than one contemporary farmstead. During the Roman period, a stabile multiple-farmstead settlement developed. A total of thirteen houses were documented for the 1st and 2nd century AD settlement phases. The settlement consisted of two and possibly three contemporary farmsteads and was enclosed and organised by means of a common ditch system (approximately 150 x 150 m), created in the 1st century AD. Two relatively large *horrea* could also be dated to this period. At a distance of 200 m north of the settlement part of a grave field was documented, Jansen/Fokkens 2002.

028 Oss-IJsselstraat, B, 1970s, settlement of at least three contemporary farmsteads, probably enclosed by a ditch. In two cases, houses were rebuilt on the same spot. Settlement activity could be dated between 50 and 250 AD, Wesselingh 2000, 189-191.

029 Oss-Schalkskamp, B, 1990s, enclosed (multi-)farmstead settlement dating to the Late Iron Age and first half of the 1st century AD. One or two contemporary farmsteads, many small granaries and two relatively large granaries were part of this settlement, Wesselingh 2000, 171-182.

030 Oss-Vijver, B, 1970s, multiple-farmstead settlement. During the first decades AD one or two farmsteads existed. After 70 AD, one farm was rebuilt and a large granary was constructed. For the period between 150 and 200 AD, a house and a number of wells could be documented as well. After this period, however, the site does not seem to have been occupied. There are no indications for an enclosure ditch, Wesselingh 2000, 25-46.

031 Oss-Westerveld, A, 1980s, during the Late Iron Age, a cluster of three contemporaneous farmsteads shifted through a large territory. Towards the end of this period a stronger clustering of these farmsteads occurred. Then, in the early 1st century AD a large enclosed multiple-farmstead settlement (7.5 ha) was laid out at this same location (Wesselingh 2000, 158). The houses within the enclosure were orientated on the settlement enclosure. Separate farmsteads were recognisable, sometimes even marked by fences or ditches. During the pre-Flavian period the settlement expands rapidly up to eight or nine contemporary farmsteads and diminishes after 125 AD. Around 100 AD, one farmstead was clearly separated from the rest by a ditch, creating an internal separate compound. On this internal enclosed compound a portico-house and a large granary were situated. The settlement seems to have been occupied until the second half of the 2nd century AD, Wesselingh 2000, 71-169; Schinkel 2005.

032 Oss-Zomerhof, B, 1970s, this settlement started as an organised enclosed multiple-farmstead settlement around 70 AD. Three farmsteads were rebuilt twice at approximately the same location. The settlement was abandoned in the first quarter of the 3rd century AD, Wesselingh 2000, 47-70.

033 Overasselt, C, 1930s, rectangular building on stone foundations, consisting of large hall-like space and two small rooms at one of the short sides, of which one was heated by means of a hypocaust system (32 x 10 m). A small cellar was situated in the hall. Two other buildings were documented only fragmentarily. Of one of these buildings, three rooms could be excavated, two of which had hypocausts. Habitation could be dated to the 2nd century AD, Braat 1934, 13-18.

034 Riethoven-Heesmortel, B, 1980s-1990s, multiple-farmstead settlement that was probably enclosed by a double ditch enclosure for only part of its occupation period. Habitation could be dated from the last decades BC until the middle of the 3rd century AD. The double ditch was dated in the 1st century AD and seems to have gone out of use afterwards. The settlement consisted of several farmsteads that were rebuilt at approximately the same location, Van der Sanden 1989, 59-60; Vossen 1997; Verwers 1998, 64-66.

035 Rijswijk-De Bult, A, 1960s-1970s, this settlement started with a single farmstead, dated to the first half of the 1st century AD. The house was rebuilt and around 60-70 AD a second farmstead was founded. During the first decades of the 2nd century AD, three or four contemporary farmsteads existed, including a small granary. In this phase, or probably even somewhat earlier, the settlement was partially organised by ditches. It is only around the middle of the 2nd century, however, that the settlement is completely enclosed and organised by means of a coherent ditch system. The surrounding landscape is also organised by ditches, connected to the settlement. Next, in the first half of the 3rd century, a partly monumental house was constructed. A large granary could probably be associated with this house.[2], Bloemers 1978; Heeren 2009, 216-218.

---

[2] Bloemers interpreted this non-residential structure as a temple, but Derks (1998, 152, note 96) and Heeren (2009, 217) argue that it should be re-interpreted as a large *horreum*.

036 Tiel-Passewaaij, A, 1990s–2000s, this settlement started in the Late Iron Age with one or two and later three contemporary farmsteads. These farmsteads were dispersed over a streamridge. Around 40 AD the farmsteads started to cluster. In this period, the settlement was partly organised by ditches. In the late 1st or first half of the 2nd century, a first larger ditch system enclosed and organised the settlement. These ditches also structured the surrounding landscape. In the second half of the 2nd century a partly new settlement enclosure was created. In this phase, a large *horreum* and stable were constructed as well. In the 1st and 2nd century settlement phases, around three to five contemporary farmsteads were part of the settlement. In the 3rd century, the settlement declined and two and later one farmstead remained. There are no indications for monumentalisation within the settlement. Some changes with regard to house building, mentioned by the author, include the construction of hypothetical wooden porticoes, the use of window glass and roof tiles, and the foundation of posts on wooden planks. These may represent military architectural influences (Heeren 2009, 300), Heeren 2006, 2009.

037 't Goy-Tuurdijk, D, 1950s/2000s, house on stone foundations, probably with a portico. Fragments of painted wall plaster were also found, Bogaers 1959; Vos 2009, 52-54.

038 Weert-Kampershoek, B, 1990s, multiple-farmstead settlement dating to the Late Iron Age (1st century BC) and Roman Period (until the middle of the 3rd century AD). Within the excavated area, probably two farmsteads existed simultaneously. Some farmsteads were partly organised and enclosed by a (palisaded) ditch. At one of the farmsteads a house was rebuilt at the same location two times between 100/150 and 225/250 AD. In this period this farmstead was partly enclosed, Roymans/Tol 1996, 32-37.

039 Weert-Molenakker-Laarderweg, A, 1990s, at the location of a Late Iron Age defensive ditched structure (1.25 ha surface), a rural settlement developed from around the middle of the 1st century BC, and existed until the middle of the 3rd century. No less than 45 post-built houses were documented within a relatively small area, inside the old enclosure, which by that time had lost its function but will have been visible still. Calculated for the 300 year period of habitation, probably four or five houses existed contemporaneously, Roymans 1995.

040 Weert-Raak, B, 1990s, open multiple-farmstead settlement consisting of probably three contemporary farmsteads, shifting in location each time a farmhouse was rebuilt. Habitation could be dated between the Late Iron Age and the end of the 1st century AD, Roymans/Tol/Hiddink 1998, 25-29.

041 Nederweert-Rosveld, A, 2000s, settlement consisting of a cluster of two or three farmsteads, occupied between the early 1st century and the early 3rd century AD. Contemporary houses shared a similar orientation, but were not organised on an enclosed compound. Only during the period between 150 and 180 AD, a rectangular settlement ditch system organised settlement space. Houses were rebuilt on slightly different locations each time; they did not overlap, Hiddink 2005b.

042 Weeze-Vorselaer, B, 2000s, enclosed settlement that existed from the middle of the 1st century AD until the second half of the 3rd century. House 1 (see Archäologie im Rheinland 2008, 82, fig. 85) had a plan comparable to byre houses known from the Dutch region. House 2 had an a-typical plan and is associated with the portico-houses of Druten by the author. The character of the settlement is comparable to settlements known from the Dutch sand and clay areas. This site is the first example of larger scale rural settlement research in the German sand and clay region, Archäologie im Rheinland 2008, 81-83.

043 Wijk bij Duurstede-De Geer, A, 1960s-1990s, this settlement had a structured settlement layout comparable to that of Wijk bij Duurstede-De Horden; a rectangular settlement enclosure could be dated to the 2nd century AD. Although not so much is known about the development of this specific settlement, a development trajectory similar to that of De Horden may be suggested, Vos 2009, 105-108.

044 Wijk bij Duurstede-De Horden, A, 1970s-1980s, during the first half of the 1st century AD, the settlement at this site consisted of a small number of loosely ordered and unenclosed farmsteads. During the Claudian-Neronian period one of the farmsteads was enclosed by a ditch system. Subsequently, during the Flavian period, the complete settlement was reorganised with the construction of a new enclosure system, connecting to the existing one. During the 2nd century, ditches projecting from or connecting to the settlement organised the surrounding landscape. Besides many traditional houses, two portico-houses were documented as well. These houses could be dated to the later 2nd or early 3rd century AD. Vos associates these houses with veterans returning to their home settlements, Vos 2002; Vos 2009, 59-105.

045 Winssen-Waalbandijk, D, 1970s, several stone foundations and a hypocaust, documented at this site, will have been part of a monumental house. Traces of habitation could be documented over a terrain of 15000 m2. Find material dates habitation between the second half of the 1st and the middle of the 3rd century AD. The stone foundations were dated to the 2nd century by the author, Van Kouwen 1978.

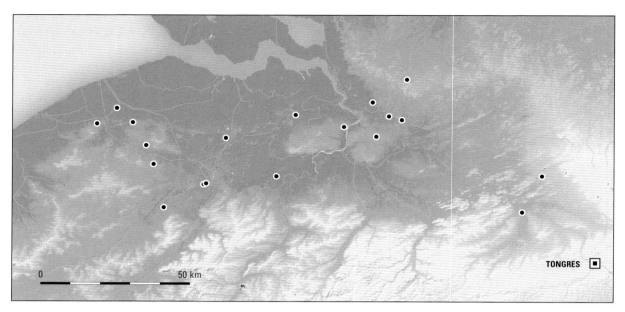

Distribution of sites in Flanders.

046 Aalter-Langevoorde, A, 2000s, in the 2nd century BC, a first enclosure was dug at this site, possibly representing a compound with ritual significance. Around the middle of the 1st century BC, a new enclosure was created, enclosing an area of 150 x 150 m. On the compound, a traditional Alphen-Ekeren type house and a number of secondary buildings -among which a large 9- and later 12-post granary- were situated against the northern enclosure ditch. Remarkably early imports, found in the enclosure ditches, could be dated to the Augustan period. Together with painted plaster and slate, the latter possibly used for roof covering, this could indicate the special status of the inhabitants. The house was rebuilt in the Flavian period and habitation continued into the 2nd century AD, In 't Ven/De Clercq 2005, 242, De Clercq 2009, 220-225.

047 Antwerpen-Mortsel, C, 1960s, two post-built houses (26.5 x 17.5 m and 16 x 20 m), probably part of a larger enclosed settlement. One of the houses seems to have had a wooden portico, resembling Druten house 1. The inner space of this house was divided into two parts; probably a byre and a residential section. A cellar, constructed of limonite and tiles, was connected to the house, De Boe 1966; Slofstra 1991, 164.

048 Beringen, B, 1990s, seemingly unenclosed settlement, consisting of one or more contemporary farmsteads. Habitation is dated between the Late Iron Age and Roman period. The houses dating to the earliest phase were of the Haps type. The Roman period houses were Alphen-Ekeren type constructions. These latter houses could be dated to the 2nd century AD. 1st century habitation activity is only suggested by pottery finds, Van Impe 2002.

049 Brecht-Zoegweg, B, 2000s, for the Iron Age, a somewhat dispersed cluster of post-built structures was documented, probably representing several phases of a farmstead. In the Roman period, traditional post-built houses were being rebuilt on approximately the same location, the settlement is organised by means of ditches and houses were arranged around a central open space.

From the 1st century AD onwards, houses were constructed with heavy central posts, typical for Alphen-Ekeren type houses. Habitation continues until the first quarter of the 3rd century, Delaruelle *et al.* 2004, 196-229.

050 Bruges-Refuge, A, 1990s, at Bruges-Refuge, an Early Roman Period settlement consisted of a cluster of two traditional houses. During the Flavian period, the settlement was reorganised with four farmsteads being enclosed by a common ditch. The farms were situated against the ditches and surrounded an open space. Each farmstead had its own secondary building and well. Around the middle of the 2nd century, a new house was built at a prominent position on the northern side of the compound. A remarkable cluster of granaries were situated around this house, De Clercq 2009, 225-228.

051 Damme-Stoofweg West, C, 1990s, small part of an enclosed, probably spatially structured settlement with one documented post-built house, orientated on the settlement enclosure. Habitation could be dated to the Roman period, In 't Ven/De Clercq 2005, 249-250.

052 Damme-Antwerpse Heirweg, B, 1990s, fragmentarily documented, spatially structured and enclosed rural settlement with several post-built structures. Habitation could be dated to the Roman period, In 't Ven/De Clercq 2005, 249-250.

053 Donk, B, 1970s-1980s, after the middle of the 1st century AD, a more or less structured, enclosed settlement was founded, with buildings arranged around an open space (Van Impe 1983, 82). These buildings were post-built Alpen-Ekeren type constructions, with heavy central posts, measuring between 18 and 27 m in length. According to the author (Van Impe 1983, 1984), buildings H, I, J and K were simultaneously occupied, each having (partly) different functions. Habitation continued until the first half of the 3rd century AD, Van Impe 1983, 1984; Van Impe/ Strobbe/Vynckier 1984, 1985; Slofstra 1991, 150.

054 Ekeren-Het Laar, B, 2000s, several post-built houses and a number of secondary buildings represent Late Iron Age (probably four houses) and Roman period habitation (three houses and two secondary buildings). Individual ditches can probably be interpreted as part of a Roman period settlement enclosure, Delaruelle *et al.* 2004, 189-196.

055 Evergem-Kluizendok, A, 2000s, at this large site, measuring a total of 170 hectares, three areas, Zandeken (4 ha), Hultjen (12 ha) and Puymeersen (1 ha), have been excavated. The sites comprise groups of more or less connected enclosed farmsteads, situated on the slightly higher parts of the relatively low sandy area. The excavations, as well as paleo-ecological research indicate that the area was not inhabited before the 2nd century AD, when forest will have dominated the area. Within the three areas, a total of fifteen farmsteads were documented. Although no strict planned layout seems to have been present, the settlements formed a coherent complex, respecting each others boundaries. A road probably functioned as a structuring element in the area. This layout, combined with the limited time depth of the complex, seems to indicate that the area was colonised in the 2nd century AD. Colonisation of this marginal area can probably be related to increasing pressure on land in this period, De Clercq 2009, 229-234; Laloo *et al.* 2008.

056 Knesselare-Kouter zone 1, B, 2000s, partly documented enclosed settlement, situated along a road. Two occupation phases could be defined, each consisting of two post-built structures. During the latest phases, granaries were part of the settlement as well, De Clercq 2009, 228-229.

057 Kruibeke-Hogen-Akkerhoek, B, 2000s, Roman-period single farmstead, enclosed by a squarish ditch system. The Roman enclosure cuts an Iron Age predecessor, De Clercq 2009, 234; Van Vaerenbergh 2007.

058 Machelen-Posthoornstraat, B, 2000s, partly documented, enclosed and spatially structured settlement with a number of post-built structures, among which an Alpen-Ekeren type house, a five-post granary and a secondary building, Verbrugge 2008.

059 Oelegem, B, 1970s, settlement traces including five or six houses and a number of smaller secondary buildings and four-post granaries. The houses with comprehensible plans were two-aisled Alphen-Ekeren type farms with heavy central and wall posts. The settlement, which will have consisted of a maximum of two contemporary farmsteads, could be dated from the late 1st or early 2nd until the early 3rd century AD. There is no clear indication for settlement organisation reaching beyond the level of the individual farmstead, De Boe/Lauwers 1980.

060 Sint-Denijs-Westrem-Vliegveld and 'The Loop', B, 1990s, two partly documented rural settlements, consisting of an unenclosed settlement area with post-built structures. Both settlement were founded just after the middle of the 1st century AD and were occupied until the late 2nd century. Each habitation phase was represented by a single farmstead, consisting of a post-built house and a secondary building. The Vliegveld site was situated along a road. At the 'The Loop' site a trail could be documented, De Clercq 2009.

061 Sint-Denijs-Westrem-Zone 1, B, 2000s, three Roman-period farmsteads, consisting of a post-built house, secondary building and a well. The settlement was possibly enclosed by a ditch. The farmsteads were not contemporary. One of them could be dated in the late 1st or early 2nd century AD, another in the late 2nd or early 3rd century, Hoorne 2008.

062 Sint-Gillis-Waas-Kluizenmolen, A, 1990s, three enclosed farmsteads, situated along a sand road, dated to the Roman period, De Clercq 2009, 234-235; Vermeulen *et al.* 1998.

063 Wijnegem-Steenakker, B, 1970s, the excavated settlement traces include two and possibly three post-built houses and three smaller buildings. The houses shared a similar orientation and were situated 30-50 m apart. They were of an Oss-Ussen type and did not show characteristics of the more sturdy Alphen-Ekeren type houses. The settlement could be dated to the Late Iron Age and/or Early Roman period. Settlement space was not organised by means of ditches. It remains unclear whether the documented houses were contemporary or not, Cuyt 1991.

064 Zele-Kamershoek, B, 1990s, fragmentarily documented, structured and enclosed rural settlement with several post-built structures, In 't Ven/De Clercq 2005, 249-251.

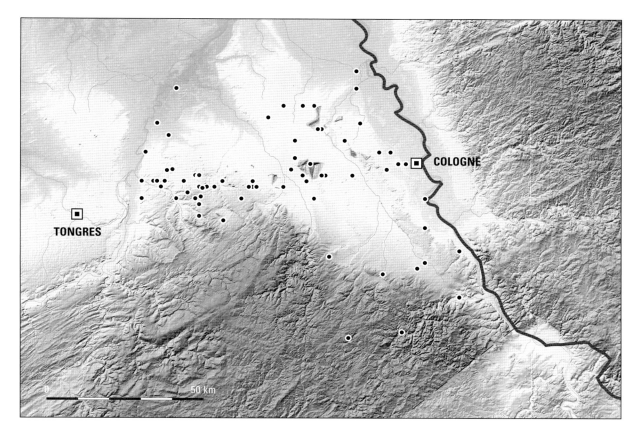

Distribution of sites in the Dutch and German loess region.

065 Aken-Süsterfeld, C, 1980s, multi-roomed house on stone foundations and a separate bath build-ing. The house was built in the 1st century AD and extended in the 2nd or 3rd century. In that latter period the separate bath house was constructed, Archäologie im Rheinland 1993, 78-80.

066 Aldenhoven-Langweiler / Siedlung 32, B, 1990s, part of a Roman period settlement with post-built houses. Building 4 could probably be interpreted as the main house. Buildings 1-3 probably belong to the oldest phase, 4 and 5 to the younger phase. One or more buildings possibly had a tiled roof, Lenz 1999, 143-147.

067 Aldenhoven-Schleiden / Siedlung 15, C-D, 1850s, large multi-roomed house on stone founda-tions which was partly excavated in 1850. In 1968, the site has been re-studied by means of aerial photography. The house measured around 90 x 35 m and had a façade with two projecting wings. The triple apsidal room at the southern corner could possibly be interpreted as a *triclinium*, Bonner Jahrbücher 16, 81-90; Lenz 1999, 120-121.

068 Alsdorf-Hoengen-Bachfeld / Siedlung 31, C, 1990s, multi-roomed house on stone foundations (37 x 19 m) that was built in the late 1st century AD and abandoned in the 4th century. The house consisted of a central rectangular hall with a number of small rooms around it, Lenz 1999, 142.

069 Alt-Inden / Weisweiler 122, C, 2000s, during the earlier 1st century AD, single-aisled framework houses with squarish wall posts were constructed on this site. The site is situated along the river Inde and near a road that was constructed during the Augustan period. In the late 1st or early 2nd century the framework buildings were replaced by a large house on stone foundations. The L-shaped house consisted of a main section of 120 x 29 m and a transverse section of 40 x 50 m. As no secondary buildings were situated around the house, the author suspects that their functions were integrated in the main house (a so-called *Kompaktanlage*). Near the house a separate bath building was situated, consisting of three large rooms, a *piscina* and an *alveus*. Two building phases could be recognized, of which the second one was dated in the second half of the 2nd century. The bath was supplied with water through a 600 m long clay pipe system (see Archäologie im Rheinland 2005, 89-90), Archäologie im Rheinland 2005, 86-88.

070 Bad Neuenahr-Ahrweiler-Silberberg, C, 1980s, a first known house at this site could be dated around the middle of the 1st century AD. Of this house, only fragmentary stone foundations, a cellar and a *praefurnium* were preserved. A separate bath section, consisting of at least five rooms, was much better perseved. This first house was torn down in the second half of the 1st century AD. After preparing the site by creating a plain of rubble and chalk, a new house was built, measuring 72 x 18-20 m. This house consisted of two large central rooms, surrounded by a number of smaller rooms, fronted by a long portico. In a second phase, this portico was extended towards the still separate bath house, situated at the same location as the previous one. Over time, a number of rooms were added to the house. The bath house was extended towards at least seven rooms, reaching a surface of 180 m2. As a result of good preservation, the elevation of the house could be reconstructed as a stone base wall of 1.70-1.80 m high, on which a framework construction was built. This framework wall was plastered on both out- and inside, Cüppers 1990, 324-325; Wegner 1985; Fehr 2003.

071 Bad Neuenahr-Ahrweiler Tiefenbachtal, C-D, 1950s, monumental settlement complex with three documented buildings on an enclosed compound (110 x 75 m). The complex was documented by survey only, Bonner Jahrbücher 160, 301-312; Cüppers 1990, 326-327.

072 Bedburg-Garsdorf, B, 1950s, part of an enclosed compound settlement with five buildings. Probably, none of these constructions can be interpreted as the main house. During a first phase, all the buildings were post-built. In a second phase, one of the buildings was rebuilt in stone, while preserving the rectangular layout (divided in two spaces). The settlement was founded around the middle of the 1st century AD and was abandoned in the 4th century. Outside the Roman period compound, an Iron Age settlement has been partly documented, Bonner Jahrbücher 159, 382-384.

073 Bedburg-Königshoven / Frimmersdorf 80, D, 1980s, rectangular settlement enclosure, measuring 100 x 108 m (1,080 HA = 4 Iugera), that was part of an enclosed compound settlement. Because of the limited extent of the excavations, traces of habitation on the enclosed compound were not documented, however. A small, separately enclosed area in the northeastern corner of the compound contained at least three graves, Bonner Jahrbücher 188, 406-408.

074 Bedburg-Morken-Harf, C, 1950s, large monumental house. The earliest habitation on this site were sunken-floor huts as well as a framework building with construction timbers set in hewn blocks of natural stone. This latter building is interpreted as a shed or granary and could be dated to the second half of the 1st century AD. In the early 2nd century AD, a large house on stone foundations was built. This house had a 104 m long portico-risalith façade. In the southeast corner of the house a bath section was situated. The choice for such a remarkably long-rectangular plan may be associated with the local geography, as the house is situated on a ridge between two streams and a 'deeper' design would not have been possible, Hinz 1969a, Bonner Jahrbücher 157, 453-454.

075 Margraten-Berg-Backerbosch, B-C, 1870s-1880s, three monumental buildings were excavated by Habets in the later 19th century. The main house had an 82.7 m long façade and contained exotic building materials. Two other buildings (one measuring 20 x 9 m) probably also had residential functions. This site was dated between the early 2nd and 3rd century AD. During recent excavations, traces of at least two other buildings on stone foundations were documented, of which one measured 10 x 20 m, Habets 1895; De Groot 2006.

076 Blankenheim-Hülchrath, B, 1890s, 1910s, 1930s, monumental, axially organised complex. Only of the main house the development has been reconstructed. A first monumental house was constructed during the 1st century AD and consisted of around 20 rooms (48 x 17 m). Already during this first phase a hypothetical bath section was situated in the west corner of the house. Around the middle of the second century the house was destroyed by fire, however. At the same location, even using existing foundations, the house was rebuilt, this time without projecting risaliths. From this phase on, the house developed towards a 30+-room plan, with several rooms heated by hypocausts. The bath section was extended with among others an apsidal basin. During the two last phases, the central open hall was subdivided into a number of smaller rooms, Lenz 1998, 54; Horn 1987, 361-363, Bonner Jahrbücher 123, 210-226.

077 Bonn-Friesdorf, C, 1860s, 1920s, 1950s, fragmentarily documented monumental house (68 x 37 m). The structure of this house is not well documented. Remarkable are the circular rooms that were probably part of the bath section. The house was occupied at least during the 2nd century AD, Bonner Jahrbücher 159, 380-382.

078 Born-Buchten, C, 1920s, monumental house with a symmetrical layout, consisting of a central room, several smaller rooms and a fronting portico-risalith façade (25 x 12 m), Oudheidkundige Mededelingen uit het Rijksmuseum van Oudheden te Leiden 9, 2.

079 Bornheim-Botzdorf, C-D, 2000s, fragmentarily documented settlement complex. The main house, a multi-roomed house on stone foundations, had a relatively simple plan, with a bath section that was added during a later phase (the reconstructed size of the house is 20 x 11 m). Four other constructions can be interpreted as secondary buildings. Settlement activity was dated to the 1st and 2nd century AD, Archäologie im Rheinland 2002, 89-92.

080 Broichweiden-Würselen, C, 1970s, a rectangular post-built house was constructed in the 1st century AD. Then, during a next phase, this house was replaced by a simple house on stone foundations, situated at exactly the same location (26 x 15 m). This latter house consisted of a rectangular hall, fronted by a portico-risalith façade. The site seems to have been occupied until the 4th century, Bonner Jahrbücher 177, 577-580.

081 Düren-Arnoldsweiler, C, 1980s, house on stone foundations (23 x 14 m) and two secondary buildings. Settlement activity could be dated from the 1st until the 4th century AD, Bonner Jahrbücher 186, 599-600.

082 Elsdorf-Etzweiler / Hambach 127, A, 1990s, well-structured compound settlement measuring 145 x 150 m (2,25 ha). Three buildings were excavated; some more were recognized in the field. The main house was relatively simple (23 x 31 m) and could be dated to the 1st century AD. In the early 2nd century, a bath section was added to the existing house. A secondary house (16 x 31,5 m) with a portico-risalith façade was situated close to the main house. The third building was a large, rectangular storage building, consisting of a large room with a raised floor and a very small room on one of the short ends of the building (10.5 x 25 m). On the east and west sides of the compound, many graves were documented. Besides simple cremation graves, a small monumental structure is mentioned, but not well published. The graves date settlement activity between the 1st and 3rd century AD, Archäologie im Rheinland 2000, 73-76.

083 Elsdorf-Neu-Etzweiler / HA 132, B-C, 1970s, several buildings forming a settlement (of which five were excavated). No enclosure was documented. The main house consisted of a hall and a number of small rooms, fronted by a portico-risalith façade (28.5 x 16.5 m). A bath section and hypocaust were probably later additions to the existing house. Another building can be interpreted as a large storage building (15.5 x 14 m). Metal working and glass production, documented at this site, were probably relatively late phenomena. Settlement activity could be dated between the second half of the 1st century and the late 4th century AD, Brüggler 2009.

084 Erkelenz-Commerden, B-C, 1990s, three buildings that were part of a settlement. The main house was of a well-known type with a portico-risalith façade and measured 20 x 17 m (reconstructable size). For the other buildings, a function could not be reconstructed. Settlement activity was dated between the middle of the 2nd and the 3rd century AD, Archäologie im Rheinland 1994, 67-70.

085 Eschweiler-Laurenzberg / Siedlung 63, B-C, 1960s, several monumental buildings that were part of a settlement complex. A simple stone house, consisting of a large central space and smaller surrounding rooms, could probably be interpreted as the oldest structure (21 x 17 m). During a second phase, a new, much larger house with projecting wings was constructed just behind the old house (probably not before this old house was torn down). Of the six (partly) documented secondary buildings, building 1 can be interpreted as a large storage building (35 x 15 m). Settlement activity could not be dated more precisely than to the reign of Trajan, Lenz 1999.

086 Euskirchen-Kreuzweingarten, C, 1830s-1880s, monumental house (87 x 56 m). The northern part of the house had as a typical structure, with several rooms fronted by a portico-risalith façade (around 60 m wide). Behind this part, an open court, surrounded by rooms, was attached. A room, situated centrally on the south side of the court, had a mosaic floor and could possibly be interpreted as a *triclinium*. Habitation was dated between the second half of the 1st century and the middle of the 4th century AD. Although probably the house had multiple building phases, these were not reconstructed, Horn 1987, 426-427.

087 Frechen-Königsdorf, C, 2000s, monumental house, measuring 32 x 21 m. Habitation activity could be dated between the 1st and 4th century AD. Remarkable elements of the house were a large rectangular basin and a cistern, used for filtering and storing water respectively, Archäologie im Rheinland 2004, 94-96.

088 Alt-Etzweiler/Hambach 133, A, 2000s, well-structured enclosed compound settlement of about 1 hectare. The first rectangular compound, created around the middle of the 1st century AD, was later extended with a new long rectangular section, interpreted as a garden. Here, a number of graves were situated. During another phase, the enclosure ditches were replaced by a palisade. Thirteen buildings were documented, of which most were post-built. The main house was constructed on stone foundations and had a simple plan, consisting of a few rooms fronted by a portico-risalith façade (around 25 x 15 m). One building, deviating from the generally respected orientation, could perhaps be interpreted as the oldest element of the settlement, dating to the Early Roman period. This situation is possibly similar to that at the settlement of Hambach 412. A large rectangular stone building with buttresses possibly had a storage function and could probably be associated with a later settlement phase, Archäologie im Rheinland 2007, 111-114.

089 Heerlen-Heerlerbaan-Bovenste Caumer, C, 1920s, monumental house (25 x 20 m) consisting of a bipartite central hall, surrounded by a number of smaller rooms and fronted by a portico-risalith façade. In the western section of the house, a *preafurnium* and hypocaust were documented. Habitation was dated between the middle of the 2nd and the middle of the 3rd century AD, Peters 1930.

090 Heerlen-Meezenbroek, C, 1950s, not so well documented monumental house, measuring 40 x 16 m. At least two rooms were heated by a hypocaust. Habitation was dated between the 2nd and early 3rd century AD, Berichten van de Rijksdienst voor het Oudheidkundig Bodemonderzoek 1950, 42.

091 Heerlen-Trilandis, A, 2000s, probably enclosed settlement, consisting of several Alphen-Ekeren type post-built houses and a number of wells. Although the houses shared a similar orientation, the settlement was not rigidly structured on a compound, comparable to many settlements in the region. Only at a single location, gravel traces of a foundation were documented. The author does not associate this foundation with a monumental house, however, Tichelman in prep.

092 Herzogenrath-Merkstein, A, 2000s, during the 1st century AD, an enclosed settlement (123 x 144 m) was founded. Parallel to the northern enclosure ditch, three buildings were situated. These were interpreted as a byre house, a secondary building and a granary by the author. During the 2nd century AD, another granary and a building interpreted as a stable were constructed. In this same century, or somewhat later in the 3rd century, several new buildings were also constructed. One of these was constructed with horizontal beams on stone footings. In the 3rd century AD, the enclosure ditch was backfilled. The settlement was abandoned around the early 4th century AD, Archäologie im Rheinland 2008.

093 Houthem-Kloosterbos (Rondenbosch), D, 1850s, two buildings on stone foundations. The fragmentarily documented main house measured 20 x 15.5 m and probably had a portico-risalith façade. The other building had a simple rectangular plan and measured 10 x 25 m. Habitation could be dated to the 2nd century AD, Schuermans 1867.

094 Jüchen-Altgarzweiler-Elsmar / FR 131, A-B, 1990s, organised compound settlement with two documented buildings (compound dimensions 50 x 95 m). The main house was a simple hall-type construction with timber framework walls. Two building phases were recognised. The first building measured 15 x 10 m, the second 24 x 11 m. These houses were not built on stone foundations and probably did not have a tiled roof. Settlement activity could be dated between the middle of the 1st and the middle of the 2nd century AD, Archäologie im Rheinland 1999, 76-79.

095 Jüchen-Auf dem Fuchsberg / FR 129, A, 1990s, this settlement started as an unenclosed cluster of buildings, probably representing a farmstead. This early habitation phase could be dated to the first half of the 1st century AD. During this phase, the main house was a simple post-built rectangular construction measuring 16 x 6 m. During a second phase, in the later 1st or early 2nd century AD, an enclosed compound was created (150 x 100 m), containing a number of buildings, arranged along the ditches and surrounding an open space. At the location of the previous main house, a new house, measuring 18 x 13 m, was constructed. This wooden house had its posts resting in postholes with packings of gravel, quartzite and tile fragments, Archäologie im Rheinland 1997, 53-55.

096 Jüchen-Neuholz, A, 1990s, site with a well-reconstructable habitation history. The earliest habitation consisted of small single-aisled post-built houses measuring around 6.5 – 9.0 m by an average 3.5 m (consisting of four or five opposing pairs of posts). Two-aisled houses with lengths between 7.5 and 9.0 m could also be documented. Excavated four-post constructions were interpreted as granaries. This settlement was not enclosed or organised by means of ditches or palisades. On the chronology of this habitation phase views have shifted over time. Originally, the phase was dated to the Middle to Late La Tène period, thus possibly connecting the Roman-period habitation. However, new research has shown that the Late La Tène habitation phase should actually be dated earlier, to the Early Iron Age.[3] Around the start of the 1st century AD, two sunken-floor huts and a hypothetical building, consisting of ditches (possibly foundations trenches) and postholes, were constructed a short distance to the northwest. During this phase, a first geometrical ditch system organised settlement space, although it does not seem to have created a coherent compound. Settlement shifted in location again around the middle of the 1st century, when a small enclosed compound was created (80 x 80 m). On this enclosed compound, eight post-built constructions were situated, not yet strictly organised along the enclosure ditches. These buildings were traditional in plan and construction, although somewhat larger than earlier examples. Later in the 1st century, two larger single-aisled framework houses were constructed on this same compound. These houses, considerably larger than preceding ones, were orientated on the enclosure ditches. One of the houses had an internal cellar. Probably around 100 AD a new, larger palisade-enclosed compound was created at the same location (measuring at least 140 x 120 m). The main house on stone foundations had a typical plan with a portico-risalith façade (measuring around 36 x 20 m). Three or four secondary buildings, of which one constructed on linear stone foundations and one on stone footings, were organised along the palisade and around a central open space. Three small clusters of graves could be dated between the late 1st and 2nd century AD. The main house was destroyed by fire around the end of the 2nd century. Artisanal activity was also documented, dating to the 3rd century. Archäologie im Rheinland 2000, 69-72; Andrikopoulou-Strack 1999 *et al.*; Frank/Keller 2007.

097 Jüchen-Neuotzenrath, B, 1990s, part of an organised compound settlement with six documented buildings. The main house was a rectangular timber framework construction, with walls constructed on stone footings. A single risalith, situated at one of the corners of the house, was constructed on a linear stone foundation. The secondary buildings were also built on stone footings. Habitation could be dated between the early 2nd and early 3rd century AD. One of the secondary buildings, however, could be dated to the 4th century, Archäologie im Rheinland 1999, 82-84.

---

[3] This new analysis is presented in a not yet published dissertation by Stephan Weber (Bonn University). Pers. comm. Prof. Dr. Jürgen Kunow.

098 Jülich-Stetternich / HA 47, C, 1970s, three non-monumental buildings that represent the periphery of a rural settlement. These buildings were equally large (around 8 x 15 m) and probably had functions as shed or stable. Remarkably, these structures were situated very close to the main road (only tens of meters), Gaitzsch 1983, 349-352; Bonner Jahrbücher 182, 494.

099 Jülich-Welldorf / HA 23, C, 1970s, monumental house and secondary building. The fragmentarily documented house had a regular plan with a portico-risalith façade (24 x 18 m). The secondary building measured 15 x 11 m and can probably be interpreted as a granary on the basis of its plan. Settlement activity could be dated between the middle of the 2nd and the first half of the 3rd century AD, Gaitzsch 1983.

100 Kerkrade-Holzkuil, A, 2000s, this settlement was founded as a well-structured, yet unenclosed settlement during the late 1st century AD. During this phase, the settlement consisted of two opposing axes of post-built structures, with a central open space in between. The main building was an Alphen-Ekeren type farmhouse. During the early 2nd century AD, this post-built house was replaced by a simple rectangular house on stone foundations and the settlement compound was being enclosed. During the next phases, the main house was rebuilt and extended again, resulting in a multi-roomed house with a portico-risalith façade, a cellar and a bath section, the latter being attached to the existing house is a later phase. The basic structure of the settlement was preserved through time. On the central open space, a pond was created, Tichelman 2005.

101 Kerkrade-Spekholzerheide, C, 1930s-1940s, at this site, a post-built, probably single-aisled framework construction (12.5 x 7.5 m), was dated to the 1st century AD. A hypothetical older post-built construction could possibly even be dated before the middle of the 1st century AD. Then, around the end of the 1st century AD, a multi-roomed house on stone foundations was constructed. During a first phase, the house consisted of a number of rooms, fronted by a simple portico. In a second phase, a bath section, a large room at the back of the house, and two risaliths were added (the final house measured 52 x 22 m). A hypothetical secondary building measured 18 x 12.5 m. Habitation continued until the early 3rd century AD, Braat 1941; Koster/Peterse/Swinkels 2002, 48 ff.; Brunsting 1950.

102 Kerkrade-Winckelen, C-D, 2000s, four Alphen-Ekeren-type post-built farmhouses could be dated between the second half of the 2nd and the first half of the 3rd century AD. Finds of building material points at the nearby presence of a monumental house, although structural traces have not been found. If correct, the post-built houses could be interpreted as secondary buildings belonging to a larger villa settlement, Dijkstra 1997.

103 Kerpen-Sindorf, B, 2000s, part of an enclosed compound settlement. Three buildings (building 100 and two two-aisled houses) represent the first settlement phase that could be dated to the 1st century AD. During this period, a compound of 1 hectare was defined by a ditch. During a second phase, the compound was extended 0.3 hectares. Habitation continued until the late 4th century AD, Archäologie im Rheinland 2002, 87-89.

104 Cologne-Braunsfeld, C, 1920s, multi-roomed house on stone foundations. The first phase, dated to the 2nd century AD, entailed a simple rectangular framework house. Then, in the 3rd century AD, a monumental house with a central hall fronted by a portico-risalith façade was constructed. During the 4th century, a bath section was created within the existing house. A number of very rich sarcophagi can be associated with this building phase, Horn 1987, 506; Van Ossel 1992, 198.

105 Cologne-Müngersdorf, A-B, 1920s, well-excavated enclosed compound settlement. The earliest documented house, situated at the same location as the later main house, was dated as early as the first half of the 1st century AD by Fremersdorf, but was re-dated to the middle of the 1st century AD by Horn. What the settlement looked like during this early phase is not clear. During a second phase, dated in the second half of the 1st century AD, a larger main house, a secondary house and two hall-type houses -barns or stables-, were part of the settlement. They were arranged around an open space. The façade of the main house seems to have been facing away from the secondary buildings, overlooking a part of the compound that is clear of structures; possibly a garden. The wall, enclosing the settlement, did not exist during the earliest settlement phases. It is not clear if the settlement was enclosed in another way during these phases. A large granary, built in the middle imperial period, indicates an economic shift towards the intensified and specialised production of corn. Several other buildings, interpreted as byres by Fremersdorf, point at the importance of livestock. The main house was situated at the same location for over three centuries: from the middle of the 1st century until the later 4th century. In the 3rd century, a tower-like granary was constructed within an existing building, indicating the need for safety precautions. This phenomenon can also be documented at other settlements, among which Voerendaal-Ten Hove, Fremersdorf 1933; Horn 1987, 505.

106 Cologne-Widdersdorf, B, 1990s, fragmentarily documented enclosed compound settlement. Of this settlement, the squarish enclosure (around 80 x 80 m) could be documented, together with two buildings. These buildings were dated to the second half of the 2nd century AD. By this time, the enclosure ditch was backfilled and the settlement boundaries were defined by means of a fence. The earlier ditched enclosure could be dated to the second half of the 1st century AD at the earliest. The structure of this settlement is similar to the many compound settlements known from the Hambach region, Spiegel 2002.

107 Landgraaf-Binnenring, D, 2000s, part of a rural settlement consisting of two Alphen-Ekeren type houses and a long ditch, that can probably be interpreted as the settlement enclosure ditch. During a first phase, posts were set in postholes. Later, another, still traditional house was built with posts set on gravel footings. The authors suggest that these traces could have been part of a villa settlement comparable to that of Kerkrade-Holzkuil. Both houses could be dated in the 2nd century AD, Van Hoof/Van Wijk 2007.

108 Maasbracht-Brachterbeek-Steenakker, C, 1980s, a first monumental house was constructed in the late 1st century AD and consisted of a central hall and several smaller rooms, fronted by a portico-risalith façade. In the late 2nd century, rebuilding activities enhanced the monumentality and appearance of the house (now measuring 30 x 50 m). First of all, the existing risaliths were replaced by larger ones with deeper foundations, indicating a tower-like appearance. These risaliths were now like projecting wings, containing several rooms. Secondly, at the centre of the portico, a monumental entrance was created. At the back of the house a cellar was built. The large amount of rich painted plaster, collected during the excavations, could be dated to this period was well. At the east side of the house, a gallery connected the second phase risalith with an unexcavated structure, probably the bath building. In both phases a number of rooms were heated by hypocausts. A second phase hypocaust was situated in a room in the eastern risalith. The house seems to have been abandoned during the second half of the 3rd century AD, Stuart/De Grooth 1987.

109 Meerssen-Onderste Herkenbergh, D, 1860's, many stone foundations were documented at this site. According to the excavator these belonged to a single monumental house. A well-preserved cellar and a bath suite were documented as well. During recent excavations at this site, two other buildings were partially documented. Yet another building on stone foundations was excavated in 2001. This building, which probably had a simple rectangular plan, could be dated to the 2nd century AD, Schuermans 1867; Habets 1871; De Groot 2005, 2007.

110 Mönchengladbach-Herrath, C, 1970s, simple monumental house, consisting of two rooms front-ed by a portico-risalith façade (25 x 15 m). This house can de dated to the 2nd century AD. Part of an enclosure was documented as well, Ausgrabungen im Rheinland 1978, 106-107.

111 Neuss-Meertal, C, 1990s, simple multi-roomed house on stone foundations. The first phase of this house, dated to the late 1st century AD, consisted of a hall and a room, fronted by a portico-risalith façade. During a next phase, extra rooms and a hypothetical bath section were added to the existing core (measuring 29.5 x 10 m), Archäologie im Rheinland 1995, 60-62.

112 Neuss-Rommerskirchen/Nettesheim, C, 1980s, in the late 1st century AD, a framework house was constructed at this site. Next, around the middle of the 2nd century, a simple house on stone foundations replaced it. During a first phase, the house consisted of a hall, fronted by a façade with a portico and single risalith. In a second phase, a second risalith, several small rooms and a bath section were added to the existing house. Later, the bath section was abandoned and rebuilt in a slightly different location. In this latter phase, the house measured 32 x 16 m. The site was abandoned around 275 AD, Archäologie im Rheinland 1987, 80-81; Bonner Jahrbücher 189, 398-405.

113 Neuss-Weckenhoven, C, 1950s, during the second half of the 1st century AD, a rectangular, single-aisled house was constructed (18 x 7.5 m). The postholes in the walls were more or less square. During a next phase, a larger house on stone foundations was constructed (37 x 17 m) at exactly the same location. This house consisted of at least six rooms and a portico-risalith façade, situated at the northeastern short side of the house. The site was inhabited until the second half of the 3rd century AD, Haupt 1968.

114 Nideggen-Wollersheim-Am Hostert, B-C, 1950s, partly documented monumental settlement complex, consisting of at least six monumental buildings and a grave monument. The complex can probably be reconstructed as a rectangular compound with a main house at one of the short ends and secondary houses on both of the long sides in front of the main house. The main house had a typical plan with a portico-risalith façade (measuring at least 35 x 20 m). Next to the main house, a smaller secondary house was situated (measuring 12 x 16 m). One of the other buildings (number IV in Pertikovits 1956, 102) was interpreted as a *horreum* (15.5 x 18 m). Remarkable is the group of graves, located les than 100 m to the northwest of the complex. One of the graves can be reconstructed as a grave pillar. One of the other, of which a rectangular stoned foundation remained, also has a monumental character, Petrikovits 1956.

115 Niederzier / HA 69, A, 1980s, enclosed compound (0.9 ha) settlement with buildings arranged around an open court. At least eight buildings were documented. The main house consisted of a number of rooms, fronted by a façade (15 x 10 m). Traces of a post-built structure could represent a predecessor. The fragmentarily documented building next to this main house was interpreted as a secondary house. Six other buildings were interpreted as secondary buildings, among others for holding livestock. On the south side of the compound, many cremation graves were documented. Furthermore, two sarcophagi were situated 100 meter from the settlement. Habitation was dated between the 2nd and 4th century AD, Gaitzsch 1986; Bonner Jahrbücher 183, 652-654.

116 Niederzier / Hambach 74, C, 1970s, at this partly excavated settlement, the main house consisted of a central hall, a number of smaller rooms and a fronting façade (20 x 14 m). The documented secondary building was a simple rectangular structure, measuring 6.5 x 10 m. West of these buildings, around 20 m of enclosure ditch was documented. The settlement was inhabited until around 200 AD, Ausgrabungen im Rheinland 1978, 119-120.

117 Niederzier / Hambach 403, A, 1980s, enclosed compound settlement with buildings around an open court (total surface: 0.75 ha). The main house consisted of a hall and a smaller room, fronted by a portico-risalith façade (28.5 x 16 m). A smaller building next to this house can be interpreted as a secondary house (16.5 x 9 m). The other buildings can be interpreted as sheds, granaries or stables. The settlement was founded around the middle of the 1st century AD and abandoned around the late 2nd century. The enclosure ditch was backfilled in the early 2nd century and replaced by a palisade. In the late 3rd and 4th century, the site was re-occupied. During this phase, the economic focus had shifted artisan production, however, Bonner Jahrbücher 185, 474-476; Bonner Jahrbücher 186, 617-626.

118 Niederzier / Hambach 516, A, 1980s, this settlement took a start in the Claudian-Neronian period. During this phase, an open settlement consisting of two buildings, a well and four graves existed. In the later 1st century a settlement enclosure was dug. The buildings were now orientated on this enclosure. Graves were situated outside the compound. The main house was extended considerably and building 2 was rebuilt on gravel foundations. During the first half of the 2nd century four new buildings were constructed and the main house was extended with a risalith at one corner, built on gravel foundations. In this same period the enclosure ditch was filled up and replaced by a palisade. During the 3rd century, the agriculturally orientated settlement was given up and ovens were constructed around and inside the existing buildings. In this period, the economic focus changed from agriculture to artisan production; a phenomenon known from many of the Rhineland settlements, Bonner Jahrbücher 186, 627-628; Kaszab-Olchewski 2006.

119 Niederzier-Hambach / Hambach 425, B, 1990s, part of an enclosed compound settlement. Parts of three buildings were documented here. The only completely excavated building measured 15 x 8 m and can be interpreted as a secondary building. A corn drying oven was probably added during a later phase. The compound was defined by a double palisade. Habitation could be dated between the 2nd and 4th century AD. Fourteen graves were situated directly along a road, close to the settlement compound, Archäologie im Rheinland 1990, 50-53.

120 Niederzier-Hambach / Hambach 56, C, 1970s, four monumental buildings that were part of a settlement complex. The main house started as a simple rectangular hall with porticoes. Later, small rooms and a bath section were added. This building measured 32 x 20-25 m. The other buildings can be interpreted as a shed or granary. One of the buildings had a basilical plan, which was quite rare for this region. Habitation was dated between the middle of the 2nd century and around 270/280 AD, Ausgrabungen im Rheinland 1978, 108-112.

121 Niederzier-Hambach / Hambach 66, C, 1970s, two monumental buildings. The main house consisted of a hall and several smaller rooms, fronted by a portico-risalith façade (18 x 27 m). The secondary building had two phases. During the first phase, a 10 x 10 m building existed that can possibly be interpreted as a *horreum* (Heimberg 2002/2003, 121). The superseding building was larger (19.5 x 16 m) and could have had a similar function. However, a residential function could also be suggested for this latter building. Habitation activity could be dated to the late 2nd and 3rd century AD, Rech 1983.

122 Niederzier-Hambach / Hambach 512, A, 1980s, the first habitation phase on this site could be dated around the middle of the 1st century AD. To this phase belong a wooden building, a well, a sunken floor hut, two *bustum*-type graves and some simple cremation graves. The wooden house, of which the exact plan remained eligible, was situated at the location of the later stone-built house. During this earliest phase, the settlement was not yet enclosed. During the second half of the 1st century AD, however, a compound of 2.5 hectares was separated from the surrounding landscape by a ditch. The main building, still a post-built construction (although possibly on sandstone bases), was situated in the north corner of the compound, with four secondary buildings arranged along the enclosure ditches, surrounding an open court. At the southern part the enclosure a group of graves was situated. During the first half of the 2nd century, the enclosure ditch was filled up and replaced by a palisade. Just like in the previous phase, besides the main house, four secondary buildings were situated on the compound. Also during the early 2nd century AD, a first house on stone foundations was built. This house consisted of a large hall and a number of smaller rooms, fronted by a portico-risalith façade. Next, a complete new building with a slightly different orientation was connected to the existing house, by means of a tapering section, constructed between the two buildings. In a number of phases the house developed towards a structure of fifteen to twenty rooms, fronted by a portico-risalith façade. A hypothetical bath section was situated in the tapering section just mentioned, Gaitzsch 1986; Bonner Jahrbücher 184, 617-622; Kaszab-Olschewski 2006.

123 Niederzier-Steinstrass / Hambach 264, C, 1970s, monumental house, measuring 39 x 17 m. The house consisted of several small and large rooms, fronted by a portico. Habitation could be dated to the 2nd and 3rd century AD, Gaitzsch 1983; Ausgrabungen im Rheinland 1978, 115-116.

124 Niederzier-Steinstrass / Hambach 382, A-B, 1980s, part of an enclosed compound settlement. At least three buildings were documented. The main house consisted of a large central hall and two or more porticoes (16.5 x 18.5 m). The other buildings can be interpreted as a shed and workshop respectively. The compound had a surface of at least 2 hectares. In the northwestern part of the compound, a group of cremation graves was situated, Bonner Jahrbücher 183, 648-652.

125 Niederzier-Steinstrass / Hambach 59, A, 1980s, four development phases can be reconstructed for this settlement (see Hallmann-Preuss 2002/2003, 395 ff.). During the first phase, dated to the 1st century AD, a fairly small enclosed compound contained a simple house on stone foundations and two secondary buildings, arranged along the sides. The earliest house on stone foundations seems to have been constructed during the later 1st century and consisted of a central hall, a portico on three sides and probably three non-projecting risaliths. Around the transition from the 2nd to the 3rd century, a bath section and hypocausted rooms were added to the house on the west side. The presence of a post-built house, preceding the stone house, could be documented only fragmentarily. As a south ditch could not be documented, the compound measured at least 80 x 95 m (0.76 ha). During the second phase, dated to the 2nd century, the compound was extended considerably. The main house was now positioned centrally against the northern enclosure ditch and six secondary buildings were arranged in two rows in front of the main house, creating an almost axial layout. The compound, only partially enclosed by ditches, now covered a surface of 1.5 hectares. During the third phase, around the late 2nd and early 3rd century AD, the compound was extended to 1.78 hectares, this time towards the east. For a fourth phase no enclosure ditches could be documented. Apart from the main house, only two or three secondary buildings existed at this time. By now, the 3rd century, the settlement had clearly started declining, Gaitzsch 1990; Van Ossel 1992, 217; Hallmann-Preuss 2002/2003.

126 Niederzier-Steinstrass / Hambach 412, B, 1980s, the first phase of this settlement, dated to the early 1st century AD, consisted of six similarly orientated post-built structures, partly constructed on horizontal foundation beams. Still in the first half of the 1st century, five new post-built buildings were erected, differing slightly in orientation. Three of these buildings were long rectangular two-aisled structures. During these two phases, the settlement was unenclosed and not yet organised around a central open space. Then, during the early second half of the 1st century, a rectangular enclosed compound was created, on which at least four buildings were built against the enclosure ditches and around a central open space. The now monumental main house consisted of a hall fronted by a portico-risalith façade. This house existed for around 200 years and was partly reconstructed several times. Secondary buildings were also rebuilt in the same location. The enclosure ditch was backfilled and replaced by a palisade, parallel to many other settlements in the German Hambach region. The settlement was occupied until the first half of the 3rd century AD. Like in many other settlements, the site was re-occupied during the Late Roman period, as traces of a building and several ovens indicate, Archäologie im Rheinland 2007, 69-71.

127 Niederzier-Steinstrass-Lich / Hambach 224, B, 1990s, partly documented compound settlement. The compound had a surface of 1.13 hectares (150 x 75 m) and was defined by means of a ditch and palisade. The hypothetical main house (it has also been suggested that this building is not the main house) was a single-aisled post-built structure (22 x 11 m), comparable to houses at Frimmersdorf 131 and Jüchen-Neuotzenrath. The secondary building was a smaller, also single-aisled post-built structure. The ditch system could be dated to the 1st century AD. During the second half of the 3rd century, a *burgus* was constructed on this site that remained occupied until the 4th century, Bonner Jahrbücher 195, 516-518.

128 Nuth-Arensgenhout-Scherpenbek (Steenland), B-C, 1870s, rectangular enclosed compound (95 x 256 m) with two opposing buildings on the short sides. The main building measured 40 x 20 m and contained a cellar and hypocaust. The other building was somewhat smaller (17 x 20 m), Habets 1882.

129 Nuth-Op den Billich / Valkenburg-Ravensbosch, C, 1900s, two monumental buildings, situated less than 100 m from each other. The building referred to as Nuth-Op den Billich was a monumental house consisting of several rooms fronted by a portico-risalith façade (31.5 x 14 m). The other building, referred to as Valkenburg-Ravensbosch, was equally large (30 x 15.5 m) and also consisted of a number of rooms, fronted by a portico-risalith façade. Both buildings were occupied at least during the 2nd and early 3rd century AD, Goossens/Holwerda/Krom 1907.

130 Nuth-Terstraten, D, 2000s, simple rectangular house on stone foundations. This building had a structure similar to traditional Alphen-Ekeren farmhouses. It superseded a post-built granary and, nearby, traces of another post-built structure were documented as well. According to the author, these buildings can be interpreted as part of a villa settlement. The building on stone foundations could be dated to the late 2nd or 3rd century AD. The post-built constructions were somewhat older, perhaps reaching back into the 1st century AD, Hiddink/De Boer 2003, 22-41.

131 Nuth-Thull-Zandbergsweg/Vaasrade, C, 1930s, monumental house consisting of a central hall and several smaller rooms, fronted by a portico-risalith façade (30 x 20 m). Two rooms, heated by means of hypocausts, were interpreted as part of a bath section. Habitation could be dated between the 2nd and the early 3rd century AD, Braat 1934.

132 Pulheim-Brauweiler, A, 1990s, the first phase of this settlement could be dated to the latest Iron Age or earliest Roman period[4] and comprised a loosely ordered cluster of small buildings. Around the middle of the 1st century AD, an enclosed compound was created, containing small, wooden buildings, partly built on horizontal foundation beams and orientated on the enclosure ditch. This compound was inhabited until the end of the 1st century AD. Around the same time, a new compound was created just west of its predecessor. On this new compound, three large post-built constructions, one building on horizontal foundation beams and four sunken-floor huts were situated, arranged parallel to the enclosure ditches and surrounding an open space. The main house measured 28.5 x 13 m and had a single-aisled plan with walls of timbers set in pairs, partly on stone footings, Archäologie im Rheinland 1999, 72-75; Andrikopoulou-Strack *et al.* 2000.

133 Rheinbach-Baumarkt, B-C, 1990s, partly documented compound settlement. At least four buildings could be recognised. Only one corner of the main house was excavated. A secondary building on stone foundations measured 20 x 8 m. Near the northern settlement boundary, sixteen cremation graves were situated. Habitation could be dated between the 2nd and 4th century AD, Archäologie im Rheinland 1997, 65-66.

134 Rheinbach-Flerzheim, B-C, 1970s-1980s, partly documented compound settlement. Four buildings were excavated. The main house consisted of a large hall and a number of smaller rooms, fronted by a portico-risalith façade (37 x 20 m). A bath section was probably added during a later phase. The first monumental phase could be dated to the first half of the 2nd century AD. Preceding this phase, a framework structure existed. A secondary residential building actually was a smaller version of the main house (22 x 10 m). Two secondary buildings on stone foundations were interpreted as a shed and *horreum* respectively. A group of graves, comprising sarcophagi and simple cremations graves, was situated north of the main house. Around 275 AD, the settlement was destroyed by fire. During the Late Roman period, a *burgus* was built on this site, Gechter 1990.

135 Schaesberg-Overstenhof, C-D, 1920s, partly documented monumental house, measuring 35 x 20 m, Peters 1922.

136 Schuld, C, 1960s, monumental house, measuring 52.5 x 26 m. The house consisted of a central large space, surrounded by several smaller rooms and fronted by a portico-risalith façade (at least 20 rooms). At the back of the house, two large corner risaliths were present. Traces of mosaic floors were documented in this house. Habitation could be dated in the 2nd and 3rd century AD, Cüppers 1990, 547-549.

[4] In an earlier publication (Archäologie im Rheinland 1999, 82-84) a pre-Roman settlement phase was suggested, but later (Andrikopoulou-Strack *et al.* 2000) this first phase was re-dated to the earliest Roman period. Find material as well as house building were still heavily rooted in Iron Age tradition in this period.

137 Simpelveld-Bocholtz (Vlengendaal), C, 1910s, three monumental buildings, situated next to each other. The main house measured 44 x 31 m and consisted of a central hall, surrounded by several smaller rooms and fronted by a portico-risalith façade. At the back of the house, a similar portico-risalith façade was situated. A bath section was situated in the west corner of the house. In at least three rooms traces of mosaic were documented. In front of the house, a hypothetical basin was situated. There is mention of finds dating to the Early Roman period (Sprokholt 1988, 142-143). The two secondary buildings are relatively simple rectangular constructions. Habitation could be dated between the first half of the 2nd until the early 3rd century AD, Goossen 1916.

138 Simpelveld-Remigiusstraat/Stampstraat, C, 1930s, two partly excavated monumental buildings, situated only 50 m from each other. The main house probably had a regular plan with a fronting portico. The second building was somewhat smaller and also consisted of a few rooms, fronted by a portico. The famous Simpelveld sarcophagus was found near these buildings. Habitation could be dated between the late 1st and early 3rd century AD, Braat 1941.

139 Sittard-Nusterweg, B-C, 2000s, two post-built houses of the Alphen-Ekeren type (15 x 7 and 18 x 7.5 m). A ditch, situated parallel to the long side of house 1, was interpreted as a portico-construction. Two other long ditches organised settlement space. House 1 could be dated to the 2nd and 3rd century AD. House 2 was older and could be dated to the 1st and earlier 2nd century AD, Wetzels 2001.

140 Stein-Gemeentehaven, C, 1920s, two monumental buildings. The largest building had an a-typical plan. It is not sure if this structure can be interpreted as part of a villa settlement (48 x 30 m). Some authors have suggested that it should be interpreted as a peristyle-type villa house. Others suggested a function as *praetorium*. The second building was smaller rectangular structure with a portico on three sides (13 x 27 m), Remouchamps 1928, Bogaers 1986.

141 Titz / Hambach 303, B-C, 1980s, partly documented compound settlement with a surface of around 4 hectares. Four buildings were documented. The main house consisted of a central part with four corner risaliths and a portico. This house was preceded by a post-built structure, probably dating to the 1st century AD. Three buildings on stone foundations were documented as well. Remarkable is a small monumental grave complex, situated near one of the settlement enclosure ditches. Habitation could be dated in the 1st and 2nd century AD. A *burgus* was constructed during the later Roman period, Bonner Jahrbücher 186, 635-636; Van Ossel 1992, 223-224.

142 Vaals-Lemiers-Platte Bend, C, 1930s, monumental house and separate bath building. The house consisted of a large central room, a number of smaller rooms and a portico-risalith façade on both long sides of the house (32 x 17 m). Northwest of the house, a separate bath section was situated, consisting of four rooms. One of these had an apsis, Braat 1934.

143 Valkenburg-Heihof, C-D, 1900s, at this site, two buildings were documented. The first house measured 16.75 x 11.25 m, the second 10 x 7 m. Both buildings were constructed on gravel footings. Recently, three more, somewhat smaller buildings were excavated at this site. These houses were constructed on footings as well, Holwerda/Goossens 1907; De Groot 2007.

144 Valkenburg-Vogelenzang, C, 1920s, at this site, two buildings were documented. The main house consisted of a number of rooms fronted by a portico-risalith façade (37 x 16 m). A bath section, connected to the house on the southwestern side, was probably a later addition to the existing core. At this house, famous inscriptions mentioning patronage relationships were found. The secondary building was a simple rectangular structure measuring 16 x 8 m. Habitation can dated between the early 2nd and early 3rd century AD, Remouchamps 1925; for a discussion on the inscriptions also see Slofstra 1983.

145 Voerendaal-Colmont-Stockveld (Ubachsberg), C, 1920s, monumental house consisting of a hall, fronted by a portico-risalith façade (34 x 14 m). Habitation could be dated between the late 1st and late 2nd or early 3rd century AD, Remouchamps 1923.

146 Voerendaal-Ten Hove, A, 1890s, 1950s, 1980s, the oldest traces of habitation at this site could be dated to the Late Iron Age. In this period, a seemingly fortified compound, enclosed by large ditches, was constructed. Comparable Late Iron Age 'forts' have also been documented in Germany and Belgium (Niederzier, Jülich and Latinne). These latter sites seem to have been abandoned around the middle of the first century BC. Wether this is also the case at Voerendaal remains unclear, unfortunately. In the period between 50 BC and 50 AD, a large rectangular enclosure was created. Contrary to the preceding enclosure, this one does not seem to have had defensive functions. Various post-built structures were documented on this compound, but chronology remains problematic, as these structures have not been published until now. It seems likely, however, that an enclosed settlement, with several post-built houses and secondary buildings, existed during this period. Around the middle of the 1st century AD, a first simple stone house, consisting of two central rooms, a number of smaller rooms and risaliths, was constructed on the compound. This house probably took a central position within the settlement. Several post-built buildings can also be dated to this period. Then, around the turn of the 1st to the 2nd century AD, the simple stone house was abandoned and the settlement was reorganised in a radical way. Directly behind the old house –that was torn down–, a planned and coherent monumental complex was laid out, consisting of a main house, granary, a separate bath building and other secondary buildings. These buildings were connected by a large portico, creating a visually coherent monumental complex with a visually impressive façade, Braat 1953, Willems/Kooistra 1986, 1987, 1988.

147 Wesseling-Gut Eichholz, 1980s, B, at this site, several buildings that were part of a settlement complex were documented. The main house consisted of a hall fronted by a portico-risalith façade (22 x 20 m). Two other monumental buildings were somewhat smaller and can be interpreted as secondary buildings (20 x 12 and 22 x 15 m). Still other buildings were only very fragmentarily documented. A group of cremation graves, situated on the west side of the settlement, belonged to the early habitation phases. Habitation could be dated between the middle of the 1st and the 4th century AD, Archäologie im Rheinland 1987, 74-75.

148 Wilre-In den Vroenhof-Louwberg, C-D, 1870s, fragmentarily documented monumental building, measuring 23 x 38 m, Habets 1895, 264-266.

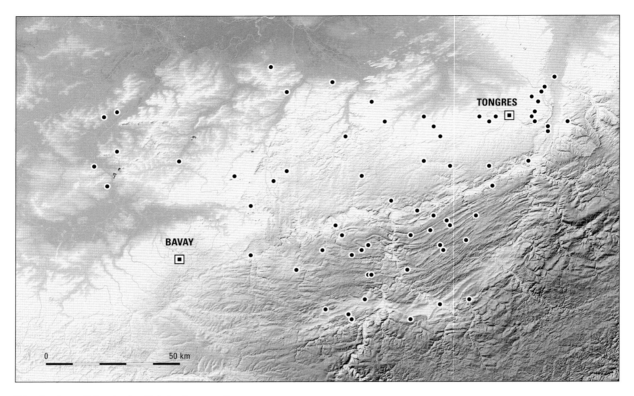

Distribution of sites in the Belgian loess region.

149 Aiseau-Presles, D, 1870s, at this site, three monumental buildings were documented. The main house, that was documented only fragmentarily, seems to have been of a winged type and had an internal bath section. A second, smaller house had a façade with two risaliths. A third structure is a small separate bath building. The precise layout of the settlement complex remains unclear, De Maeyer 1937, 63; Brulet 2009, 303-304.

150 Ambresin, C, 1870s, monumental house with around 15 rooms, fronted by a portico-risalith façade. A large court, defined by walls, was attached to the house. Remarkable is a round room, heated by a hypocaust. The site was occupied at least during the 2nd and 3rd century AD, De Maeyer 1937, 71; Brulet 2009, 438-439.

151 Anthée-Grand Bon Dieu, B, 1860s-1880s, large monumental, axially organised villa complex. The total complex measured 646 x 212 m and thus covered a surface of approximately 13 hectares. The main house was situated on the residential compound that was divided from the working compound by means of a wall. This house had a long rectangular plan with projecting wings and was over 100 m wide. On the working compound 24 secondary buildings were documented. Several of these building will have had residential functions, which was especially clear for the buildings closest to the main residential compound. One of these latter buildings even had five hypocausts, a cellar and a mosaic floor. In total, nine buildings had a cellar and four had a hypocaust. Three buildings seem to have had metallurgical functions, De Maeyer 1937, 77, 81; Brulet 2009, 561-564.

152 Arquennes-Maleville, C, 1870s, simple monumental house that, during a first phase, consisted of a few rooms fronted by a portico-risalith façade. During a next phase, two cellars were constructed within -and attached to- the existing building and a separate bath building was connected to the house. No absolute chronology is available for this site, De Maeyer 1937, 72; Brulet 2009, 365-366.

153 Ath-Meslin-l'Évêque/Ghislenghien, B, 1980s-1990s, two settlement cores were documented at this site, 1.5 km apart. The oldest settlement activity was documented along the river Sille. The small post-built structures found here could be dated between 40 and 10 BC. At another part of this site, a rectangular enclosed settlement compound with post-built structures could be dated to the first half of the 1st century AD. At least one of the buildings was identified as an Alphen-Ekeren type house by the author (Deramaix *et al.* 2010, 47). Then, during the later 1st century, the settlement was directly superseded by a monumental, axially organised settlement complex that respected the existing orientation. The complex measured at least 5 hectares and was dominated by a large house with a 110 m long façade. At again another part of the site, an enclosed settlement dated between the second half of the 1st century and the first quarter of the 2nd century AD. Three buildings could be defined as Alphen-Ekeren type constructions. Remarkably, one of the buildings was separately enclosed by means of a ditch, Deramaix/Sartieaux 1994; Houbrachts 1994; Braekeleer 1994; Brulet 2009, 309-310; Deramaix *et al.* 2010.

154 Bassenge-Int' les Deux Voyes, D, 1990s, a post-built structure, measuring 11,5 x 6,5 m could be dated to the Iron Age. To the Roman period (2nd and early 3rd century AD) belong fragmentary traces of a number of monumental buildings, Close 1997.

155 Basse-Wavre-L'Hosté, C, 1900s, large monumental house with over fifty rooms, of which ten were heated by a hypocaust. The fronting gallery was 110 m wide. Habitation could be dated between the middle of the 1st century AD until the middle of the 3rd century. During the 2nd century, a bath section was constructed and connected to the existing house on the west side. Secondary houses were documented during a survey, covering a surface of 4 hectares. Hypothetical reconstruction of the villa estate has resulted in an estimated surface of between 250 and 300 hectares for this estate, De Maeyer 1937, 73; Brulet 2009, 297-299.

156 Bierbeek, C, 1970s, monumental house consisting of a number of rooms fronted by a portico-risalith façade (16 x 33 m). A cellar was situated in the west corner of the house. Local sandstone ('Diestiaanse steen') was used for its construction. Habitation could be dated between approximately 100 and 300 AD, Deweerdt/Provoost 1982.

157 Broekom-Sassenbroekberg, B, 1980s, Late Iron Age settlement activity consisted of fragmentary habitation traces. During the second half of the 1st century AD, a house on stone foundations, consisting of a large hall, some smaller rooms and a fronting portico-risalith façade, was built (20 x 10 m). Next, during the first half of the 2nd century, the house was extended with a large room towards the east. At the same time, the façade was extended as well, requiring the construction of a new risalith. In the western risalith a basement was created. At the end of the 2nd century, the house was extended considerably. Seven rooms were added to existing house and a new portico façade with projecting wings was created at the south side of the house. Possibly, this side of the house was now the new front. On the southwest side of the house, an apsidal room was constructed, heated by a hypocaust. This room could have functioned as a *triclinium* or a bath. Building B, to the north of the house, could possibly be interpreted as a separate bath house, although the author interprets this building as a secondary residence (24 x 9.5 m). This building could be dated between the 2nd century and the middle of the 3rd century. Building C consisted of a 15 m long wall and four masonry pillar bases. Building D was an a-typical long rectangular building (69 x 13 m), dated in the Flavian period or early 2nd century. This building seems to have had at least partly residential functions, Vanvinckenroye 1988.

158 Bruyelle-Haute Éloge, B, 1990s, fragmentarily documented, axially organised settlement complex. Of the main house, only the bath section has been preserved. The first building phase of this bath section could be dated before the early 2nd century AD. During this same period, the wall dividing the main residential compound from the working compound was constructed. During the second half of the 2nd century, the bath section was extended. This bath existed until the 4th century. On the working compound, a number of monumental buildings could be dated to the 2nd century AD. Besides the architectural elements, other archaeological traces could be dated between the first half of the 1st century AD and the first half of the 4th century AD, with emphasis on the Flavian period and first half of the 2nd century, Corbiau 1997, 319-322; Brulet 2009, 305-309.

159 Clermont-sous-Huy-Arvy, D, 1960s-1970s, fragmentarily documented large monumental house. The house was over 100 m long, only 15 m deep and had a fronting portico-risalith façade. A bath section was connected to the southwest side of the house. The earliest phase could be dated to the late 1st century AD. During later phases, a portico, risalith and bath section were added. The house was probably occupied until the middle of the 3rd century AD. Under the bath section, traces of a post-built house were documented. This house could be dated to the second half of the 1st century AD, Brulet 2009, 405-406.

160 Dinant-Gemechenne-Chiautes, C, 1970s, monumental house, comprising a number of rooms fronted by a portico-risalith façade. This house was constructed during the 1st century AD. During the early 2nd century, a separate bath house was constructed just north of the existing house, Brulet 2009, 516-517.

161 Champion-Le Emptinne, A, 1980s, axially organised settlement complex. The complex seems to have been laid out as a coherent whole during the second half of the 1st century AD. The monumental main house was situated at one of the short sides of the long rectangular compound. In front of this main house, on both sides of the central axis of the compound, two rows of post-built structures were present. There are indications that the monumental house was preceded by a post-built structure, but this phase could not be well documented. During the 2nd century AD, a number of hypocausted rooms were added to the main house, the bath building was extended considerably and was connected to the house by means of a hallway. Some secondary buildings were also rebuilt during this phase. In the late 2nd and early 3rd century, the enclosure went out of use, some changes or additions were made to the house and bath, and one of the secondary buildings was rebuilt on stone foundations. The other post-built structures were abandoned. During the later 3rd century, only part of the main house was being occupied, habitation reaching into the 4th century, Van Ossel/Defgnee 2001; Corbiau 1997, 323-327; Brulet 2009, 540-546.

162 Erps-Kwerps, D, 1980s-1990s, fragmentary traces indicate habitation activity during the Late Iron Age at this site. The earliest houses, however, could be dated to the Early Roman period. Two Alphen-Ekeren type houses had a northeast-southwest orientation. During the late 1st century AD, a stone-built house (51 x 23 m), with an orientation parallel to the wooden houses, was constructed a short distance to the northwest. This house was of a well-known type with several rooms fronted by a portico-risalith façade. Three post-built constructions were also part of the settlement during this phase. Around the middle of the 2nd century, the house was extended with a portico at the back. One of the secondary buildings was reconstructed on stone foundations. Habitation continued until the end of the 3rd century, Verbeeck 1995.

163 Evelette-Résimont, C, 1960s, fragmentarily documented monumental house, consisting of a number of rooms, fronted by a hypothetical portico-risalith façade. A large room formed the core of the house. To the sides, a hypocausted room, a cellar and a small bath section were situated. The house was occupied at least during the 2nd and 3rd century AD, Willems 1966; Brulet 2009, 559.

164 Froyennes, C, 1960s, simple monumental house (22 x 17 m), consisting of a central room, surrounded by a number of smaller rooms and fronted by a portico-risalith façade. Two rooms were heated by means of a hypocaust. The house was probably built in the 1st century AD, Brulet 2009, 366-367.

165 Gerpinnes, C, 1870s, monumental house, consisting of a central hall, fronted by a portico-risalith façade. During later building phases, several smaller rooms were added to the central hall. A short distance from the house, a separate bath house was situated, De Maeyer 1937, 85-87.

166 Gesves-Sur le Corria, B, 2000s, the earliest phase of this settlement was represented by the fragmentarily documented building 1, which was directly superseded by building H and, later, the stone-built bath section (see fig. 1 in Lefert 2008). Building H and building G were simple post-built houses, sharing the same orientation, and probably dating to the late pre-Roman period. The earliest Roman-period habitation comprised buildings J, I and C; all two-aisled houses with an orientation deviating from the earlier houses. During a next phase, a simple stone house was constructed, consisting of five rooms and a fronting portico. Unfortunately, an absolute chronology is not available for these developments. During later phases, the stone house was extended with a new section on the west side. Probably during this same phase, a separate bath section was constructed some fifty meters south from the house. Later on, this baths section was extended with a number of rooms and connected to the house by a corridor, which also provided a monumental entrance to the yard in front of the house, Lefert/Bausier 2006; Lefert 2008; Brulet 2009, 531-535.

167 Graux-Al Ronce, C, 1890s, simple monumental house. During its first phase, the house consisted of a few rooms, fronted by a portico-risalith façade. During a second phase, a bath section and some rooms were attached to the existing core. Fifty meters from this main house, two connected secondary buildings on stone foundations were situated, De Maeyer 1937, 57; Brulet 2009, 549-550.

168 Haccourt, C, 1960s, at this site, the pre-Roman settlement phase comprised traces of several post-built houses within a settlement, organised by ditches. A first Roman-period post-built structure could probably be dated to the middle of the 1st century AD. Continuity between these two phases is a possible scenario (De Boe 1974, 43-44). Unfortunately, little is known about the plans of these houses. After the middle of the 1st century AD, probably around 70, a new house was built, of which only the cellar was preserved. The superseding house probably had a simple plan, built on stone foundations, without hypocausts and concrete floors. A capital, found in the cellar,

does indicate the existence of a portico, however. Several decades later, probably before the end of the 1st century, a new house was built. This house consisted of a long part, comprising several rooms, and a bath section at the south end of the building, together creating a house with a length of 78,5 m. During the early 2nd century, the existing bath house was partly put out of use, and in the *frigidarium* a mosaic floor was created. At the back of the building a new bath section was built, to which a new portico was connected. Next, during the first half of the 2nd century, it seems that this house was deliberately torn down, as plans for creating a much larger house were to be executed. This new house measured 103 x 46 meters. The monumental façade consisted of two projecting wings with a portico in between. A centrally positioned portal accentuated the entrance. This portal led to the main hall that was surrounded by an open court on three sides. In front of the portico a long basin was situated. The rest of the house comprised a large number of rooms and two open courts. A separate bath building was situated south of the main house. Later, with the extension of this bath section, it was also connected to the house by means of a portico-gallery. The considerable luxury of this house was illustrated by the presence of three rooms with mosaics, many rooms with painted wall plaster and even marble plates, used in the most important spaces. With regard to the orientation of this house, it is remarkable that what seems to be the main façade, was orientated away from the settlement complex that is reconstructed on the southwest side of the house. Looking at the relief map, it seems that the house was situated on a small hill, overlooking the surrounding landscape. It was the most visible side of the house that needed to have an elaborate façade, it seems. The settlement complex, outside the main house, was not excavated. Surveys have indicated that this complex probably had a length of around 500 m. An axial layout seems a probability for this complex, De Boe 1974, 1975, 1976; Lensen 1987; Brulet 2009, 425-429.

169 Haillot-Matagne, C, 2000s, simple monumental house, consisting of a hall, fronted by a portico-risalith façade. During a second phase, a small bath section was added at the west side of the house, Brulet 2009, 560.

170 Haltinne-Strud, C, 1960s, simple monumental house with a hall and possibly some other rooms, fronted by a portico with a single risalith. The occupation of this house could be dated between the late 1st and second half of the 3rd century AD, Hazee 1969, Brulet 2009, 535.

171 Hamois-Sur le Hody, A, 1990s-2000s, a first settlement phase can probably be dated around the middle or the second half of the 1st century AD. During this period, the settlement consisted of post-built structures, arranged in two opposing axes, similar to the Kerkrade-Holzkuil settlement. During the earlier settlement phases, wooden two-aisled houses dominated. Later on, within these houses, central posts were replaced by pairs of wall posts supporting the roof, thereby creating a single-aisled structure. This development was visible at building N, which developed from a two-aisled to a single-aisled post-built construction and later to a building on stone foundations. At the end of the 1st or early 2nd century AD, the wooden house, positioned centrally on the northern axis, was rebuilt as a house on stone foundations, developing further in a number of phases. The original house consisted of large central rooms and several smaller rooms, fronted by a portico-risalith façade. After the first extension of the main house towards the west, a bath section was constructed and the house was extended still two more times, creating a façade of around 50 m wide. Possibly, this house was not the first one on stone foundations, however. The simple rectangular, bipartite house on stone foundations, directly overlaying the wooden house, possibly represented a first stone phase. This cannot be proven, however. Parallel to Kerkrade-Holzkuil, this settlement was founded as a well-structured, planned compound settlement, Lefert/Bausier/Nachtergael 2000, 2001, 2002; Brulet 2009, 535-540.

172 Heestert, B, 1980s, a rectangular post-built house, measuring 17 x 7.5 m, could be dated around the middle of the 1st century AD and represented the earliest structure on this site. During the early 2nd century, a house on stone foundations (21.5 x 15 m) and a separate bath section (4 x 6 m) were constructed. The house had a typical layout, with a portico-risalith façade. The settlement was enclosed by a ditch system. Habitation continued until the third quarter of the 3rd century AD, Van Doorselaer 1995.

173 Houdeng-Goegnies, C, ?, at this site, two monumental buildings were documented. The building interpreted as the main house, consisted of a relatively large number of rooms and had two projecting wings. The second building also seems to have had residential functions and a layout with a portico-risalith façade, De Maeyer 1937, 83-85.

174 Rochefort-Jemelle-La Malagne, A-B, 1890s, 1990s, large part of a monumental villa complex with a pseudo-axial organisation. The oldest core of the stone-built main house had two rooms that perhaps could be interpreted as *tricliniae*. This house was probably constructed during the late 1st century AD. No pre-monumental building phase was documented. During later phases, the main house was extended considerably by the construction of a new section around and next to it. A bath section was constructed within this new section, connecting to the oldest core. The house was destroyed by fire around 270-275 AD. A walled court in front of the house probably represented a garden. The complex seems to have been laid out as a planned unit. Five secondary buildings were documented. Both buildings G and H (see Brulet 2009, 571) were interpreted as residential. During the 4th century, economic focus shifted towards iron and bronze working. The site was occupied until the early 5th century, Mignot 1996; Mignot 1997; Brulet 2009, 570-573.

175 Jette, C, 1960s, monumental house, consisting of a central hall, fronted by a portico-risalith façade (measuring approximately 23 x 14 m). Find material dates habitation to the 2nd and 3rd century AD, Matthys 1973.

176 Kerkom-Boskouterstraat, C, 1990s, monumental building, consisting of a large central space and a number of smaller spaces around it (37 x 19 m). Indications for preceding post-built structures were also documented, In 't Ven/De Clercq 2005.

177 Kesselt, A, 2000s, settlement consisting of a number of post-built houses, arranged around a central open space on which wells and ponds were situated. Settlement space does not seem to have been enclosed. This settlement could be dated to the 2nd and 3rd century AD. An earlier settlement phase could be dated to the Late Iron Age. The settlement phases cannot be connected, however, publication in prep.

178 Lanaken-Smeermaas-Kerkveld, D, 1990s, during the Late Iron Age or Early Roman period, probably two contemporary farmsteads with post-built, Alphen-Ekeren type houses, existed at this site. An excavated ditch indicated that these farmsteads were situated on an enclosed compound. During a next phase, dated to the late 1st or 2nd century AD, a monumental house was constructed. Of this house, only the cellar had been preserved. This house was probably destroyed by fire in the 2nd or early 3rd century, Pauwels/Creemers 2006.

179 Landen-Betzveld, C, ?, monumental house and secondary building. The house had a long rectangular plan (54 x 10 m) with two projecting corner rooms. The bath section was situated in the northwestern corner of the house and probably represented a later addition. The secondary building had a simple plan, consisting of a large and small room, and measured 15 x 9 m, De Maeyer 1937, 68-70.

180 Latinne-Les Grandes Pièces, B, 1970s, fragmentarily documented villa settlement on a rectangular compound, with several buildings arranged around and open space. The main house had a 43 m-long portico-risalith façade. Habitation activity can probably be dated back to the 1st century AD, although the documented structures can only be dated to the 2nd and early 3rd century, Plumier 1984; Brulet 2009, 398-399.

181 Le Roux-lez-Fosses-Vigetaille, C, 1900s, at this site, three buildings on stone foundations were documented. The main house consisted of three rooms, fronted by a portico-risalith façade (22 x 13 m). One of the risaliths was heated by a hypocaust. Near the house, a large granary, measuring 9 x 16 m, was situated. Another, long rectangular secondary building (32 x 6 m) was documented south of the main house, De Maeyer 1937, 52; Brulet 2009, 528.

182 Luik-La Place Saint Lambert, C, 1970s-2000s, monumental house with four corner risaliths and a central risalith at the back of the house. The house was constructed around the late 1st century and was occupied at least until the first half of the 3rd century. The bath section, located in the northwest risalith, represents a later addition to the existing house, Brulet 2009, 421-423.

183 Maillen-Al Sauveniere, C, 1880s, a long rectangular monumental house, consisting of a residential section to the west and a connected building, which probably had economic functions. The main room of the residential part was a pseudo-apsidal space. A bath section was attached at the back of the house. The house was occupied from the 2nd until the 4th century AD, De Maeyer 1937, 97-99; Brulet 2009, 510-511.

184 Maillen-Arche, C, 1880s, simple monumental house, consisting of two rooms, a cellar in a risalith and a small bath section. The house was occupied from the 1st century AD until the Late Roman period, De Maeyer 1937, 54; Brulet 2009, 511.

185 Maillen-Ronchinne, C, 1890s, three monumental buildings, situated on a single axis. The main house was a long rectangular structure with a fronting portico, measuring 110 m. In the western part of the house, small rooms were arranged around an apsidal reception room. The bath section was also situated here. A small building south of the main house consisted of a large room heated by a hypocaust. West of the house, two secondary buildings were documented. One could be associated with metallurgical activity, the other probably had residential functions. No chronology is available for this site, De Maeyer 1937, 95; Brulet 2009, 509-511.

186 Matagne-La-Petite-Aux Murets, C, 1980s, monumental house with projecting wings (total width 60 m). The house was built as a winged house with a small bath section and was later extended with a new fronting portico. The construction of the house is dated to the 2nd century AD. It was destroyed by fire in the second half of the 3rd century AD, Rober 1980; Plumier 1987, 61; Brulet 2009, 523-524.

187 Matagne-La-Petite-La Plaine de Bieure, C, 1970s, the first phase of a monumental house, dated to the second half of the 1st century AD, was represented by a typical plan with a portico–risalith façade. During the early 2nd century, a new hall and portico–risalith façade were constructed at the back of the house. During the 3rd century, a number of small rooms were added along the sides of the central hall and a hypocaust was constructed in the west risalith, Plumier 1987, 65; Brulet 2009, 523.

188 Merbes-Le-Chateau-Champs de Saint-Eloi, C, 2000s, monumental house that, in its most elaborate stage, measured 91.5 x 19 m (1843m2). The oldest core of the house was around 50 m in length and consisted of around 20 rooms, fronted by a portico. In this part, the bath section was situated. Subsequently, the house was extended on both sides. Both new sections were in fact separate houses with a larger central room, surrounded by smaller rooms and fronted by the extended portico that ran along the full length of the house. Only on the south side, a risalith projected sideward from the house, in line with the portico, Authom/Paridaens 2008.

189 Merchtem-Dooren, C, 2000s, monumental house, measuring 38 x 17.5 m. The house consisted of a long rectangular central hall with central roof-supporting posts, surrounded by a number of smaller rooms and fronted by a portico. Habitation is dated between the late 1st and late 2nd century AD. A simple rectangular building, measuring 9.75 x 28.5 m, was interpreted as a secondary building. Near the house, an enclosed grave field was documented, containing eight simple cremation graves. Most graves could be dated to the first half of the 2nd century AD, Van Den Vonder 2008.

190 Mettet-Bauselenne, B, 1890s-1900s, partly excavated, highly monumental, axially organised villa complex. On the main residential compound, a number of connected buildings had access to a number of open courts. This compound was separated from the working compound by a wall. On this latter compound, a number of monumental secondary buildings were situated. The complex could be dated between the 1st and late 4th century AD, De Maeyer 1937, 101; Brulet 2009, 547-549.

191 Mettet-Try Salet, C, 1900s, simple monumental house, consisting of six rooms, fronted by a (portico-)risalith façade, De Maeyer 1937, 56; Brulet 2009, 549.

192 Miecret-Saint Donat, C-D, 1960s, fragmentarily documented monumental house. During a first phase, a simple rectangular structure existed. Later, a long rectangular house with an internal bath section was constructed. To the northeast of this house, a separate bath building was situated. No absolute chronology is available, Materne 1969; Brulet 2009, 546-547.

193 Modave-Survillers, C, 1880s, monumental house with a simple core, consisting of a few rooms, fronted by a portico-risalith façade. Probably during a later phase, a number of heated rooms and a bath section were attached to the west side of the existing house, De Maeyer 1937, 61; Brulet 2009, 424-425.

194 Montenaken-Weyerbampt, C, ?, at this site, two monumental buildings were documented. The best excavated building had a long rectangular plan with projecting corner rooms at the northern short side (the long side had a length of 50 m). A partly excavated building was situated at a distance of 75 m, De Maeyer 1937, 76.

195 Neerharen-Rekem, A, 1980s, during the early phases, probably the Late Iron Age and Early Roman period, an enclosed settlement with post-built houses existed at this site. It is not entirely clear whether the settlement enclosure existed already during the Late Iron Age, though. Next, during the Flavian period, a monumental house was being erected at the previous location of one of the two-aisled farms. Interestingly, it was around this particular post-built house that a remarkable number of granaries had been situated. The monumental house was built as a simple construction with a portico-risalith façade. During later phases, a rear façade, an apsidal room and a bath section were added. Although no clear picture of the complete layout of the complex could be reconstructed, it seems that the main house took a central position, with the secondary buildings arranged in front of it on both sides. One of the secondary buildings was interpreted as a secondary residence, De Boe 1982, 1985a, 1987.

196 Nivelles-La Tournette, B, 1980s, this settlement consisted of eight monumental buildings. The buildings were arranged on a single axis, with the main house (A) taking a central position. No settlement enclosure was documented. The main house consisted of a number of rooms, fronted by a portico-risalith façade. A building behind this house, measuring 10.5 x 24 m, represented the oldest monumental building within the settlement. Another residential building, consisting of a hall fronted by a portico-risalith façade, was documented a short distance to the northwest. Southeast of the main house, a small separate bath building was situated. The other secondary buildings were fairly simple constructions. At building B (see Brulet 2009, 291, fig. 22) Samian ware from southern Gaul was found. This building could be dated to the 1st century AD, it seems. The other buildings were probably constructed during the early 2nd century and occupied until the third quarter of the 3rd century, Corbiau 1997, 342-344; Brulet 2009, 290-291.

197 Piringen-Mulkenveld, C-D, 1980s, earliest habitation at this site could be dated to the Flavian period and consisted of a small a-typical house on stone foundations, consisting of only a few small rooms and lacking a portico-risalith façade. As a result of severe erosion, several post-built secondary buildings around this house could not be documented in any detail. During the 2nd century AD, habitation shifted towards the north, where a new and probably larger house was built. Unfortunately, this house was not excavated. Occupation of this settlement continued until the middle of the 3rd century, Vanvinckenroye 1990.

198 Riemst-Lafelt, B, 1990s, at this site, four Alphen-Ekeren type houses were excavated, of which only the central postholes were preserved. During a later phase, a house on stone foundations was built at the same location. Only parts of this house were preserved. Without any more chronological detail, habitation at this site covered the period between the 1st and 3rd century AD. Possibly, a development similar to Lanaken-Smeermaas-Kerkveld could be suggested, Vanderhoeven/Creemers 1999.

199 Rognee-le Péruwelz, B-C, 1880s, monumental house, built around a central open court (measuring 65 x 70 m). The rooms of the house were situated on the northeastern and northwestern sides of the court. The two other sides were not well documented. In the centre of the court, a cistern was situated. A bath section was constructed in the northwestern part of the house. The find material dates the site between the 1st and 3rd century AD, De Maeyer 1937, 104; Brulet 2009, 580-583.

200 Roly-La Crayellerie, C, 1970s, monumental house, consisting of a hall and two small rooms, fronted by a portico-risalith façade. The house was constructed during the 1st century AD. During the second half of the 2nd century AD, a number of rooms, of which two were heated by a hypocaust, were attached to the existing core of the house, Dewert 1980; Brulet 2009, 566.

201 Rosmeer-Diepestraat, C, 1970s, the earliest Roman-period habitation was represented by traces of a post-built house. During the second half of the 1st century AD, a house on stone-foundations was built in the same location. Although only partly documented, the plan of the house can probably be reconstructed as consisting of a large room, surrounded by smaller rooms and fronted by a portico-risalith façade. During the third quarter of the 3rd century, the house was abandoned. Traces of Iron Age habitation were documented, but their chronological relationship to the Roman-period settlement could not be determined, De Boe/Van Impe 1979.

202 's Gravenvoeren-Het Steenbosch, C-D, 1840s, large monumental house that, according to De Maeyer, was inhabited during the Roman period as well as during the early and later Medieval period. The not so well documented structure was over 150 m in length. It remains unclear which parts could be dated to the Roman period, De Maeyer 1937, 119.

203 Saint-Georges-sur-Meuse-Warfée, C-D, 1940s-1960s, monumental house, consisting of a few rooms, fronted by a portico-risalith façade. Two rectangular rooms, projecting to the sides, were added to the risaliths, creating a 30 m long façade. One of the main rooms behind the façade was heated by a hypocaust, Destexhe 1973; Brulet 2009, 431-432.

204 Saint-Gérard-Try Hallot, B-C, 1880s, 1960s, fragments of a very large, monumental, and probably axially organised villa complex (19 ha). In the northern section of the compound, parts of the main house were excavated. The part of the main house that was excavated had a long rectangular plan with a fronting portico. Besides this main house, four secondary building on stone foundations were documented. The complex was occupied during the 2nd and 3rd century and until the 4th century AD, Brulet 1970; Brulet 2009, 550-551.

205 Sauveniere-Arlansart, C, 1890s, the first phase of this simple monumental house (28 x 18 m) comprised a few rooms, fronted by a portico-risalith façade. During a next phase, a larger risalith with a cellar and a room, heated by a hypocaust, were added, De Maeyer 1937, 159; Brulet 2009, 530-531.

206 Serville-Pré des Wez, C, 1890s, simple monumental house, consisting of a hall, fronted by a portico-risalith façade. The house was abandoned in the second half of the 3rd century AD, De Maeyer 1937, 51; Brulet 2009, 565.

207 Soignies-La Coulbrie, C, 1980s, simple monumental house, consisting of a few rooms, fronted by a portico-risalith façade. The house was built around the middle of the 1st century AD and, only during a second phase, risaliths were added. In the third quarter of the 2nd century, the house was destroyed by fire, Scholl 1987; Dewert 1980; Brulet 2009, 366.

208 Tiegem, C-D, 1980s, early habitation is represented by a 24 m long post-built structure, dated to the (later) 1st and 2nd century AD. During a second phase, a house on stone foundations was constructed, preserving the orientation of the preceding house. Occupation continued until the first half of the 3rd century, Van Doorselaer 1995, De Cock 1988.

209 Treignes-Les Bruyères, C, 1980s, during the early phases, the second half of the 1st century AD, buildings on stone foundations could be associated with metallurgical activity. Next, around the middle of the 2nd century, an a-typical monumental house was constructed, consisting of a bipartite central space with smaller rooms around it on all four sides. Around 225 AD a cellar was constructed, which was destroyed by fire around 260 AD. The house was occupied until around 375 AD, Bott/Cattelain 1997; Bott/Cattelain 2000; Doyen 1985, 1987, Brulet 2009, 577-579.

210 Val-Meer-Meerberg, C-D, 1970s, the earliest traces of habitation were represented by postholes and pits, dated to the later pre-Roman or proto-historic period. Probably during the later 1st or 2nd century AD, a house on stone foundations was constructed. This portico-risalith type house had an internal cellar and a bath section. Occupation continued until the second half of the 3rd century, De Boe 1971.

211 Vechmaal-Middelpadveld, B, 1990s, pre-Roman habitation comprised two fragmentarily preserved two-aisled houses and a settlement enclosure ditch. Probably around the middle of the 1st century AD, another two-aisled house was built, containing a small internal cellar. The authors suggest the presence of a (probably partly) tiled roof. During the early 2nd century AD, a stone-built house was constructed. During a first phase, two rectangular rooms were fronted by a portico-risalith façade. Subsequently, during the late 2nd or early 3rd century AD, a bath section was connected to the existing house by a section of five new rooms. Habitation activity seems to have continued until the middle of the 4th century, Vanvinckenroye 1997.

212 Vechmaal-Walenveld, C, 1980s, monumental house, consisting of a number of rooms, fronted by a portico-risalith façade (40 x 15 m). In two of the central rooms, divided by a narrow hall-like space, a hearth was found. A cellar was situated in one of the risaliths. Many fragments of daub were found here, suggesting that the elevation of the house consisted of a framework construction. The house could be dated to the 2nd and 3rd century AD, although find material dates back to the Flavian period. Settlement traces from this early period have probably been erased by the severe erosion. Directly south of the house, a rectangular secondary building was documented (19.5 x 11 m). This buildings was (partly) heated by a hypocaust and was constructed only during the later 2nd century AD, Vanvinckenroye 1990, 21 ff.

213 Vedrin-Berlacomines, C, 1980s, simple monumental house (23.75 x 11m), consisting of a hall, fronted by a portico. Attached to this portico were a single risalith and a heated room, De Maeyer 1937, 55; Plumier 1988, 305 ff.; Brulet 2009, 558-559.

214 Velaines-Popuelles-Le Moreux, B, 1960s-1970s, part of a monumental, probably axially organised settlement complex. Part of the main residential compound has been excavated, including a small section of the main house, two secondary buildings and a portico and porch (the latter separating the main residential compound from the working compound). The complex has only been approximately dated between the 1st and 3rd century AD, Lambert 1971; Brulet 2009, 321-322.

215 Veldwezelt, A-B, 2000s, a trapezoidal enclosure at this site can probably be dated to the Late Iron Age. The oldest documented building superseded this enclosure, but predates the Alphen-Ekeren type houses at this site. Eight of these Alphen-Ekeren type houses were documented. One of them had its posts set on tile fragments. A phasing could not be reconstructed, however. The north and south settlement boundaries were defined by a small ditch and a road respectively.

An interesting element was a small, partly stone-lined cellar. Although no traces of a superseding structure, to which this cellar belonged, was documented, such a structure could well have existed. Like at several other sites, erosion probably erased the traces of such a building, that was possibly built on shallow stone or horizontal beam foundations. Within the settlement, several ponds, probably used for watering livestock, were situated, Pauwels 2007; Vanderhoeven *et al.* 2006.

216 Vezin-Namêche, A, 1990s, first habitation activity could be dated to the late 1st century AD. However, no structural traces belonging to this period were documented. During the 2nd century, an enclosed settlement developed, consisting of at least five post-built houses. During the late 2nd or early 3rd century, one of the houses was rebuilt on stone foundations. A portico-risalith façade was later added to this existing house. Probably during the same phase, two secondary houses on stone foundations were constructed as well. During the Late Roman period, metal working activity developed on this site and the settlement was only abandoned in the early 5th century, Robinet 2004; Brulet 2009, 505-509.

217 Villers-le-Bouillet-Vi-Tchestia, C, 1930s, 1970s, 1990s, at this site, two monumental houses were fragmentarily documented. One of the houses had a typical layout, with a number of rooms fronted by a portico-risalith façade. At one of the rear corners, a bath section was attached, probably during a later phase. The second house was less well documented and seems to have consisted of a central room, surrounded by several smaller rooms. A heated room and a cellar were documented just west of this structure. The site was occupied at least until the 4th century AD, Brulet 2009, 435-436.

218 Villers-sur-Lesse, C, ?, simple monumental house of around 20 m in length, De Maeyer 1937, 67.

219 Visé-Lixhe-Loën, C, 1960s, parts of several buildings on stone foundations were documented at this site. Best preserved was a rectangular building, divided into three aisles by two rows of roof supporting posts or columns (13.6 x 27 m). Near this building, a cellar and a single room were documented. They were part of buildings that have been eroded beyond recognition. The three-aisled building was constructed around the end of the 1st century AD and was abandoned after a fire in the 3rd century. This building could possibly be interpreted as a granary or artisan workshop, Van Ossel 1983; Brulet 2009, 437-438.

220 Vodelée-Vieille Terre au Couvent, C, 1980s, monumental house, consisting of a hall and two small rooms, dated to the second half of the 2nd century AD. During a second phase, a portico-risalith façade was added to the existing house. In the 3rd century, a second portico-risalith façade was added, a cellar was dug, several hypocausts were constructed and a bath section was integrated into an existing risalith. The house was destroyed by fire in the second half of the 3rd century, Rober 1987; Brulet 2009, 524-525.

221 Wahanges-Beauvechain-l'Ecluse-Leckbosch, C, 1930s, 1940s, 1970s, monumental house with a wide façade (51 m). The house could only be approximately dated to the 2nd and 3rd century AD, Van Ossel 1984; Dewert 1980; Brulet 2009, 283.

222 Wancennes-La Couturelle, B, 1880s, 1960s, 1980s, settlement complex of a 'dispersed plan' (Brulet 2009, 511), consisting of eight buildings, covering a settlement surface of 2 hectares. The main house was not very well documented, but seems to have been organised around a central open

space and measured at least 33 x 37 m. A bath section was documented as well. Habitation could be dated between the 1st century AD and around 275 AD, Devillers 1971, 1987; Van Ossel 1992; Brulet 2009, 511–512.

223 Wange-Damekot, C, 1980s, pre-Roman post-built houses were excavated at this site. The plans of these house have not been published, however. The houses dated to the Early Roman period and were still traditional post-built structures, although the associated material culture was clearly influenced by Roman-style imports. According to the author, there was a continuous development from pre-Roman to Roman period habitation. Somewhere during the 2nd century AD, a house on stone foundations was built, consisting of several rooms, fronted by a portico–risalith façade (measuring 38 x 15 m). One or more rooms were heated by a hypocaust and the eastern risalith had a cellar, where fifteen *dolia* were dug into the ground. During a second phase, a bath section was constructed against the west side of the house. The house was destroyed by fire in the third quarter of the 3rd century, Lodewijckx 1995.

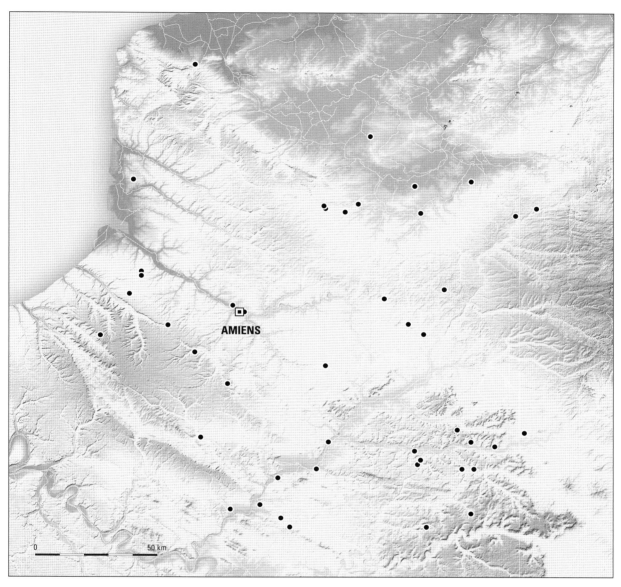

Distribution of sites in northwestern France.

224 Amiens-Le Champ Pillard, B, 2000s, a settlement enclosure ditch and a number of quite hypothetical post-built constructions were dated to the late 1st century AD. For the second habitation
phase, during the 2nd and 3rd century, several post-built constructions and two cellars, lined by
chalkstone blocks, were documented. Of the hypothetical main house, only a number of posts
were preserved. During the 3rd century, a framework house on horizontal foundation beams and
a roof, covered with tiles, was constructed (12 x 7 m). A large cellar with stairs was situated within
this house, bilan scientifique de la région Picardie 2004, 92-94.

225 Amiens-Renancourt - Rue Haute-des-Champs, B, 1990s, the oldest traces of habitation comprise
ditches and some post-built structures, situated on the eastern part of the site. Then, during the

latest pre-Roman period (La Tène D2B), habitation shifted towards the west, where a rectilinear ditch system was created. This compound was divided into two courts, separated by a palisade. Several post-built structures could be recognised here. The settlement existed until the earliest decades AD. Then, around the middle of the 1st century AD, monumental buildings were constructed. A bath section was added during a second phase (several decades later). The site was abandoned already in the early 2nd century AD, bilan scientifique de la région Picardie 1997, 84-85.

226 Arras-Actiparc /Delta 3, A, 1990s-2000s, large-scale settlement research, providing insight into the way the landscape was settled during the Iron Age and Roman period, was carried out at this site. At Delta 3, several rectangular and trapezoidal enclosures existed during the period between the 2nd century BC and the 1st century AD, situated only short distances from each other. The surface of these enclosed compounds varied from 1300 to 6000 m². A number of these enclosures can be associated with continuous settlement activity from the Late Iron Age until the middle of the 2nd century AD. At one location, a simple house on stone foundations was constructed (measuring 24 x 5 m). This building was situated on an enclosed compound, measuring 110 x 65 m and containing several other buildings. At Actiparc, five settlements were documented. One of these was interpreted as a high status settlement (named 'Les Soixante'). It consisted of a large enclosed compound with a monumental entrance and at least two relatively large houses. On this compound, traces of salt and bronze working have been found. The other four settlements (at sections called 'Les Quarante' and 'Le Buisson') could be dated between the Late Iron Age and the High Empire. At 'Le Buisson', three enclosed compounds were situated less than 50 meters apart. They probably represented single farmsteads. The construction of a small Roman military fort and the construction of a road, mark the reorganisation of the area under direct influence of the Romans administration. At a certain point in time, a stone house is constructed at 'Les Quarante'. As this site has only been pre-published, no more detailed chronology is available at this point, Blancquaert/Prilaux 2003.

227 Arras-Villa du Mont Saint-Vaast, C, 1980s, monumental house, measuring 22 x 16 m. The simple core of the house is surrounded by a portico on three sides. Find material indicated that the site was inhabited between the Tiberian period and the early 2nd century AD, carte archéologique de la Gaule 62/1, 153-154.

228 Bazoches-La Foulerie, A, 1990s, during the La Tène D1 period, two zones were inhabited at this site. At one zone, a trapezoidal enclosure of 100 x 60 m existed. In the period La Tène D2 and the earliest Roman period, habitation shifted somewhat toward the southeast. Here, a more or less rectangular double enclosed settlement was founded (94 x 84 m). A traditional post-built house was situated in the northeast corner of the compound. Later research has shown that the settlement extended towards the west, where a row of post-built constructions was documented. Ben Redjeb, Duvette and Quérel reconstructed this settlement as a more or less axially organised complex with a residential compound (the inner compound of the above mentioned double enclosure) and a court (working compound), with building on at least one side (Ben Redjeb/ Duvette/Quérel 2005, fig. 12). During the 1st century AD, settlement space decreased in size. The settlement now only comprised a small enclosure and a small number of post-built constructions. No traces of monumental buildings were documented at this site, Collart 1996, 137 ff.

229 Beaurieux-Les Greves, A, 1980s, at this site, a rectilinear enclosed compound, with several buildings arranged around an open court, could be dated to the Late Iron Age. The three larger buildings seem to have been residences, whereas two other buildings were probably barns or byres. At this stage, the settlement had an almost axial layout, with a house situated at one of the short ends, overlooking rows of buildings on either side of an imaginary axis. Other than at some other complexes, however, the axial organisation of the settlement did not develop further. During the earlier 1st century AD, the compound was reduced, and in the middle or later 1st century, the ditch was finally backfilled. Around this period, or somewhat later, a number of buildings were rebuilt in stone. The main houses took a central position, flanked by buildings arranged along the the backfilled enclosure ditches, Haselgrove 1996, 155-161; carte archéologique de la Gaule 02, 118.

230 Beauvais-Rue de Witten-'Les Champs Dolents', B, 1990s, first habitation activity at this site could be dated to the La Tène C1/C2 period. For later periods, several enclosures were documented. A first settlement enclosure dated to the La Tène D1/D2 period (zone 1[5]). Another one, just to the east, could not be dated precisely, but probably belonged to the Early Roman period (zone 2). The trapezoidal enclosure at zone 4 probably dated to the Tiberian-Claudian period and was abandoned already in the second half of the 1st century AD. The youngest enclosure at this site, superseding the older enclosure in zone 4, had a long rectangular shape, interpreted as a villa settlement by the author. Of this compound, a surface of 18000 m2 was documented, the total surface being estimated at 30000 m2. The main residential section was situated in the northern part of the enclosed area, the working compound in the southern part. During a later phase, possibly the later 3rd century, the compound was extended considerably, but the general layout was maintained. Of the internal habitation, only few traces were documented. Along the enclosure ditches, two granaries, ovens and stone floors were found. On the northern residential compound, a stone-lined cellar was documented, that could be dated in the 1st century AD and was abandoned already at the end of that same century. It was replaced by a new cellar, constructed with limestone, flint and chalkstone. Near this cellar, a hypocaust was documented as well. Both will have been part of the main house, of which the foundations have been completely eroded, bilan scientifique de la région Picardie 1996, 50-52, bilan scientifique de la région Picardie 1999, 46, bilan scientifique de la région Picardie 2002, 64-65.

231 Beauvais-Le Brin de Glaine- ZAC du Haut Villé, B, 1990s-2000s, during the La Tène D1 period, an enclosure with a surface of 1 hectare contained a small post-built house and a number of small secondary buildings. These buildings were situated on the inner compound. The other part of the settlement had non-residential functions. During the 1st or 2nd century AD, the inhabited surface decreased as the settlement now consisted of a trapezoidal enclosure. A stone-built granary (13 x 8 m) was dated to the second half of the 2nd or first half of the 3rd century. For this later period, no houses were documented, bilan scientifique de la région Picardie 2000, 56-57, bilan scientifique de la région Picardie 2004, 60-61.

232 Behen-Au Dessus des Grands Riots, A, 1990s, first settlement activity at this site could be dated to the 2nd century BC and comprised a small double curvilinear enclosed compound. This first compound was replaced by a somewhat larger one around the end of the Augustan period. Around the middle of the 1st century AD, the inner compound was doubled in surface and now got a more or less rectangular layout. Unfortunately, internal habitation was not documented for these early periods. During the Flavian period, settlement space was restructured again and in the

[5] For these zones see bilan scientifique de la région Picardie 2002, 65.

first half of the 2nd century, the axial structure of the settlement took form. Around the middle of the 2nd century, the residential compound was divided from the working compound by means of a palisade. Until the middle of the 2nd century, only the south side of the compound was lined with buildings. It was only during the second half of the 2nd and the earlier 3rd century that buildings were constructed on the north side as well. Most 1st-century buildings were constructed as framework structures on simple flint foundations. Chalkstone foundations were constructed from the late 1st or early 2nd century AD onwards. The oldest monumental core of the main house consisted of a row of four rooms. During a later phase, a portico-risalith façade and a few rooms were added to this core. The bath section could be dated to the second half of the 2nd century, Bayard 1996, 169-177.

233 Bohain-en-Vermandois, A-B, 2000s, a trapezoidal enclosure could be dated between the middle of the 1st and the middle of the 2nd century AD. Ditches organised internal settlement space. Most buildings were situated on the central part of the compound, defined by these ditches. During the second half of the 1st century AD, a traditional two-aisled house was situated in the northeast corner of the compound. During a next phase, dated to the first half of the 2nd century AD, a single-aisled house with heavy wall posts, a stone-lined cellar and a tiled roof, was constructed, centrally against the western enclosure ditch. Already before the middle of the 2nd century AD, the settlement was abandoned, archéologie en Picardie 2004 (nr. 28), bilan scientifique de la région Picardie 2000, 19-20.

234 Callengeville-Mont Cauvet, B, 1990s, axially organised settlement complex with a simple monumental main house and a number of post-built constructions. The latter were probably representing preceding settlement phases, Bayard 1996, 175.

235 Chavignon-Terres de la Malmaison, B-C, 2000s, this settlement was founded during the second half of the 1st century AD. The oldest structure was a ditch system, orientated on a road. During the late 1st or early 2nd century AD, two buildings on stone foundations and a number of smaller structures were constructed. In the 2nd century, two new buildings on stone foundations were constructed on an enclosed compound, subdivided by means of internal ditches. Another habitation phase could be dated to the late 2nd or early 3rd century. During this phase, a house on stone foundations, a nine-post granary and two other buildings were part of the settlement complex. All buildings were abandoned in the 4th century, bilan scientifique de la région Picardie 2003, 28-29.

236 Chambly-Le Chemin Herbu - La Remise Ronde, D, 2000s, this site has three habitation phases. The first phase could be dated to the 1st century AD and comprised three post-built structures, ditches, holes and a palisade. Space was structured by means of two ditches. In the late 1st and 2nd century, the central settlement space was reorganised; a road and parcelling system were constructed. One possible building can be recognized. During the late 2nd and 3rd century, east of the road, houses on stone foundations were constructed. The author states that the minimum length of the settlement complex was 200 m, comparable to complexes like Verneuil and Roye, bilan scientifique de la région Picardie 2002, 72-73.

237 Courmelles-La Plaine du Mont de Courmelles (ZAC), A, 2000s, a rectangular enclosed settlement compound with a wooden house on horizontal beams, a small secondary building and a pond could be dated between 70 and 120 AD. In the 2nd century, the enclosure ditches were backfilled, and two buildings, one post-built, the other on horizontal foundations, were built. Early 3rd century, the settlement is abandoned, bilan scientifique de la région Picardie 2005, 22.

238 Épaux-Bézu-ZID de l'Omois, B, 2000s, La Tène period habitation comprised a rectangular enclosure of circa 4000 m2, with internal palisades and several buildings. Around the middle or the second half of the 1st century AD, only a short distance to the west, a new settlement was founded. Here buildings were constructed on horizontal beams. During this period, the spatial structure of the settlement was radically reorganised, creating an axial layout. Of the main house, orientated towards the north, only a hypocaust and basement were preserved. This house overlooked two rows of secondary buildings, on both sides of a central axis, bilan scientifique de la région Picardie 2004, 28-30.

239 Famechon-Le Marais, B, 1970s-1980s, a Late La Tène settlement at this site was abandoned well before a settlement complex was laid out during the earliest Roman period. At the location of the later working compound, however, a ditch, palisade and a four-post building could be dated to the La Tène D2 period. These latter structures had an orientation and spatial layout, exactly parallel to the settlement complex that developed here from the earliest Roman period onwards. On the residential compound of this axially organised complex, a 12 m building on flint and chalkstone foundations was constructed in the Augustan-Tiberian period. In this same period, four buildings on chalkstone foundations were built on the working compound, following the existing La Tène D2 habitation. Next, around the middle of the 1st century AD, the main house was rebuilt as a 23 m long structure on chalkstone foundations. In three of the buildings on the working compound, a hearth was found, indicating a residential function fot these buildings. During the next phases, the main house was extended and decorated, and around the middle of the 2nd century, the houses on the working compound developed towards multi-roomed buildings on massive chalkstone foundations. Around the late 3rd century, the buildings were probably abandoned, although habitation seems to have continued on the working compound until the end of the 4th century, Collart 1996, 146-149.

240 Gouvieux-La Flâche, B, 1990s, at this site, continuity between the Late Iron Age and the Roman period could be documented. The Late Iron Age habitation comprised a settlement enclosure, but internal structures were not documented as a result of severe erosion. During the 1st century AD, settlement space was reorganised with the creation of a more orthogonal layout. The earliest use of stone, dating to the 1st or 2nd century AD, was documented for a cellar, with the superseding structure, probably a framework house, no longer being traceable. The settlement compound measured 80 x 80 m and contained a main house and two rows of buildings, ordered around an open court. Only during the second half of the 3rd century, buildings with heavy stone foundations were constructed on this site, archéologie en Picardie 1998 (nr. 2), bilan scientifique de la région Picardie 1997, 57-58.

241 Hamblain-les-Près, C, 1980s, a first post-built house could be dated to the late La Tène period. Then, during the first decades of the 1st century AD, two post-built constructions, probably a house and a granary, were built. Subsequently, possibly already during the second quarter of the 1st century, a house on stone foundations was constructed. This rectangular house, measuring 29 x 13 m, consisted of a number of rooms, with a portico at the rear and a single risalith at the front. During a next phase, dated to the the Claudian period, a second risalith was constructed. One or more rooms of this house was probably heated by a hypocaust and decorated with wall paintings and even mosaic. At the end of the 1st century AD, the addition of new rooms around the existing core resulted in a significantly larger house, measuring 65 x 20 m. This larger house probably also contained a bath section. During the 2nd century, apart from a number of small changes, the basic structure of the house remained the same. The settlement seems to have been abandoned after the 2nd century, although habitation activity was documented again for the 4th century, Jacques/Tuffreau-Libre 1984, carte archéologique de la Gaule 62/2, 487-489.

242 Hargnies-Foret de Mormal - Brai Préchon, C, 1920s-1950s, monumental house, consisting of a number of rooms, fronted by a portico-risalith façade (22 x 11 m), carte archéologique de la Gaule 59, 321-322.

243 Hordain-ZAC la Fosse à Loups, A, 2000s, at this site, large-scale settlement research covered a number of settlement cores, dated between the Iron Age and Roman period. In sector 6, a rectangular enclosed compound, measuring 100 x 60 m, was created in the early 1st century AD. Habitation, consisting of one traditional post-built house and a number of secondary buildings, was concentrated on one half of the compound. The other half was clear of built structures and might have been used for agro-pastoral activities. During the second phase, this internal division was marked by a ditch. Around the middle of the 1st century AD, the compound was extended to the north and east, doubling its surface. During this period, the main house was also rebuilt as a simple rectangular house on stone foundations. Directly to the north of the settlement a road was constructed. Remarkably, after its abandonment in the early 2nd century AD, the settlement was re-established in the 3rd century, following the main layout of the 1st-century compound. On the residential part of the compound, three stone buildings were situated, Archeologie en Nord-Pas-de-Calais 2007.

243 Hornoy-Le-Bourg - A 29 - L'Ancien Grand Bois, B, 2000s, of the earliest habitation, dated to the La Tène period, only a limited number of pits were documented. Around the middle of the 1st century AD, however, a small enclosure with a monumental entrance was constructed. Inside the new enclosure, during the first half of the 2nd century, two wooden buildings were built. Then, during the second half of the 2nd century, the sites was reorganised, internal space being segmented by two ditches. A pond was situated in the southern part. Only during the fourth phase, which was difficult to date, a large building on flint foundations was constructed, bilan scientifique de la région Picardie 2003, 109-110.

244 Juvincourt-et-Damary-Le Gué de Mauchamps, B, 1980s-1990s, during the earliest Roman period, a large, probably long rectangular complex was laid out, measuring at least 210 x 192 m. Following an axial layout, buildings were arranged along the enclosures on both sides of a central axis. These buildings were of a traditional type, known from the La Tène period. Despite the considerable dimension of this early settlement, it did not develop towards a monumental complex, like documented for other sites. A small settlement core continued to be inhabited until the 5th century on this location, however, carte archéologique de la Gaule 02, 265-267; Collart 1996, 144-146.

245 La Chapelle-en-Serval - La Riolette, B, 2000s, fragmentary settlement activity could be dated before the middle of the 1st century AD. Around the middle of the 1st century, two stone-built structures were constructed. However, already at the end of the 1st century, the settlement was abandoned, bilan scientifique de la région Picardie 2005, 61-62.

246 Lépine-Ébruyeres, C, 1970s, monumental house, measuring 56 x 26 m, that consisted of a central part, with three rooms and two projecting wings. A hypocaust was constructed during the second half of the 2nd century AD. Habitation continued until the late 3rd century, carte archéologique de la Gaule 62/2, 442.

247 Limé-Pont-d'Ancy-Les Terres Noires, C, 1880s, 1970s-1980s, highly momumental complex, measuring 800 x 300 m. Probably, the development of this complex can be related to abandonment of the Limé-Les Terres Noires settlement, carte archéologique de la Gaule 02, 288 ff.; bilan scientifique de la région Picardie 2002, 36-38.

248 Limé-Les Terres Noires-Les Fraiches Terres, B, 1990s, earliest habitation, dated to the Late La Tène period, comprised an enclosure system and a small settlement. During the Augustan period, a larger orthogonal ditch system was laid out, respecting the existing La Tène orientation. Then, during the early 1st century AD, a large settlement complex was created. This complex could be reconstructed as an axially organised settlement with traditional wooden buildings arranged along the enclosure ditches. Internal settlement space was segmented by ditches. Between the end of the 1st and the end of the 2nd century AD, the working compound of the settlement was abandoned. Like at Juvincourt, the settlement did not develop towards a monumental villa complex. It is important to emphasise that the Limé settlement was created within an existing Late La Tène structure, bilan scientifique de la région Picardie 1998, 32-34; carte archéologique de la Gaule 02, 285-291.

249 Maubeuge-Bois Brulé, C, 1960s, during the 1st or 2nd century AD, a 19 x 11 m house on stone foundations, consisting of a number of rooms and a fronting portico, was constructed. During a second phase, the house was enlarged considerably by adding two risaliths and a long room. The house now measured 30 x 16 m. One of the risalith rooms was heated by a hypocaust and the other contained as a cellar. A hypocaust and adjacent basin possibly indicated the existence of a small bath section, carte archéologique de la Gaule 59, 392-393.

250 Mercin-et-Vaux-Le Quinconce, D, 1890s, 1990s, fragmentarily documented remains of an axially organised monumental settlement complex. The main house, which itself was not excavated, was fronted by a basin. A wall and gate divided the main residential compound from the working compound. The first monumental structures, like the basin and a building in the northeast sector of the excavated area, could be dated to the period between 50 and 70 AD. Fragments of wall paintings, found in the basin, can be dated to the period before 70 AD. The settlement was occupied until at least the 5th century, carte archéologique de la Gaule 02, 303-309.

251 Monchy-le-Preux, A, 2000s, at this site, a La Tène D2 curvilinear double compound settlement was reorganised during the latest decades BC. The La Tène enclosure was abandoned and at the same location a new, more or less rectangular enclosure was created, covering a surface of 5607 m2. Both the orientation of the enclosure and the position of the entrance were similar to the preceding enclosure. During this phase, two new buildings were constructed. During the second half of the 1st century the first developments in house building became apparent, as new materials and techniques were adopted. A house on stone foundations, with a typical portico-risalith layout, was constructed. The settlement complex had a fixed axial layout, with the main house at one of the short sides, overlooking two rows of buildings, situated on both sides of a central axis, Gricourt/Jacques 2007.

252 Neuville-Saint-Amand-La Vallée de Neuville, B, 2000s, at this site, part of an axially organised settlement was documented. Of the main house, only two cellars were preserved. The compound on which this house was situated, was divided from the working compound by means of a ditch. On this latter compound, two buildings could be fragmentarily documented. Settlement activity was dated between the late 1st and the early 2nd century AD, bilan scientifique de la région Picardie 2005, 31-33.

253 Plailly-La Butte Grise, B, 1980s, an enclosure, consisting of two compounds, could be dated to the Augustan-Tiberian period. On one compound, two larger wooden buildings and a small secondary structure were situated. With only one small secondary building, the other compound was mainly empty. Around the middle of the 1st century AD, a third, eastern compound was created, resulting in a new bipartite spatial structure. A stone-lined cellar was also be dated to this phase. During the second half of the 1st century, settlement space was reorganised and segmented by ditches. Next, during the 2nd century, a monumental house was built on the eastern compound and two rows of buildings were situated on both sides of a central axis, in front of this house. A wall divided the main house from these secondary buildings. The axial structure of the 2nd-century monumental complex seems to have been present already in the layout of the 1st-century non-monumental settlement phases, carte archéologique de la Gaule 60, 375; Gallia Informations 1989, 233-235.

254 Ploisy-Le Bras de Fer, A, 2000s, at this large site, several zones were excavated. At Zone 1, during the La Tène D2 period, an enclosure was created only a short distance away from a La Tène C1 enclosed settlement. This new enclosure consisted of a rectangular residential part and a curvilinear part, probably used for livestock. Besides some extensions, the enclosures remained basically the same until their abandonment, somewhere between the late 1st and middle of the 2nd century AD. In Zone 3, a small, organised settlement, comprising three buildings, was founded around the end of the 1st century AD. After a reorganisation in the second half of the 1st century, new buildings were built in the 2nd century. A stone cellar was also constructed during this phase. At the end of the 3rd and early 4th century, two buildings and an oven existed on this site. At Zone 5, during the first half of the 1st century AD, a rectangular enclosure was created. In the 2nd century, this enclosure was backfilled and at least two new buildings were constructed. At the end of the 3rd century the site was abandoned, bilan scientifique de la région Picardie 2003, 40-44.

255 Roisel-Rue du Nouveau Monde, B, 1990s-2000s, during the Early Roman period, a settlement with post-built houses existed. During a next phase, the late 1st century AD, an axially organised settlement with a stone-built house (including mosaic floors and painted walls) was constructed, bilan scientifique de la région Picardie 2004, 119-120.

256 Ronchères-Le Bois de la Forge, A, 2000s, at this site, a rectangular enclosed settlement (120 x 80 m) was dated to the Late La Tène period and Roman period. During the La Tène period, several post-built structures (probably a house, secondary building and a number of storage structures) were situated on the compound in a more or less structured manner. During the Roman period, four building with chalkstone foundations were constructed. Habitation continued until the first half of the 2nd century AD, bilan scientifique de la région Picardie 2002, 42-45.

257 Roye-Le Puits a Marne, A, 1990s, during the La Tène D2 or Augustan period, a rectangular compound was created, which general form and orientation were continued during the following centuries. Internal habitation, dating before the 2nd century AD, could not be documented, probably as a result of severe erosion. Only in the 3rd century AD, the residential compound was monumentally separated from the working compound. During the 1st century AD, three small, enclosed settlements were situated within an area of about 64 hectares. For the 2nd century, some significant changes could be documented. The settlement in zone 1 was abandoned and those in zone 3 and 5 developed towards what the author terms small exploitation units. According to this author, this development can be related to the development of a large villa complex in the near surroundings, Collart 1996, J.L. Collart pers. comm., bilan scientifique de la région Picardie 1997, 106-108.

258 Saint-Quentin-Parc des Autoroutes-A26–A29, A, 1990s, at this site, pre-Roman habitation dating to the Early, Middle and Late La Tène periods was documented. The Late La Tène remains comprise several parts of a ditch system. During the earliest Roman period, La Tène D2 or Augustan period, a road and parcelling system were laid out, restructuring the landscape, without respecting the La Tène orientation. Within this new spatial organisation, around the middle of the 1st century AD, a new rectangular enclosure was constructed, measuring 105 x 191 m (around 2 ha). Internal space was segmented by ditches and palisades, creating a division between a residential and working compound. On the residential compound, the main house developed from a post-built to a stone-built structure during the second half of the 1st century AD. Like at other axial complexes, this house was positioned perpendicular to the main axis and overlooked the working compound. A road entered the working compound on the short side, opposite the main house, and ended just in front of the residential compound. The author speaks of this settlement as a foundation *ex nihilo*. Although this seems to be correct in a strict sense, we should not forget that the development of this settlement seems to be part of a longer term, more complex settlement development trajectory, which could well involve continuous development lines of habitation. At a site nearby, Saint-Quentin-Tranche 6, a Late La Tène enclosure was superseded by an Early Roman enclosure, only 60 m to the northwest. Both had a similar orientation. At the same location, a new, larger enclosure was dug during the second half of the 1st century, containing four wooden buildings. Already around the late 1st century, however, habitation activity decreased, something that, according to the author, could possibly be related to the development of the villa settlement 600 m away, as described above. During the 2nd century, a stone-built granary with buttresses (65 m2) and a cellar (25 m2) were constructed. This seemingly open settlement was abandoned in the early 3rd century. The abandonment of yet another Early Roman period settlement, that of Saint-Quentin-ZAC du Parcs des Autoroutes-Voie de Francilly, was also related to the development of the axial villa complex by the author, carte archéologique de la Gaule 02, 397-399; bilan scientifique de la région Picardie 1999, 33-34, bilan scientifique de la région Picardie 2002, 45-46, bilan scientifique de la région Picardie 2004, 39-43, bilan scientifique de la région Picardie 2004, 40-42

259 Seclin-Les Hauts de Clauwiers, A, 1990s, four post-built structures could be dated to the Late La Tène period. A fragmentarily documented double ditch possibly enclosed this settlement. During a next phase, dated between the 1st century BC and 1st century AD, a slightly trapezoidal enclosure, measuring 137 x 144 m, was dug. This compound contained sunken-floor huts and rectangular post-built houses. A large granary measured 26 x 7 m. The enclosure ditch of this settlement followed the orientation of the pre-Roman ditches. During the 1st and 2nd century AD, the enclosure was enlarged to 149 x 163 m. Three buildings (V, S and L) were now constructed with stone foundations. Buildings P and Q were large storage buildings with a total storage capacity of 1030 m2. Subsequently, during the 2nd and 3rd century, buildings L and V were extended, and the storage capacity increased to 1275 m2. During the 4th century, the settlement declined to 50 x 36 m. During this phase, a tower granary was built. The other storage buildings went out of use. In two buildings, artisanal activities were carried out during this phase, Révillion/Bouche/Wozny 1994; carte archéologique de la Gaule 59, 395-406.

260 Somain-Derriere L'Abbaye, D, 1990s, two buildings on stone foundations that can be interpreted as secondary buildings belonging to an axially organised settlement complex (with a trapezoidal

plan). One building has three rooms (19 x 10 m), the other four (33 x 14 m). Between these two buildings, a four-post structure was documented, carte archéologique de la Gaule 59, 409-410.

261   Soupir-Le Parc, B, 2000s, part of a rural settlement. Three or four post-built structures and a number of palisades were documented. No monumental constructions were found. Occupation could be dated between the 2nd and 4th century AD, bilan scientifique de la région Picardie 2000, 42, carte archéologique de la Gaule 02, 463.

262   Translay, B, 1990s, two enclosures (enclosure 1 and 3 in Bayard 1996, fig. 8) could be dated to the late La Tène C2-Early La Tène D1 period and seem to be abandoned before the La Tène D2 period. One of these enclosures is cut by a somewhat younger one, which was also abandoned before the turn of the Millennium, however. Then, around 200 m to the north, a much larger rectangular enclosure was constructed, with buildings ranged around the sides, surrounding an open space. This sequence of enclosures being abandoned reconstructed and shifting in location over short distances, seems to be a common phenomenon in this region. A quite similar site was documented at Beauvais-Rue de Witten-'Les Champs Dolents', Bayard 1996, 164-165.

263   Trinquies, B, 1990s, the periphery of a settlement organised by ditches was documented here and could be dated between the early 2nd century BC and the early 1st century AD. Still during the Augustan period, a new enclosed settlement was founded somewhat to the north. This settlement did not exist for more than 50-100 years, however. Then, around the middle of the 1st century AD, a new enclosure was constructed around 200 m to the south. This axially organised settlement would remain stabile for the following centuries, Bayard 1996, 165.

264   Verberie-Les Gats/La Plaine D'Herneuse, B, 1990s, during the earlier La Tène periods, extensive, dispersed habitation existed, of which ditches, silos and several post-built constructions were part. In time, habitation became increasingly concentrated. During the Late La Tène period, a rectangular enclosed compound was created, containing three houses, a secondary building, silos and a number of granaries. During a second phase, a new enclosure was dug, following a new orientation, bilan scientifique de la région Picardie 1998, 88-90, bilan scientifique de la région Picardie 1999, 68-71.

265   Villers-Vicomte - A La Rosière, B, 1990s, during the La Tène D2 period, an enclosed settlement existed. Then, during the late 1st century AD, a house with flint foundations was constructed on what was probably an axially organised settlement complex. The settlement was abandoned in the 3rd century, carte archéologique de la Gaule 60, 503-504.

266   Onnaing-Toyota, A, 1990s-2000s, at this site, from the La Tène C1 period onwards, space was structured by means of ditches and habitation was concentrated within enclosures. Nine of these enclosed settlements, on a distance of a few hundred meters from each other, could be dated to the Late Iron Age phase. Like at many other sites, the La Tène D2 phase is less well represented archaeologically. Local geography plays an important role in the choice of location for founding these Iron Age enclosures. With regard to settlement development trajectories, a heterogeneous image appears. Some settlements existed for one or two generations, without changing (sites 4, 6, 17, 19 and 21), others shifted over short distances (sites 8 and 9), and yet others had longer life-spans and changed gradually over time (sites 14 and 16). During the pre-Roman period, three or four contemporary settlements existed within the excavated area, at a distance of between 800 and 1500 m from each other, each having 60 to 80 hectares as their territory. For the Roman period, eight rectangular, enclosed settlement compounds were documented, orientated on two

main axes, of which one had pre-Roman roots. Two roads could be dated to the Roman period. The Roman-period compounds were clearly larger than their predecessors: for example 8200, 12900 and 10750 m2. One of the compounds, number 5, contained a house on stone foundations, as well as a granary and a pond. During the first half of the 1st century AD, four relatively dispersed settlements existed. Three of these were already inhabited from the La Tène period onwards. Remarkably, two of these three continuous settlements were then abandoned in the second half of the 1st century AD. During this period, however, four new settlements were created, situated within the landscape in an ordered manner and separated by only a few hundred meters. Settlement within the landscape thus seem to have become increasingly clustered and organised in the course of the 1st century AD, Roger/Catteddu 2002; Clotuche 2009.

267 Verneuil-en-Halatte-Le Buffose, B, 1950s, 1980s, at this site, it was difficult to establish the character and importance of pre-Roman habitation activity, as it remained largely unstudied. In the Augustan-Tiberian period, a long rectangular enclosed compound with wooden buildings was constructed. At one side of the enclosed compound, a U-formed area was defined by palisades. This area can probably be understood as the predecessor of the *pars urbana*, which was later separated from the rest of the compound (*pars rustica*) by a wall. Within this U-formed area, a wooden house was situated, overlooking the compound, and positioned perpendicular to the central axis. Thus, already in this early phase, an axial layout seemed present. Over time, settlement space was being increasingly segmented by means of ditches and palisades. During the Claudian period, the western, U-formed compound was enclosed by a stone wall, measuring 63 x 71 m. During the same phase, a cellar was constructed with walls of limestone blocks. The superseding structure of what would have been the main building, was not preserved, however. Probably, the house had wooden framework structure with shallow foundations. It was only during the Flavian period that this house was replaced by a stone house, fronted by a basin. During the course of the 2nd century, several buildings on the working compound were built or rebuilt in stone. At the same location as the post-built granary, now a large stone-built granary was constructed. The now monumental secondary buildings were situated on the outer side of a wall, defining the working compound. A number of walls, a gate and a long rectangular basin separated the working compound from the residential compound. Habitation activity could be documented until the early 5th century AD. Although the settlement complex developed in terms of size, monumentality and spatial complexity, the basic spatial structure remained similar over time, Collart 1996, 124 ff.

268 Venette-Bois de Plaisance-zone 1, A, 2000s, a small enclosed settlement, dated to the La Tène D1 period, comprised a central residential compound and an external compound with other functions. No buildings were documented for this phase. After a hiatus in habitation, during the 1st century AD, a large rectangular enclosure was created, measuring 185 x 85 m. Internal space seems to have been organised by ditches, creating separate compounds within the enclosure. Internal habitation is not well known. A 1st- or 2nd-century cellar probably belonged to a house, of which no traces were found. Isolated remains and foundations ditches indicated the existence of buildings on stone foundations for this period. Traces of habitation could be dated as late as the 4th century, bilan scientifique de la région Picardie 2004, 83 ff.

269 Venette-Bois de Plaisance-zone 4, B, 2000s, parallel to zone 1, at zone 4, a rectangular enclosure was dug during the 1st century AD. On this compound, ditches organised settlement space and created separate sections. During the earliest phase, a traditional house was situated on the compound. Two cellars could be dated to the late 1st or early 2nd century AD. This site was occupied until the second half of the 3rd century, bilan scientifique de la région Picardie 2005, 87 ff.

270 Zouafques, B, 1990s, three monumental buildings were part of a probably axially organised settlement complex. The main house consisted of a number of rooms, fronted by a portico-risalith façade and measured 30 x 13 m. Two secondary buildings were situated in front of the main house, on both sides of an imaginary central axis. This settlement was remarkably late and could be dated to the late 3rd or early 4th century AD. Occupation continued until the late 4th century, carte archéologique de la Gaule 59, 109–110.